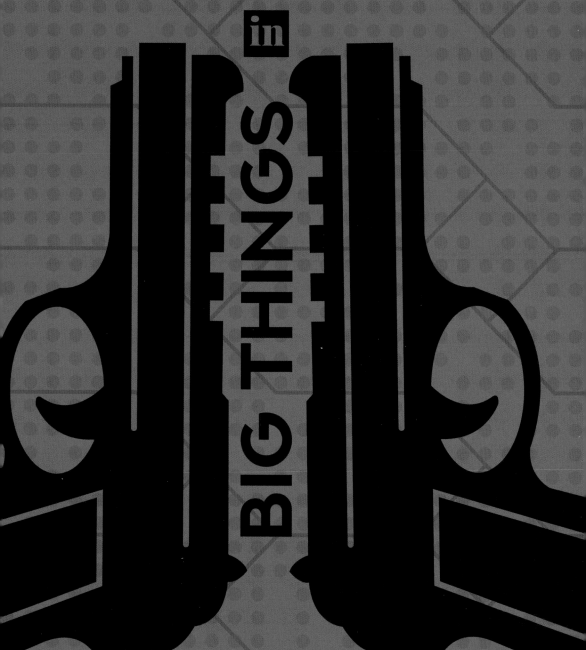

IAN FLEMING'S

JAMES BOND™

in

BIG THINGS

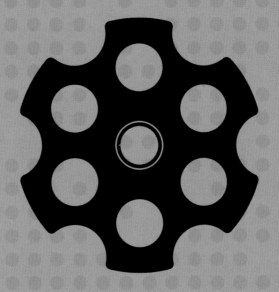

MI6.

**The Secret Intelligence
Service of the government
of the United Kingdom.**

00 Section.

**The elite level of MI6 agents.
Number of active agents, unknown.**

**00 agents are deployed directly by the
Chief of MI6, only when absolutely necessary.**

**All hold a licence to kill in the field, at his or
her discretion, to complete any mission.**

07

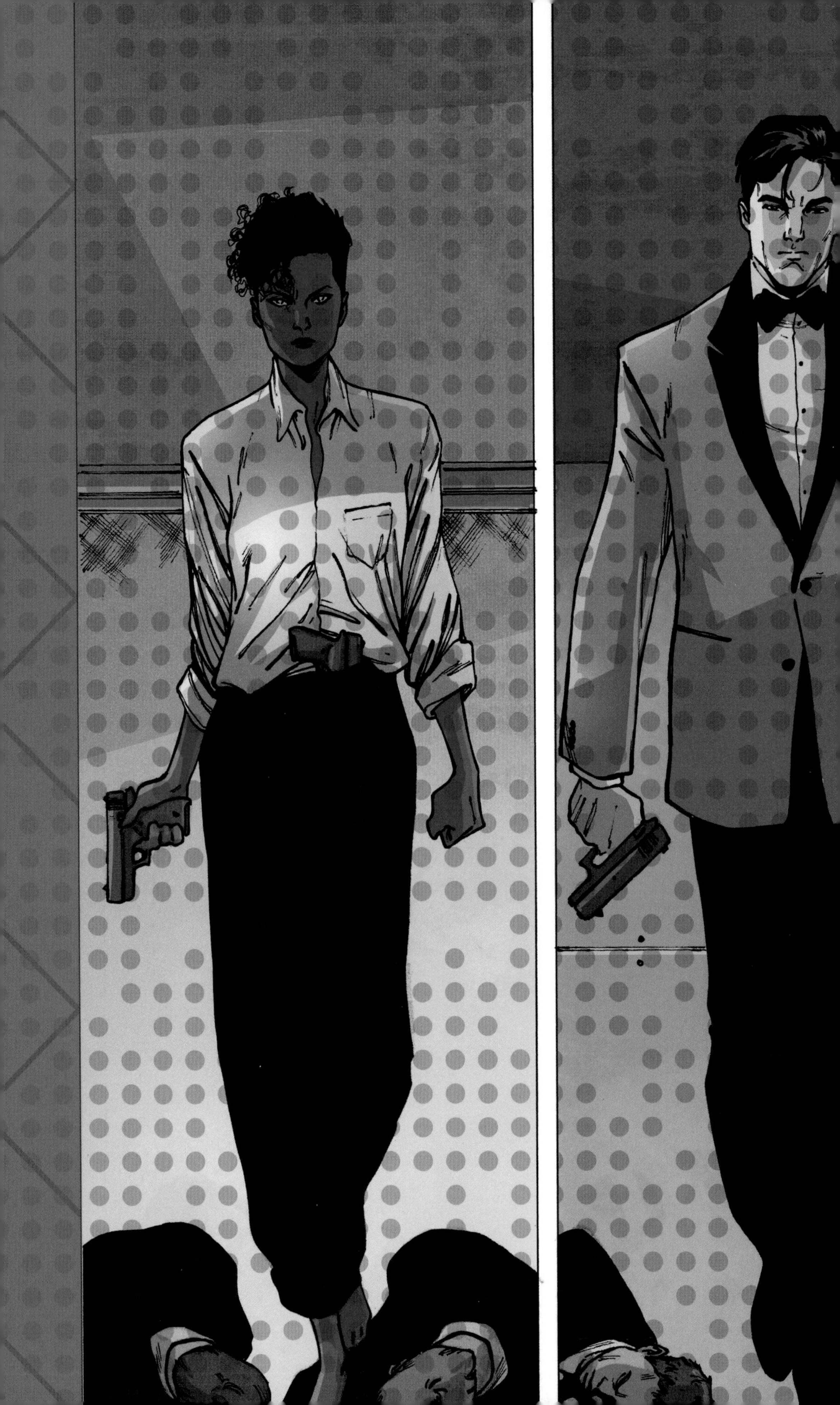

WRITERS
Vita Ayala
Danny Lore

ARTISTS
Eric Gapstur
Erica D'urso
Marco Renna
Brent Peeples

COLORISTS
Roshan Kurichiyanil with
Rebecca Nalty

LETTERERS
Ariana Maher
Hassan Otsmane-Elhrou

DYNAMITE®

Nick Barrucci, CEO / Publisher
Juan Collado, President / COO
Brandon Dante Primavera, V.P. of IT and Operations

Joe Rybandt, Executive Editor
Matt Idelson, Senior Editor

Alexis Persson, Creative Director
Rachel Kilbury, Digital Multimedia Associate
Katie Hidalgo, Graphic Designer
Nick Pentz, Graphic Designer

Alan Payne, V.P. of Sales and Marketing
Vincent Faust, Marketing Coordinator

Jim Kuhoric, Vice President of Product Development
Jay Spence, Director of Product Development

Mariano Nicieza, Director of Research & Development

Amy Jackson, Administrative Coordinator

Online at **www.dynamite.com**
On Facebook **/dynamitecomics**
On Instagram **/dynamitecomics**
On Twitter **@dynamitecomics**

ISBN 13: 978-1-5241-1911-9
First Printing 10 9 8 7 6 5 4 3 2 1

IAN FLEMING PUBLICATIONS LIMITED
www.IanFleming.com

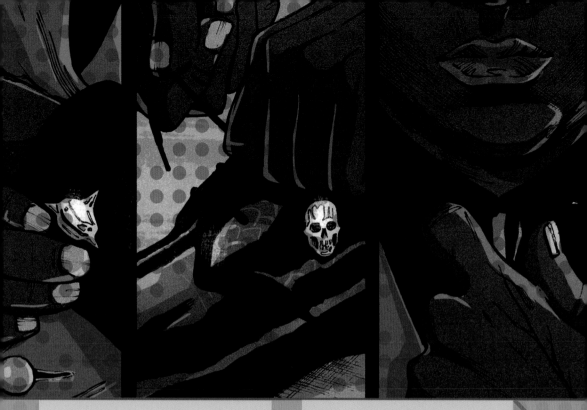

SPECIAL THANKS TO:

Chris Eliopoulos

AT IAN FLEMING PUBLICATIONS LTD.

Josephine Lane
Corinne Turner
Isabel Drake
Diggory Laycock

AT CURTIS BROWN

Jonny Geller

EDITORIAL CONSULTANT
Michael Lake

COLLECTION COVER ARTISTS
Jim Cheung &
Romulo Fajardo Jr.

LOGO DESIGNER
Geoff Harkins

COLLECTION DESIGNER
Cathleen Heard

PACKAGER & EDITOR
Nate Cosby

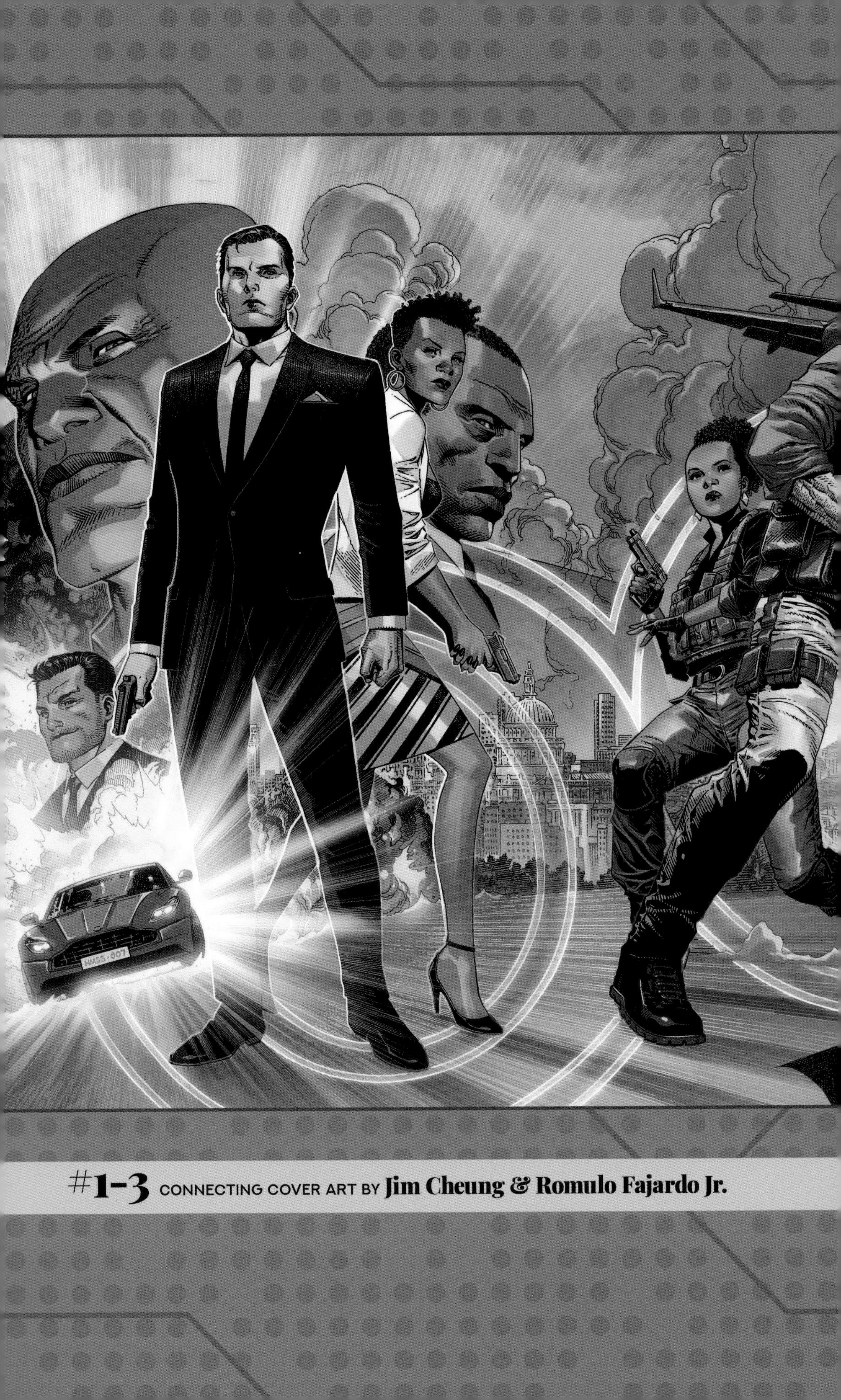
HMSS-007

#1–3 CONNECTING COVER ART BY **Jim Cheung & Romulo Fajardo Jr.**

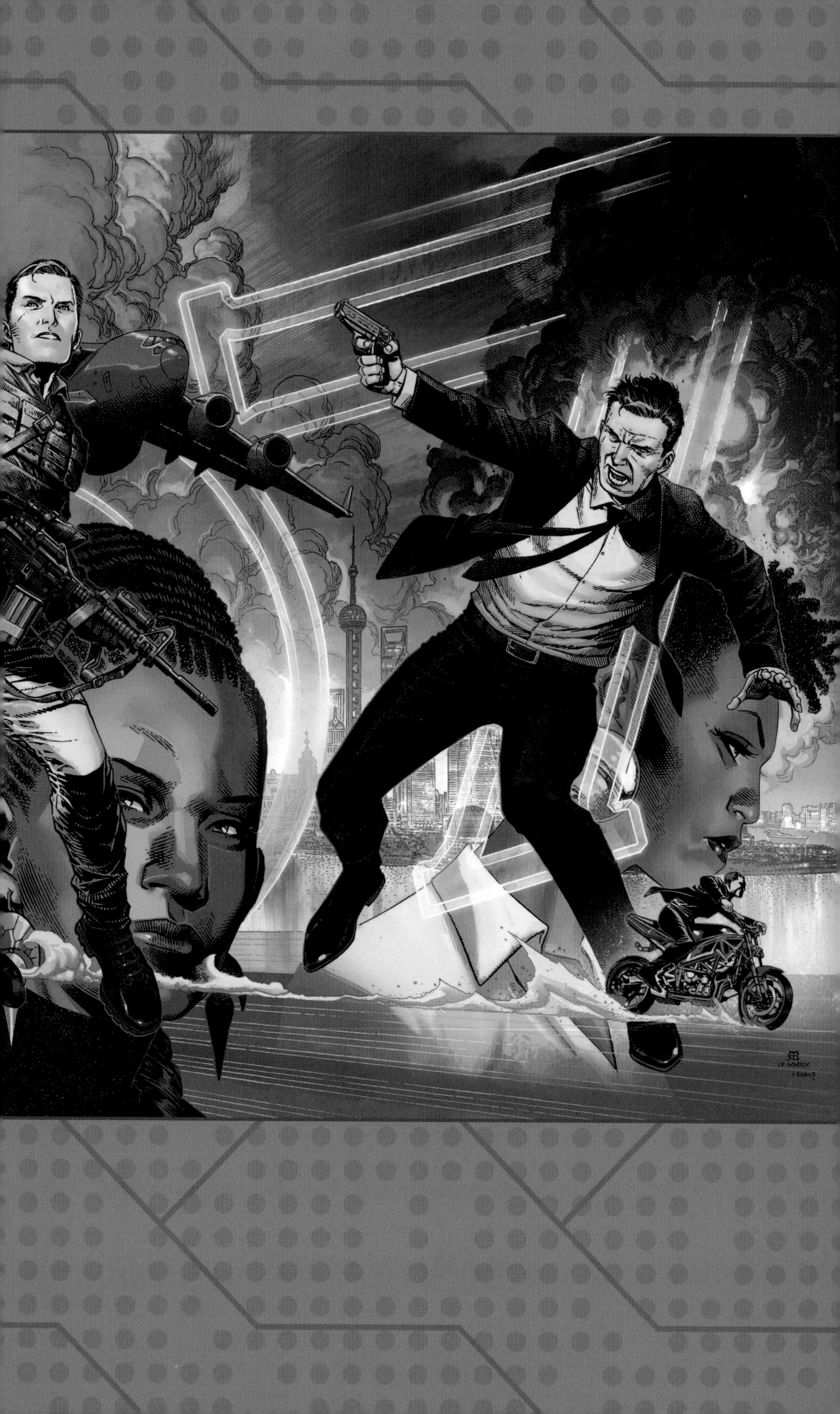
IX·MMXIX

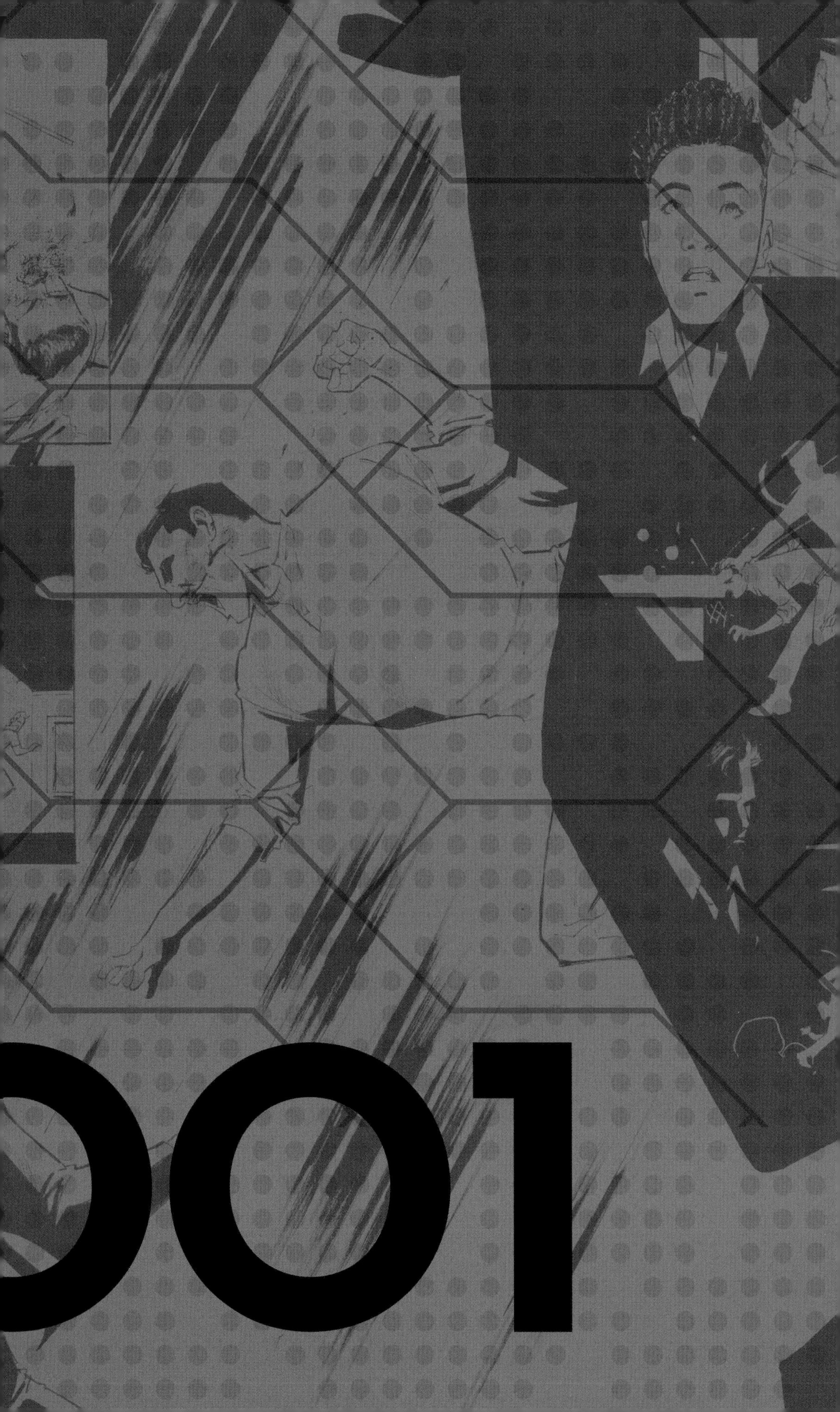
001

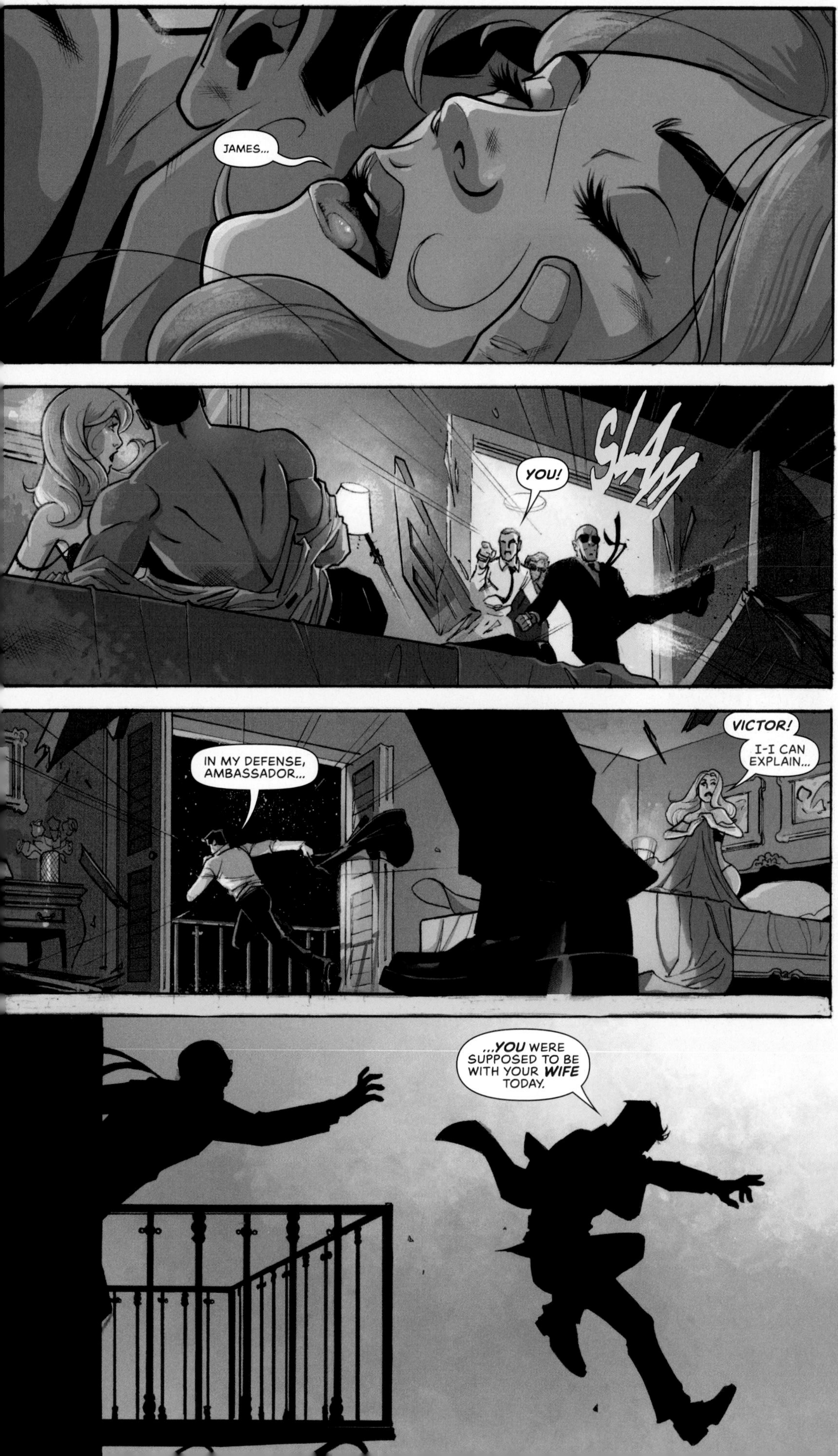
JAMES...
YOU!
SLAM
IN MY DEFENSE, AMBASSADOR...
VICTOR!
I-I CAN EXPLAIN...
...YOU WERE SUPPOSED TO BE WITH YOUR WIFE TODAY.

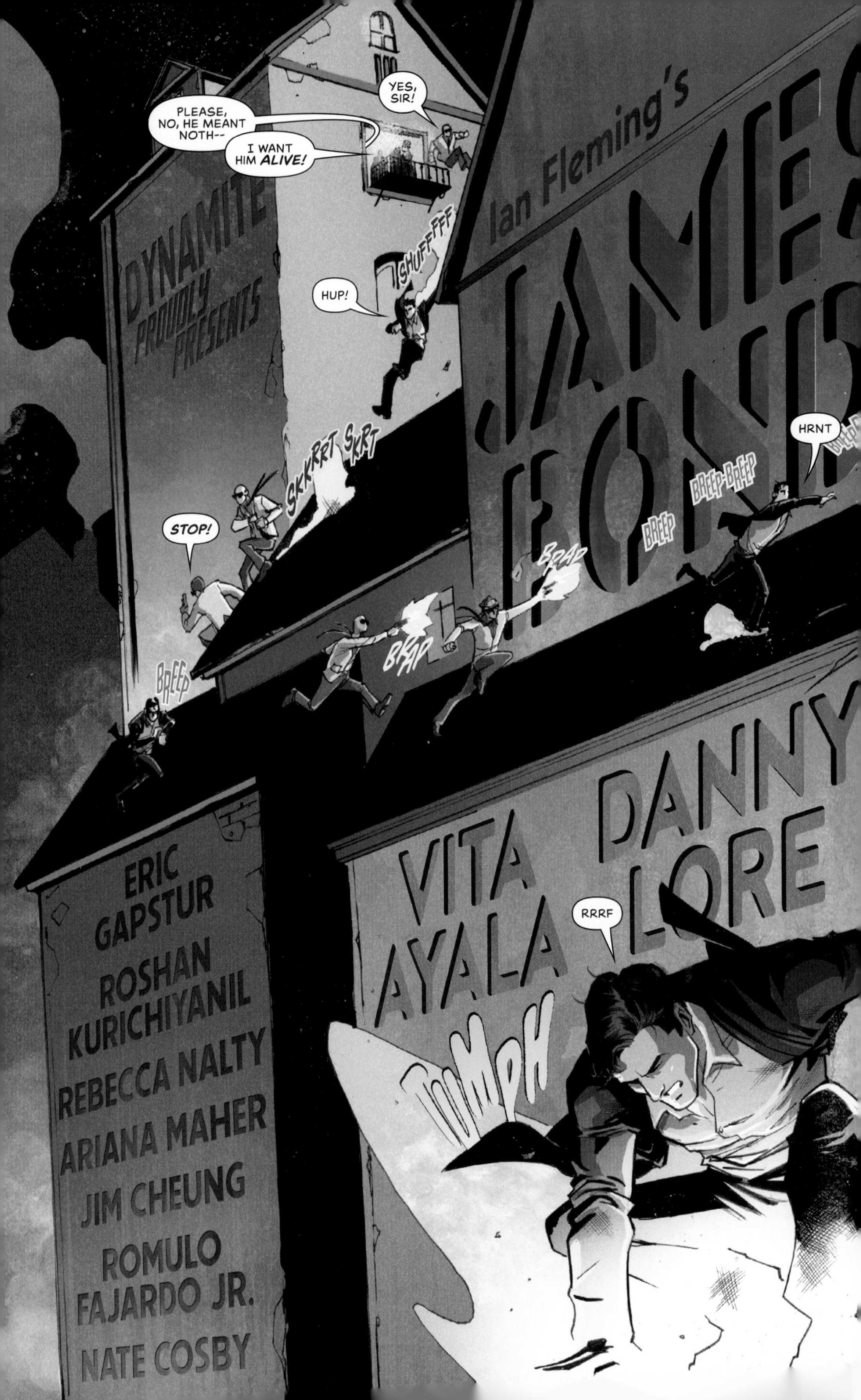

DYNAMITE
PROUDLY
PRESENTS
Ian Fleming's
PLEASE, NO, HE MEANT NOTH--
I WANT HIM ALIVE!
YES, SIR!
SHUFFFFF
HUP!
SKKRRT SKRT
STOP!
BREEP
BRAP
BRAP
BREEP
BREEP-BREEP
HRNT
ERIC
GAPSTUR
ROSHAN
KURICHIYANIL
REBECCA NALTY
ARIANA MAHER
JIM CHEUNG
ROMULO
FAJARDO JR.
NATE COSBY
VITA
AYALA
DANNY
LORE
RRRF
TOOMPH

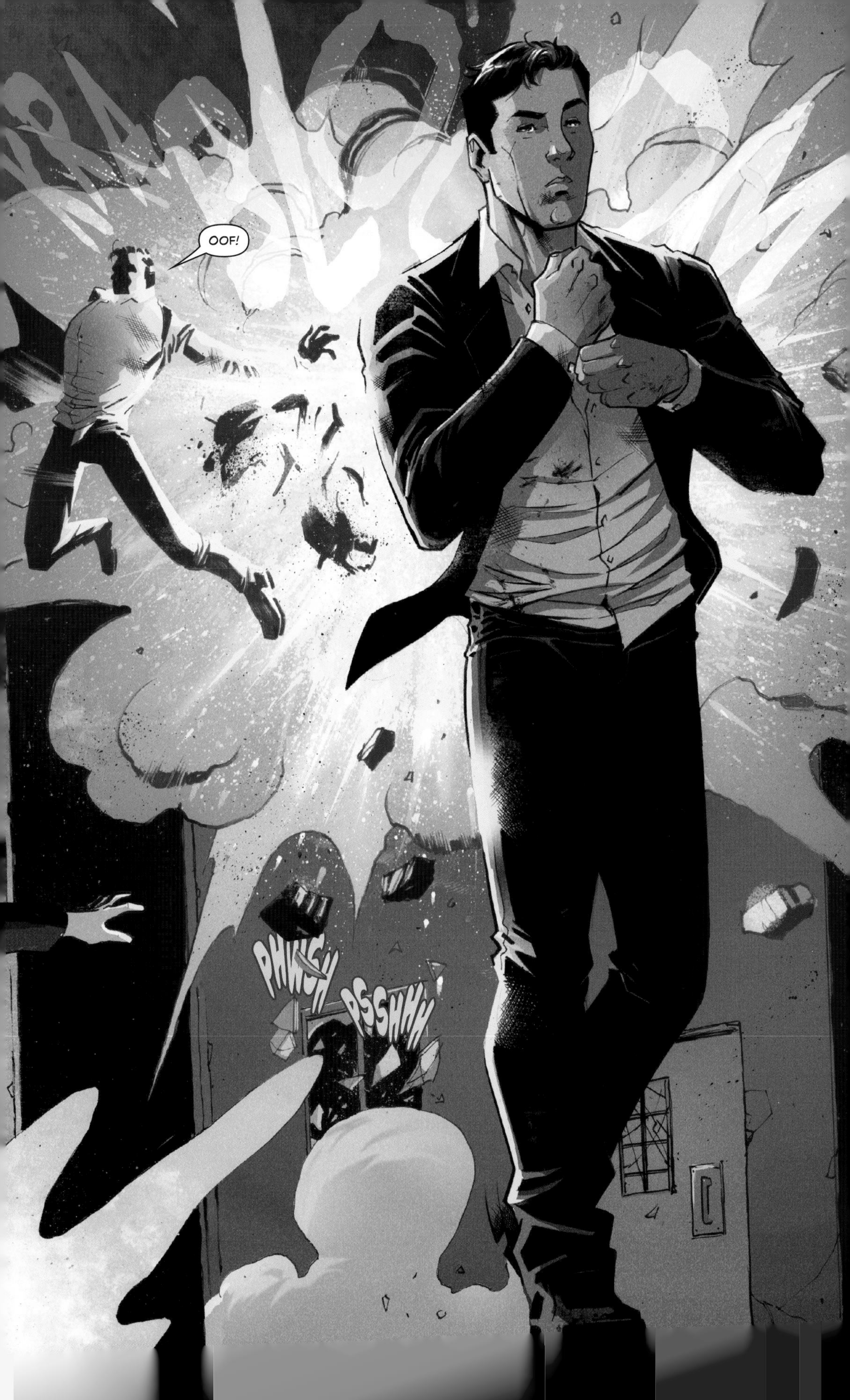
OOF!
PHWOSH
PSSHHH

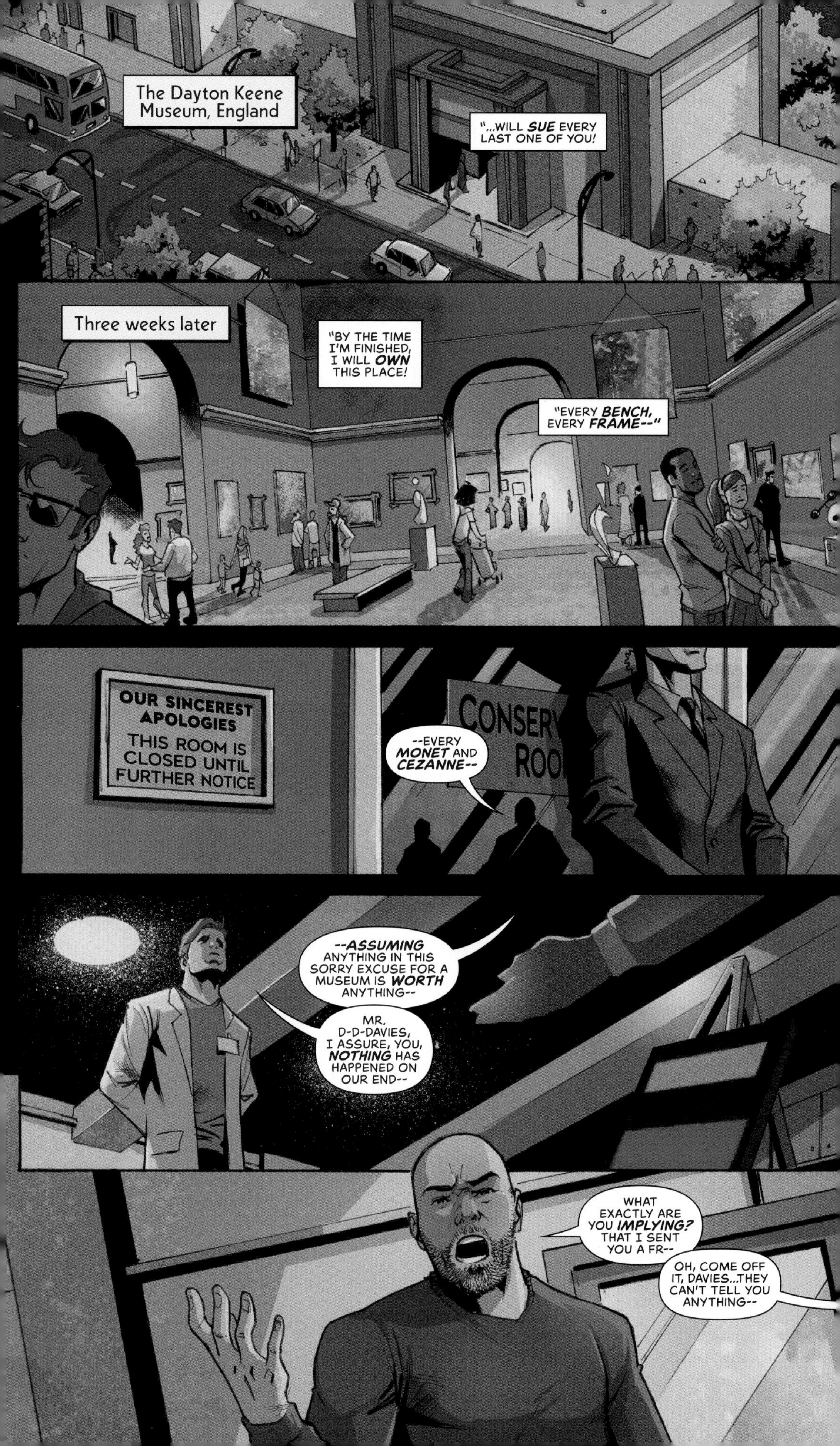

The Dayton Keene Museum, England
"...WILL SUE EVERY LAST ONE OF YOU!
Three weeks later
"BY THE TIME I'M FINISHED, I WILL OWN THIS PLACE!
"EVERY BENCH, EVERY FRAME--"
OUR SINCEREST APOLOGIES
THIS ROOM IS CLOSED UNTIL FURTHER NOTICE
--EVERY MONET AND CEZANNE--
--ASSUMING ANYTHING IN THIS SORRY EXCUSE FOR A MUSEUM IS WORTH ANYTHING--
MR. D-D-DAVIES, I ASSURE, YOU, NOTHING HAS HAPPENED ON OUR END--
WHAT EXACTLY ARE YOU IMPLYING? THAT I SENT YOU A FR--
OH, COME OFF IT, DAVIES...THEY CAN'T TELL YOU ANYTHING--

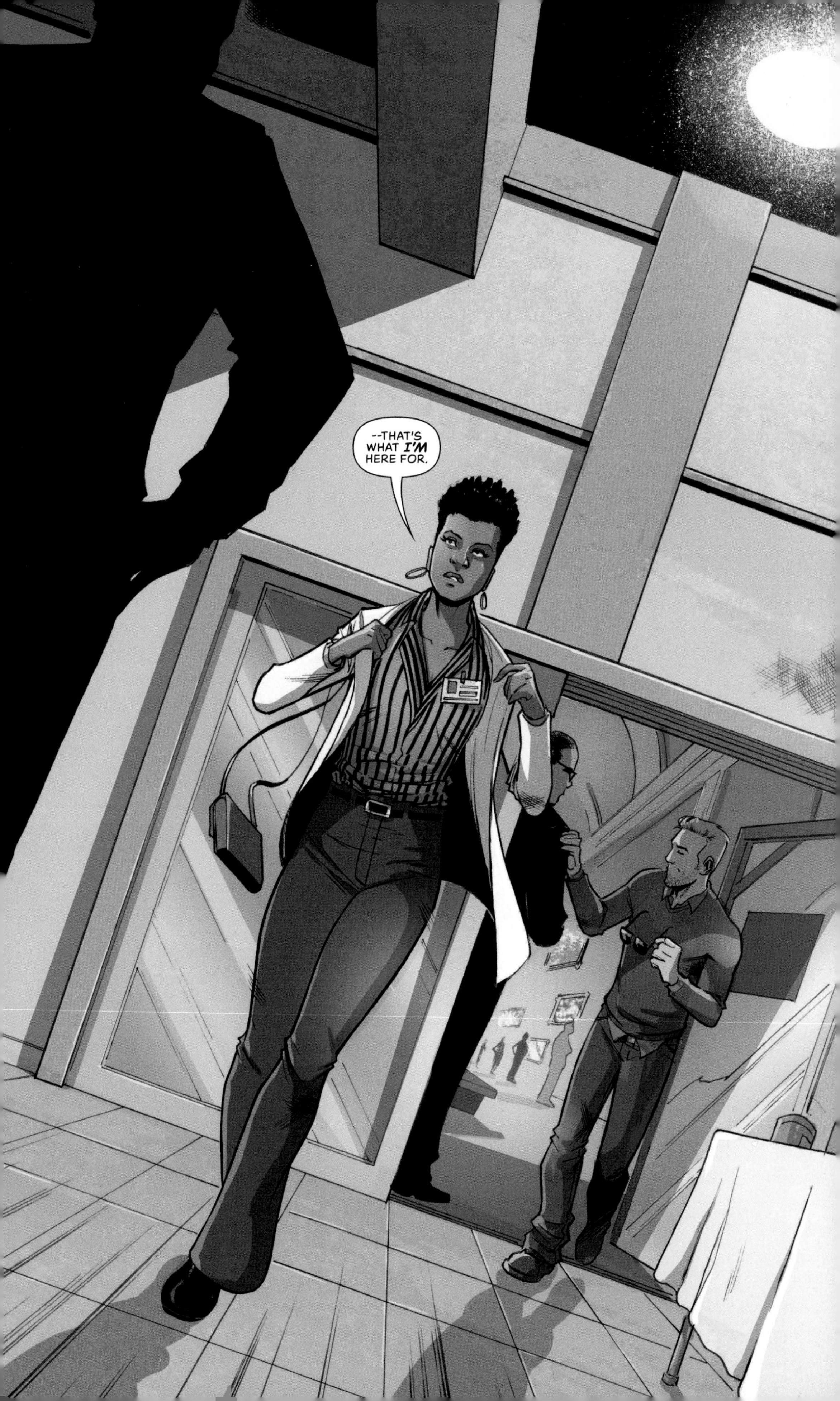
--THAT'S WHAT I'M HERE FOR.

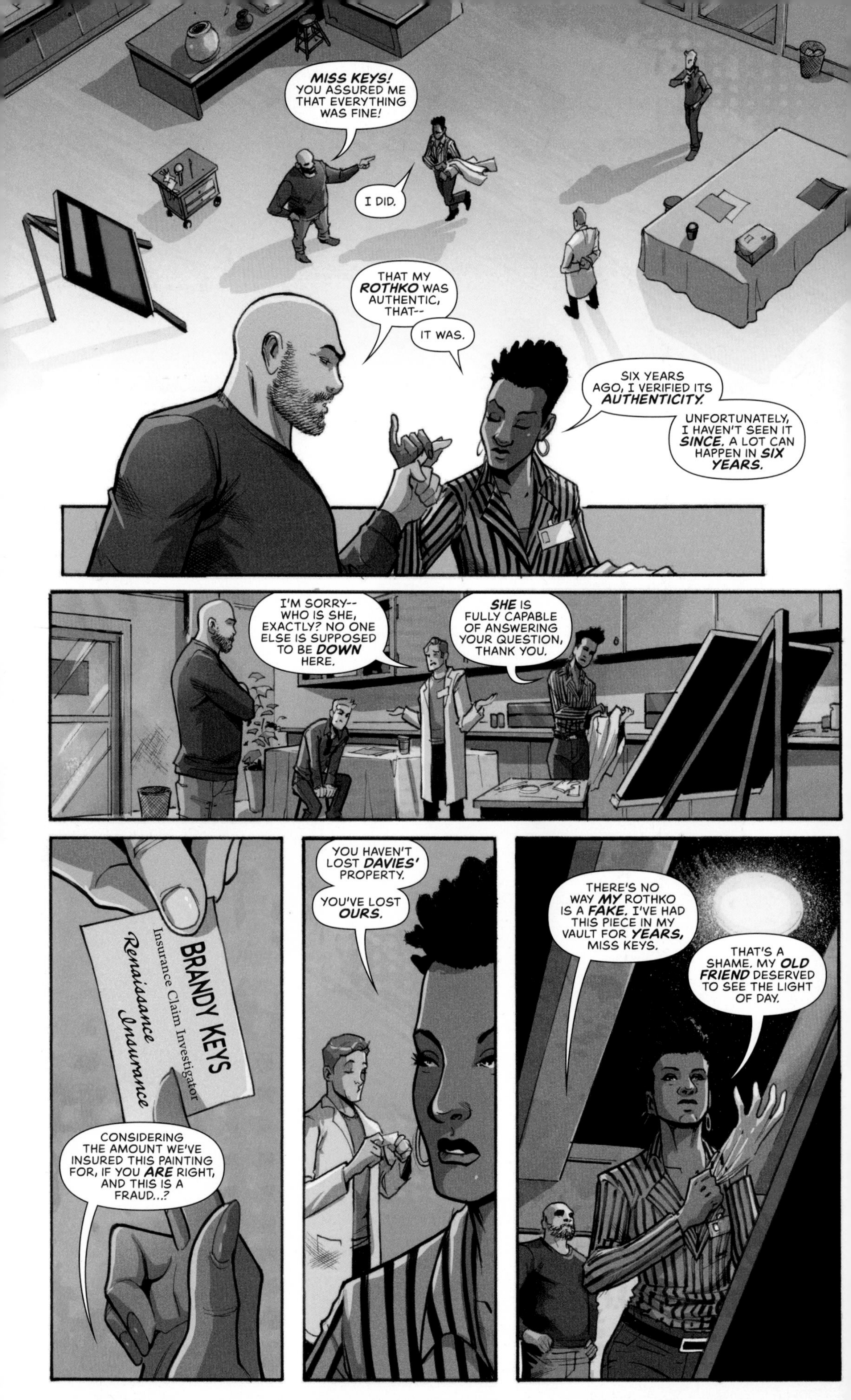

MISS KEYS! YOU ASSURED ME THAT EVERYTHING WAS FINE!
I DID.
THAT MY ROTHKO WAS AUTHENTIC, THAT--
IT WAS.
SIX YEARS AGO, I VERIFIED ITS AUTHENTICITY.
UNFORTUNATELY, I HAVEN'T SEEN IT SINCE. A LOT CAN HAPPEN IN SIX YEARS.
I'M SORRY-- WHO IS SHE, EXACTLY? NO ONE ELSE IS SUPPOSED TO BE DOWN HERE.
SHE IS FULLY CAPABLE OF ANSWERING YOUR QUESTION, THANK YOU.
BRANDY KEYS
Insurance Claim Investigator
Renaissance Insurance
CONSIDERING THE AMOUNT WE'VE INSURED THIS PAINTING FOR, IF YOU ARE RIGHT, AND THIS IS A FRAUD...?
YOU HAVEN'T LOST DAVIES' PROPERTY.
YOU'VE LOST OURS.
THERE'S NO WAY MY ROTHKO IS A FAKE. I'VE HAD THIS PIECE IN MY VAULT FOR YEARS, MISS KEYS.
THAT'S A SHAME. MY OLD FRIEND DESERVED TO SEE THE LIGHT OF DAY.

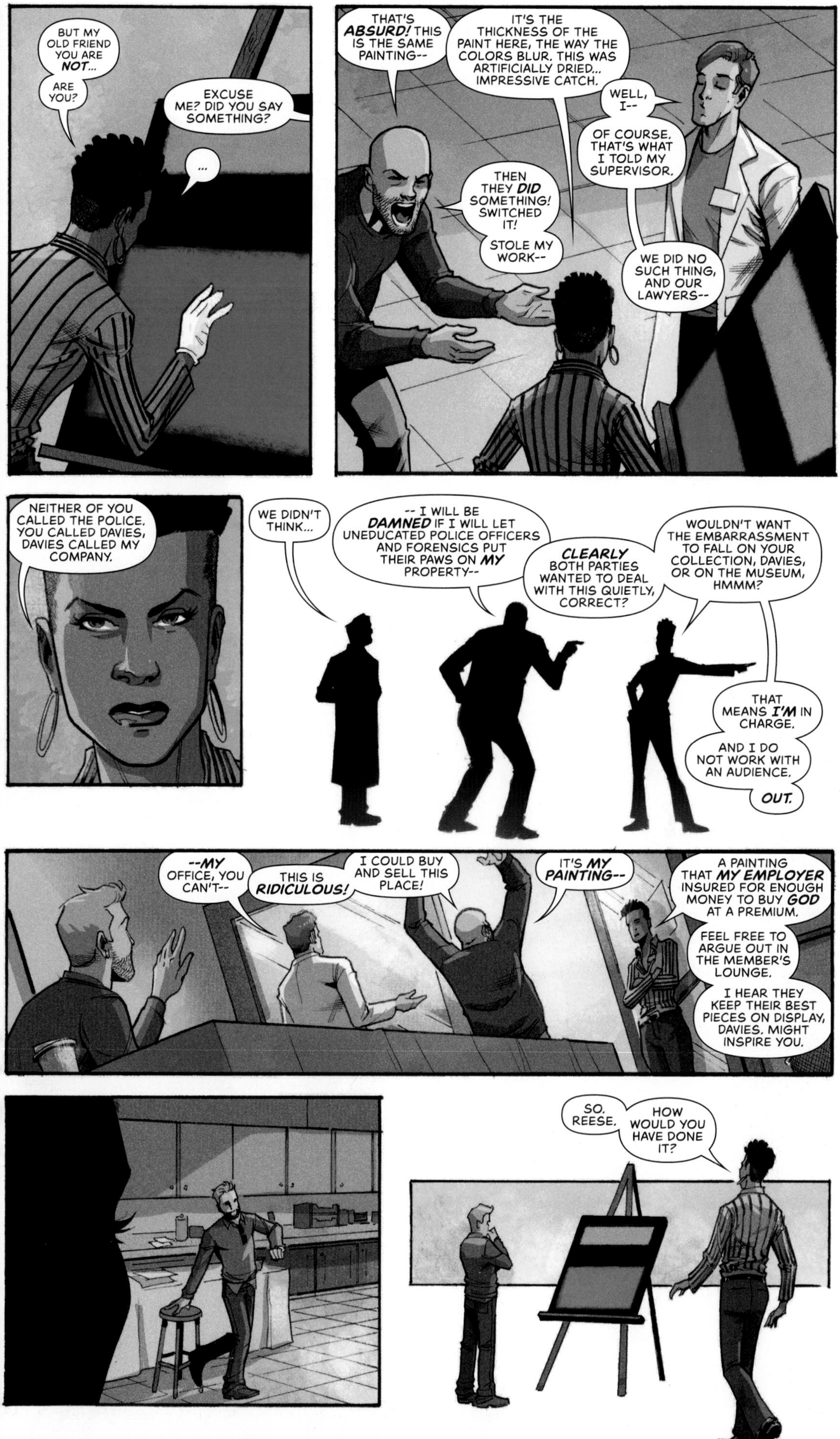
BUT MY OLD FRIEND YOU ARE NOT...
ARE YOU?
EXCUSE ME? DID YOU SAY SOMETHING?
...
THAT'S ABSURD! THIS IS THE SAME PAINTING--
IT'S THE THICKNESS OF THE PAINT HERE, THE WAY THE COLORS BLUR. THIS WAS ARTIFICIALLY DRIED... IMPRESSIVE CATCH.
WELL, I--
OF COURSE. THAT'S WHAT I TOLD MY SUPERVISOR.
THEN THEY DID SOMETHING! SWITCHED IT!
STOLE MY WORK--
WE DID NO SUCH THING, AND OUR LAWYERS--
NEITHER OF YOU CALLED THE POLICE. YOU CALLED DAVIES, DAVIES CALLED MY COMPANY.
WE DIDN'T THINK...
-- I WILL BE DAMNED IF I WILL LET UNEDUCATED POLICE OFFICERS AND FORENSICS PUT THEIR PAWS ON MY PROPERTY--
CLEARLY BOTH PARTIES WANTED TO DEAL WITH THIS QUIETLY, CORRECT?
WOULDN'T WANT THE EMBARRASSMENT TO FALL ON YOUR COLLECTION, DAVIES, OR ON THE MUSEUM, HMMM?
THAT MEANS I'M IN CHARGE.
AND I DO NOT WORK WITH AN AUDIENCE.
OUT.
--MY OFFICE, YOU CAN'T--
THIS IS RIDICULOUS!
I COULD BUY AND SELL THIS PLACE!
IT'S MY PAINTING--
A PAINTING THAT MY EMPLOYER INSURED FOR ENOUGH MONEY TO BUY GOD AT A PREMIUM.
FEEL FREE TO ARGUE OUT IN THE MEMBER'S LOUNGE.
I HEAR THEY KEEP THEIR BEST PIECES ON DISPLAY, DAVIES. MIGHT INSPIRE YOU.
SO, REESE.
HOW WOULD YOU HAVE DONE IT?

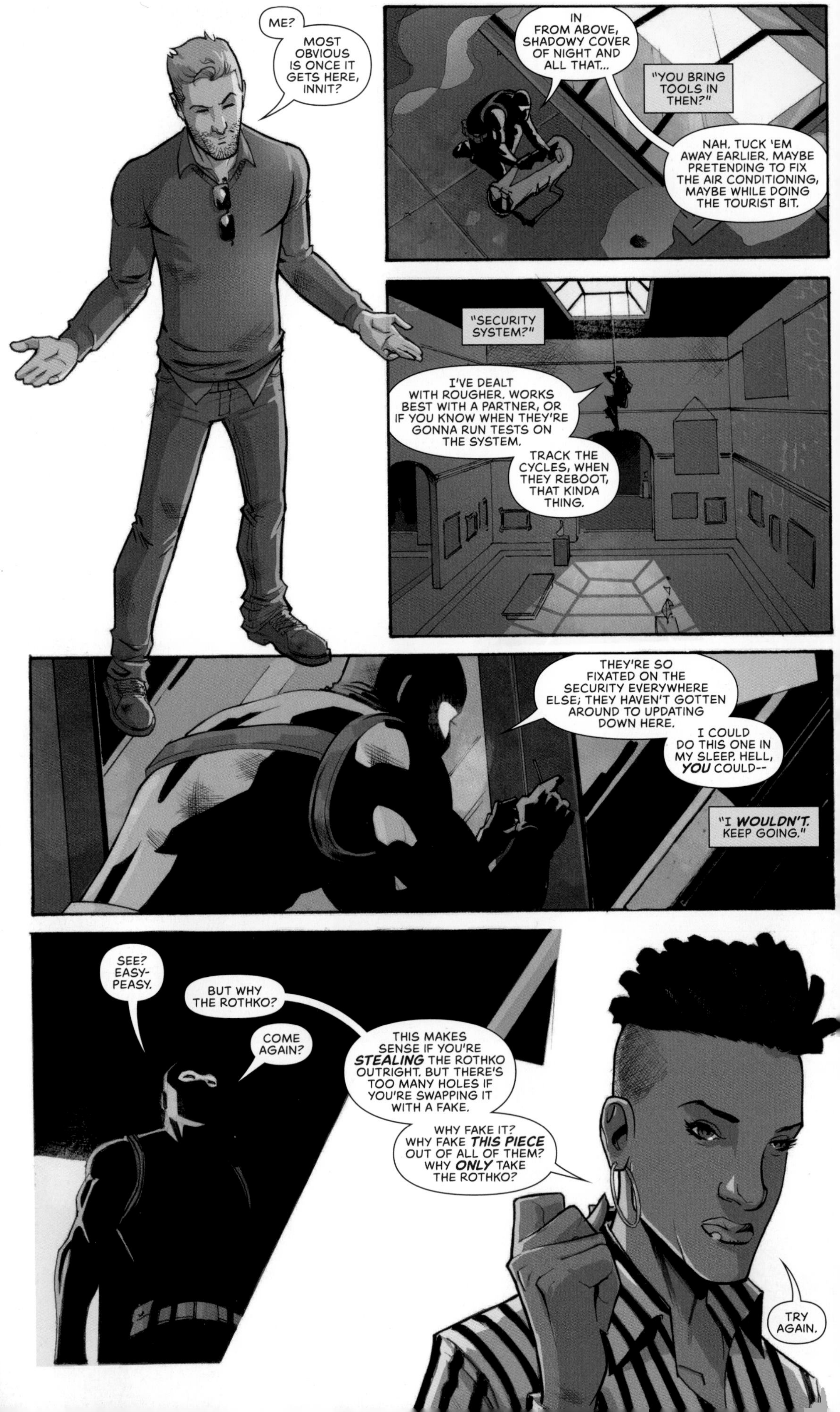
ME?
MOST OBVIOUS IS ONCE IT GETS HERE, INNIT?
IN FROM ABOVE, SHADOWY COVER OF NIGHT AND ALL THAT...
"YOU BRING TOOLS IN THEN?"
NAH. TUCK 'EM AWAY EARLIER. MAYBE PRETENDING TO FIX THE AIR CONDITIONING, MAYBE WHILE DOING THE TOURIST BIT.
"SECURITY SYSTEM?"
I'VE DEALT WITH ROUGHER. WORKS BEST WITH A PARTNER, OR IF YOU KNOW WHEN THEY'RE GONNA RUN TESTS ON THE SYSTEM.
TRACK THE CYCLES, WHEN THEY REBOOT, THAT KINDA THING.
THEY'RE SO FIXATED ON THE SECURITY EVERYWHERE ELSE; THEY HAVEN'T GOTTEN AROUND TO UPDATING DOWN HERE.
I COULD DO THIS ONE IN MY SLEEP. HELL, ***YOU*** COULD--
"I ***WOULDN'T.*** KEEP GOING."
SEE? EASY-PEASY.
BUT WHY THE ROTHKO?
COME AGAIN?
THIS MAKES SENSE IF YOU'RE ***STEALING*** THE ROTHKO OUTRIGHT. BUT THERE'S TOO MANY HOLES IF YOU'RE SWAPPING IT WITH A FAKE.
WHY FAKE IT? WHY FAKE ***THIS PIECE*** OUT OF ALL OF THEM? WHY ***ONLY*** TAKE THE ROTHKO?
TRY AGAIN.

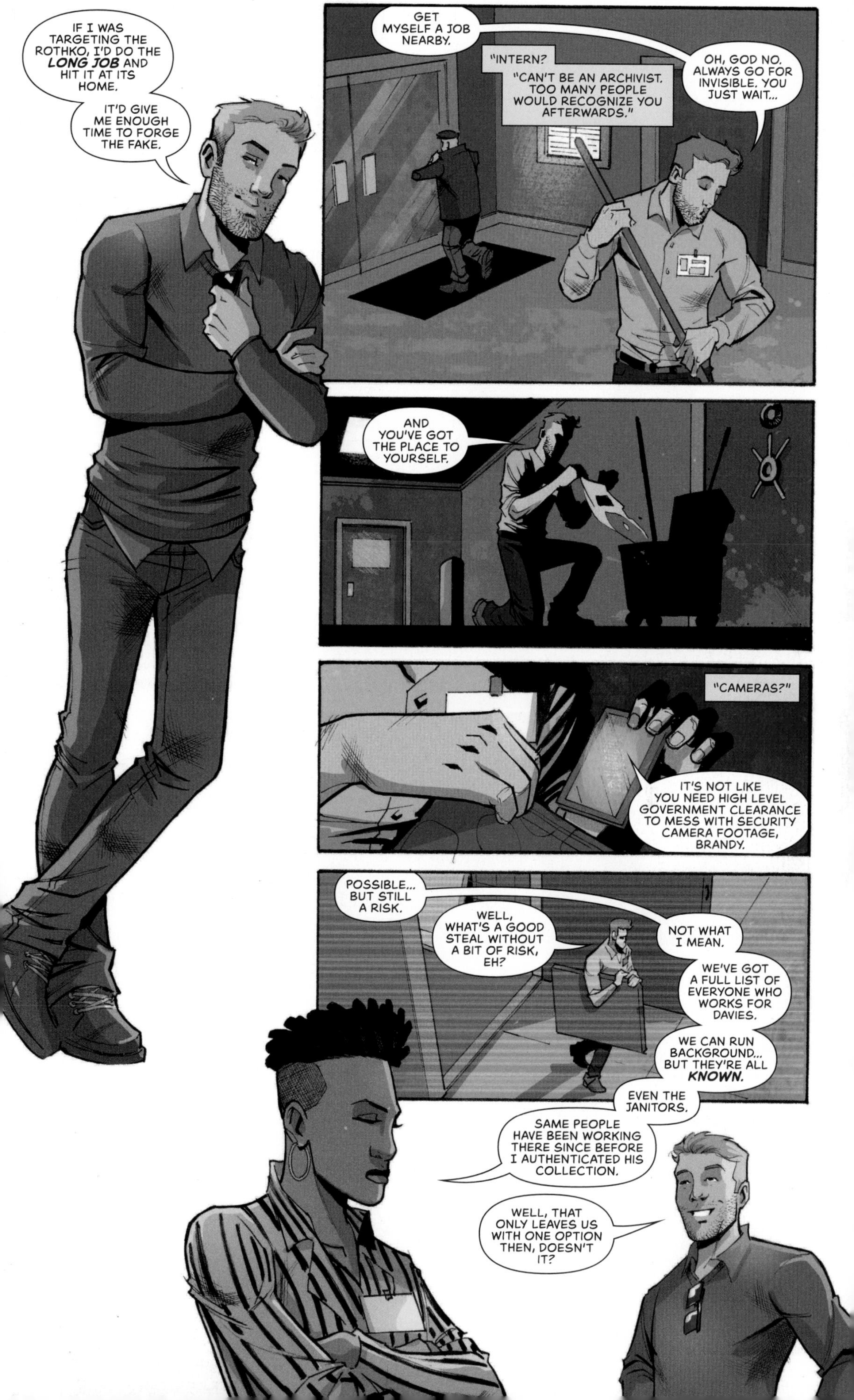

IF I WAS TARGETING THE ROTHKO, I'D DO THE ***LONG JOB*** AND HIT IT AT ITS HOME.
IT'D GIVE ME ENOUGH TIME TO FORGE THE FAKE.
GET MYSELF A JOB NEARBY.
"INTERN?
"CAN'T BE AN ARCHIVIST. TOO MANY PEOPLE WOULD RECOGNIZE YOU AFTERWARDS."
OH, GOD NO. ALWAYS GO FOR INVISIBLE. YOU JUST WAIT...
AND YOU'VE GOT THE PLACE TO YOURSELF.
"CAMERAS?"
IT'S NOT LIKE YOU NEED HIGH LEVEL GOVERNMENT CLEARANCE TO MESS WITH SECURITY CAMERA FOOTAGE, BRANDY.
POSSIBLE... BUT STILL A RISK.
WELL, WHAT'S A GOOD STEAL WITHOUT A BIT OF RISK, EH?
NOT WHAT I MEAN.
WE'VE GOT A FULL LIST OF EVERYONE WHO WORKS FOR DAVIES.
WE CAN RUN BACKGROUND... BUT THEY'RE ALL ***KNOWN.***
EVEN THE JANITORS.
SAME PEOPLE HAVE BEEN WORKING THERE SINCE BEFORE I AUTHENTICATED HIS COLLECTION.
WELL, THAT ONLY LEAVES US WITH ONE OPTION THEN, DOESN'T IT?

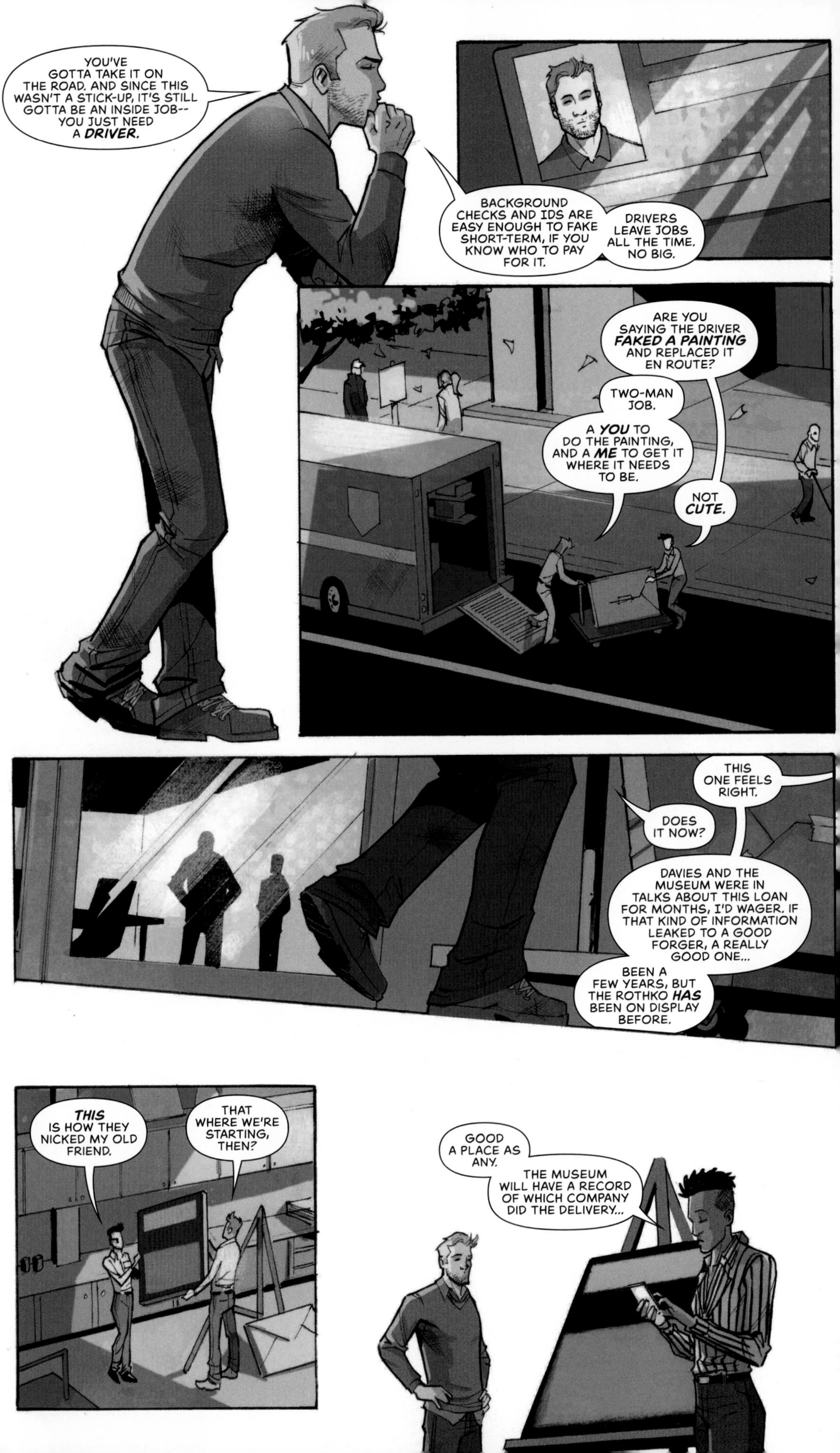
YOU'VE GOTTA TAKE IT ON THE ROAD. AND SINCE THIS WASN'T A STICK-UP, IT'S STILL GOTTA BE AN INSIDE JOB-- YOU JUST NEED A *DRIVER.*
BACKGROUND CHECKS AND IDS ARE EASY ENOUGH TO FAKE SHORT-TERM, IF YOU KNOW WHO TO PAY FOR IT.
DRIVERS LEAVE JOBS ALL THE TIME. NO BIG.
ARE YOU SAYING THE DRIVER *FAKED A PAINTING* AND REPLACED IT EN ROUTE?
TWO-MAN JOB.
A *YOU* TO DO THE PAINTING, AND A *ME* TO GET IT WHERE IT NEEDS TO BE.
NOT *CUTE.*
THIS ONE FEELS RIGHT.
DOES IT NOW?
DAVIES AND THE MUSEUM WERE IN TALKS ABOUT THIS LOAN FOR MONTHS, I'D WAGER. IF THAT KIND OF INFORMATION LEAKED TO A GOOD FORGER, A REALLY GOOD ONE...
BEEN A FEW YEARS, BUT THE ROTHKO *HAS* BEEN ON DISPLAY BEFORE.
THIS IS HOW THEY NICKED MY OLD FRIEND.
THAT WHERE WE'RE STARTING, THEN?
GOOD A PLACE AS ANY.
THE MUSEUM WILL HAVE A RECORD OF WHICH COMPANY DID THE DELIVERY...

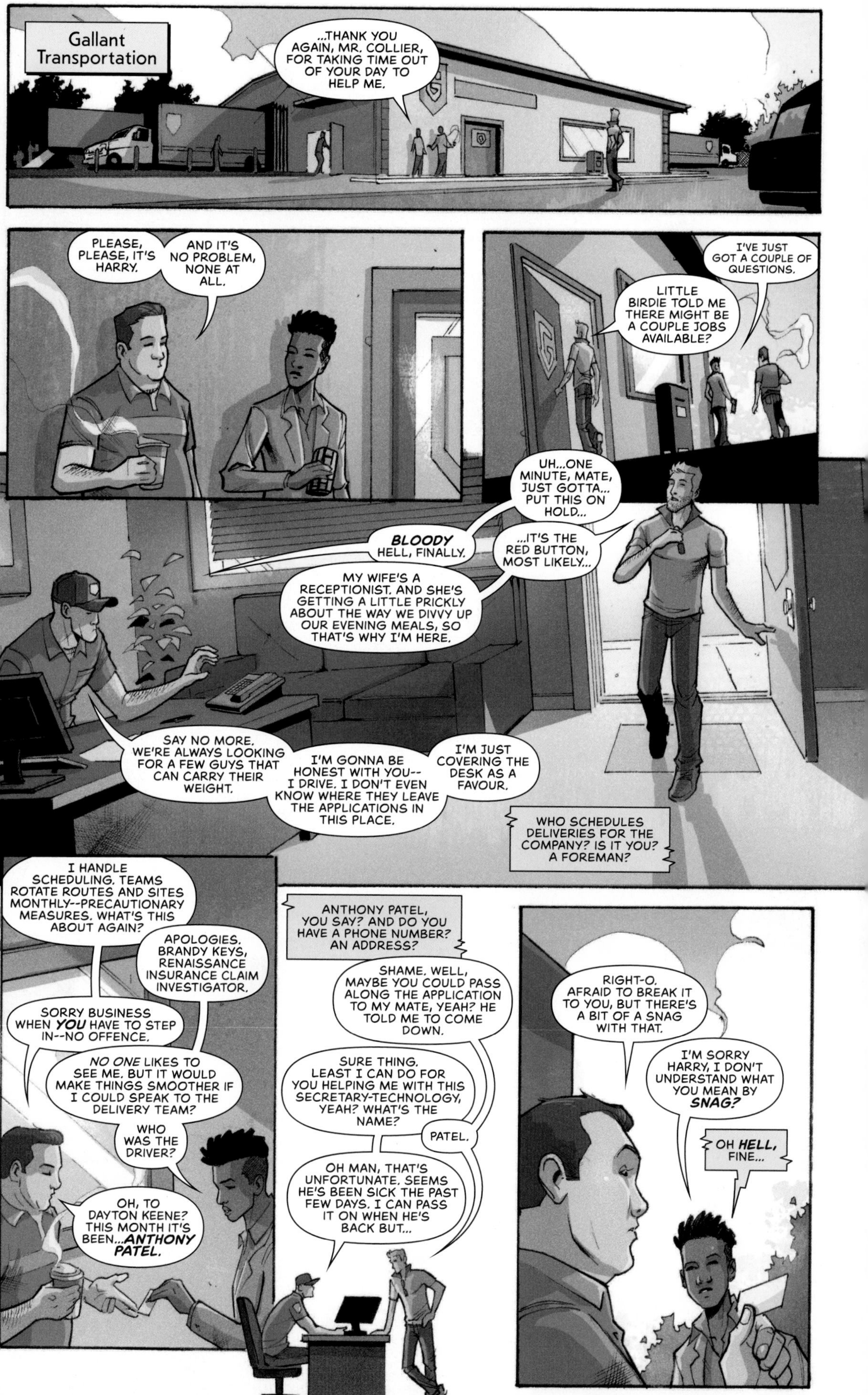

Gallant Transportation
...THANK YOU AGAIN, MR. COLLIER, FOR TAKING TIME OUT OF YOUR DAY TO HELP ME.
PLEASE, PLEASE, IT'S HARRY.
AND IT'S NO PROBLEM, NONE AT ALL.
I'VE JUST GOT A COUPLE OF QUESTIONS.
LITTLE BIRDIE TOLD ME THERE MIGHT BE A COUPLE JOBS AVAILABLE?
UH...ONE MINUTE, MATE, JUST GOTTA... PUT THIS ON HOLD...
BLOODY HELL, FINALLY.
...IT'S THE RED BUTTON, MOST LIKELY...
MY WIFE'S A RECEPTIONIST, AND SHE'S GETTING A LITTLE PRICKLY ABOUT THE WAY WE DIVVY UP OUR EVENING MEALS, SO THAT'S WHY I'M HERE.
SAY NO MORE. WE'RE ALWAYS LOOKING FOR A FEW GUYS THAT CAN CARRY THEIR WEIGHT.
I'M GONNA BE HONEST WITH YOU-- I DRIVE. I DON'T EVEN KNOW WHERE THEY LEAVE THE APPLICATIONS IN THIS PLACE.
I'M JUST COVERING THE DESK AS A FAVOUR.
WHO SCHEDULES DELIVERIES FOR THE COMPANY? IS IT YOU? A FOREMAN?
I HANDLE SCHEDULING. TEAMS ROTATE ROUTES AND SITES MONTHLY--PRECAUTIONARY MEASURES. WHAT'S THIS ABOUT AGAIN?
APOLOGIES. BRANDY KEYS, RENAISSANCE INSURANCE CLAIM INVESTIGATOR.
SORRY BUSINESS WHEN YOU HAVE TO STEP IN--NO OFFENCE.
NO ONE LIKES TO SEE ME. BUT IT WOULD MAKE THINGS SMOOTHER IF I COULD SPEAK TO THE DELIVERY TEAM?
WHO WAS THE DRIVER?
OH, TO DAYTON KEENE? THIS MONTH IT'S BEEN...ANTHONY PATEL.
ANTHONY PATEL, YOU SAY? AND DO YOU HAVE A PHONE NUMBER? AN ADDRESS?
SHAME. WELL, MAYBE YOU COULD PASS ALONG THE APPLICATION TO MY MATE, YEAH? HE TOLD ME TO COME DOWN.
SURE THING. LEAST I CAN DO FOR YOU HELPING ME WITH THIS SECRETARY-TECHNOLOGY, YEAH? WHAT'S THE NAME?
PATEL.
OH MAN, THAT'S UNFORTUNATE. SEEMS HE'S BEEN SICK THE PAST FEW DAYS. I CAN PASS IT ON WHEN HE'S BACK BUT...
RIGHT-O. AFRAID TO BREAK IT TO YOU, BUT THERE'S A BIT OF A SNAG WITH THAT.
I'M SORRY HARRY, I DON'T UNDERSTAND WHAT YOU MEAN BY SNAG?
OH HELL, FINE...

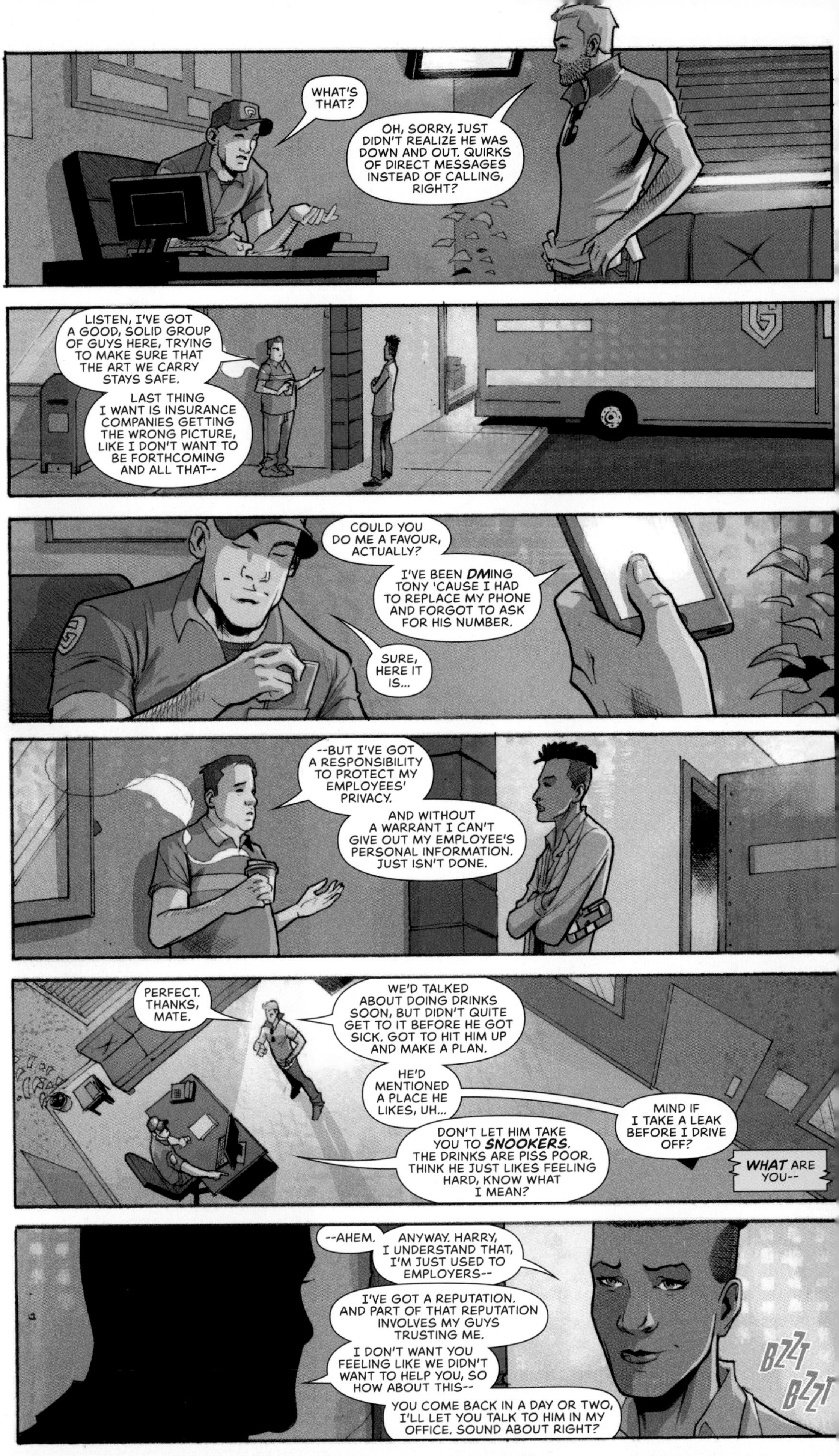

WHAT'S THAT?
OH, SORRY, JUST DIDN'T REALIZE HE WAS DOWN AND OUT. QUIRKS OF DIRECT MESSAGES INSTEAD OF CALLING, RIGHT?
LISTEN, I'VE GOT A GOOD, SOLID GROUP OF GUYS HERE, TRYING TO MAKE SURE THAT THE ART WE CARRY STAYS SAFE.
LAST THING I WANT IS INSURANCE COMPANIES GETTING THE WRONG PICTURE, LIKE I DON'T WANT TO BE FORTHCOMING AND ALL THAT--
COULD YOU DO ME A FAVOUR, ACTUALLY?
I'VE BEEN DMING TONY 'CAUSE I HAD TO REPLACE MY PHONE AND FORGOT TO ASK FOR HIS NUMBER.
SURE, HERE IT IS...
--BUT I'VE GOT A RESPONSIBILITY TO PROTECT MY EMPLOYEES' PRIVACY.
AND WITHOUT A WARRANT I CAN'T GIVE OUT MY EMPLOYEE'S PERSONAL INFORMATION. JUST ISN'T DONE.
PERFECT. THANKS, MATE.
WE'D TALKED ABOUT DOING DRINKS SOON, BUT DIDN'T QUITE GET TO IT BEFORE HE GOT SICK. GOT TO HIT HIM UP AND MAKE A PLAN.
HE'D MENTIONED A PLACE HE LIKES, UH...
DON'T LET HIM TAKE YOU TO SNOOKERS. THE DRINKS ARE PISS POOR. THINK HE JUST LIKES FEELING HARD, KNOW WHAT I MEAN?
MIND IF I TAKE A LEAK BEFORE I DRIVE OFF?
WHAT ARE YOU--
--AHEM.
ANYWAY, HARRY, I UNDERSTAND THAT, I'M JUST USED TO EMPLOYERS--
I'VE GOT A REPUTATION, AND PART OF THAT REPUTATION INVOLVES MY GUYS TRUSTING ME.
I DON'T WANT YOU FEELING LIKE WE DIDN'T WANT TO HELP YOU, SO HOW ABOUT THIS--
YOU COME BACK IN A DAY OR TWO, I'LL LET YOU TALK TO HIM IN MY OFFICE. SOUND ABOUT RIGHT?
BZZT
BZZT

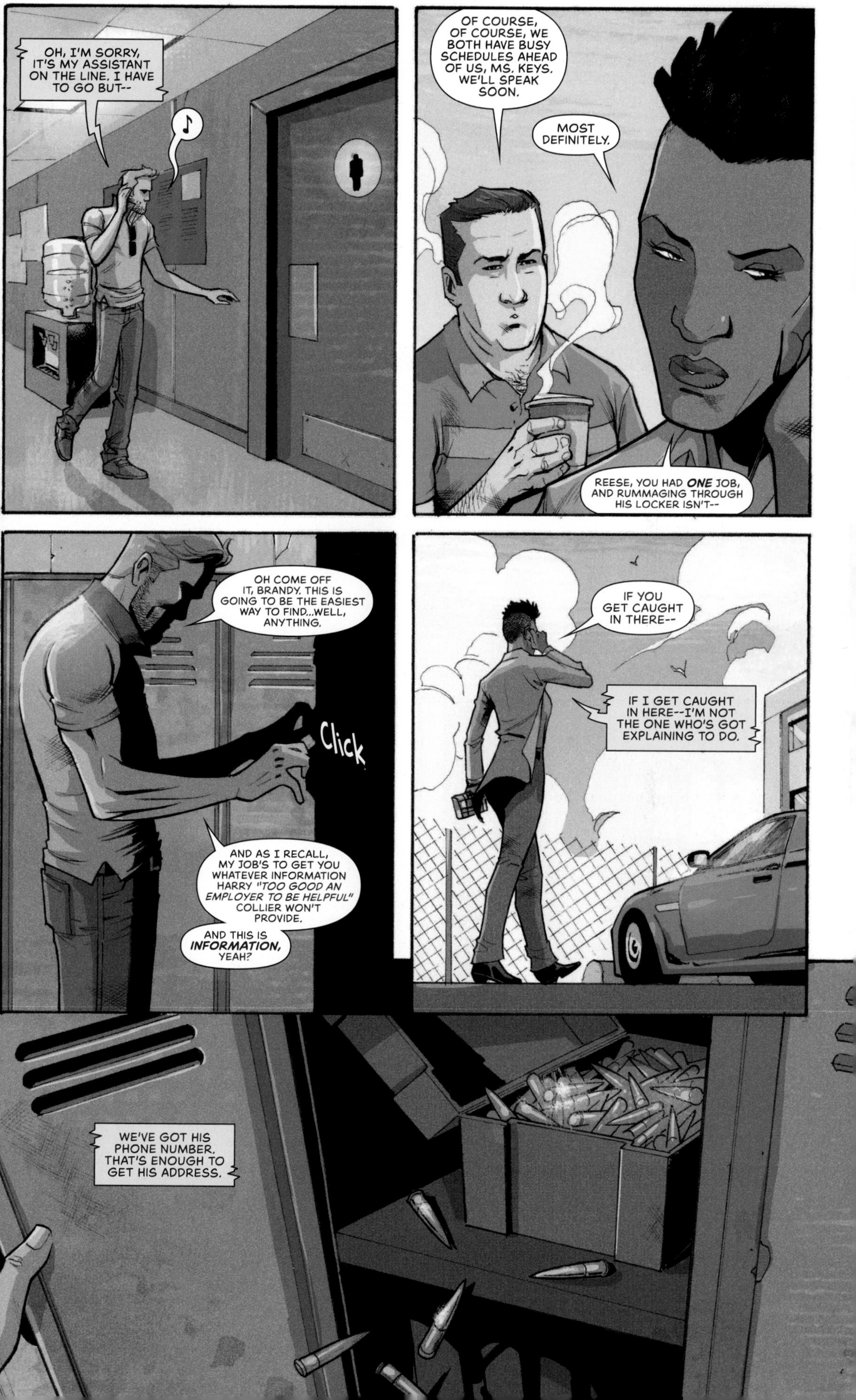

OH, I'M SORRY, IT'S MY ASSISTANT ON THE LINE. I HAVE TO GO BUT--
♪
OF COURSE, OF COURSE, WE BOTH HAVE BUSY SCHEDULES AHEAD OF US, MS. KEYS. WE'LL SPEAK SOON.
MOST DEFINITELY.
REESE, YOU HAD ONE JOB, AND RUMMAGING THROUGH HIS LOCKER ISN'T--
OH COME OFF IT, BRANDY. THIS IS GOING TO BE THE EASIEST WAY TO FIND...WELL, ANYTHING.
Click
AND AS I RECALL, MY JOB'S TO GET YOU WHATEVER INFORMATION HARRY "TOO GOOD AN EMPLOYER TO BE HELPFUL" COLLIER WON'T PROVIDE.
AND THIS IS INFORMATION, YEAH?
IF YOU GET CAUGHT IN THERE--
IF I GET CAUGHT IN HERE--I'M NOT THE ONE WHO'S GOT EXPLAINING TO DO.
WE'VE GOT HIS PHONE NUMBER. THAT'S ENOUGH TO GET HIS ADDRESS.

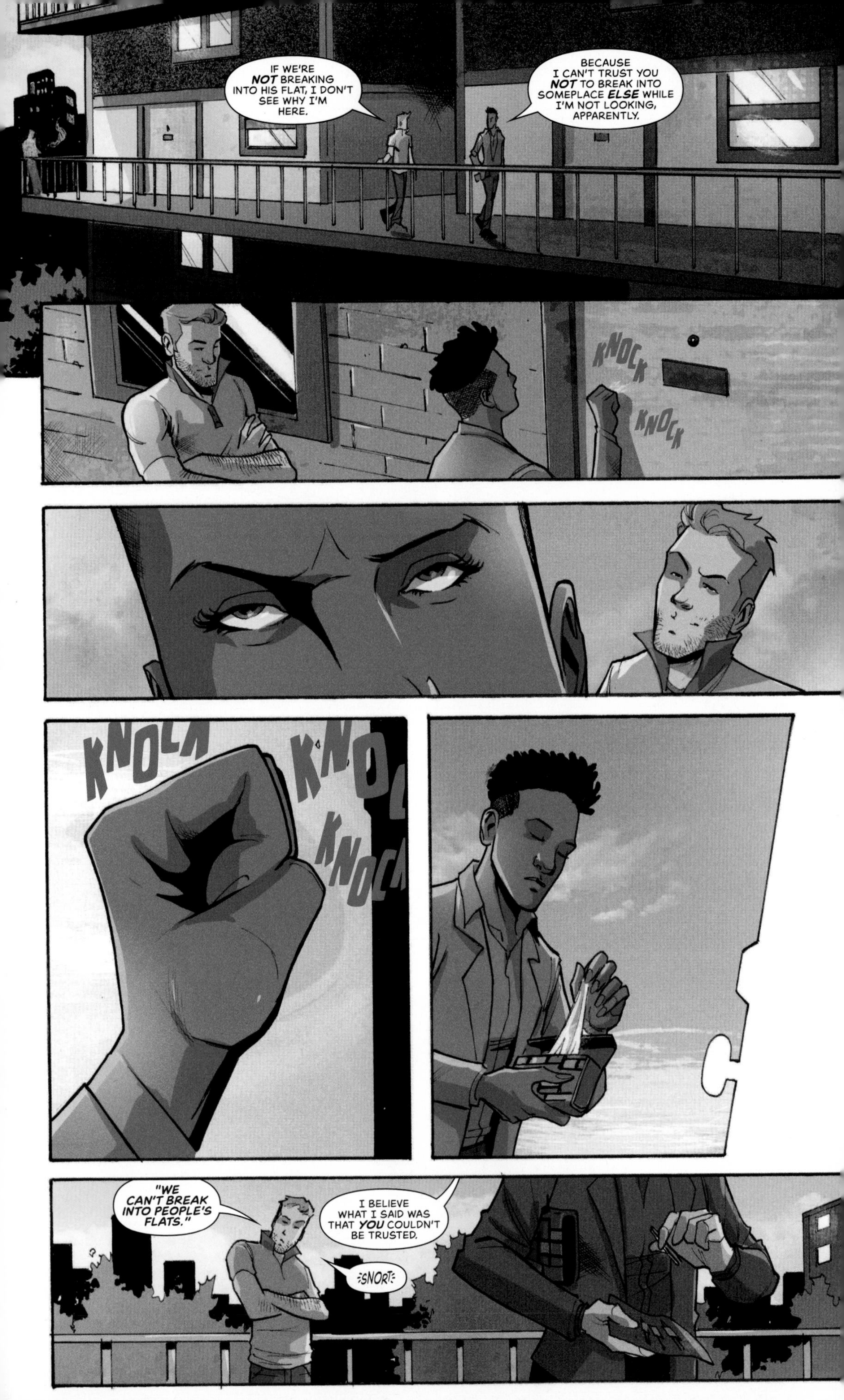
IF WE'RE NOT BREAKING INTO HIS FLAT, I DON'T SEE WHY I'M HERE.
BECAUSE I CAN'T TRUST YOU NOT TO BREAK INTO SOMEPLACE ELSE WHILE I'M NOT LOOKING, APPARENTLY.
KNOCK
KNOCK
KNOCK
KNOCK
KNOCK
"WE CAN'T BREAK INTO PEOPLE'S FLATS."
I BELIEVE WHAT I SAID WAS THAT YOU COULDN'T BE TRUSTED.
SNORT

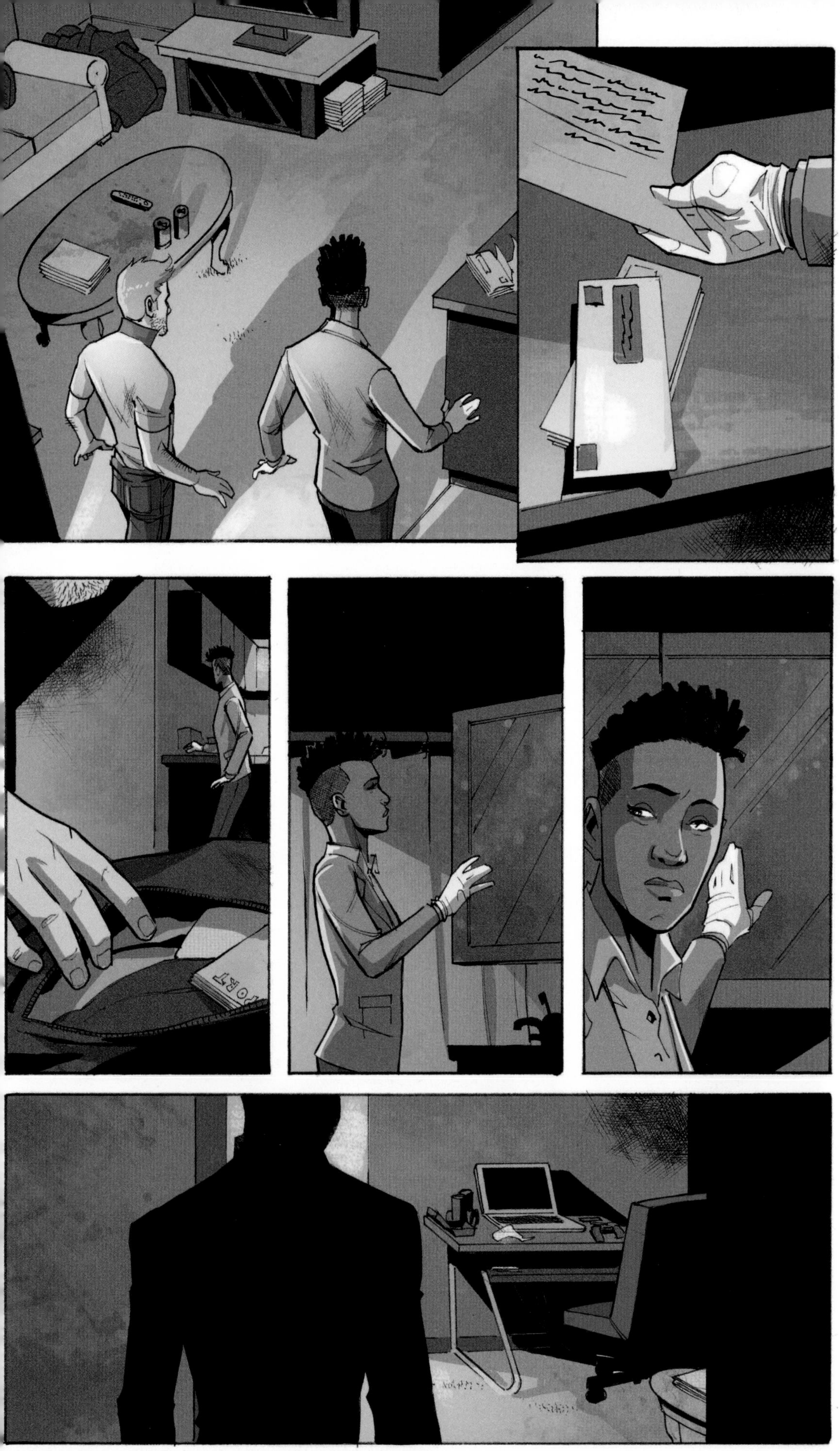

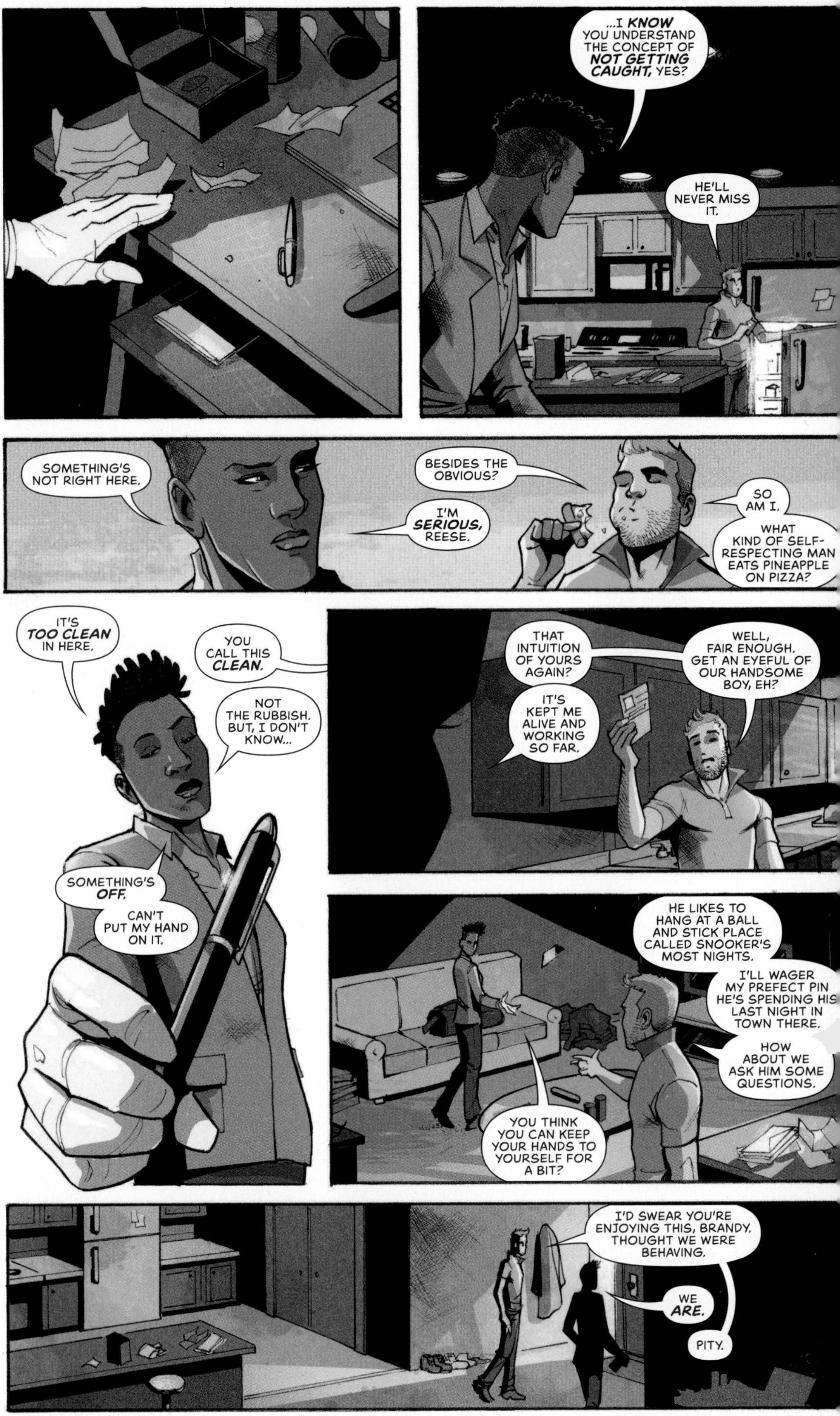
...I KNOW YOU UNDERSTAND THE CONCEPT OF NOT GETTING CAUGHT, YES?
HE'LL NEVER MISS IT.
SOMETHING'S NOT RIGHT HERE.
BESIDES THE OBVIOUS?
I'M SERIOUS, REESE.
SO AM I.
WHAT KIND OF SELF-RESPECTING MAN EATS PINEAPPLE ON PIZZA?
IT'S TOO CLEAN IN HERE.
YOU CALL THIS CLEAN.
NOT THE RUBBISH. BUT, I DON'T KNOW...
SOMETHING'S OFF.
CAN'T PUT MY HAND ON IT.
THAT INTUITION OF YOURS AGAIN?
IT'S KEPT ME ALIVE AND WORKING SO FAR.
WELL, FAIR ENOUGH. GET AN EYEFUL OF OUR HANDSOME BOY, EH?
HE LIKES TO HANG AT A BALL AND STICK PLACE CALLED SNOOKER'S MOST NIGHTS.
I'LL WAGER MY PREFECT PIN HE'S SPENDING HIS LAST NIGHT IN TOWN THERE.
HOW ABOUT WE ASK HIM SOME QUESTIONS.
YOU THINK YOU CAN KEEP YOUR HANDS TO YOURSELF FOR A BIT?
I'D SWEAR YOU'RE ENJOYING THIS, BRANDY. THOUGHT WE WERE BEHAVING.
WE ARE.
PITY.

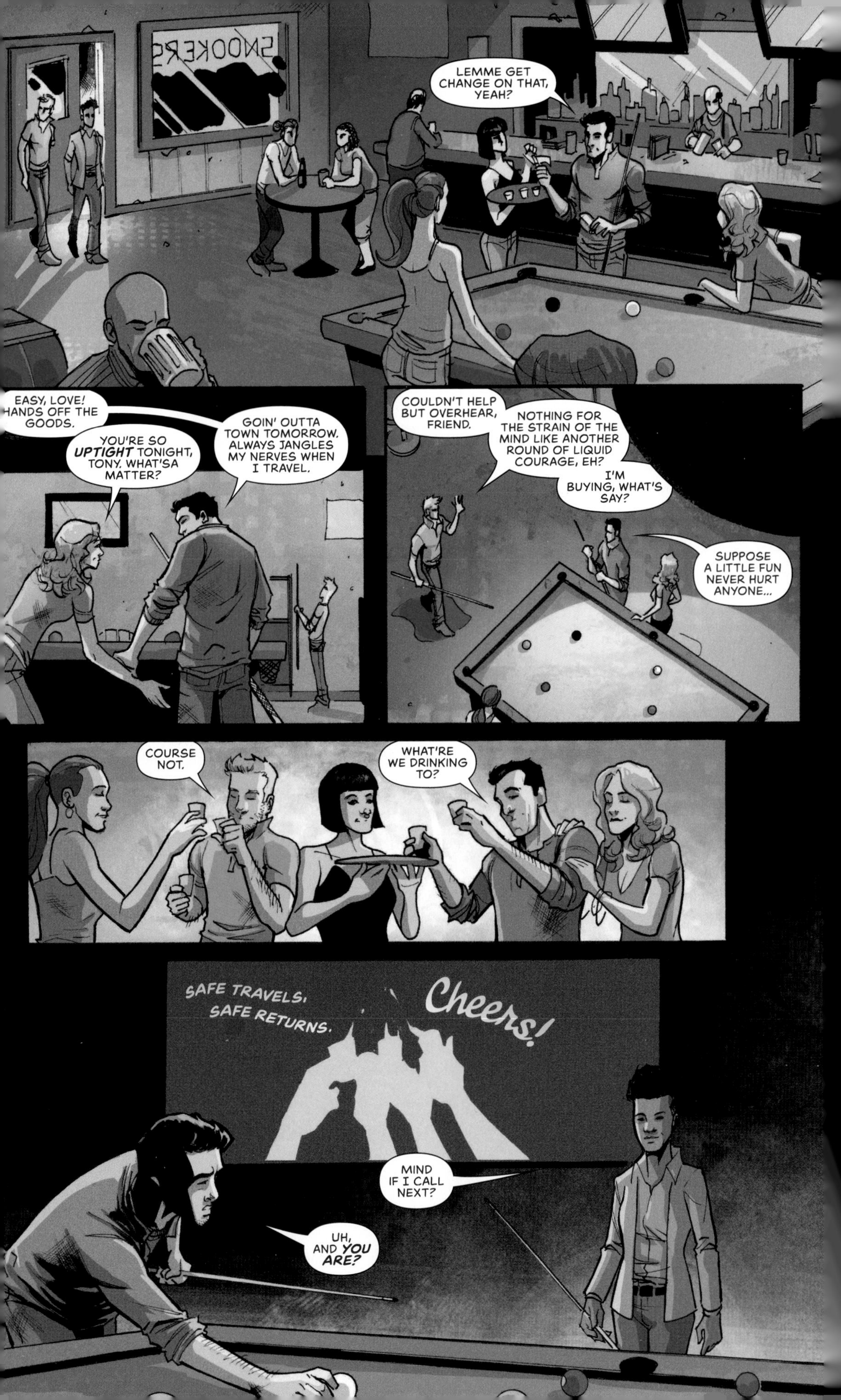
SNOOKERS
LEMME GET CHANGE ON THAT, YEAH?
EASY, LOVE! HANDS OFF THE GOODS.
YOU'RE SO UPTIGHT TONIGHT, TONY. WHAT'SA MATTER?
GOIN' OUTTA TOWN TOMORROW. ALWAYS JANGLES MY NERVES WHEN I TRAVEL.
COULDN'T HELP BUT OVERHEAR, FRIEND.
NOTHING FOR THE STRAIN OF THE MIND LIKE ANOTHER ROUND OF LIQUID COURAGE, EH?
I'M BUYING, WHAT'S SAY?
SUPPOSE A LITTLE FUN NEVER HURT ANYONE...
COURSE NOT.
WHAT'RE WE DRINKING TO?
SAFE TRAVELS, SAFE RETURNS.
Cheers!
MIND IF I CALL NEXT?
UH, AND YOU ARE?

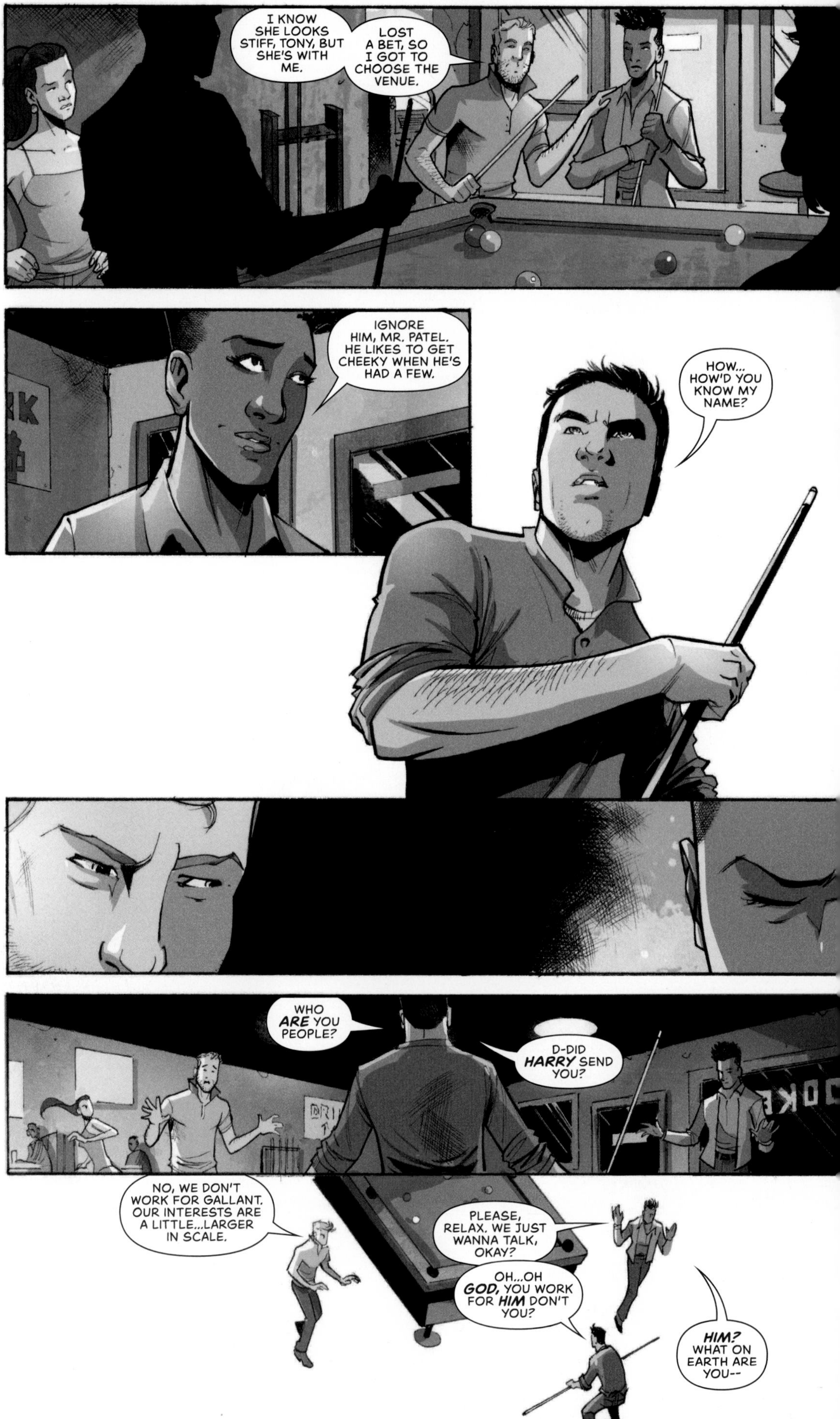

I KNOW SHE LOOKS STIFF, TONY, BUT SHE'S WITH ME.
LOST A BET, SO I GOT TO CHOOSE THE VENUE.
IGNORE HIM, MR. PATEL. HE LIKES TO GET CHEEKY WHEN HE'S HAD A FEW.
HOW... HOW'D YOU KNOW MY NAME?
WHO *ARE* YOU PEOPLE?
D-DID *HARRY* SEND YOU?
NO, WE DON'T WORK FOR GALLANT. OUR INTERESTS ARE A LITTLE...LARGER IN SCALE.
PLEASE, RELAX. WE JUST WANNA TALK, OKAY?
OH...OH *GOD,* YOU WORK FOR *HIM* DON'T YOU?
HIM? WHAT ON EARTH ARE YOU--

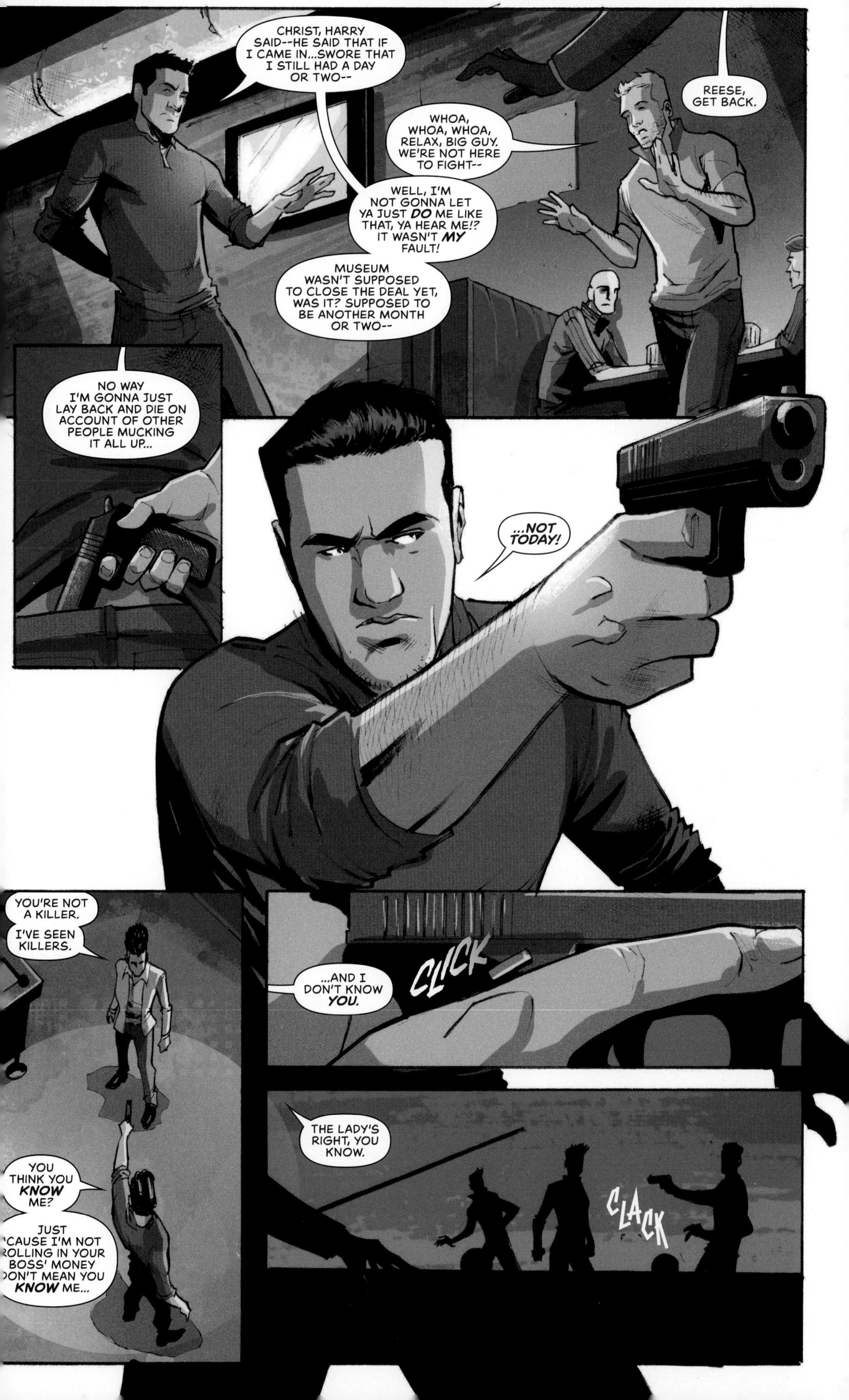
CHRIST, HARRY SAID--HE SAID THAT IF I CAME IN...SWORE THAT I STILL HAD A DAY OR TWO--
REESE, GET BACK.
WHOA, WHOA, WHOA, RELAX, BIG GUY. WE'RE NOT HERE TO FIGHT--
WELL, I'M NOT GONNA LET YA JUST DO ME LIKE THAT, YA HEAR ME!? IT WASN'T MY FAULT!
MUSEUM WASN'T SUPPOSED TO CLOSE THE DEAL YET, WAS IT? SUPPOSED TO BE ANOTHER MONTH OR TWO--
NO WAY I'M GONNA JUST LAY BACK AND DIE ON ACCOUNT OF OTHER PEOPLE MUCKING IT ALL UP...
...NOT TODAY!
YOU'RE NOT A KILLER.
I'VE SEEN KILLERS.
YOU THINK YOU KNOW ME?
JUST 'CAUSE I'M NOT ROLLING IN YOUR BOSS' MONEY DON'T MEAN YOU KNOW ME...
CLICK
...AND I DON'T KNOW YOU.
THE LADY'S RIGHT, YOU KNOW.
CLACK

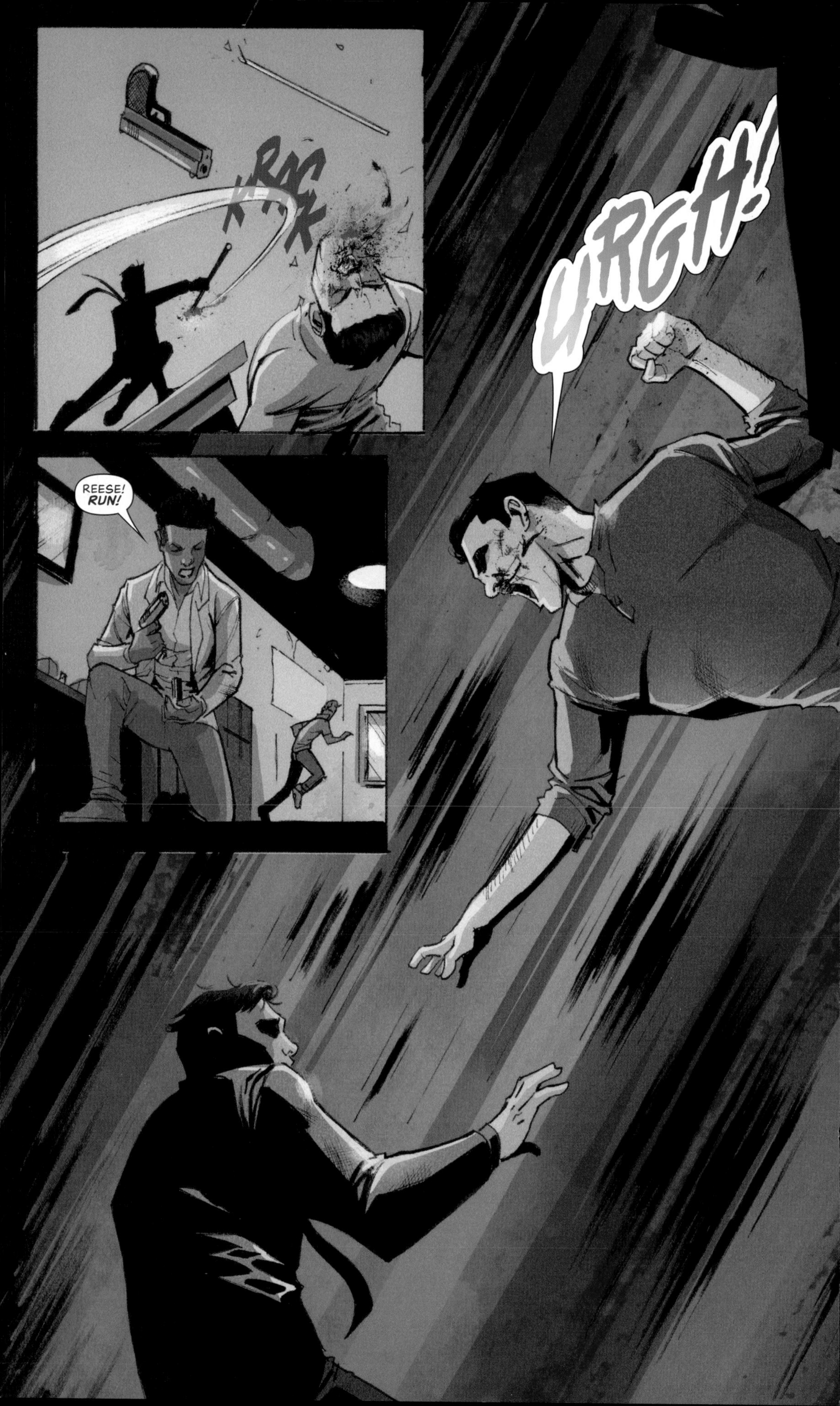
KRACK
REESE!
RUN!
URGH!

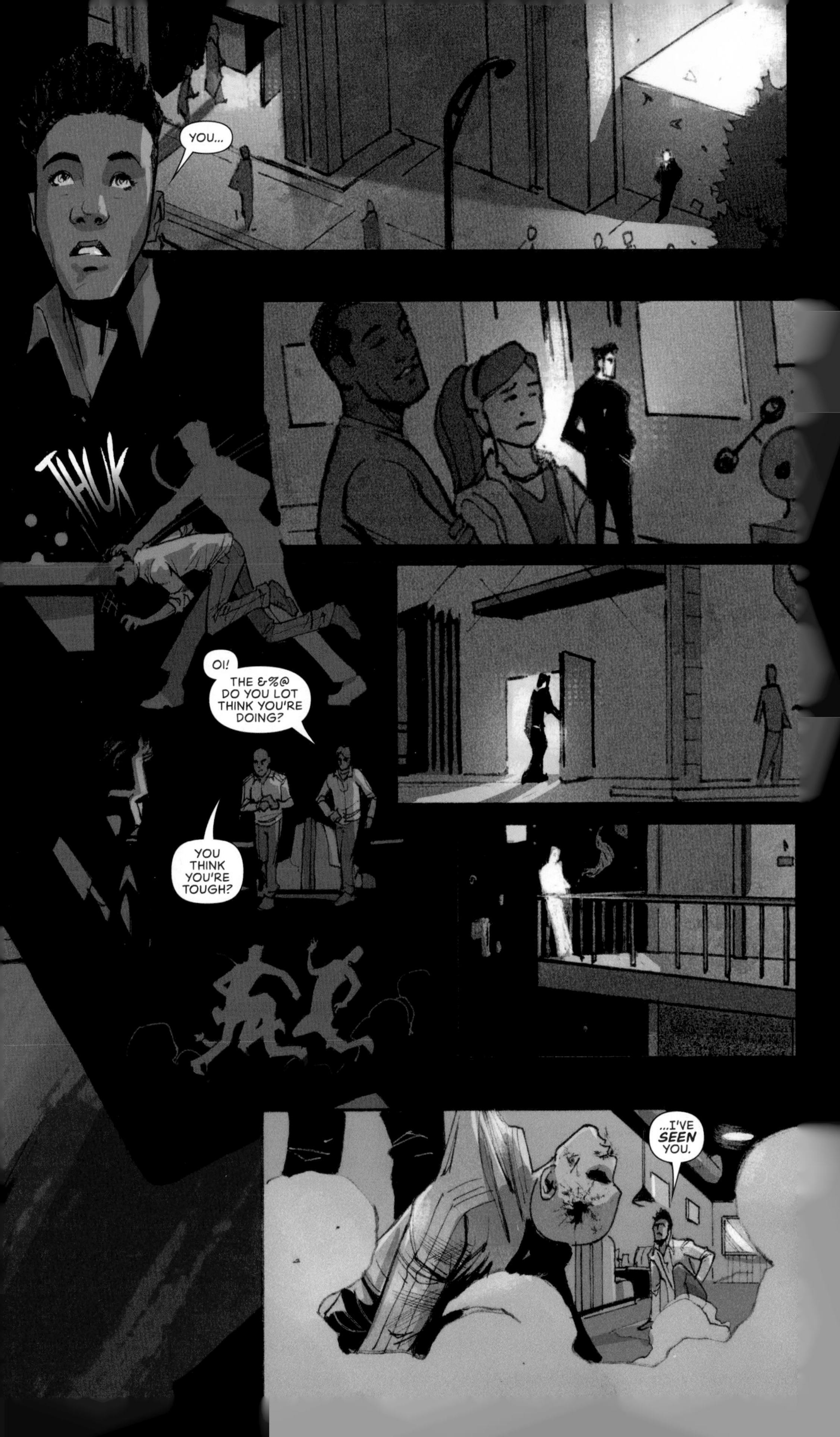
YOU...
THUK
OI!
THE &%@ DO YOU LOT THINK YOU'RE DOING?
YOU THINK YOU'RE TOUGH?
...I'VE SEEN YOU.

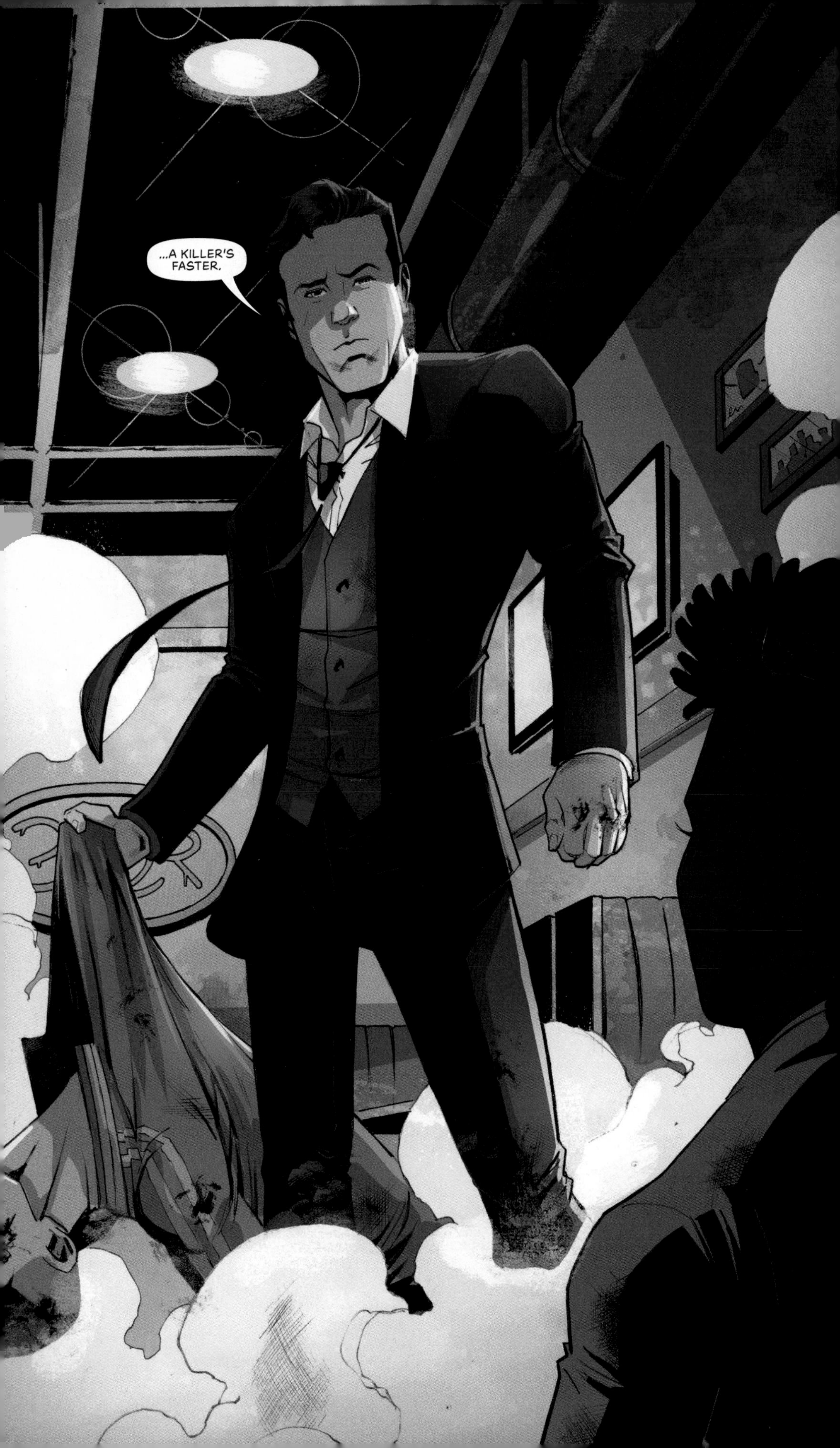
...A KILLER'S FASTER.

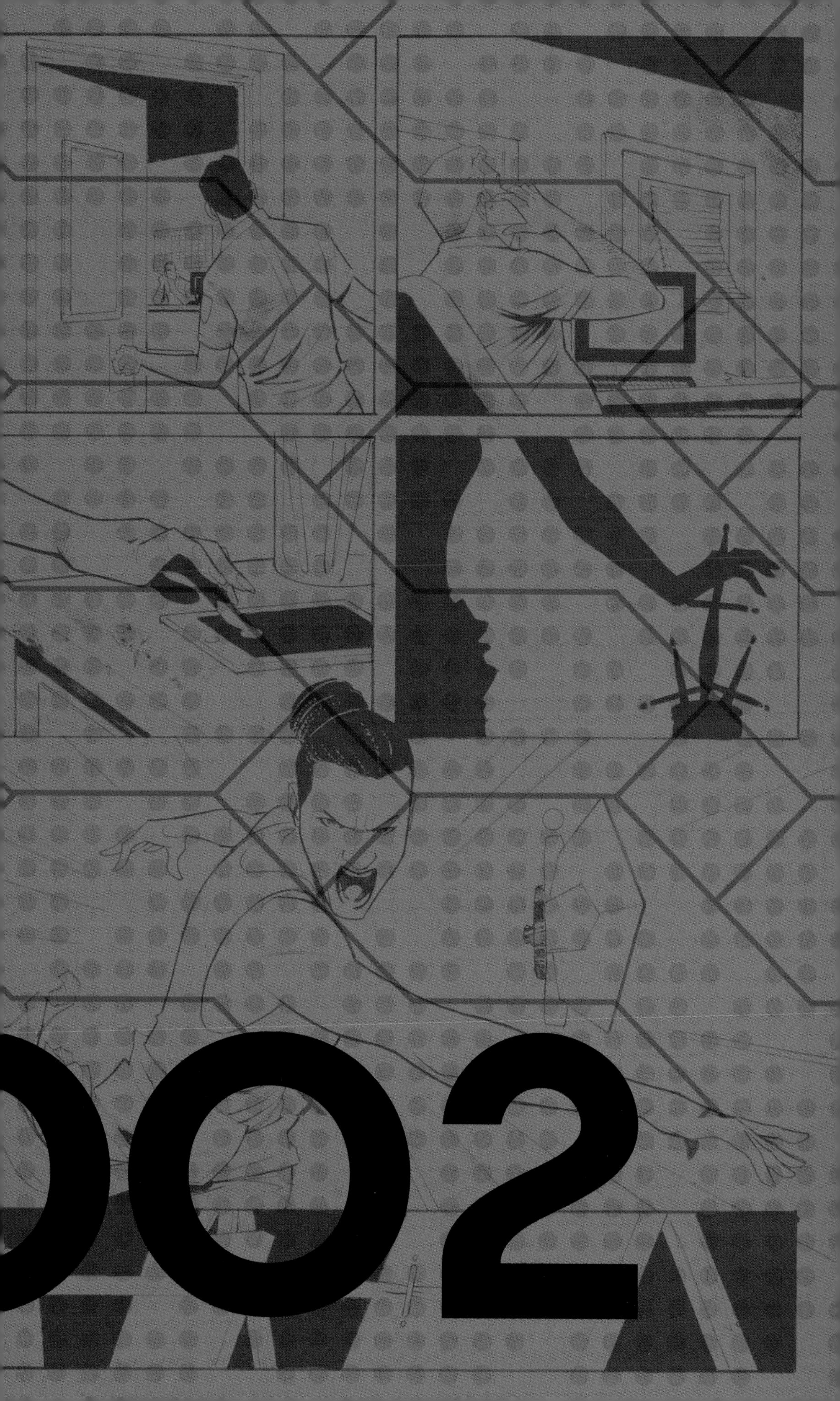
002

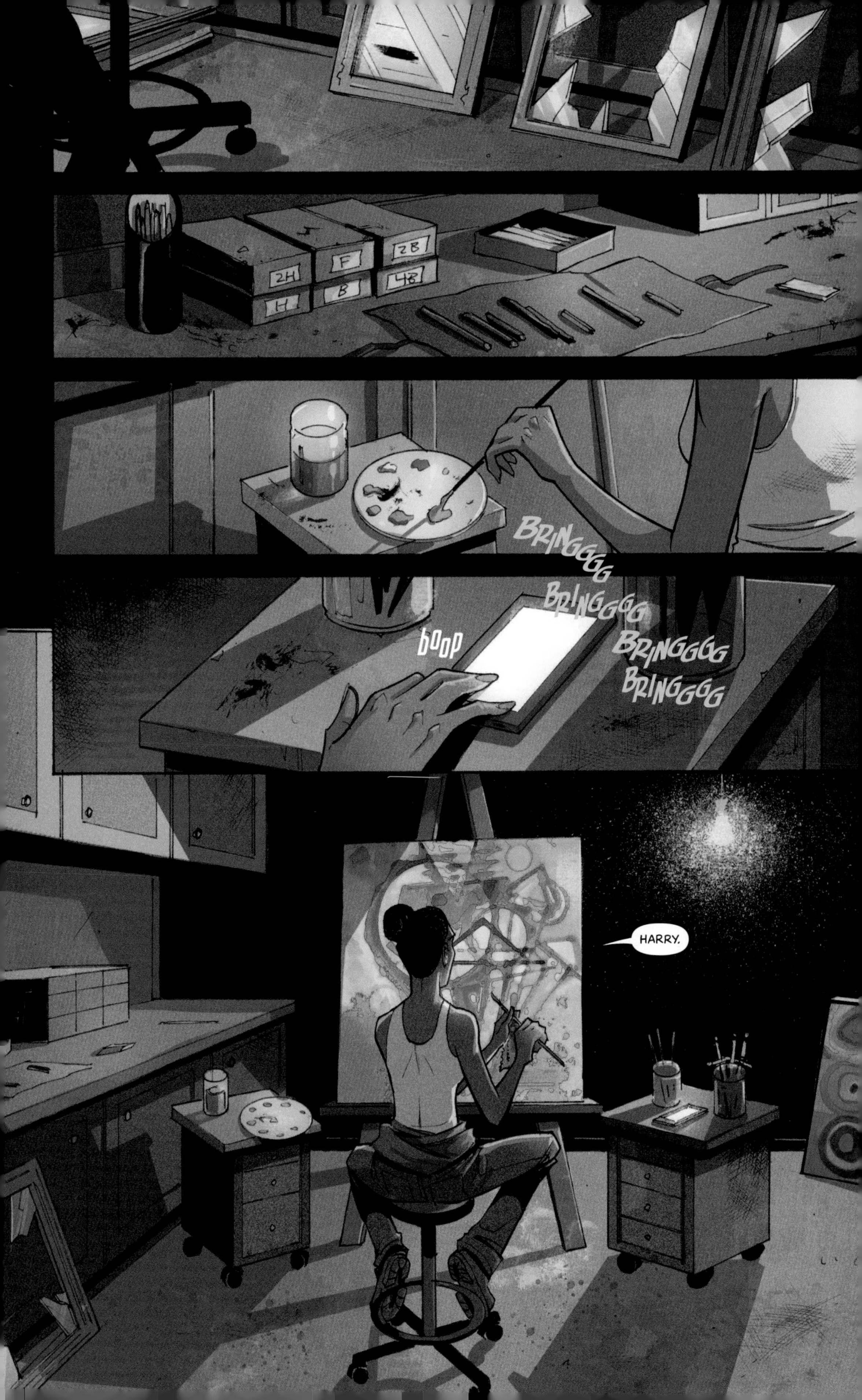
2H
F
2B
H
B
4B
BRINGGGG
BRINGGGG
BOOP
BRINGGGG
BRINGGGG
HARRY.

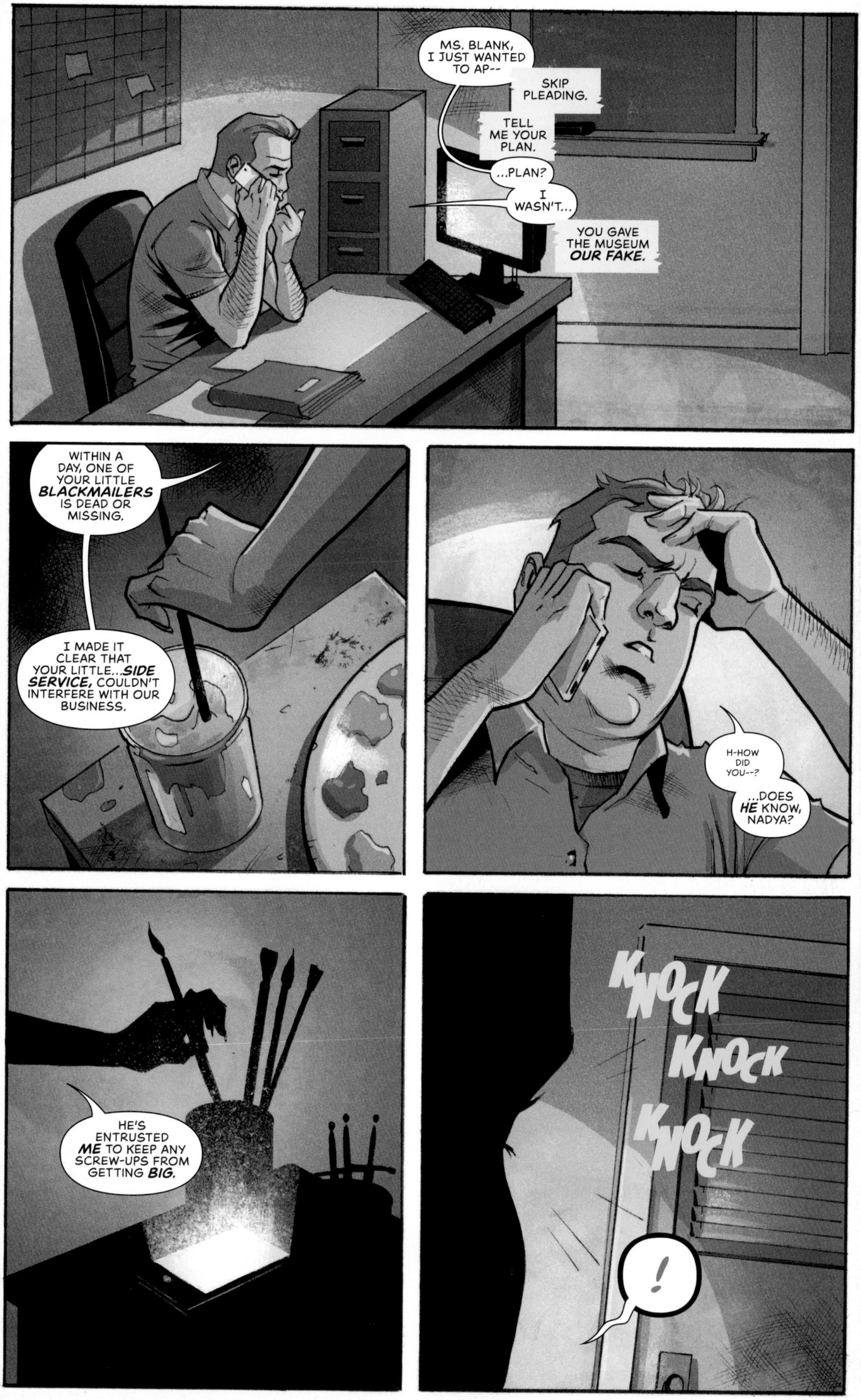
MS. BLANK, I JUST WANTED TO AP--
SKIP PLEADING.
TELL ME YOUR PLAN.
...PLAN?
I WASN'T...
YOU GAVE THE MUSEUM OUR FAKE.
WITHIN A DAY, ONE OF YOUR LITTLE BLACKMAILERS IS DEAD OR MISSING.
I MADE IT CLEAR THAT YOUR LITTLE...SIDE SERVICE, COULDN'T INTERFERE WITH OUR BUSINESS.
H-HOW DID YOU--?
...DOES HE KNOW, NADYA?
HE'S ENTRUSTED ME TO KEEP ANY SCREW-UPS FROM GETTING BIG.
KNOCK
KNOCK
KNOCK
!

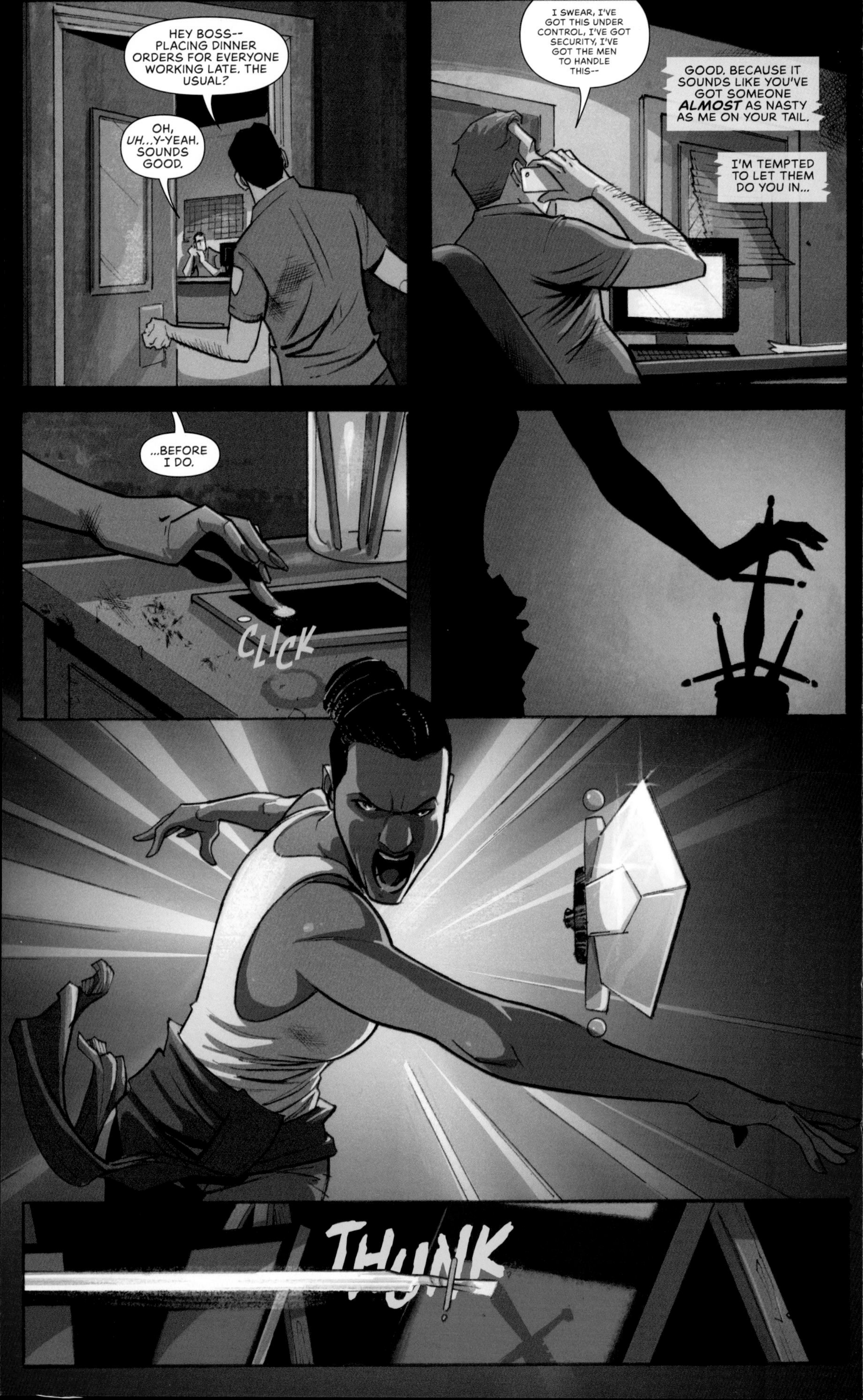
HEY BOSS-- PLACING DINNER ORDERS FOR EVERYONE WORKING LATE. THE USUAL?
OH, UH...Y-YEAH. SOUNDS GOOD.
I SWEAR, I'VE GOT THIS UNDER CONTROL, I'VE GOT SECURITY, I'VE GOT THE MEN TO HANDLE THIS--
GOOD. BECAUSE IT SOUNDS LIKE YOU'VE GOT SOMEONE ALMOST AS NASTY AS ME ON YOUR TAIL.
I'M TEMPTED TO LET THEM DO YOU IN...
...BEFORE I DO.
CLICK
THUNK

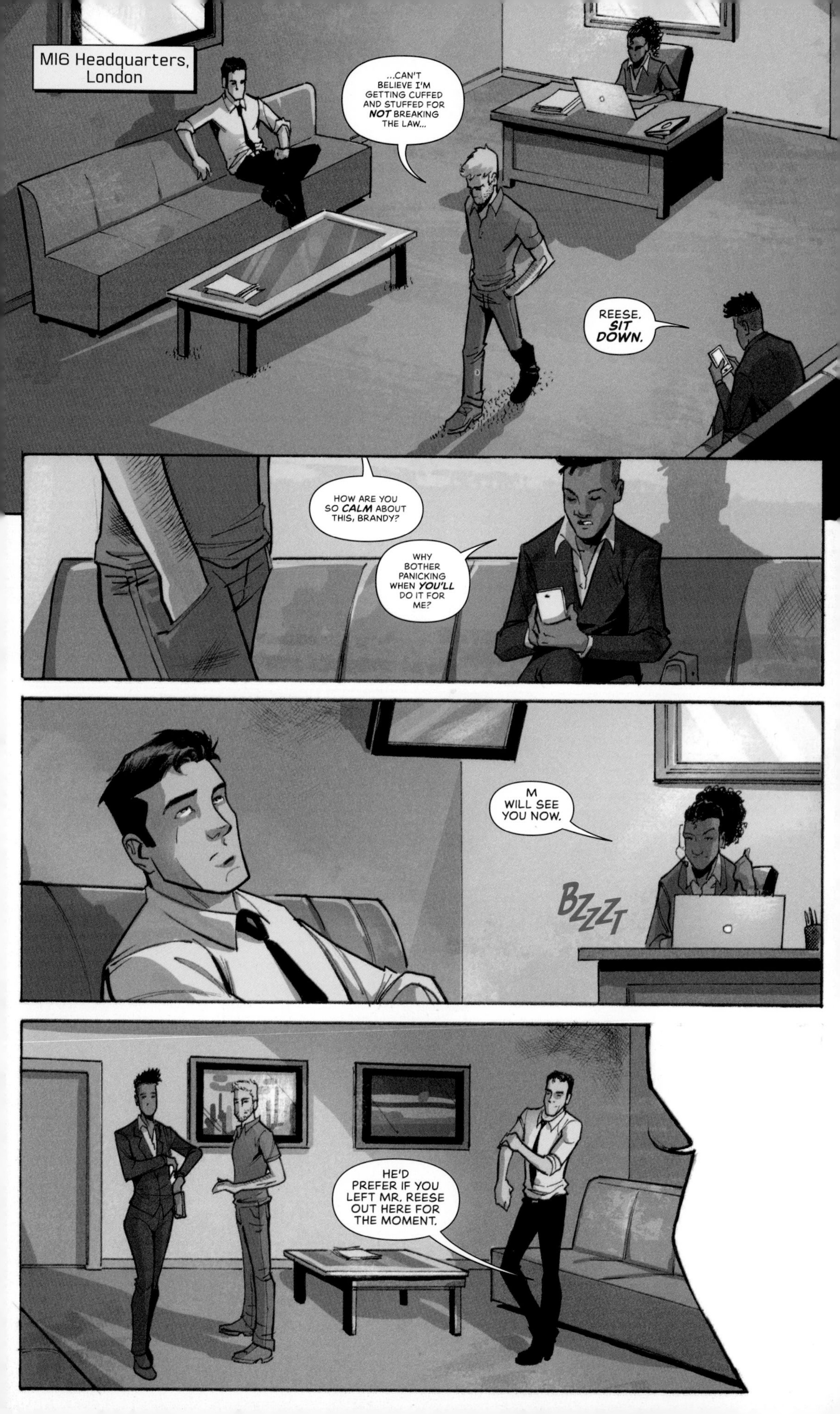
MI6 Headquarters, London
...CAN'T BELIEVE I'M GETTING CUFFED AND STUFFED FOR NOT BREAKING THE LAW...
REESE. SIT DOWN.
HOW ARE YOU SO CALM ABOUT THIS, BRANDY?
WHY BOTHER PANICKING WHEN YOU'LL DO IT FOR ME?
M WILL SEE YOU NOW.
BZZZT
HE'D PREFER IF YOU LEFT MR. REESE OUT HERE FOR THE MOMENT.

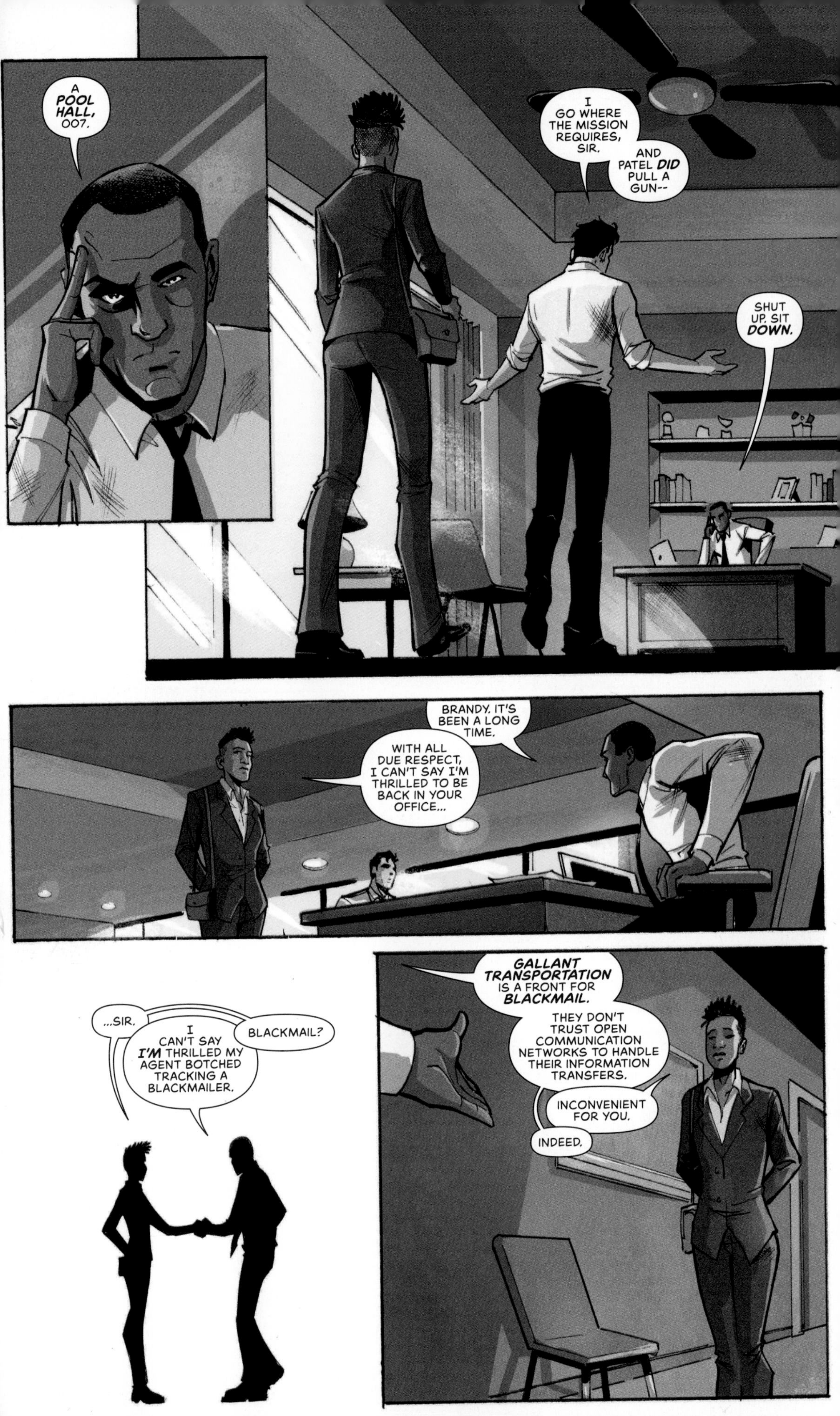
A POOL HALL, 007.
I GO WHERE THE MISSION REQUIRES, SIR.
AND PATEL DID PULL A GUN--
SHUT UP. SIT DOWN.
BRANDY. IT'S BEEN A LONG TIME.
WITH ALL DUE RESPECT, I CAN'T SAY I'M THRILLED TO BE BACK IN YOUR OFFICE...
...SIR.
I CAN'T SAY I'M THRILLED MY AGENT BOTCHED TRACKING A BLACKMAILER.
BLACKMAIL?
GALLANT TRANSPORTATION IS A FRONT FOR BLACKMAIL.
THEY DON'T TRUST OPEN COMMUNICATION NETWORKS TO HANDLE THEIR INFORMATION TRANSFERS.
INCONVENIENT FOR YOU.
INDEED.

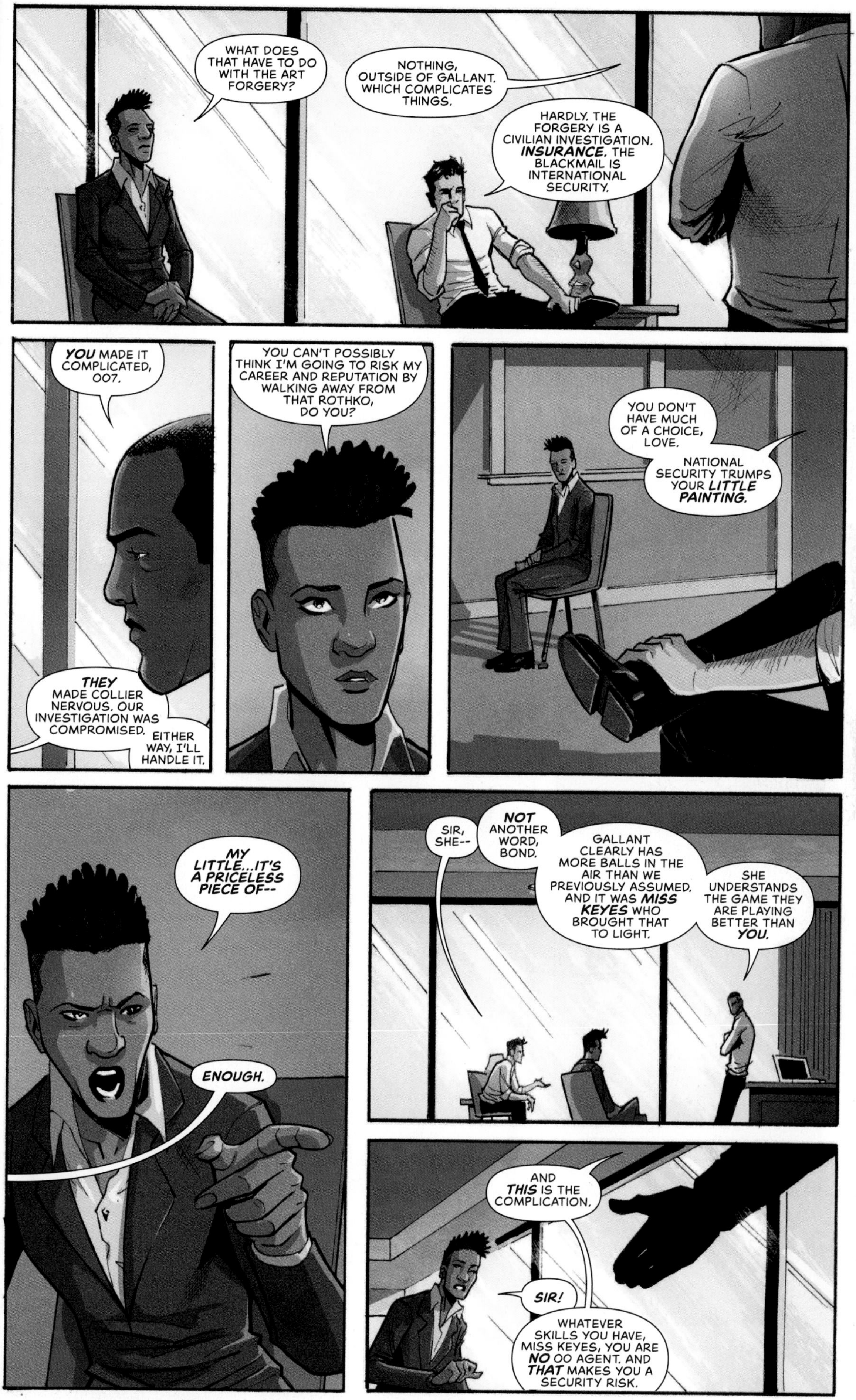
WHAT DOES THAT HAVE TO DO WITH THE ART FORGERY?
NOTHING, OUTSIDE OF GALLANT. WHICH COMPLICATES THINGS.
HARDLY. THE FORGERY IS A CIVILIAN INVESTIGATION. INSURANCE. THE BLACKMAIL IS INTERNATIONAL SECURITY.
YOU MADE IT COMPLICATED, 007.
THEY MADE COLLIER NERVOUS. OUR INVESTIGATION WAS COMPROMISED.
EITHER WAY, I'LL HANDLE IT.
YOU CAN'T POSSIBLY THINK I'M GOING TO RISK MY CAREER AND REPUTATION BY WALKING AWAY FROM THAT ROTHKO, DO YOU?
YOU DON'T HAVE MUCH OF A CHOICE, LOVE.
NATIONAL SECURITY TRUMPS YOUR LITTLE PAINTING.
MY LITTLE...IT'S A PRICELESS PIECE OF--
ENOUGH.
SIR, SHE--
NOT ANOTHER WORD, BOND.
GALLANT CLEARLY HAS MORE BALLS IN THE AIR THAN WE PREVIOUSLY ASSUMED. AND IT WAS MISS KEYES WHO BROUGHT THAT TO LIGHT.
SHE UNDERSTANDS THE GAME THEY ARE PLAYING BETTER THAN YOU.
AND THIS IS THE COMPLICATION.
SIR!
WHATEVER SKILLS YOU HAVE, MISS KEYES, YOU ARE NO 00 AGENT. AND THAT MAKES YOU A SECURITY RISK.

YOU KNOW WHAT I'VE DONE WITH MY LIFE SINCE WE MET, M.

I'VE MADE GOOD.

I DON'T WANT TO HAVE TO ASK YOU FOR ANYTHING, *AGAIN.*

IT'S NOT ABOUT THE ROTHKO.

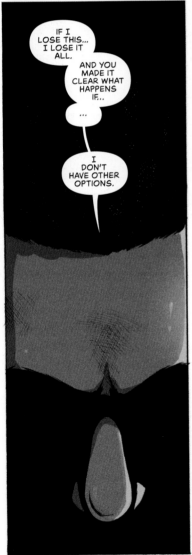

IF I LOSE THIS... I LOSE IT ALL.

AND YOU MADE IT CLEAR WHAT HAPPENS IF...

...

I DON'T HAVE OTHER OPTIONS.

PATEL REVEALED THAT HARRY COLLIER IS HAVING A BIT OF A PARTY AT HIS VILLA IN AMSTERDAM.

WE NEED A LEVEL OF EXPERTISE FOR THIS MISSION...THAT BOND DOESN'T POSSESS.

I'M QUITE ADAPTABLE, SIR...

YOU LEAVE TONIGHT.

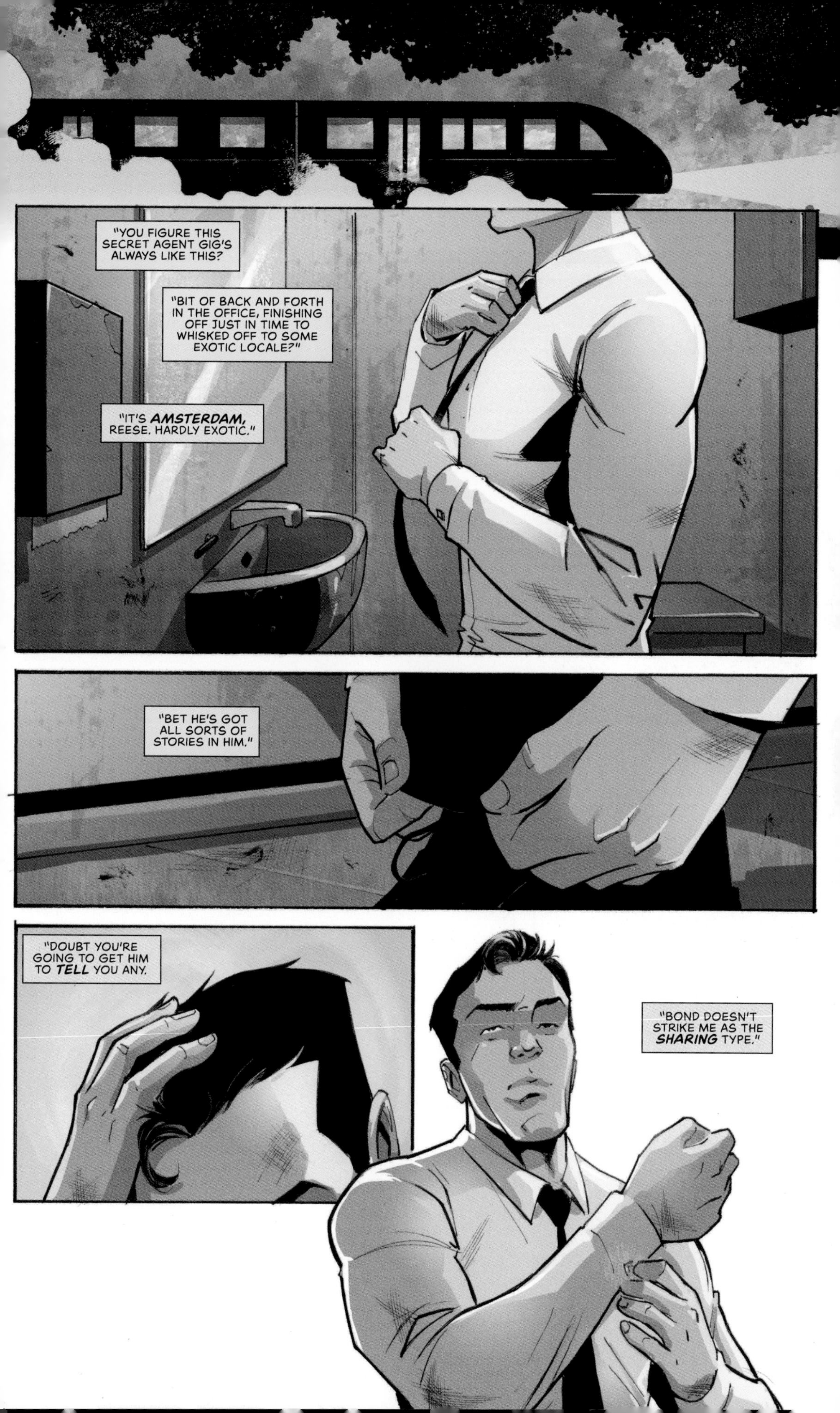
"YOU FIGURE THIS SECRET AGENT GIG'S ALWAYS LIKE THIS?
"BIT OF BACK AND FORTH IN THE OFFICE, FINISHING OFF JUST IN TIME TO WHISKED OFF TO SOME EXOTIC LOCALE?"
"IT'S **AMSTERDAM,** REESE. HARDLY EXOTIC."
"BET HE'S GOT ALL SORTS OF STORIES IN HIM."
"DOUBT YOU'RE GOING TO GET HIM TO **TELL** YOU ANY.
"BOND DOESN'T STRIKE ME AS THE **SHARING** TYPE."

VODKA
CRANBERRY.

THANK
YOU.

REAL
SHAME, INNIT?
I BET THE MAN'S
GOT SOME
AMAZIN'
STORIES.

THINK I
CAN GET HIM
TO SPILL
SOME?

I
DOUBT
IT.

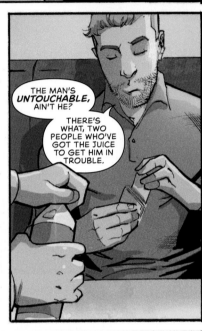

THE MAN'S
UNTOUCHABLE,
AIN'T HE?

THERE'S
WHAT, TWO
PEOPLE WHO'VE
GOT THE JUICE
TO GET HIM IN
TROUBLE.

PICTURE
IT:

"*'SCUSE ME
OFFICER, BUT THIS
GUY'S HARASSIN' ME
AND HE'S A BLOODY-
FREAKING-SECRET-
AGEN*"

IF
YOU WERE
THAT EAGER
TO CHAT...

I'D BE
OCCUPATIONALLY
BOUND TO KEEP
YOU QUIET.

OH, UH...
I...

PARDON.

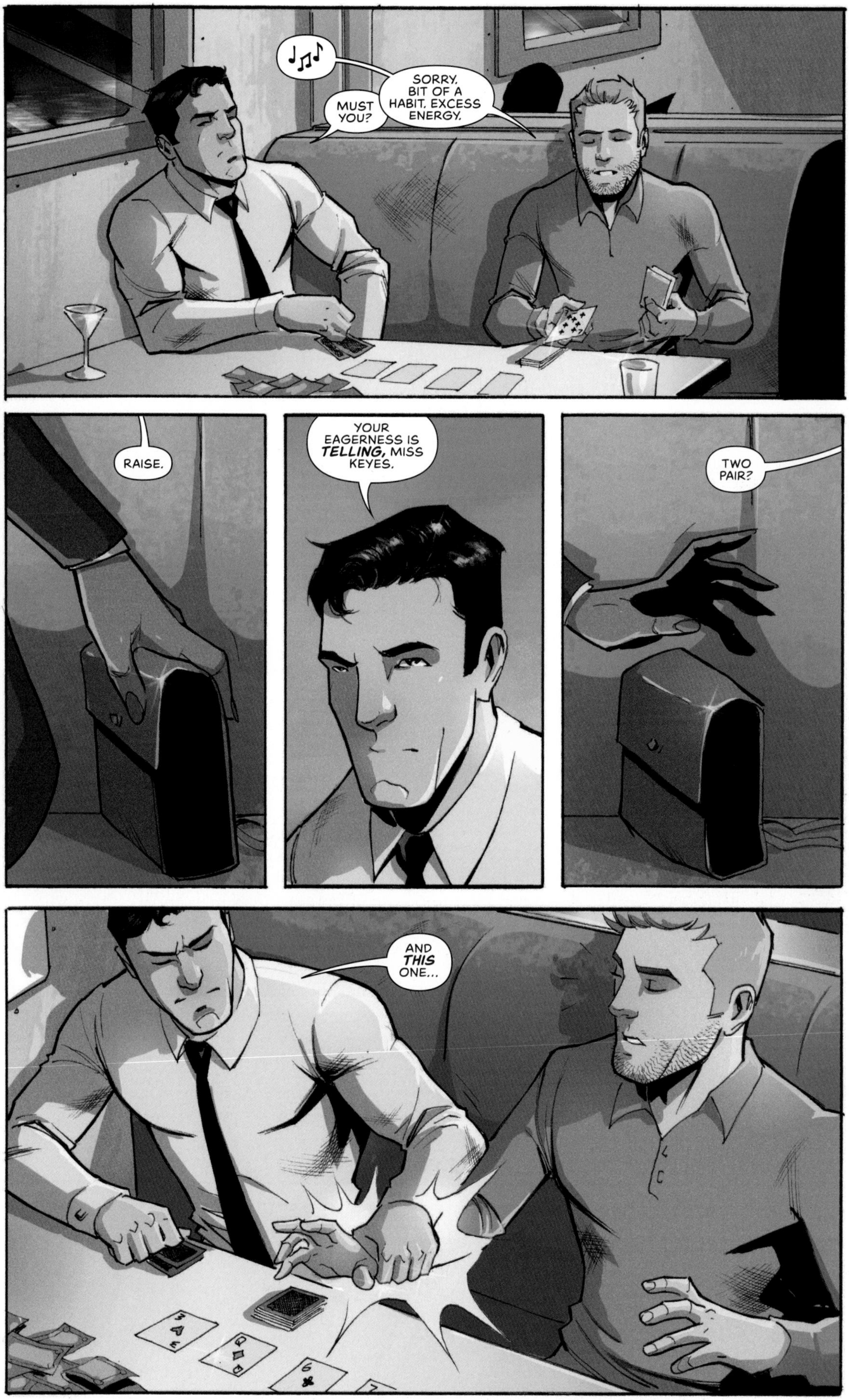

♩♫♪
MUST YOU?
SORRY, BIT OF A HABIT, EXCESS ENERGY.
RAISE.
YOUR EAGERNESS IS **TELLING,** MISS KEYES.
TWO PAIR?
AND **THIS** ONE...

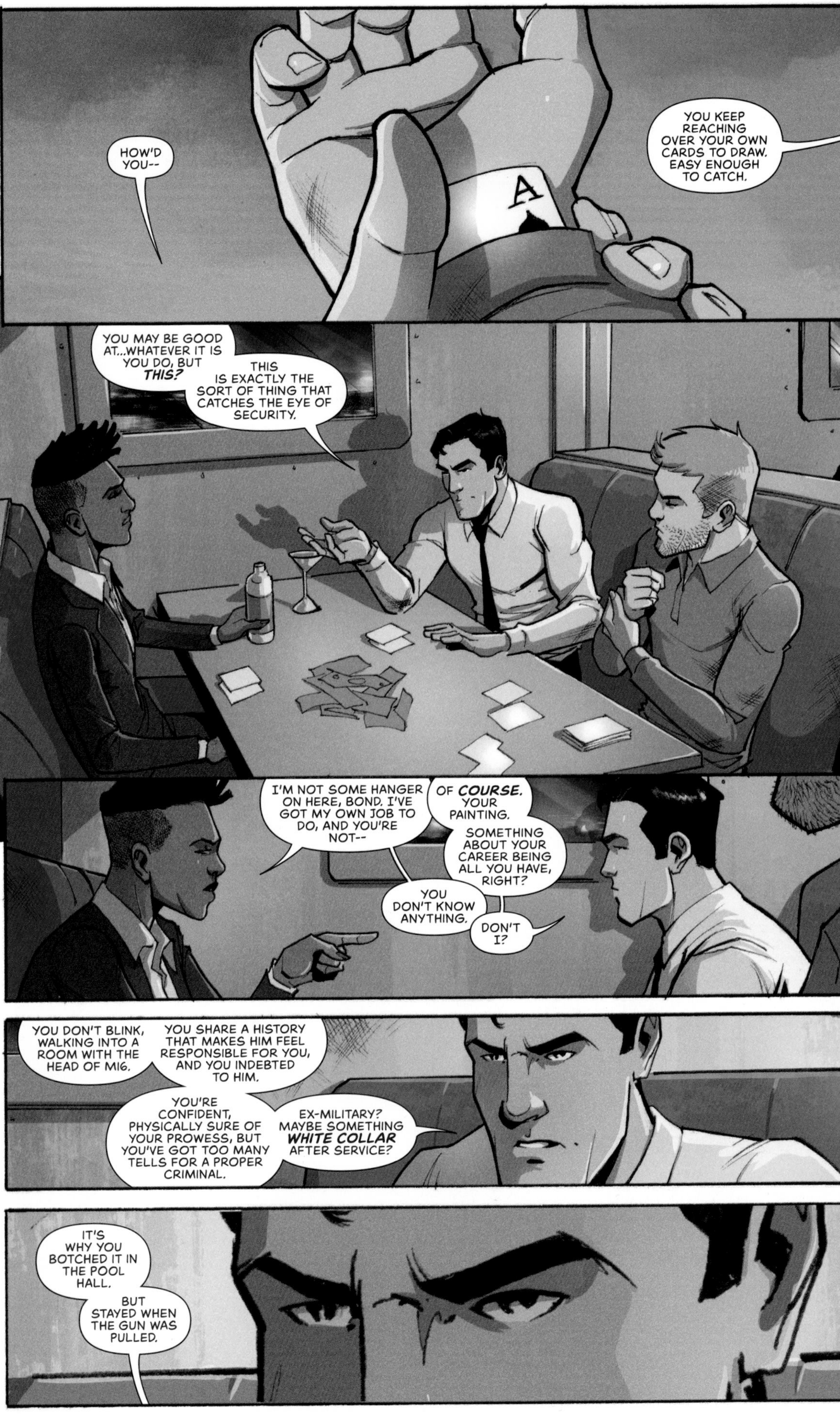
HOW'D YOU--
YOU KEEP REACHING OVER YOUR OWN CARDS TO DRAW. EASY ENOUGH TO CATCH.
YOU MAY BE GOOD AT...WHATEVER IT IS YOU DO, BUT **THIS?**
THIS IS EXACTLY THE SORT OF THING THAT CATCHES THE EYE OF SECURITY.
I'M NOT SOME HANGER ON HERE, BOND. I'VE GOT MY OWN JOB TO DO, AND YOU'RE NOT--
OF **COURSE.** YOUR PAINTING.
SOMETHING ABOUT YOUR CAREER BEING ALL YOU HAVE, RIGHT?
YOU DON'T KNOW ANYTHING.
DON'T I?
YOU DON'T BLINK, WALKING INTO A ROOM WITH THE HEAD OF MI6.
YOU SHARE A HISTORY THAT MAKES HIM FEEL RESPONSIBLE FOR YOU, AND YOU INDEBTED TO HIM.
YOU'RE CONFIDENT, PHYSICALLY SURE OF YOUR PROWESS, BUT YOU'VE GOT TOO MANY TELLS FOR A PROPER CRIMINAL.
EX-MILITARY? MAYBE SOMETHING **WHITE COLLAR** AFTER SERVICE?
IT'S WHY YOU BOTCHED IT IN THE POOL HALL.
BUT STAYED WHEN THE GUN WAS PULLED.

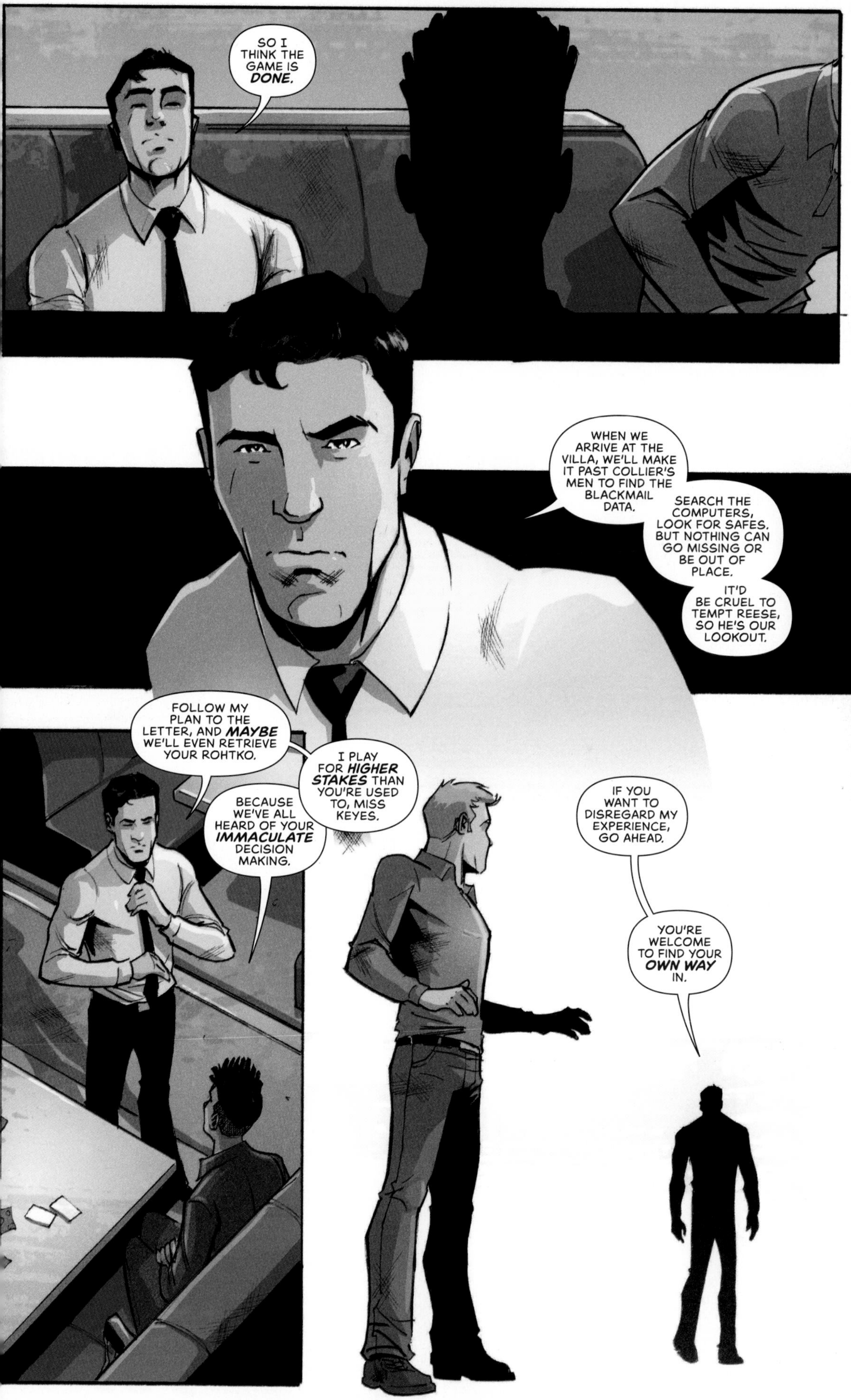
SO I THINK THE GAME IS DONE.
WHEN WE ARRIVE AT THE VILLA, WE'LL MAKE IT PAST COLLIER'S MEN TO FIND THE BLACKMAIL DATA.
SEARCH THE COMPUTERS, LOOK FOR SAFES. BUT NOTHING CAN GO MISSING OR BE OUT OF PLACE.
IT'D BE CRUEL TO TEMPT REESE, SO HE'S OUR LOOKOUT.
FOLLOW MY PLAN TO THE LETTER, AND MAYBE WE'LL EVEN RETRIEVE YOUR ROHTKO.
BECAUSE WE'VE ALL HEARD OF YOUR IMMACULATE DECISION MAKING.
I PLAY FOR HIGHER STAKES THAN YOU'RE USED TO, MISS KEYES.
IF YOU WANT TO DISREGARD MY EXPERIENCE, GO AHEAD.
YOU'RE WELCOME TO FIND YOUR OWN WAY IN.

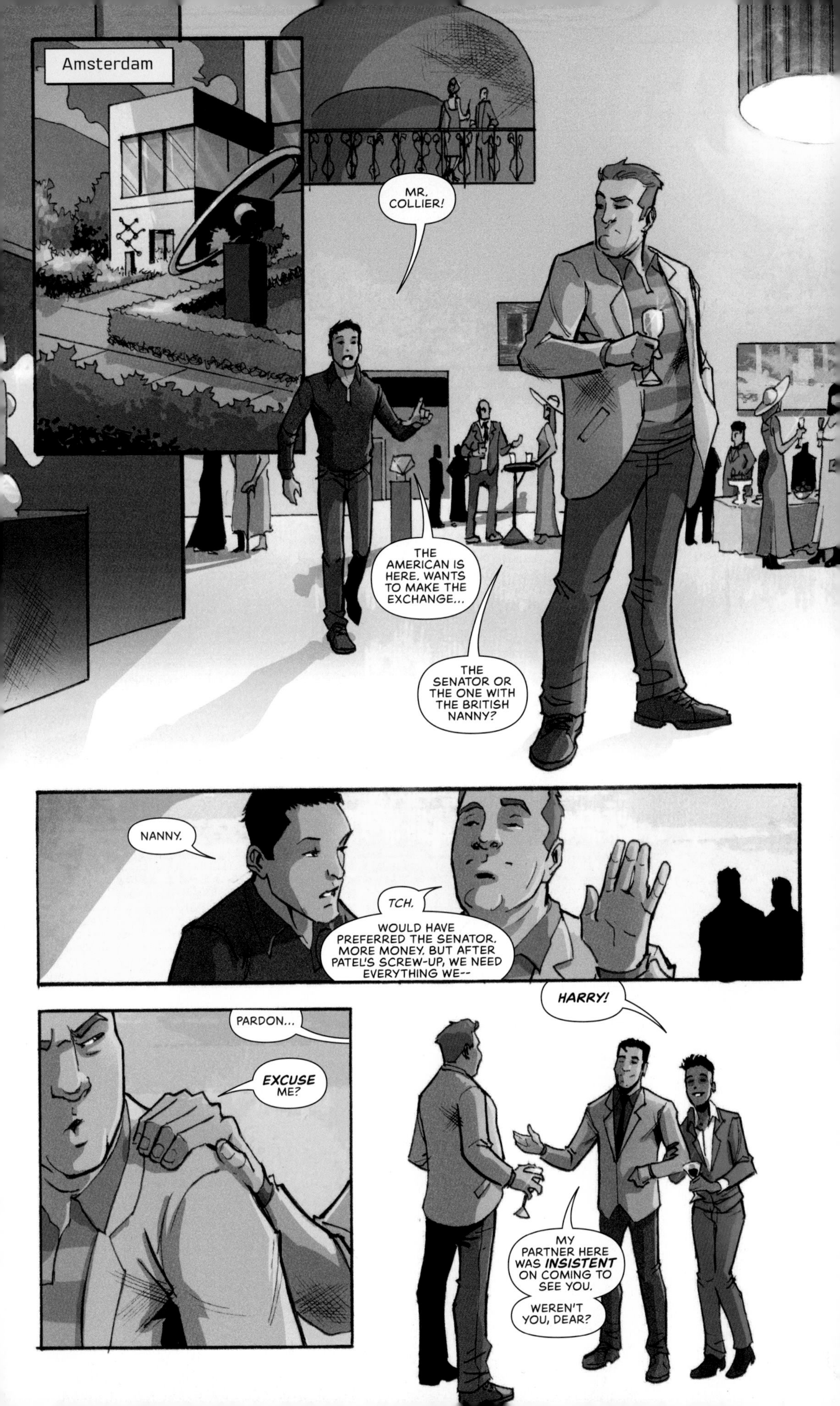
Amsterdam
MR. COLLIER!
THE AMERICAN IS HERE. WANTS TO MAKE THE EXCHANGE...
THE SENATOR OR THE ONE WITH THE BRITISH NANNY?
NANNY.
TCH.
WOULD HAVE PREFERRED THE SENATOR. MORE MONEY. BUT AFTER PATEL'S SCREW-UP, WE NEED EVERYTHING WE--
PARDON...
EXCUSE ME?
HARRY!
MY PARTNER HERE WAS INSISTENT ON COMING TO SEE YOU.
WEREN'T YOU, DEAR?

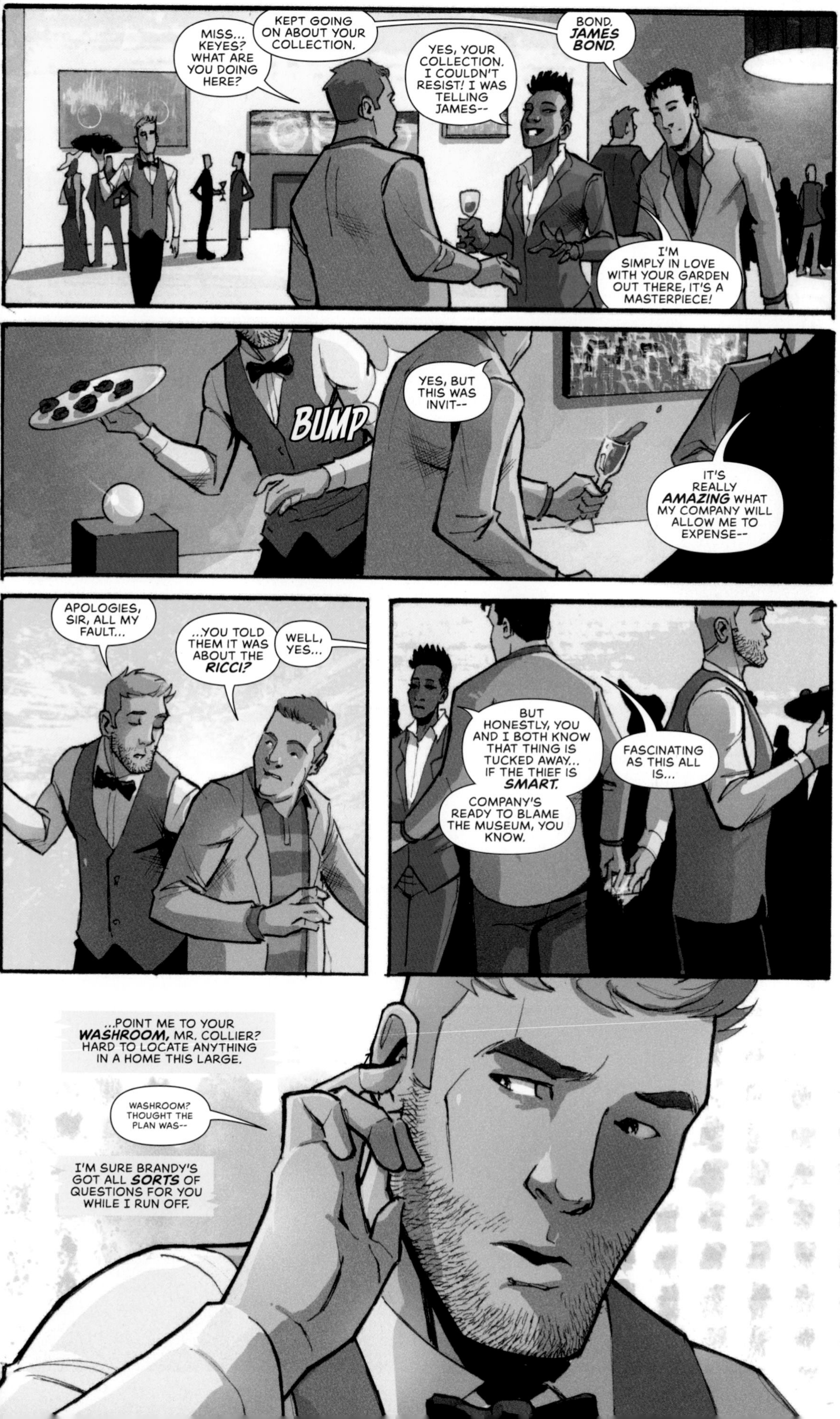

MISS... KEYES? WHAT ARE YOU DOING HERE?
KEPT GOING ON ABOUT YOUR COLLECTION.
BOND. JAMES BOND.
YES, YOUR COLLECTION. I COULDN'T RESIST! I WAS TELLING JAMES--
I'M SIMPLY IN LOVE WITH YOUR GARDEN OUT THERE, IT'S A MASTERPIECE!
BUMP
YES, BUT THIS WAS INVIT--
IT'S REALLY AMAZING WHAT MY COMPANY WILL ALLOW ME TO EXPENSE--
APOLOGIES, SIR, ALL MY FAULT...
...YOU TOLD THEM IT WAS ABOUT THE RICCI?
WELL, YES...
BUT HONESTLY, YOU AND I BOTH KNOW THAT THING IS TUCKED AWAY... IF THE THIEF IS SMART.
COMPANY'S READY TO BLAME THE MUSEUM, YOU KNOW.
FASCINATING AS THIS ALL IS...
...POINT ME TO YOUR WASHROOM, MR. COLLIER? HARD TO LOCATE ANYTHING IN A HOME THIS LARGE.
WASHROOM? THOUGHT THE PLAN WAS--
I'M SURE BRANDY'S GOT ALL SORTS OF QUESTIONS FOR YOU WHILE I RUN OFF.

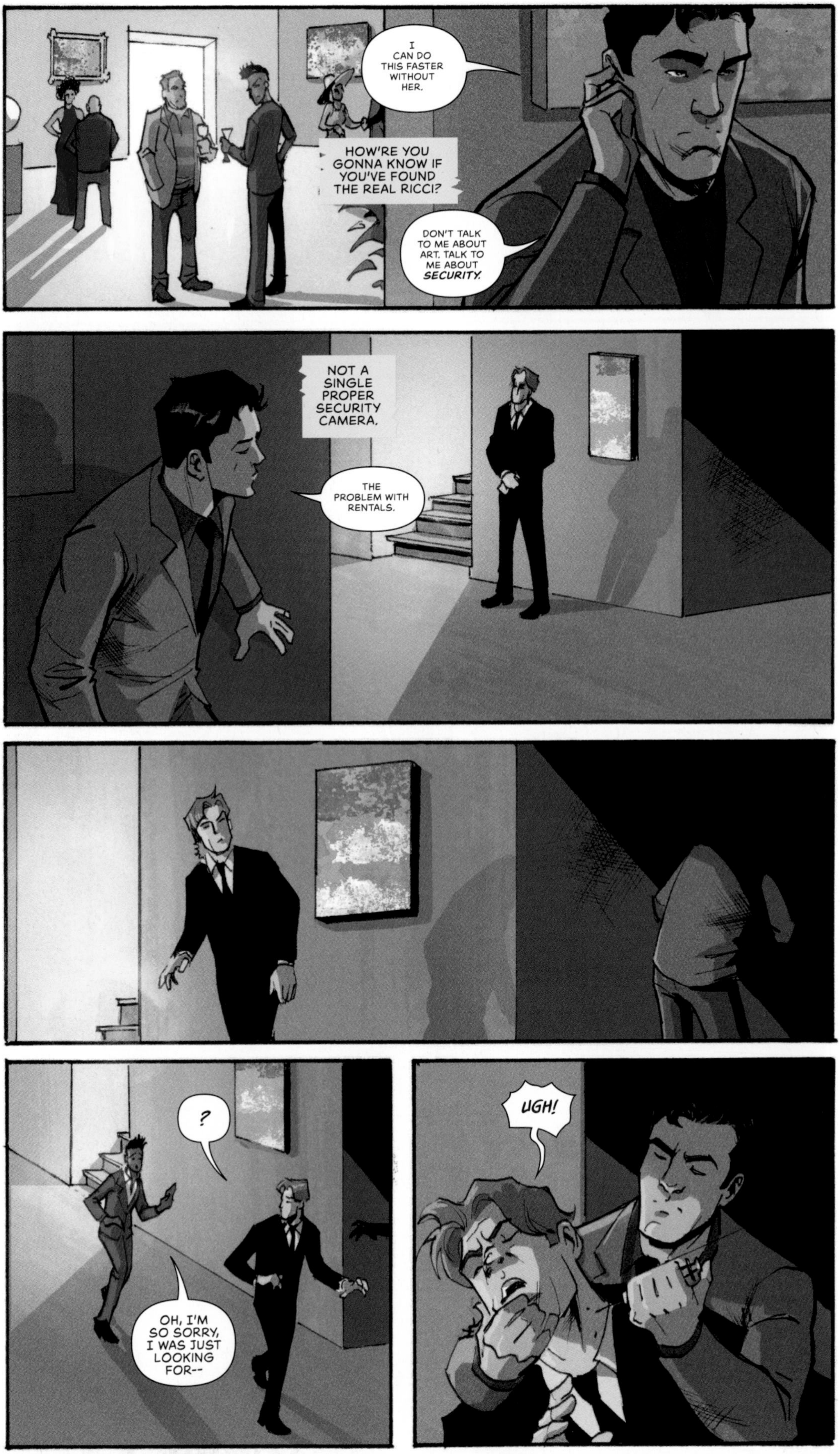
I CAN DO THIS FASTER WITHOUT HER.
HOW'RE YOU GONNA KNOW IF YOU'VE FOUND THE REAL RICCI?
DON'T TALK TO ME ABOUT ART. TALK TO ME ABOUT *SECURITY.*
NOT A SINGLE PROPER SECURITY CAMERA.
THE PROBLEM WITH RENTALS.
?
OH, I'M SO SORRY, I WAS JUST LOOKING FOR--
UGH!

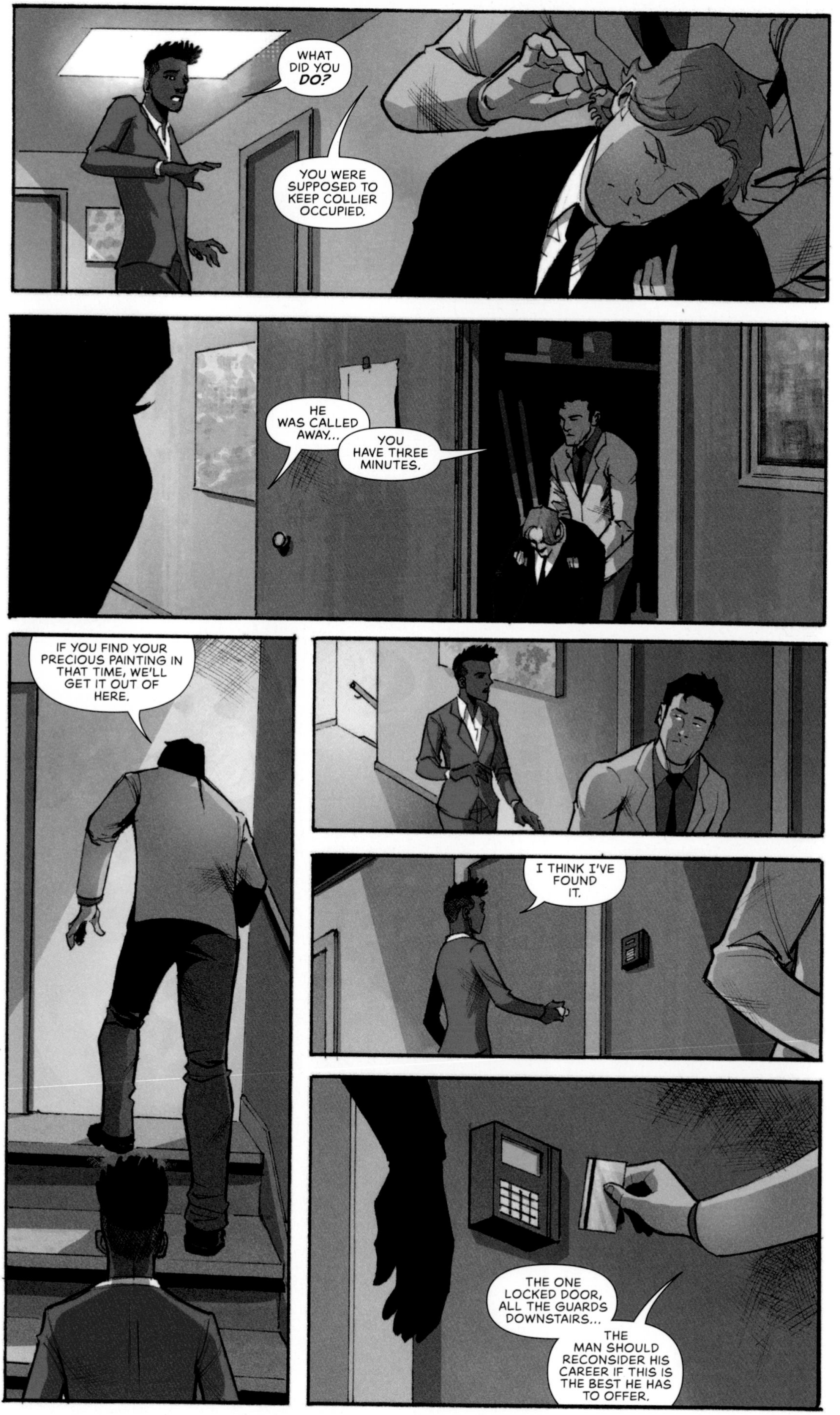

WHAT DID YOU *DO?*
YOU WERE SUPPOSED TO KEEP COLLIER OCCUPIED.
HE WAS CALLED AWAY...
YOU HAVE THREE MINUTES.
IF YOU FIND YOUR PRECIOUS PAINTING IN THAT TIME, WE'LL GET IT OUT OF HERE.
I THINK I'VE FOUND IT.
THE ONE LOCKED DOOR, ALL THE GUARDS DOWNSTAIRS...
THE MAN SHOULD RECONSIDER HIS CAREER IF THIS IS THE BEST HE HAS TO OFFER.

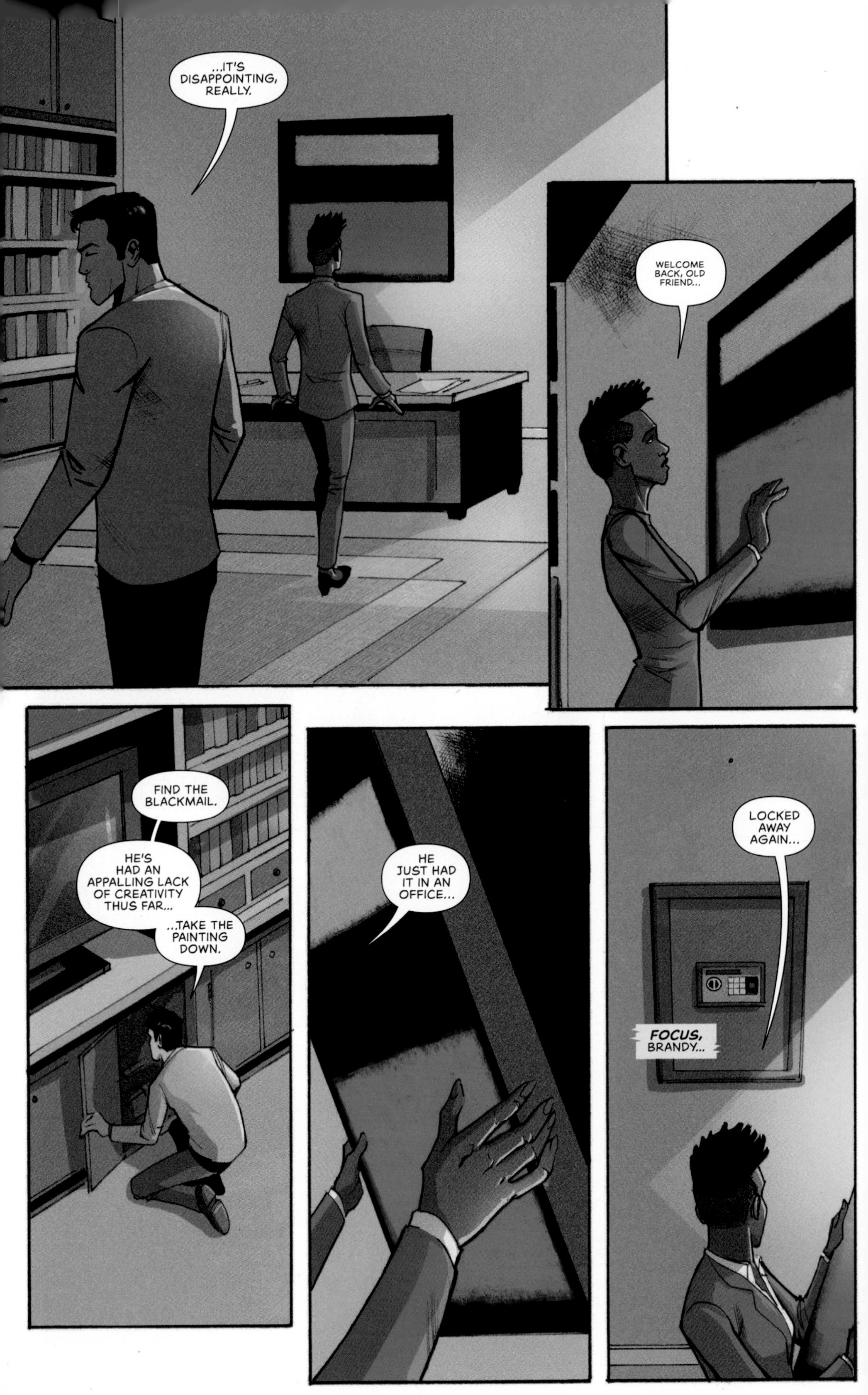
...IT'S DISAPPOINTING, REALLY.
WELCOME BACK, OLD FRIEND...
FIND THE BLACKMAIL.
HE'S HAD AN APPALLING LACK OF CREATIVITY THUS FAR...
...TAKE THE PAINTING DOWN.
HE JUST HAD IT IN AN OFFICE...
LOCKED AWAY AGAIN...
FOCUS, BRANDY...

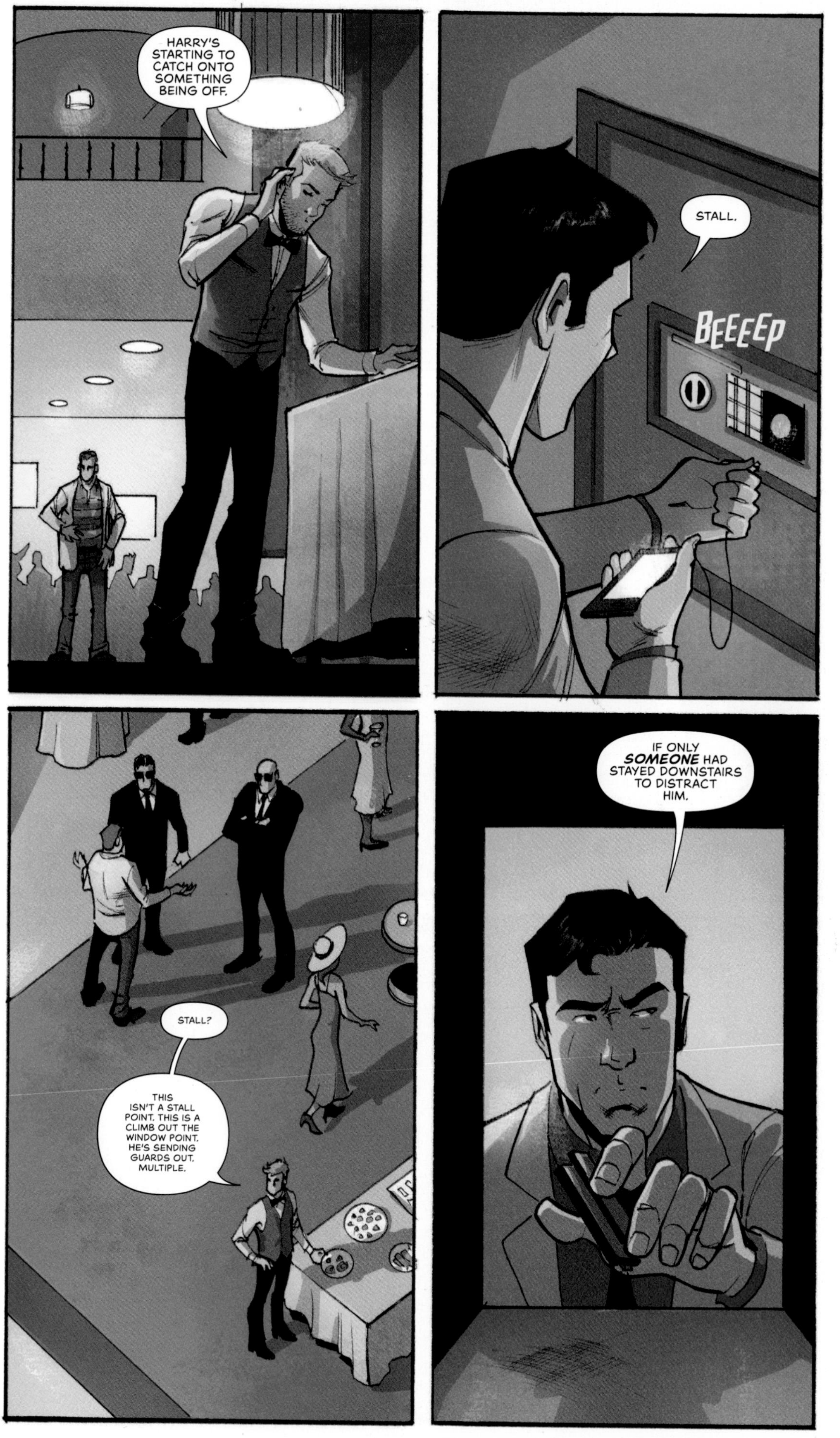
HARRY'S STARTING TO CATCH ONTO SOMETHING BEING OFF.
STALL.
BEEEEP
STALL?
THIS ISN'T A STALL POINT. THIS IS A CLIMB OUT THE WINDOW POINT. HE'S SENDING GUARDS OUT. MULTIPLE.
IF ONLY SOMEONE HAD STAYED DOWNSTAIRS TO DISTRACT HIM.

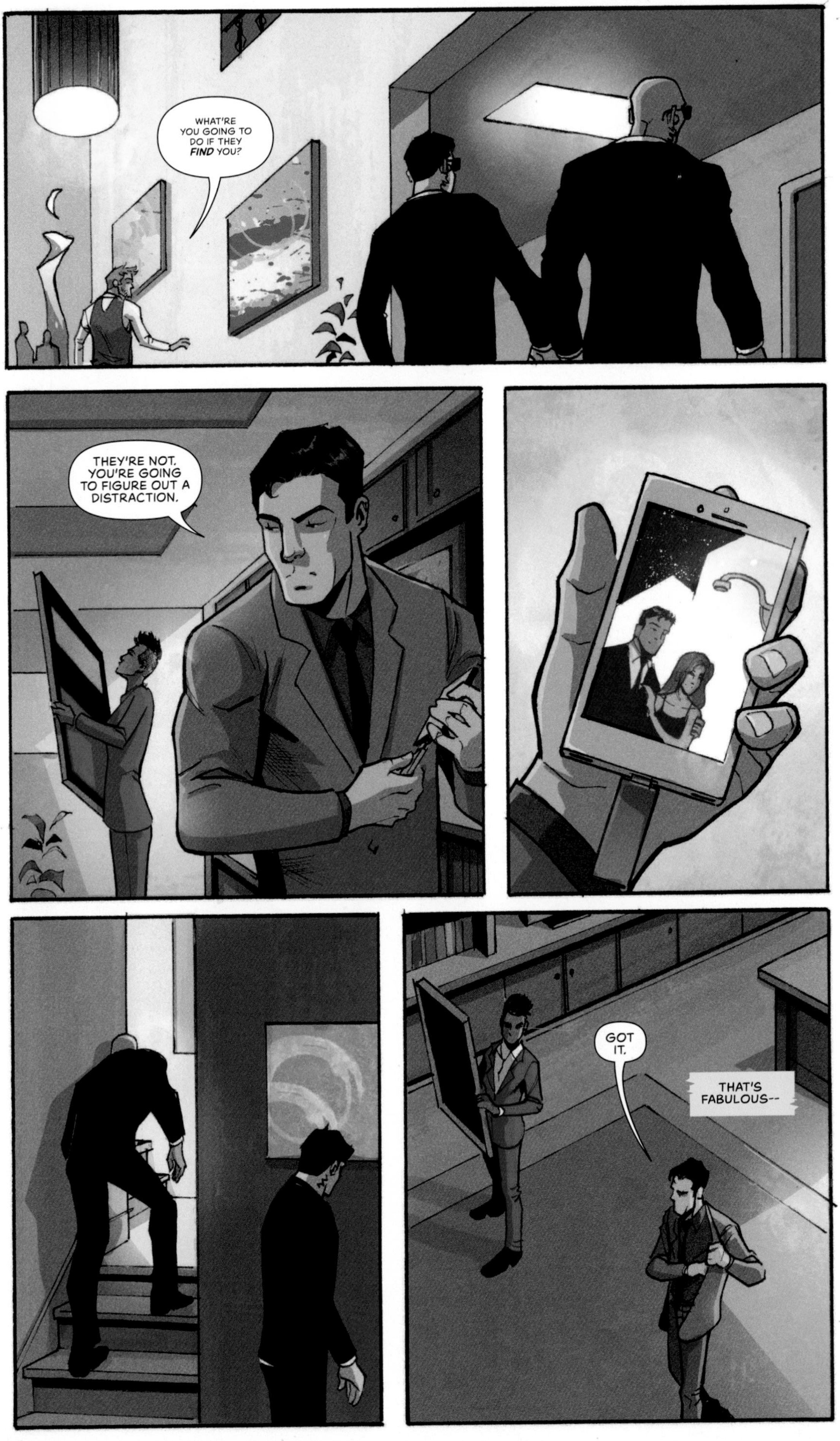
WHAT'RE YOU GOING TO DO IF THEY *FIND* YOU?
THEY'RE NOT. YOU'RE GOING TO FIGURE OUT A DISTRACTION.
GOT IT.
THAT'S FABULOUS--

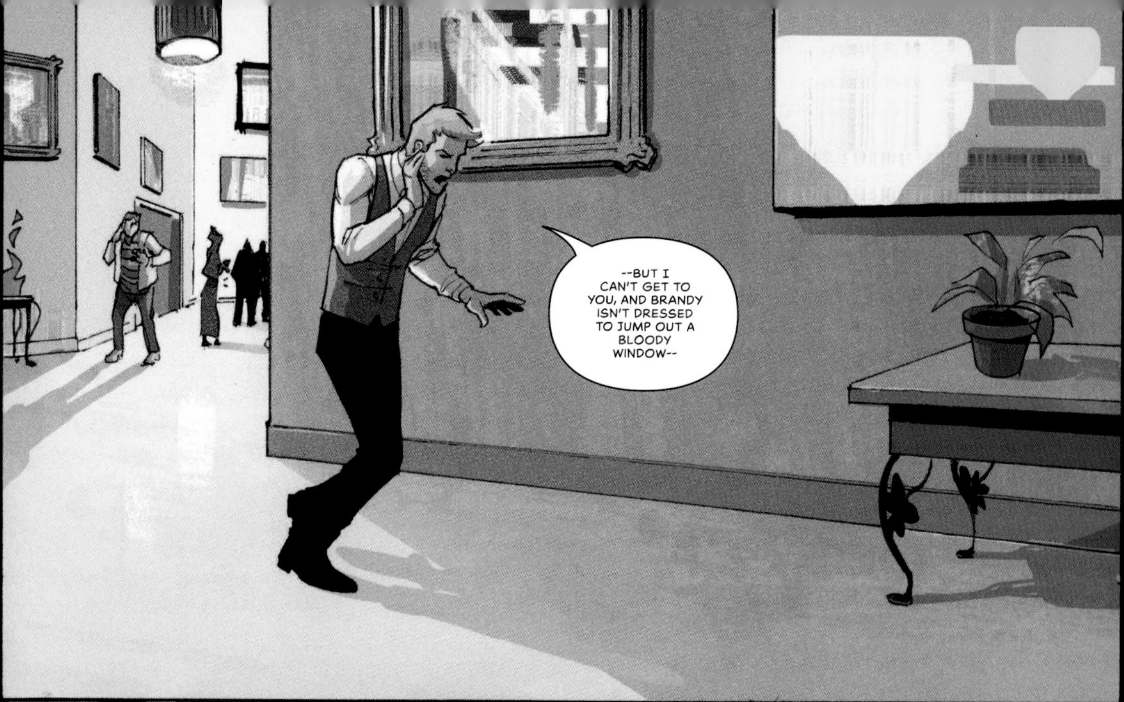
--BUT I CAN'T GET TO YOU, AND BRANDY ISN'T DRESSED TO JUMP OUT A BLOODY WINDOW--

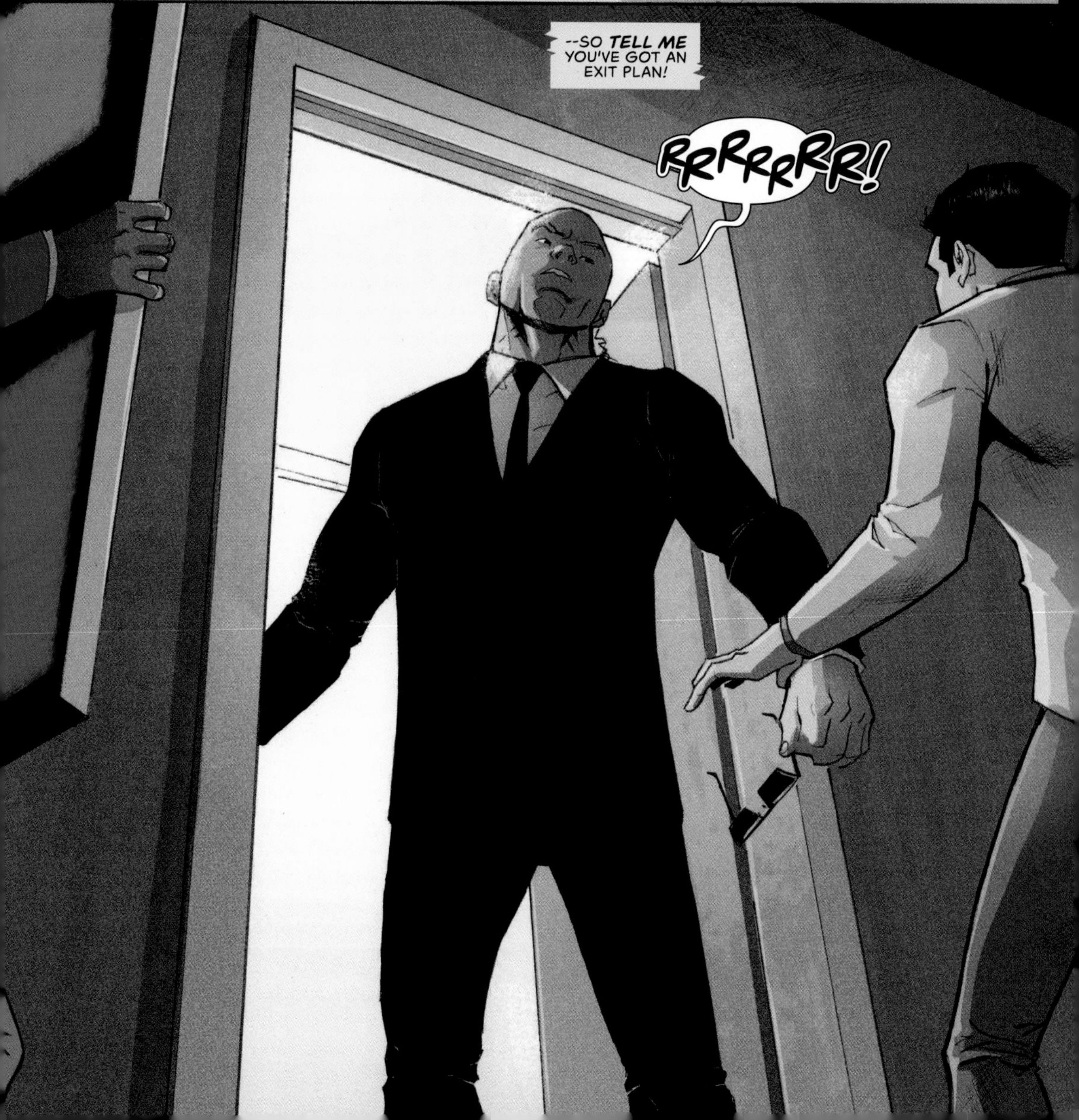
--SO TELL ME YOU'VE GOT AN EXIT PLAN!
RRRRRRR!

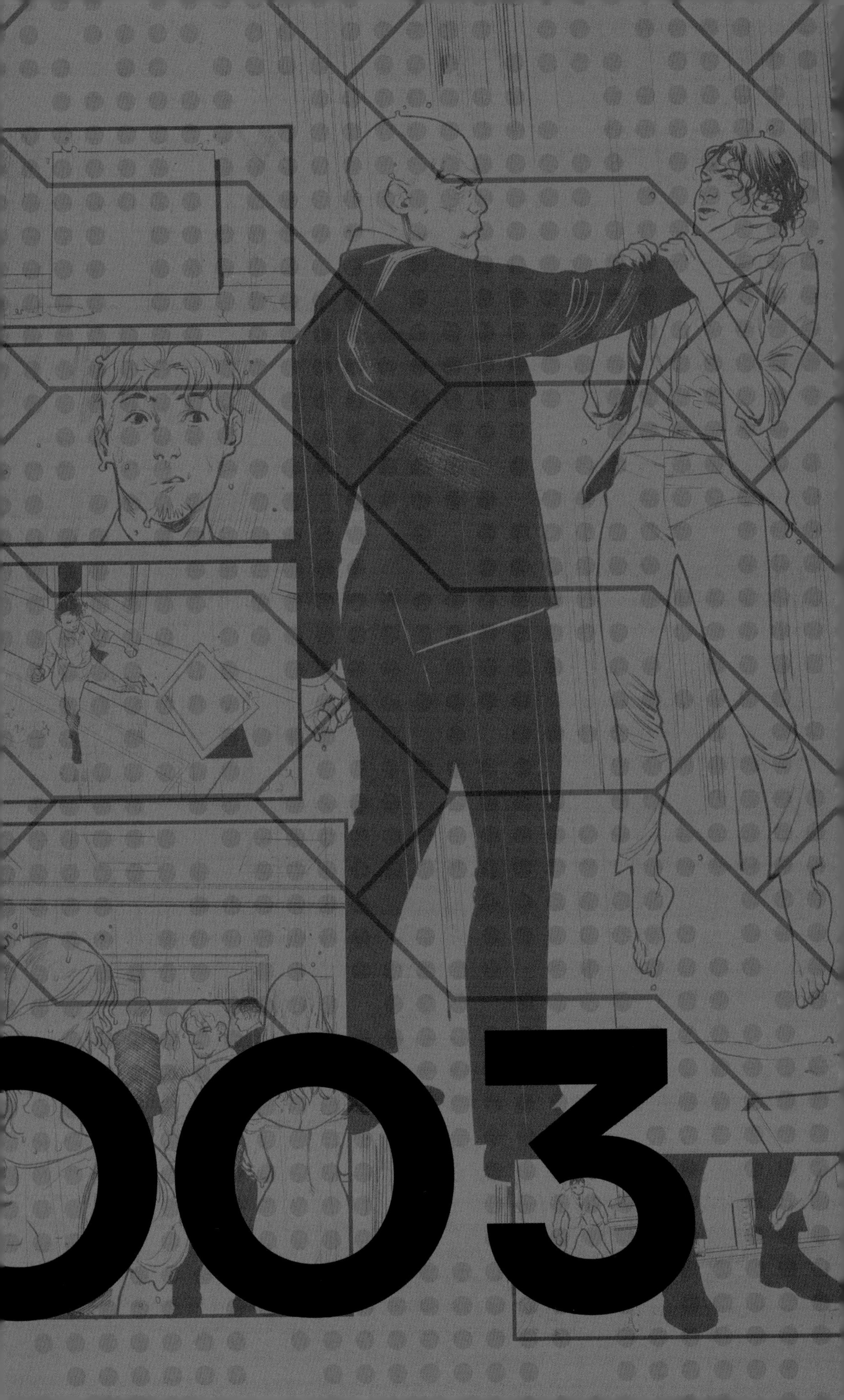
003

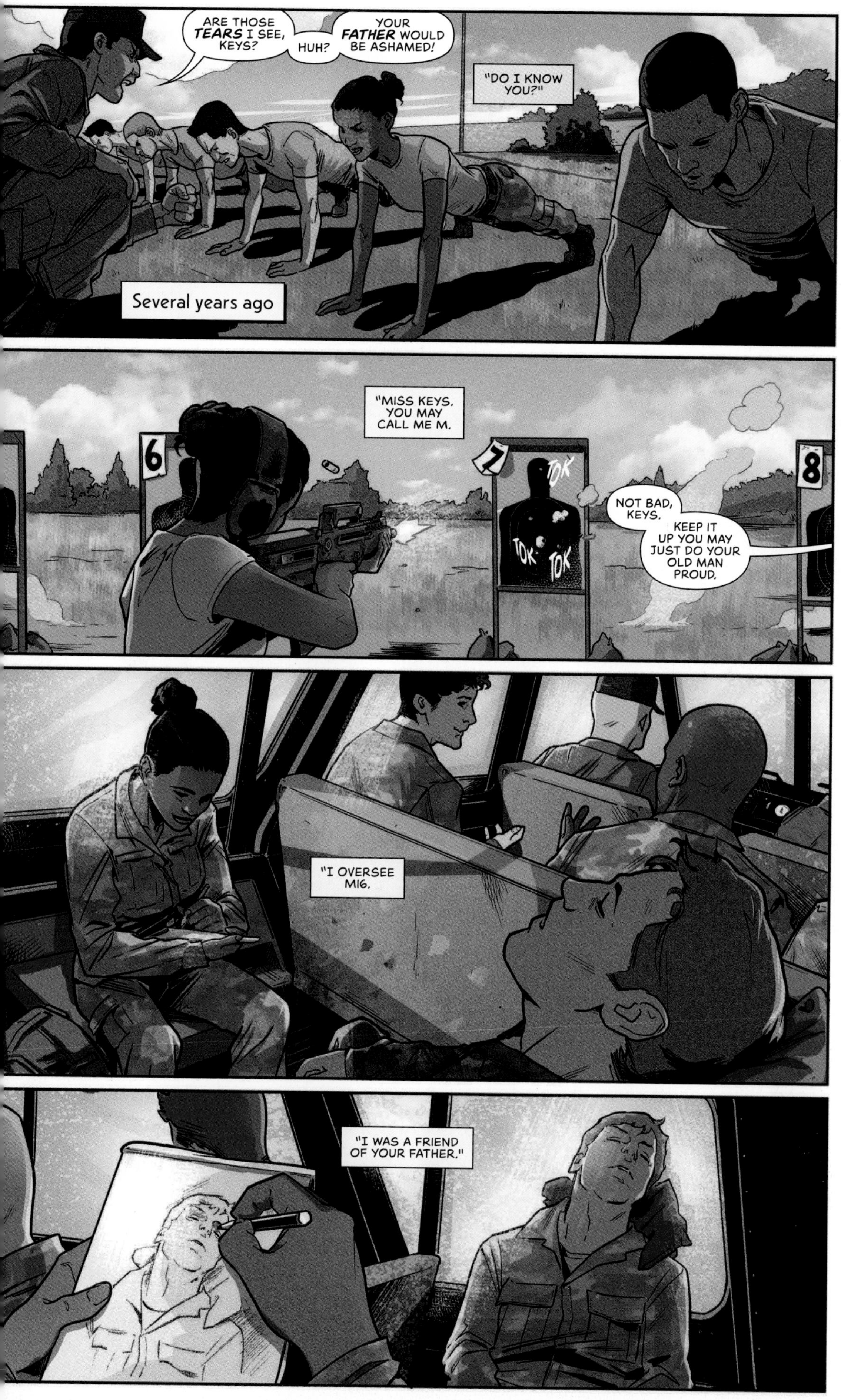

ARE THOSE TEARS I SEE, KEYS?
HUH?
YOUR FATHER WOULD BE ASHAMED!
"DO I KNOW YOU?"
Several years ago
"MISS KEYS. YOU MAY CALL ME M.
6
7
8
TOK
TOK
TOK
NOT BAD, KEYS.
KEEP IT UP YOU MAY JUST DO YOUR OLD MAN PROUD.
"I OVERSEE MI6.
"I WAS A FRIEND OF YOUR FATHER."

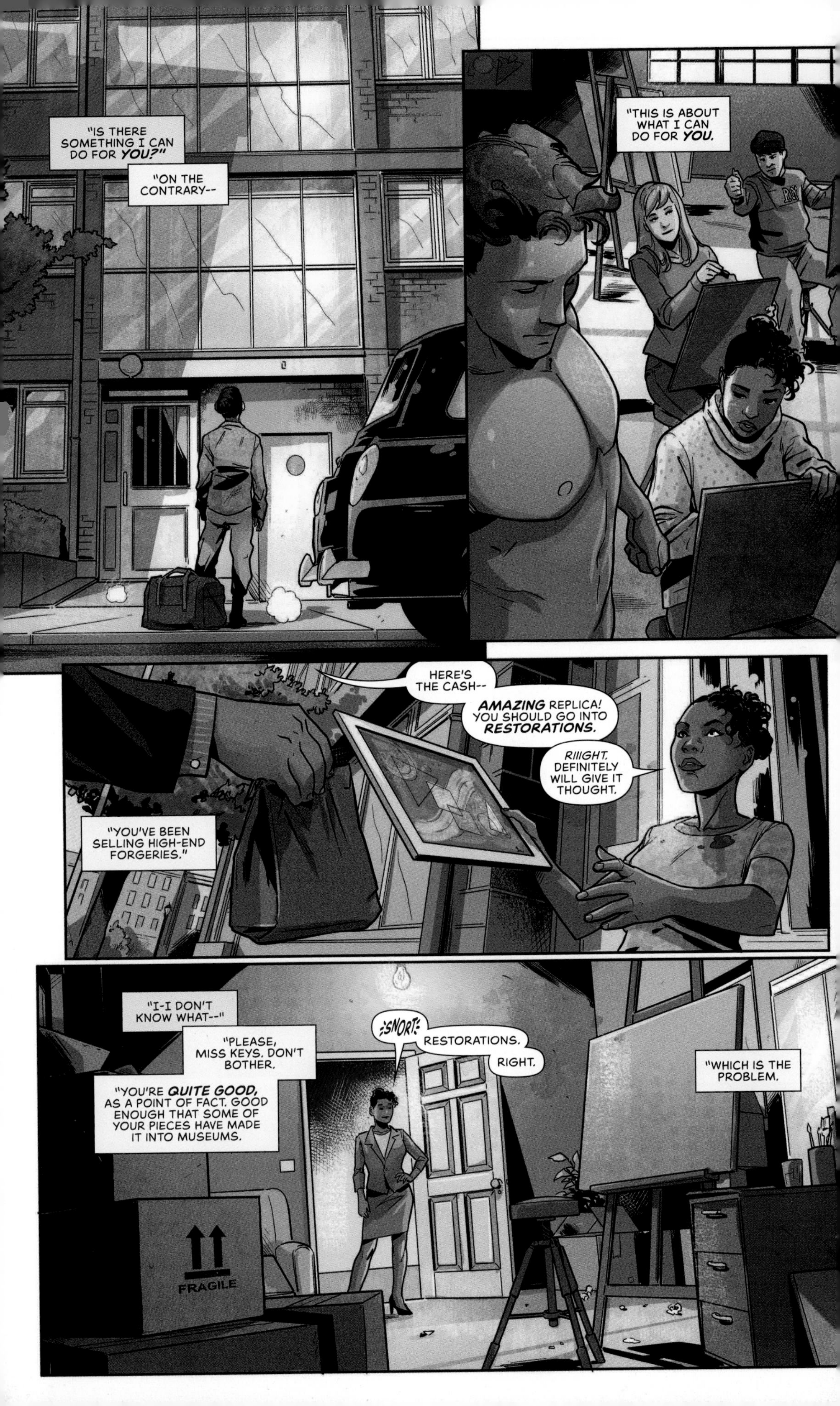

"IS THERE SOMETHING I CAN DO FOR *YOU?*"
"ON THE CONTRARY--
"THIS IS ABOUT WHAT I CAN DO FOR *YOU*.
HERE'S THE CASH--
AMAZING REPLICA! YOU SHOULD GO INTO *RESTORATIONS*.
RIIIGHT. DEFINITELY WILL GIVE IT THOUGHT.
"YOU'VE BEEN SELLING HIGH-END FORGERIES."
"I-I DON'T KNOW WHAT--"
"PLEASE, MISS KEYS. DON'T BOTHER.
"YOU'RE *QUITE GOOD*, AS A POINT OF FACT. GOOD ENOUGH THAT SOME OF YOUR PIECES HAVE MADE IT INTO MUSEUMS.
SNORT
RESTORATIONS.
RIGHT.
"WHICH IS THE PROBLEM.
FRAGILE

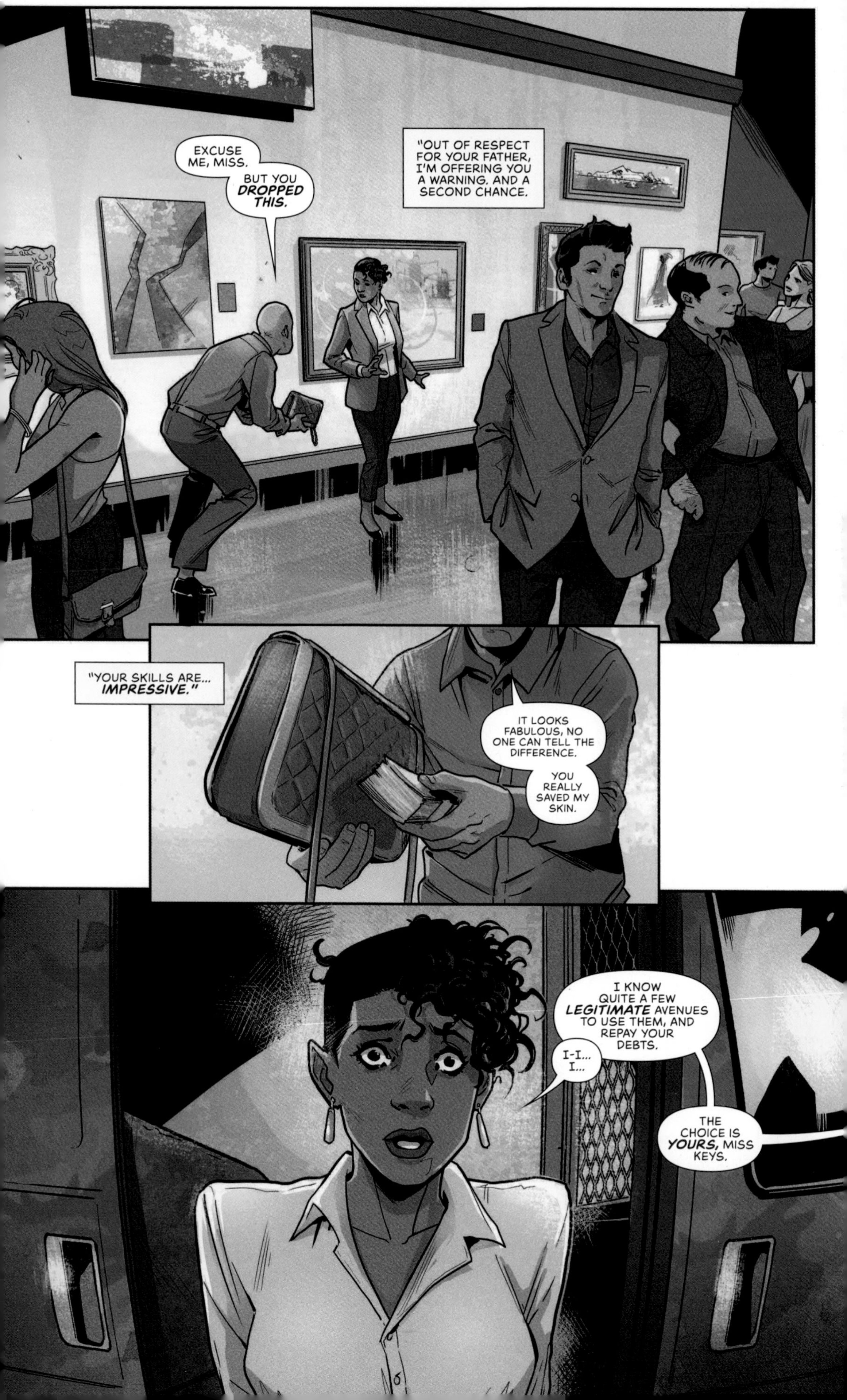
EXCUSE ME, MISS.
BUT YOU DROPPED THIS.
"OUT OF RESPECT FOR YOUR FATHER, I'M OFFERING YOU A WARNING. AND A SECOND CHANCE.
"YOUR SKILLS ARE... IMPRESSIVE."
IT LOOKS FABULOUS, NO ONE CAN TELL THE DIFFERENCE.
YOU REALLY SAVED MY SKIN.
I KNOW QUITE A FEW LEGITIMATE AVENUES TO USE THEM, AND REPAY YOUR DEBTS.
I-I... I...
THE CHOICE IS YOURS, MISS KEYS.

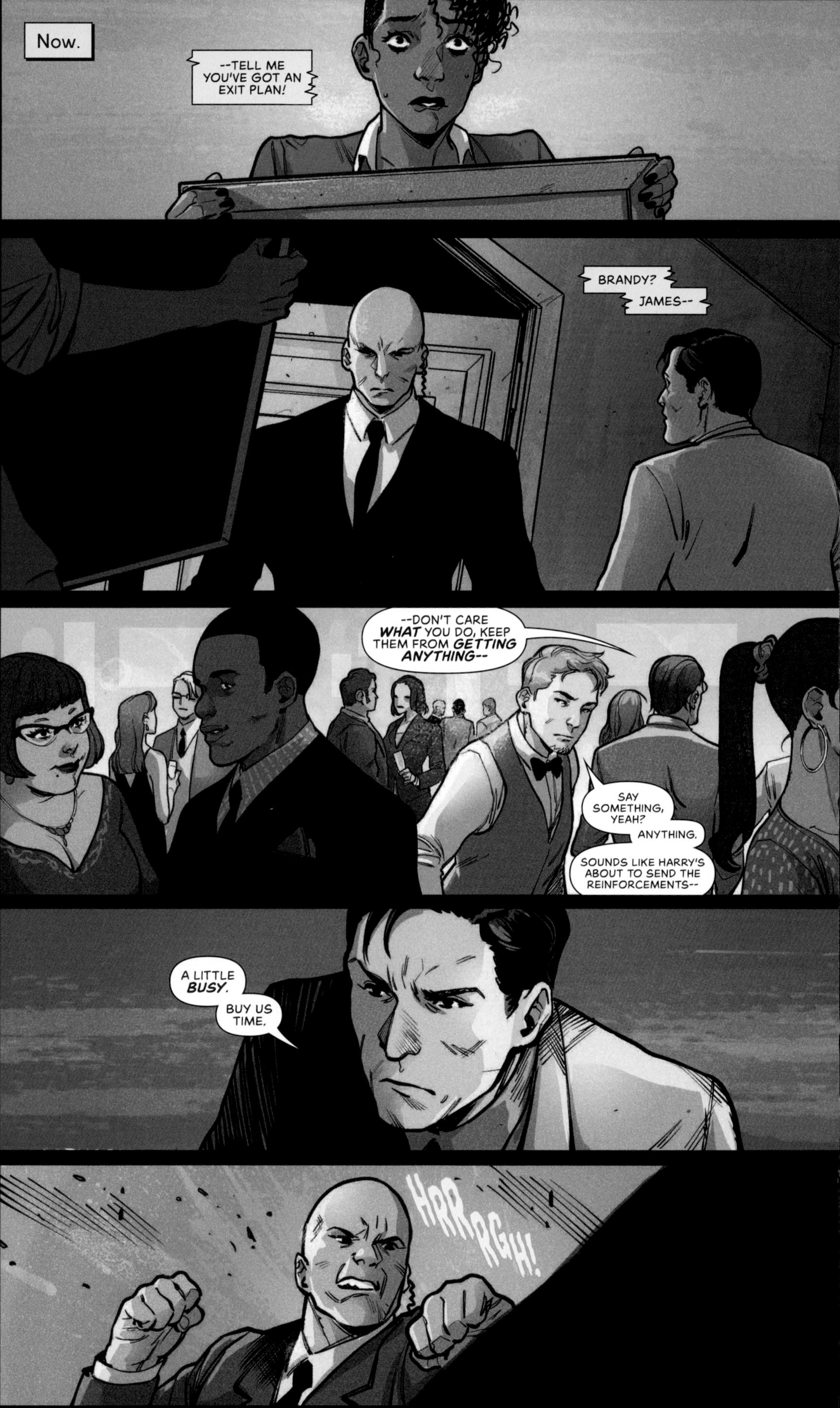

Now.
--TELL ME YOU'VE GOT AN EXIT PLAN!
BRANDY?
JAMES--
--DON'T CARE WHAT YOU DO, KEEP THEM FROM GETTING ANYTHING--
SAY SOMETHING, YEAH?
ANYTHING.
SOUNDS LIKE HARRY'S ABOUT TO SEND THE REINFORCEMENTS--
A LITTLE BUSY.
BUY US TIME.
HRRRGH!

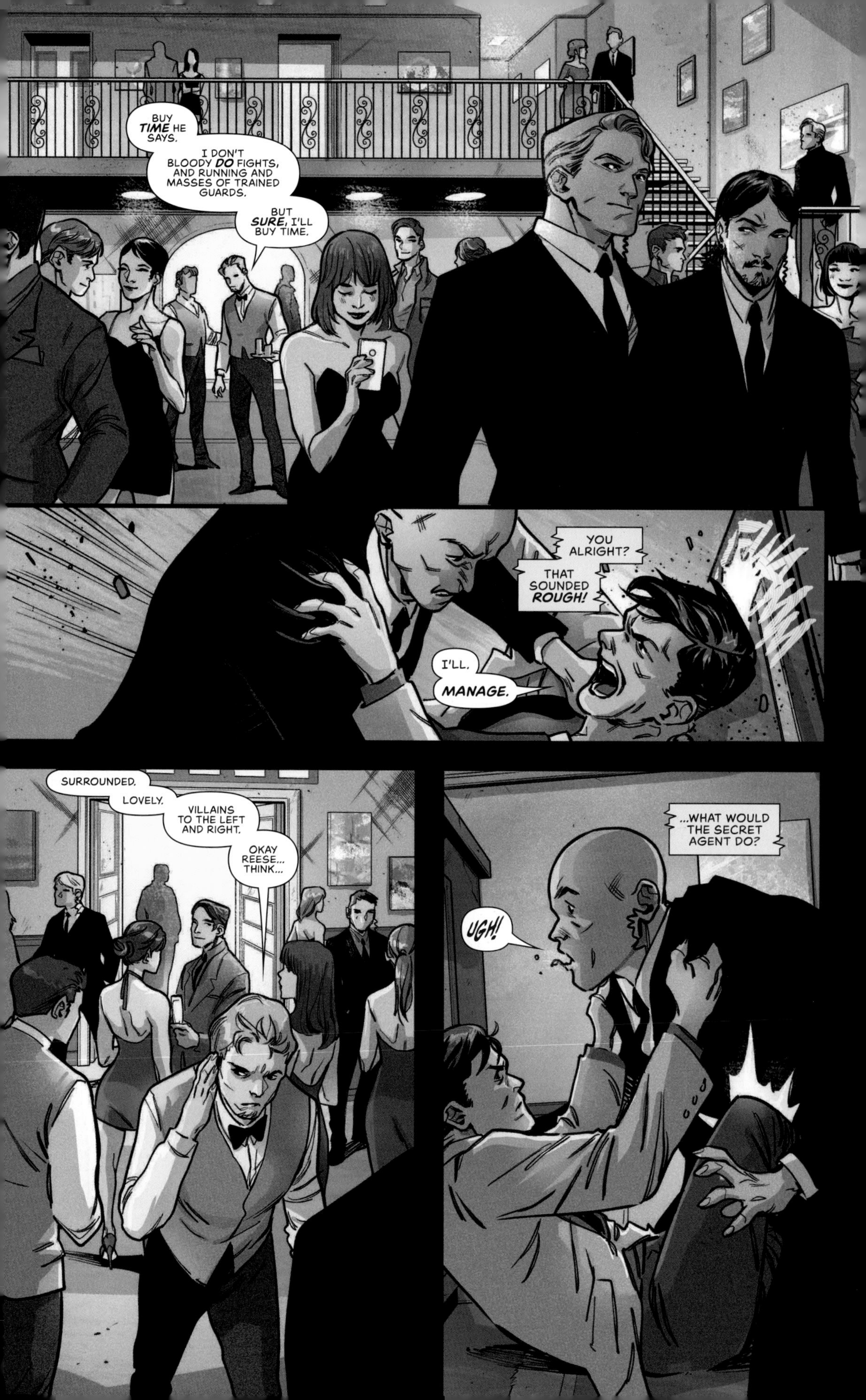
BUY TIME HE SAYS.
I DON'T BLOODY DO FIGHTS, AND RUNNING AND MASSES OF TRAINED GUARDS.
BUT SURE, I'LL BUY TIME.
YOU ALRIGHT?
THAT SOUNDED ROUGH!
I'LL.
MANAGE.
FWAM
SURROUNDED.
LOVELY.
VILLAINS TO THE LEFT AND RIGHT.
OKAY REESE... THINK...
...WHAT WOULD THE SECRET AGENT DO?
UGH!

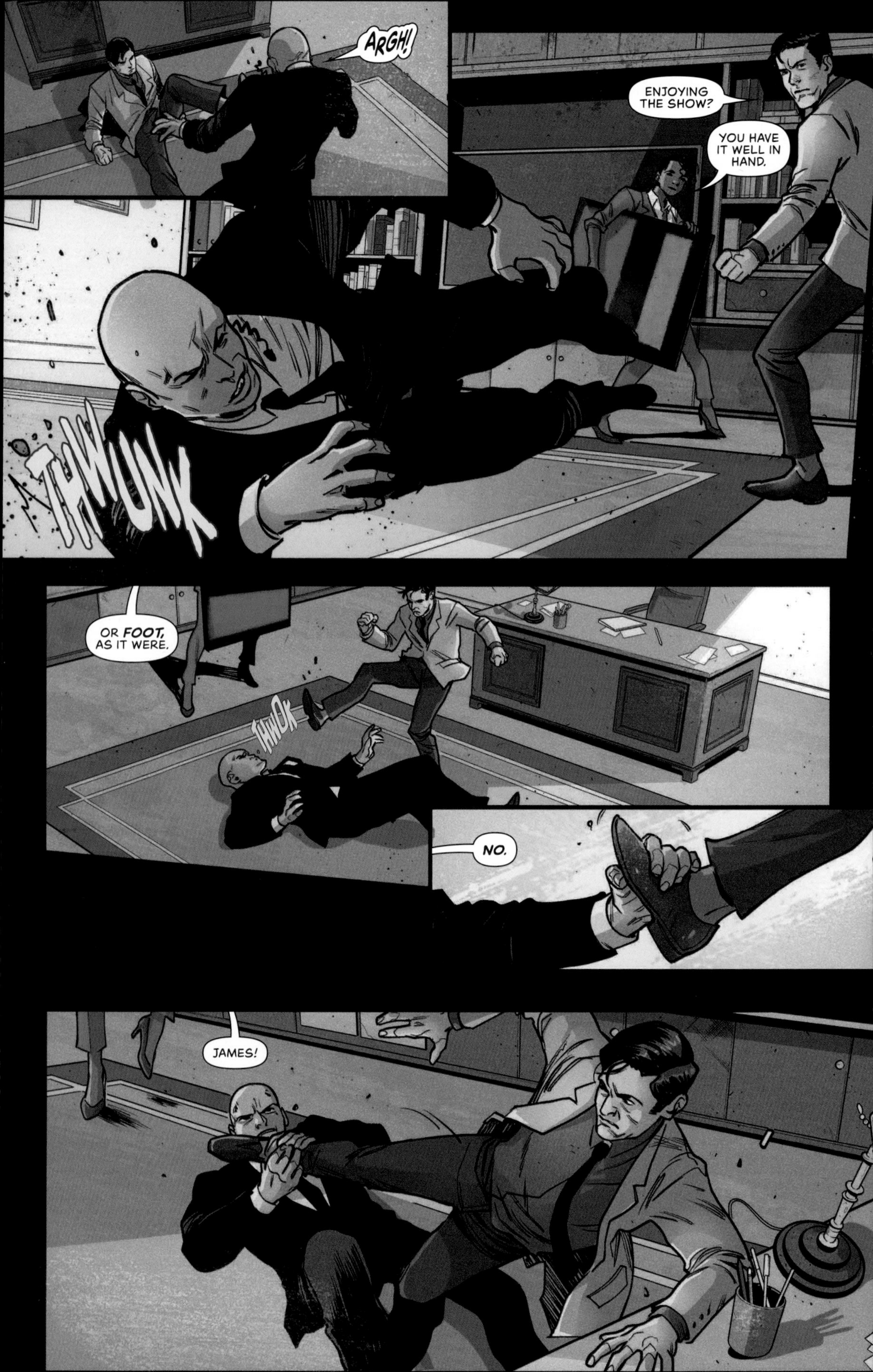
ARGH!
ENJOYING THE SHOW?
YOU HAVE IT WELL IN HAND.
THWONK
OR FOOT, AS IT WERE.
THWOK
NO.
JAMES!

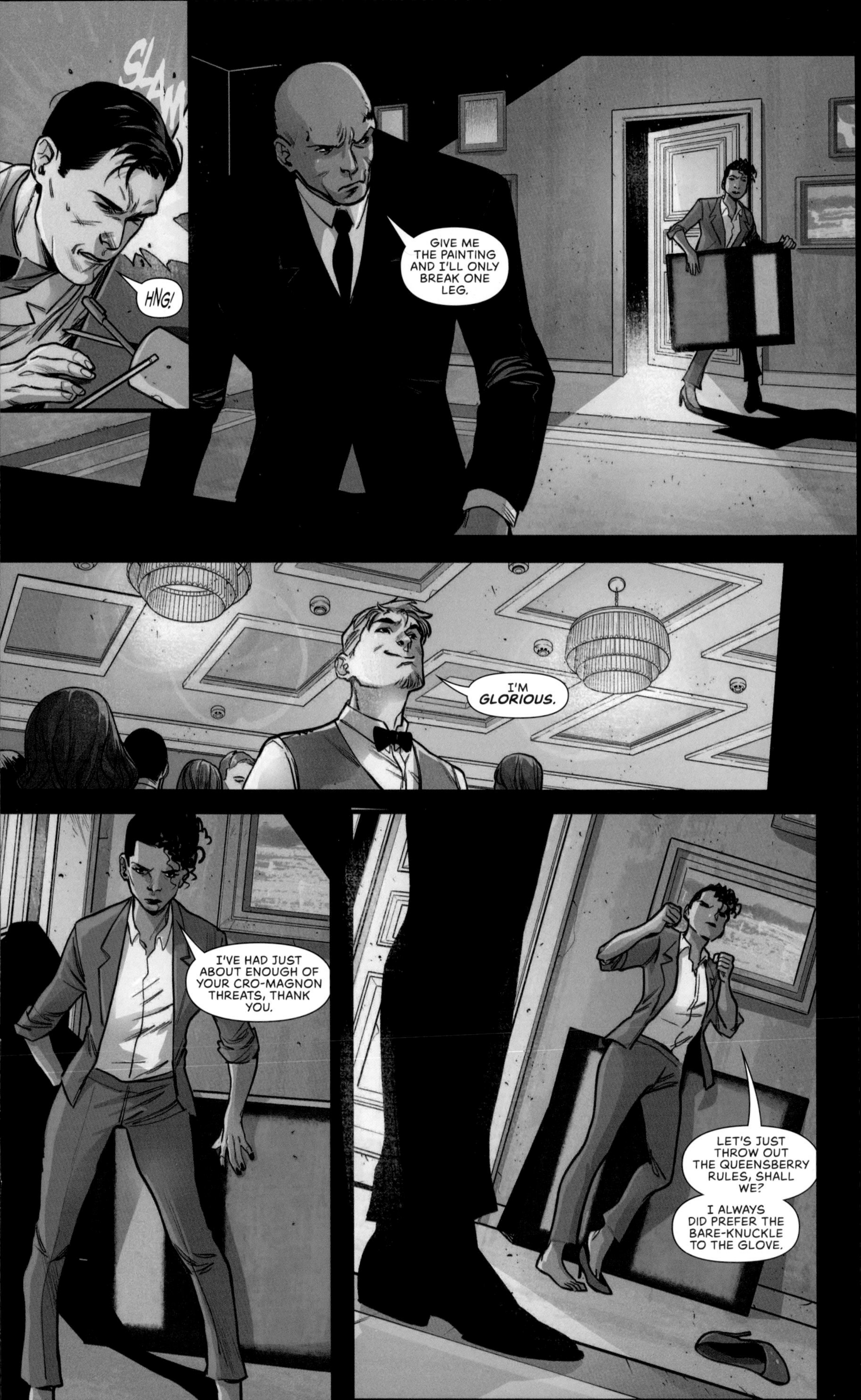
SLAM
HNG!
GIVE ME THE PAINTING AND I'LL ONLY BREAK ONE LEG.
I'M GLORIOUS.
I'VE HAD JUST ABOUT ENOUGH OF YOUR CRO-MAGNON THREATS, THANK YOU.
LET'S JUST THROW OUT THE QUEENSBERRY RULES, SHALL WE?
I ALWAYS DID PREFER THE BARE-KNUCKLE TO THE GLOVE.

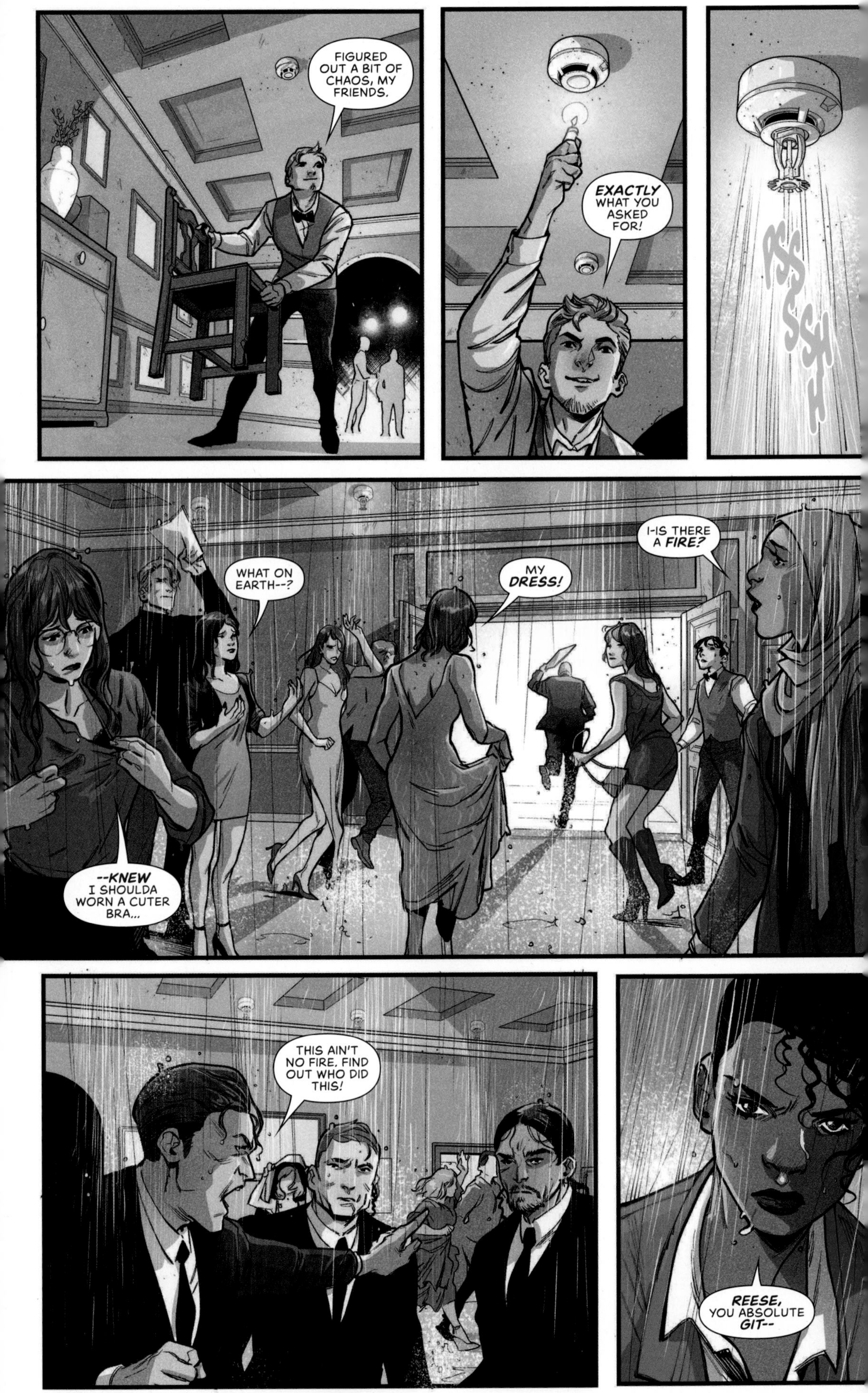
FIGURED OUT A BIT OF CHAOS, MY FRIENDS.
EXACTLY WHAT YOU ASKED FOR!
RSSSSH
WHAT ON EARTH--?
MY DRESS!
I-IS THERE A FIRE?
--KNEW I SHOULDA WORN A CUTER BRA...
THIS AIN'T NO FIRE. FIND OUT WHO DID THIS!
REESE, YOU ABSOLUTE GIT--

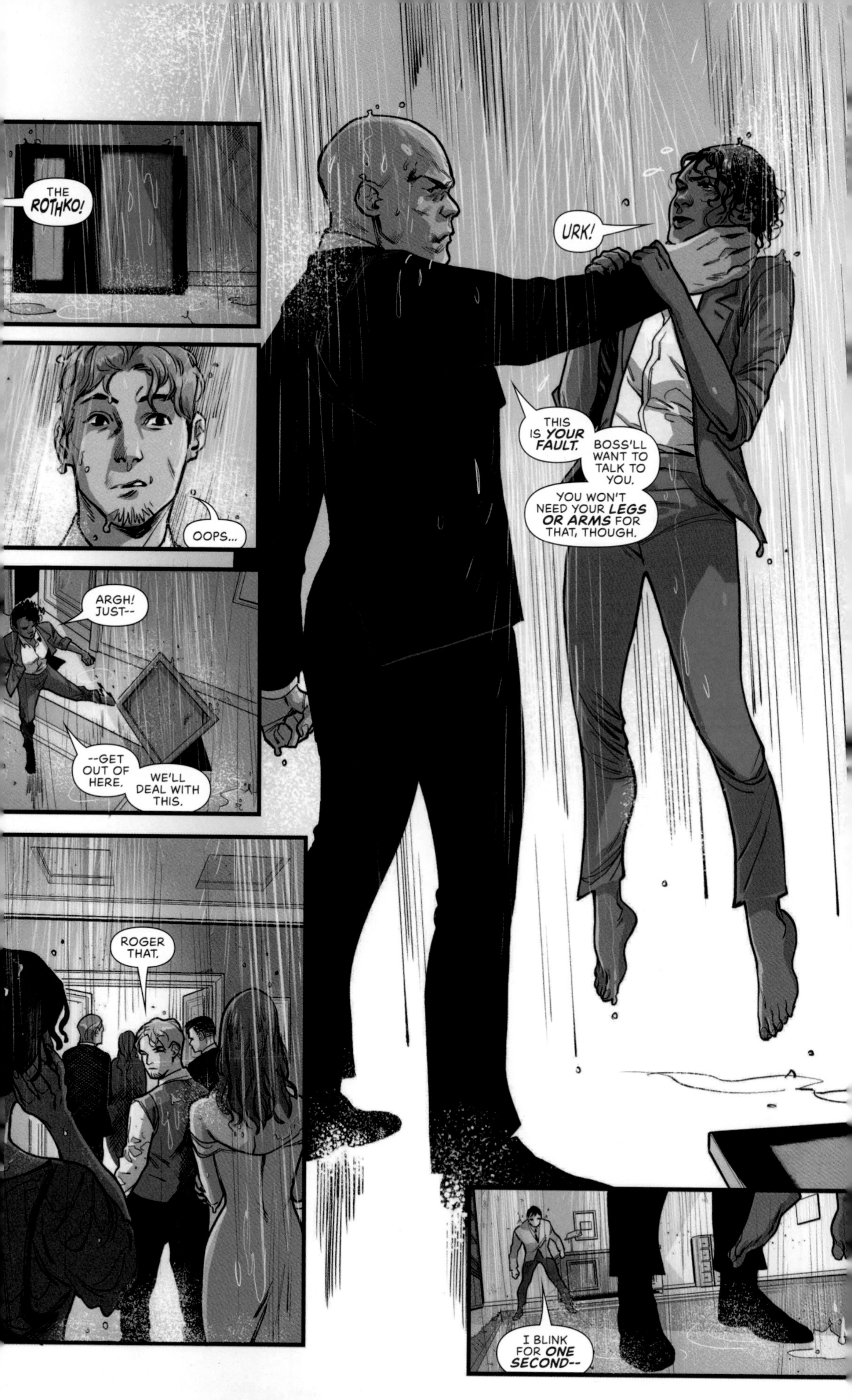
THE ROTHKO!
OOPS...
ARGH! JUST--
--GET OUT OF HERE.
WE'LL DEAL WITH THIS.
ROGER THAT.
URK!
THIS IS YOUR FAULT.
BOSS'LL WANT TO TALK TO YOU.
YOU WON'T NEED YOUR LEGS OR ARMS FOR THAT, THOUGH.
I BLINK FOR ONE SECOND--

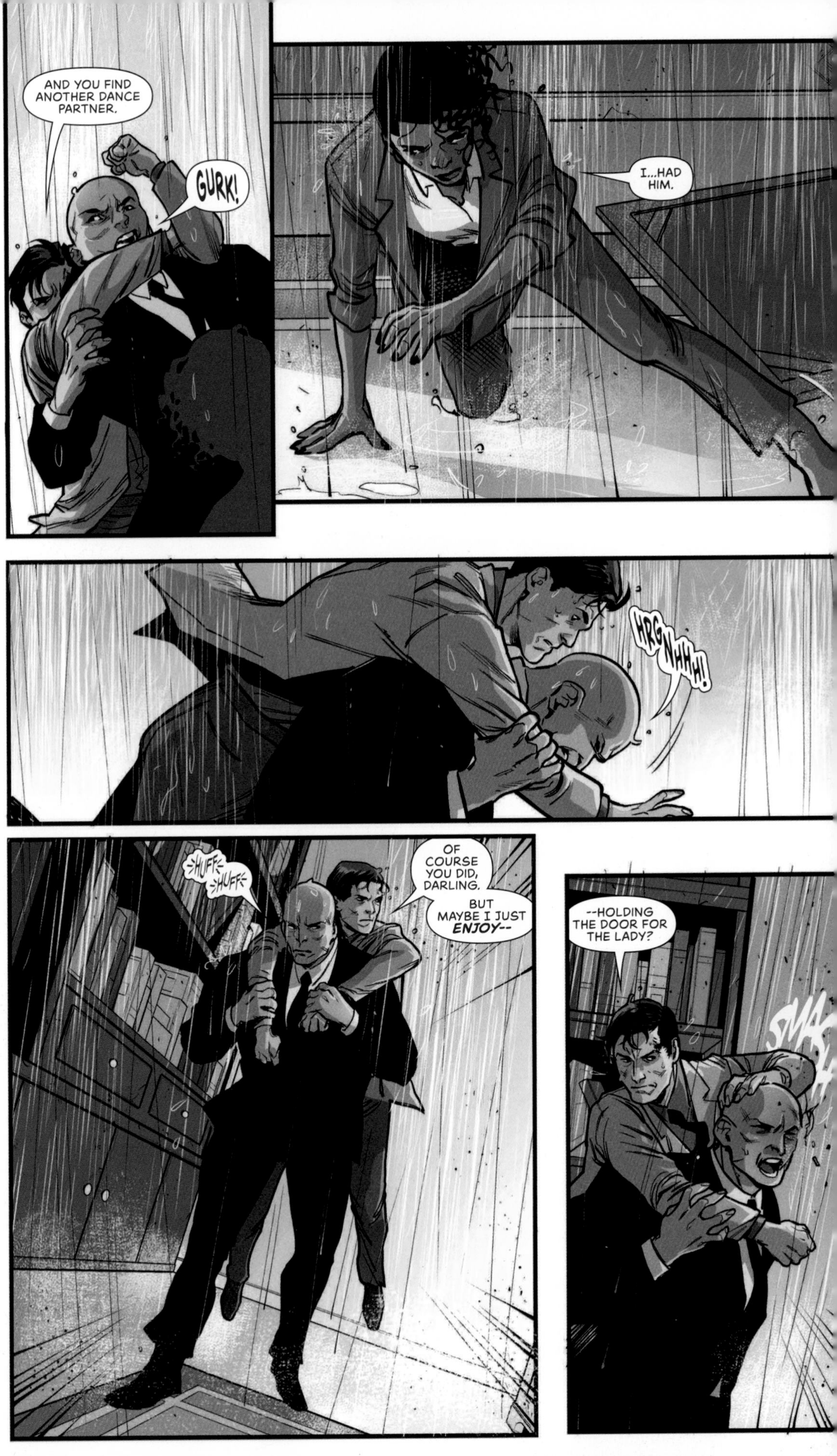
AND YOU FIND ANOTHER DANCE PARTNER.
GURK!
I...HAD HIM.
HRGNHHH!
HUFF HUFF
OF COURSE YOU DID, DARLING.
BUT MAYBE I JUST ENJOY--
--HOLDING THE DOOR FOR THE LADY?
SMASH

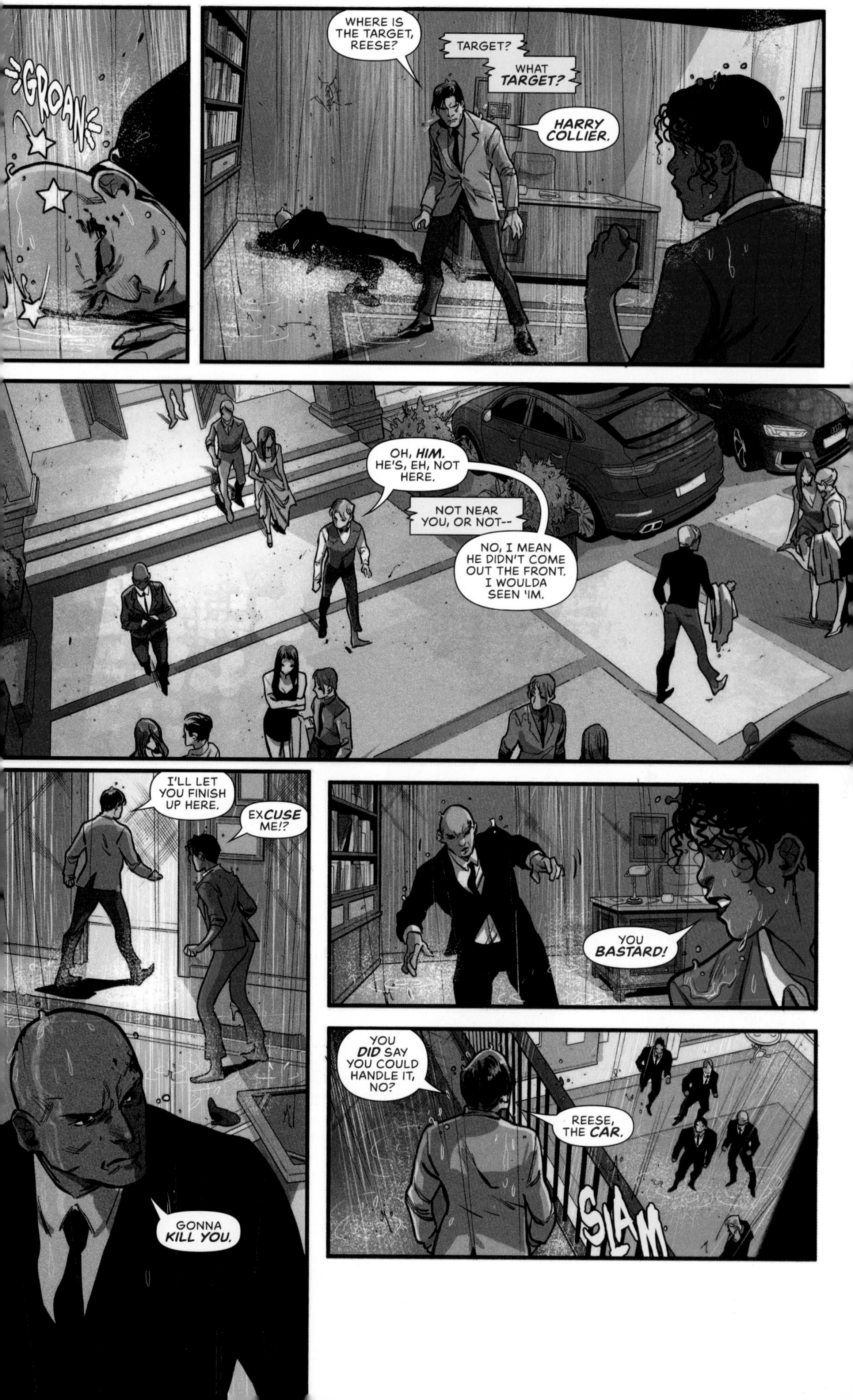
GROAN
WHERE IS THE TARGET, REESE?
TARGET?
WHAT TARGET?
HARRY COLLIER.
OH, HIM. HE'S, EH, NOT HERE.
NOT NEAR YOU, OR NOT--
NO, I MEAN HE DIDN'T COME OUT THE FRONT. I WOULDA SEEN 'IM.
I'LL LET YOU FINISH UP HERE.
EXCUSE ME!?
GONNA KILL YOU.
YOU BASTARD!
YOU DID SAY YOU COULD HANDLE IT, NO?
REESE, THE CAR.
SLAM

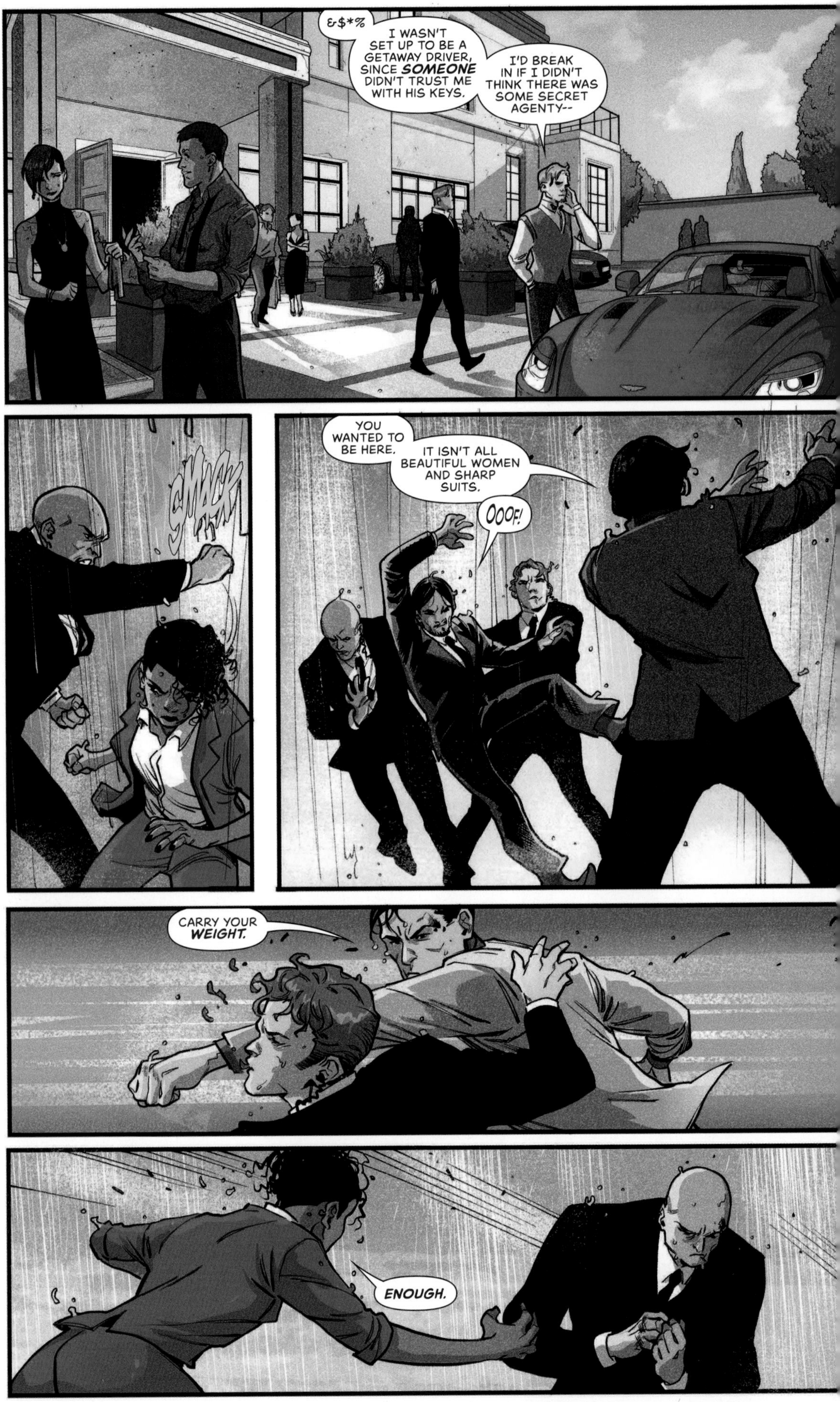

&$*%
I WASN'T SET UP TO BE A GETAWAY DRIVER, SINCE SOMEONE DIDN'T TRUST ME WITH HIS KEYS.
I'D BREAK IN IF I DIDN'T THINK THERE WAS SOME SECRET AGENTY--
SMACK
YOU WANTED TO BE HERE.
IT ISN'T ALL BEAUTIFUL WOMEN AND SHARP SUITS.
OOOF!
CARRY YOUR WEIGHT.
ENOUGH.

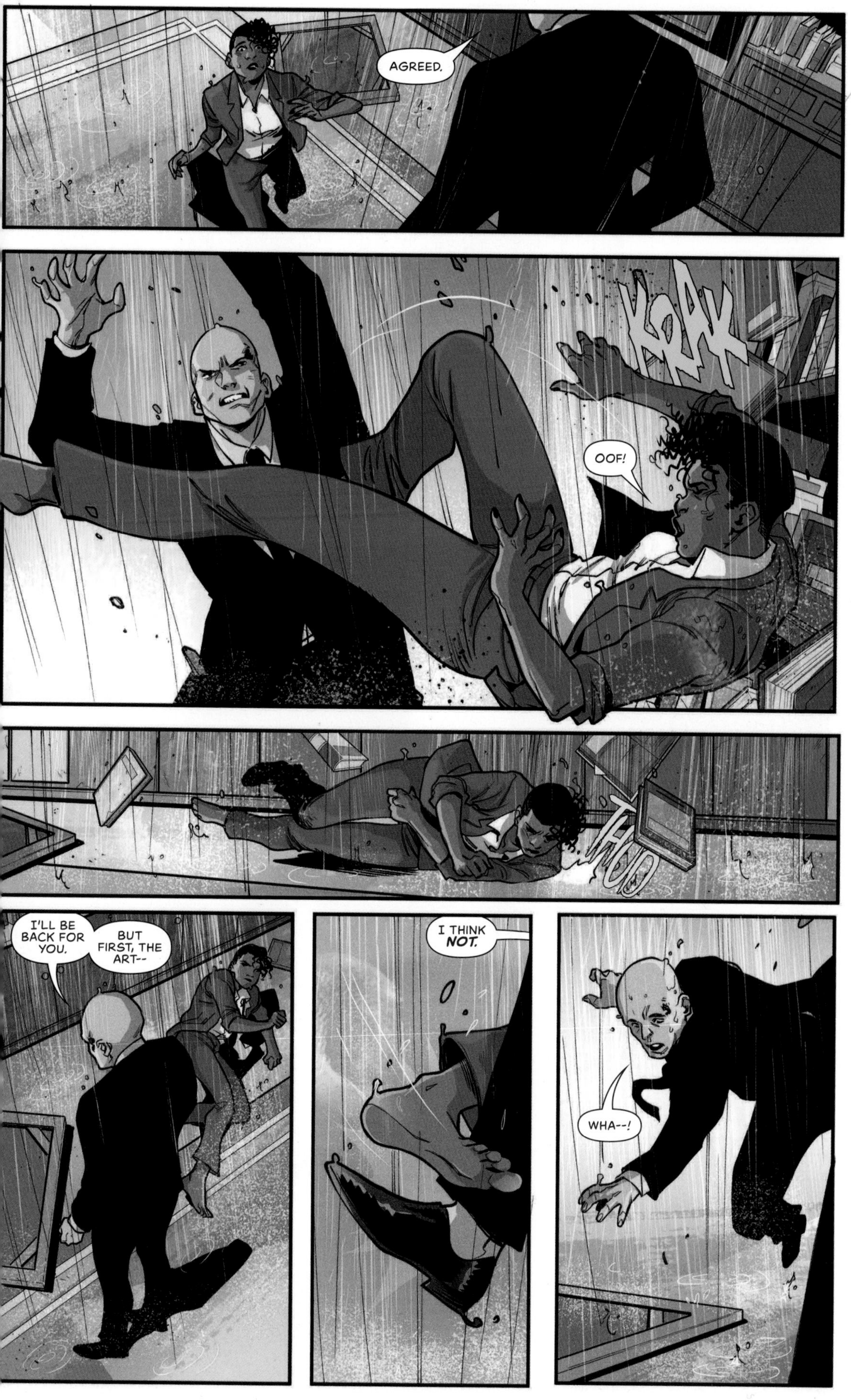
AGREED.
KRAK
OOF!
THUD
I'LL BE BACK FOR YOU.
BUT FIRST, THE ART--
I THINK NOT.
WHA--!

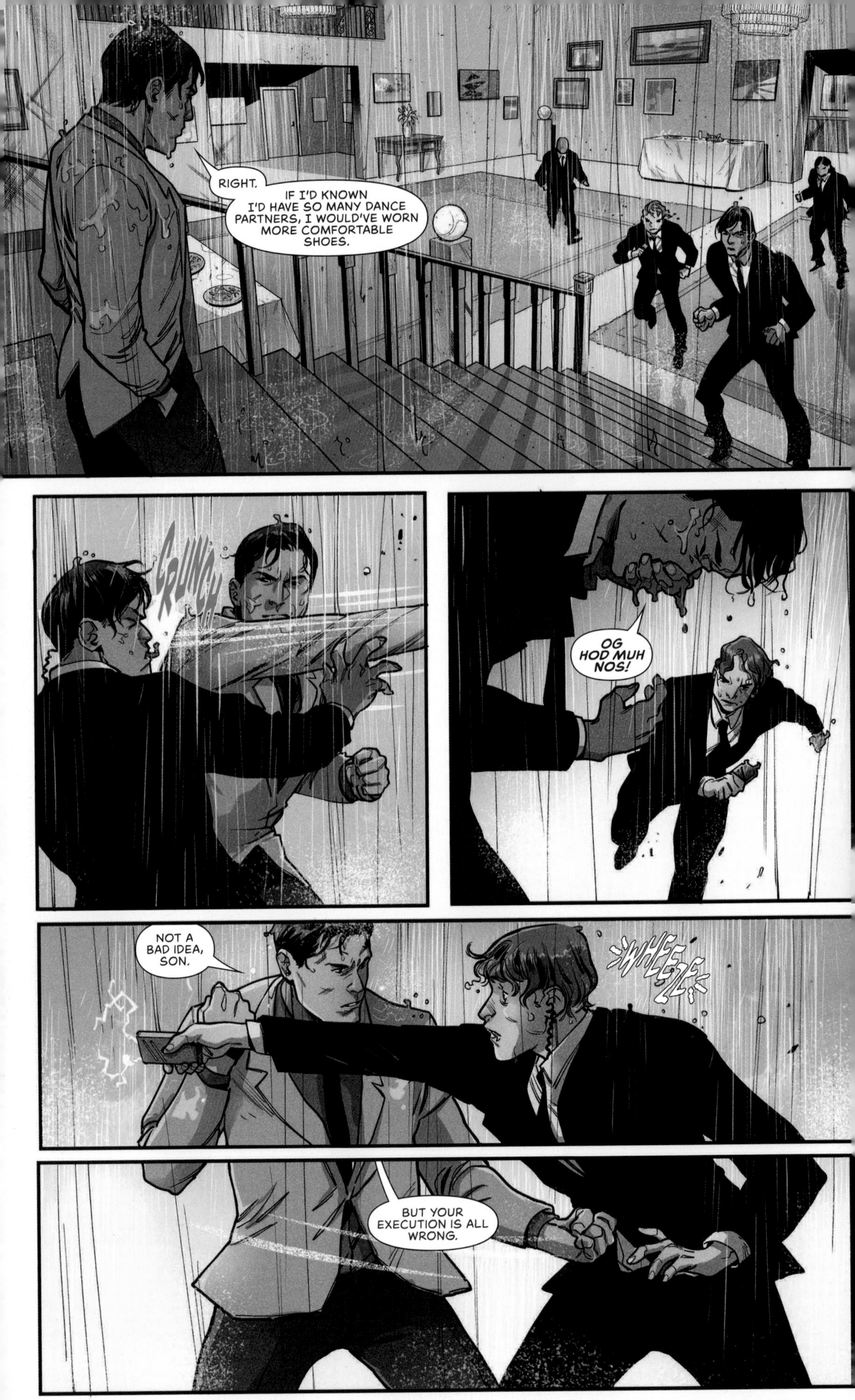
RIGHT.
IF I'D KNOWN I'D HAVE SO MANY DANCE PARTNERS, I WOULD'VE WORN MORE COMFORTABLE SHOES.
CRUNCH
OG HOD MUH NOS!
NOT A BAD IDEA, SON.
WHEEZE
BUT YOUR EXECUTION IS ALL WRONG.

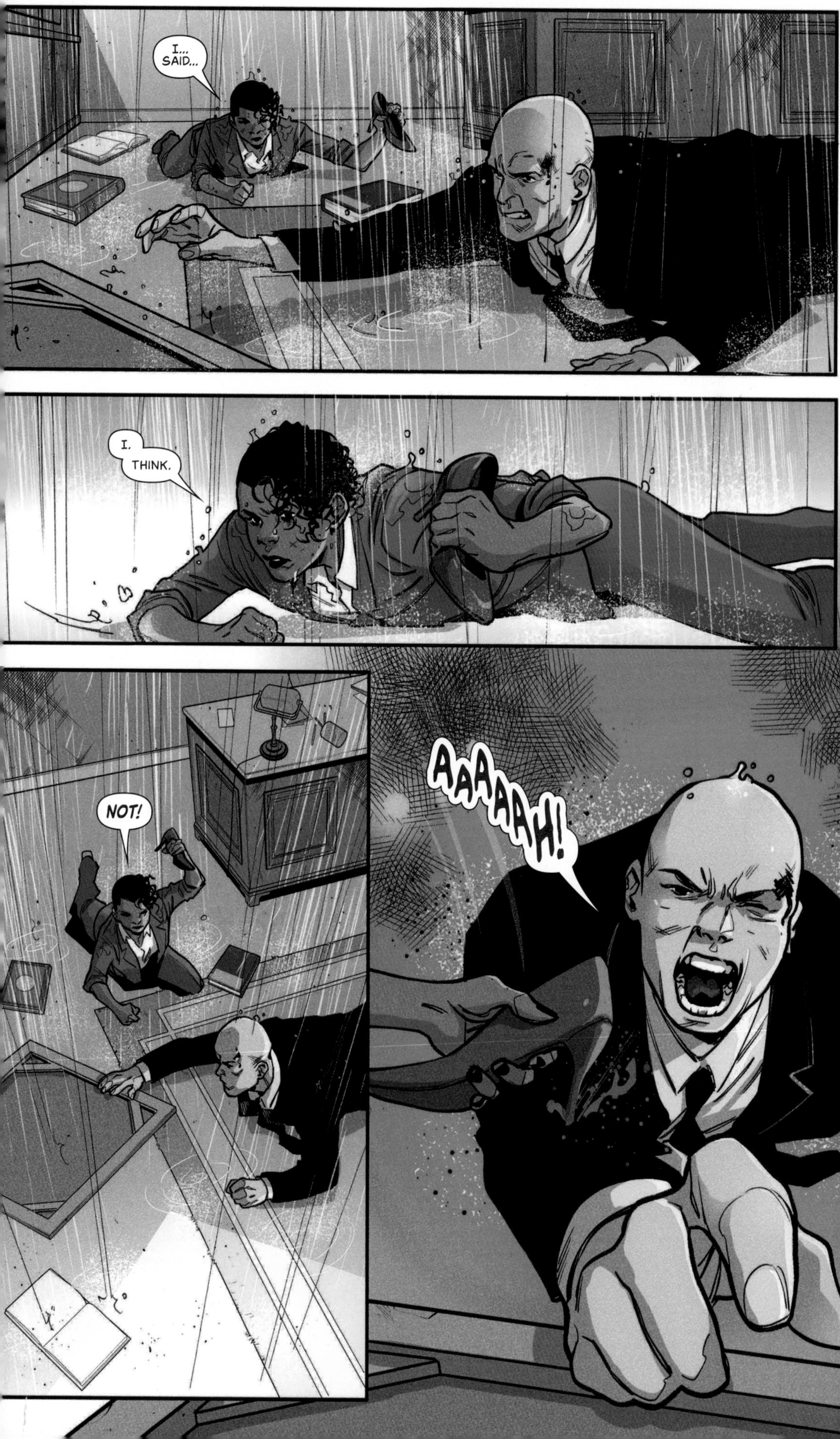
I... SAID...
I. THINK.
NOT!
AAAAAH!

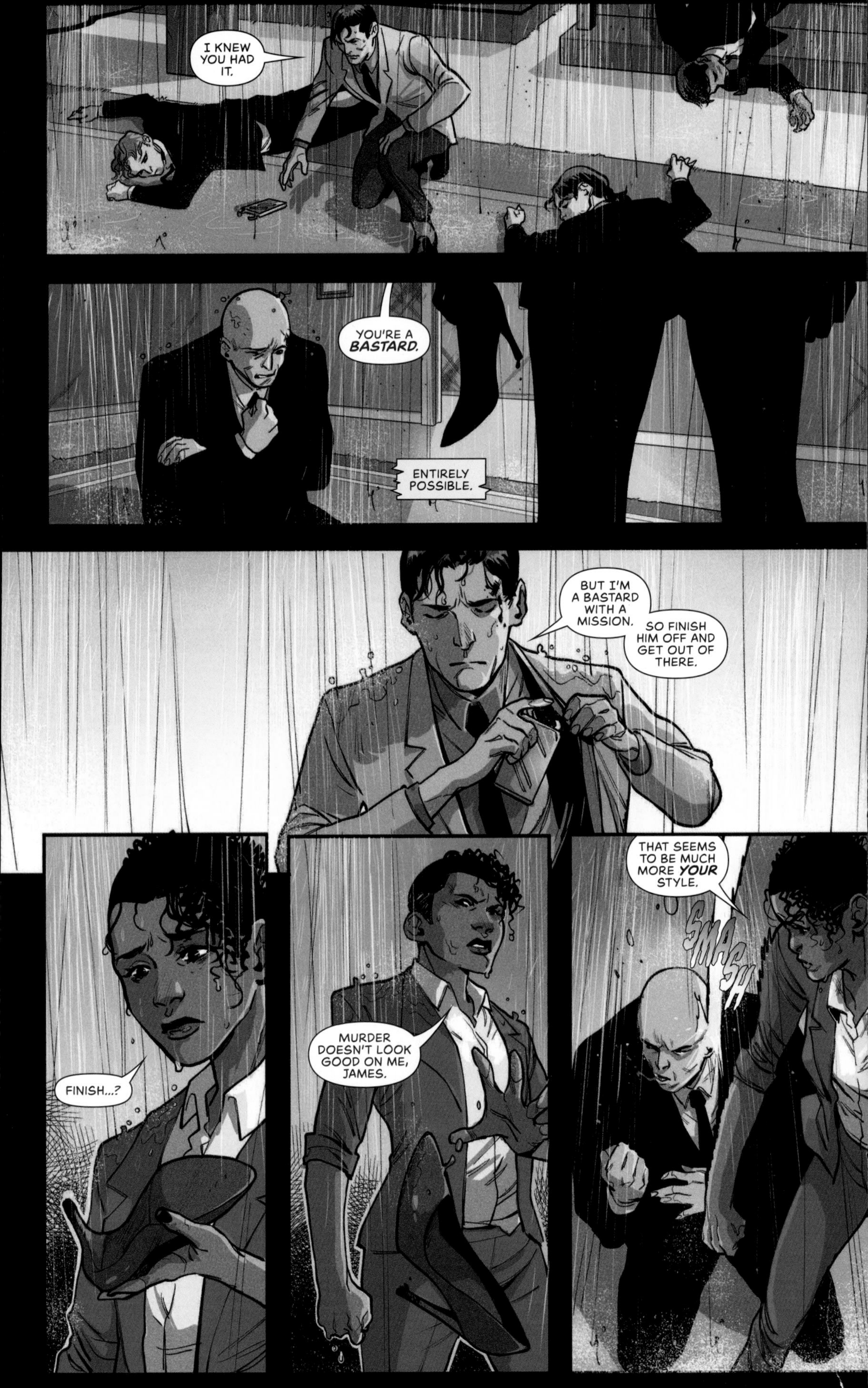

I KNEW YOU HAD IT.
YOU'RE A **BASTARD.**
ENTIRELY POSSIBLE.
BUT I'M A BASTARD WITH A MISSION.
SO FINISH HIM OFF AND GET OUT OF THERE.
FINISH...?
MURDER DOESN'T LOOK GOOD ON ME, JAMES.
THAT SEEMS TO BE MUCH MORE ***YOUR*** STYLE.
SMASH

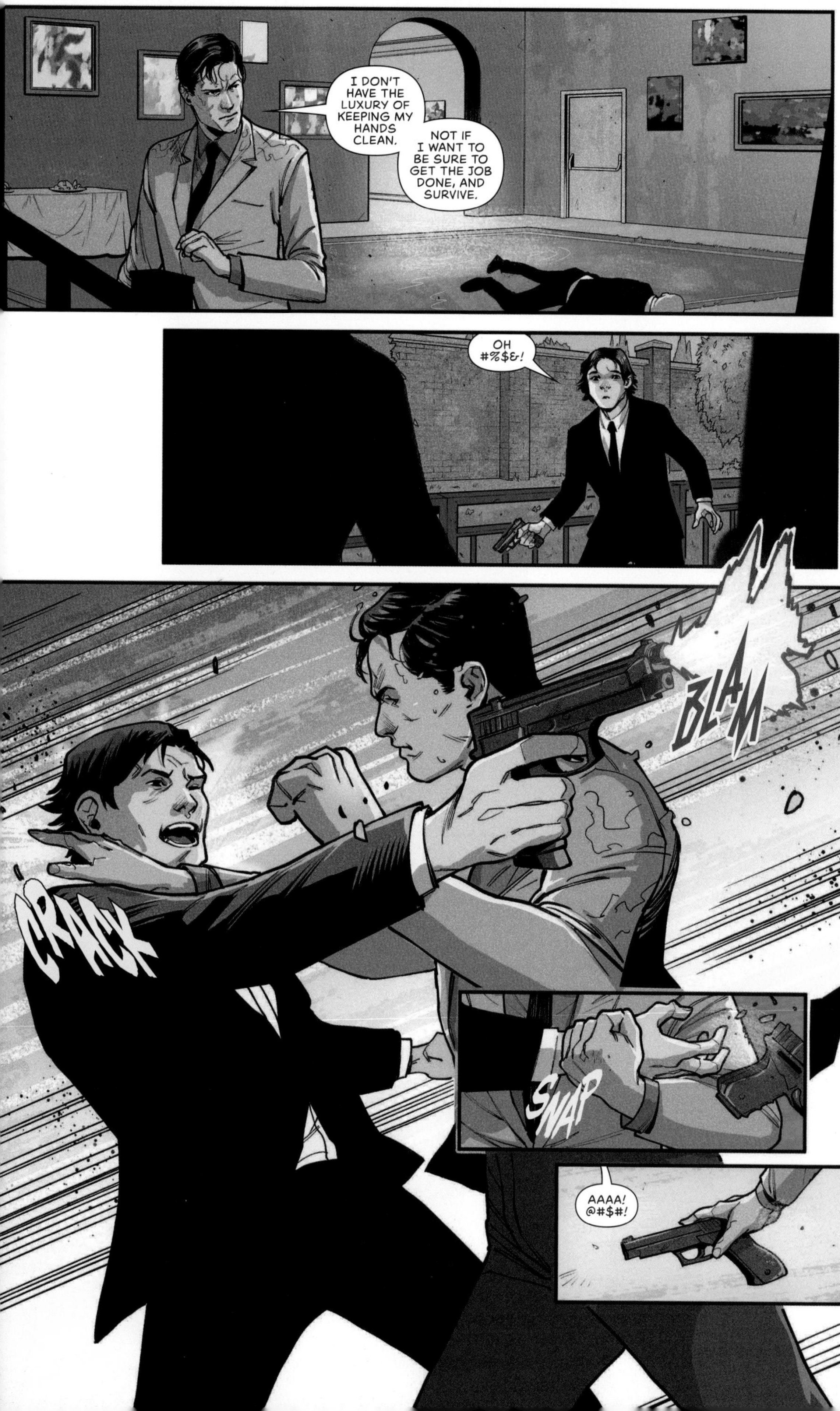
I DON'T HAVE THE LUXURY OF KEEPING MY HANDS CLEAN.
NOT IF I WANT TO BE SURE TO GET THE JOB DONE, AND SURVIVE.
OH #%$&!
BLAM
CRACK
SNAP
AAAA! @#$#!

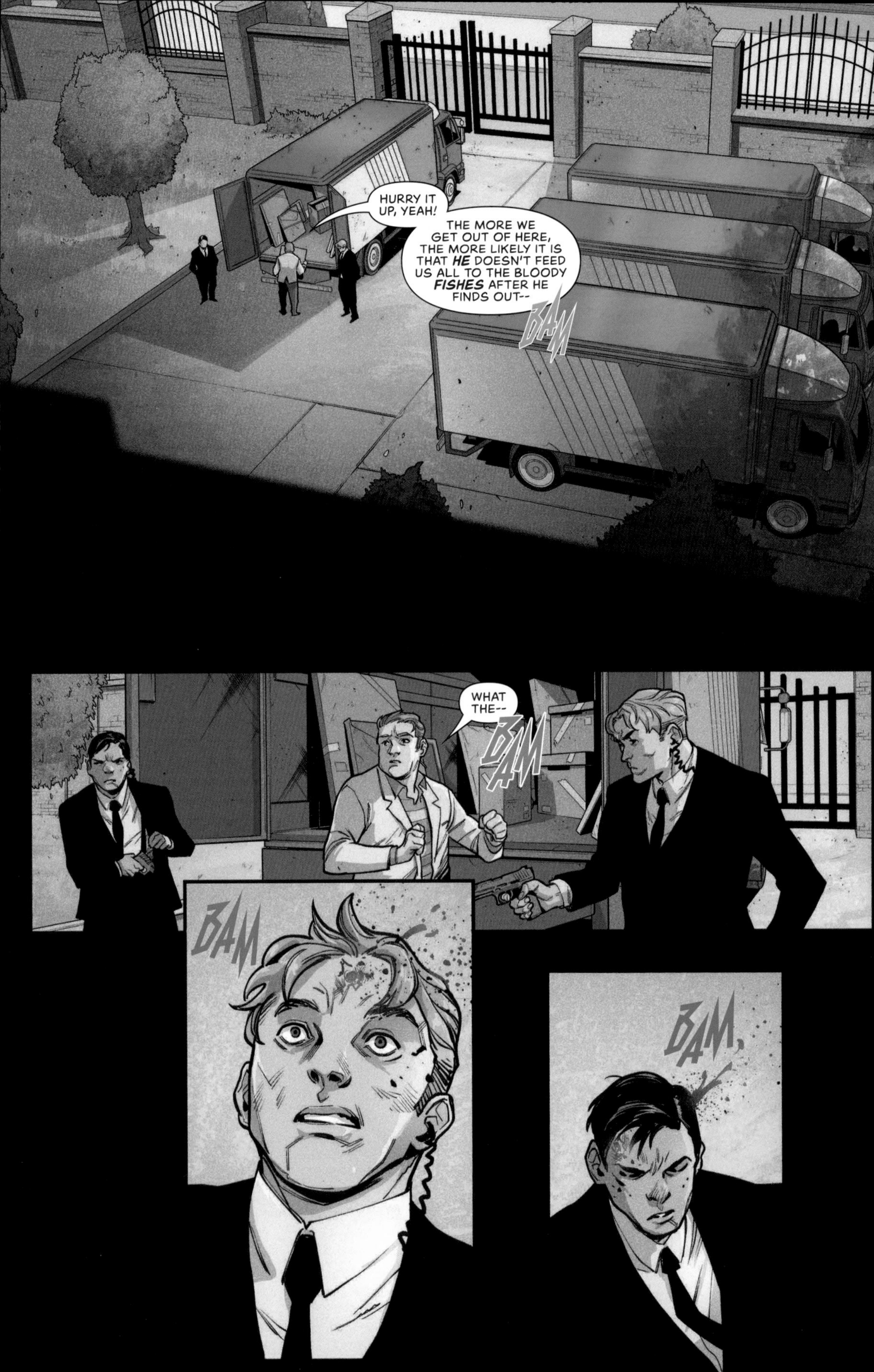
HURRY IT UP, YEAH!
THE MORE WE GET OUT OF HERE, THE MORE LIKELY IT IS THAT HE DOESN'T FEED US ALL TO THE BLOODY FISHES AFTER HE FINDS OUT--
BAM
WHAT THE--
BAM
BAM
BAM,

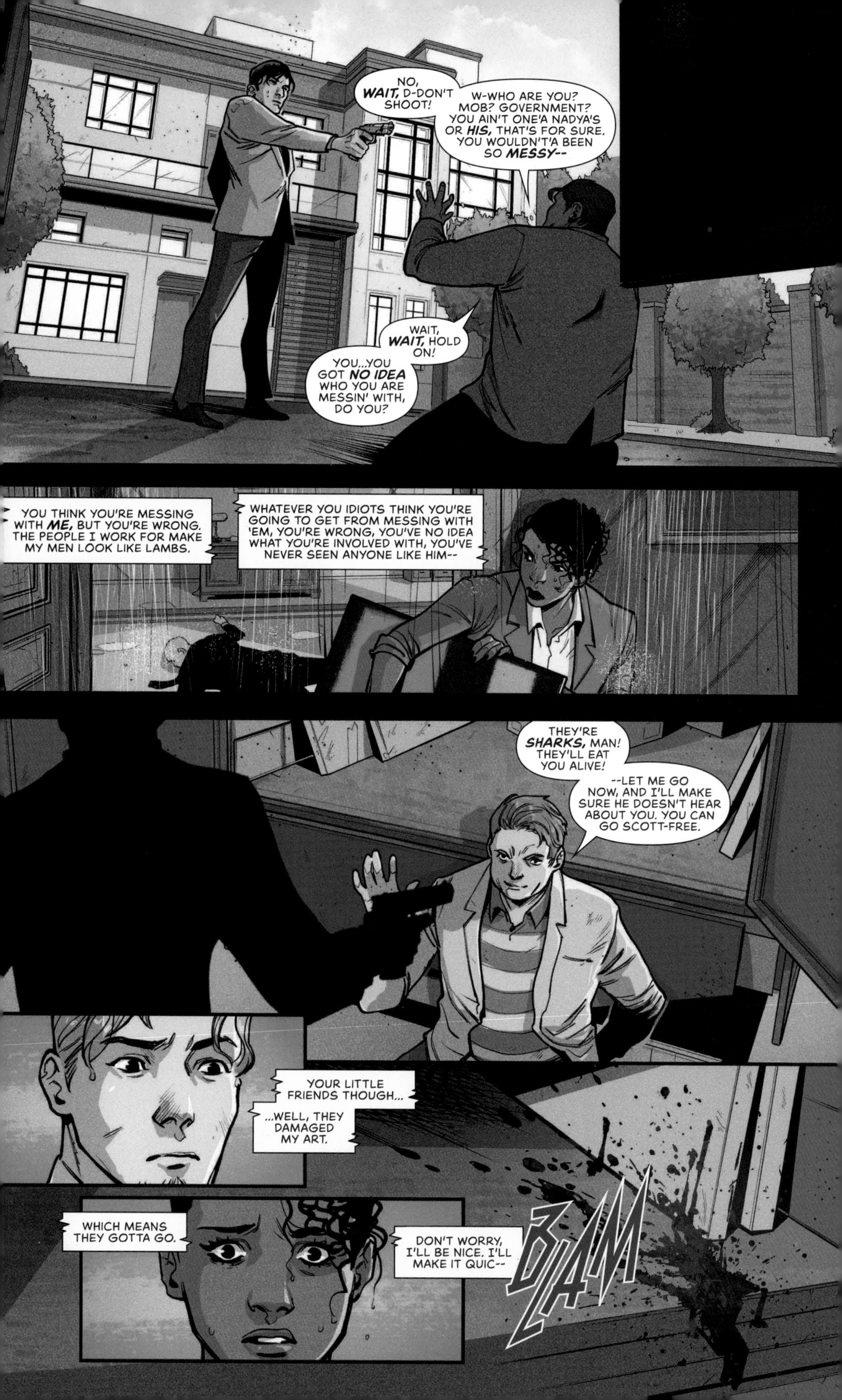
NO, WAIT, D-DON'T SHOOT!
W-WHO ARE YOU? MOB? GOVERNMENT? YOU AIN'T ONE'A NADYA'S OR HIS, THAT'S FOR SURE. YOU WOULDN'T'A BEEN SO MESSY--
WAIT, WAIT, HOLD ON!
YOU...YOU GOT NO IDEA WHO YOU ARE MESSIN' WITH, DO YOU?
YOU THINK YOU'RE MESSING WITH ME, BUT YOU'RE WRONG. THE PEOPLE I WORK FOR MAKE MY MEN LOOK LIKE LAMBS.
WHATEVER YOU IDIOTS THINK YOU'RE GOING TO GET FROM MESSING WITH 'EM, YOU'RE WRONG, YOU'VE NO IDEA WHAT YOU'RE INVOLVED WITH, YOU'VE NEVER SEEN ANYONE LIKE HIM--
THEY'RE SHARKS, MAN! THEY'LL EAT YOU ALIVE!
--LET ME GO NOW, AND I'LL MAKE SURE HE DOESN'T HEAR ABOUT YOU. YOU CAN GO SCOTT-FREE.
YOUR LITTLE FRIENDS THOUGH...
...WELL, THEY DAMAGED MY ART.
WHICH MEANS THEY GOTTA GO.
DON'T WORRY, I'LL BE NICE. I'LL MAKE IT QUIC--
BLAM

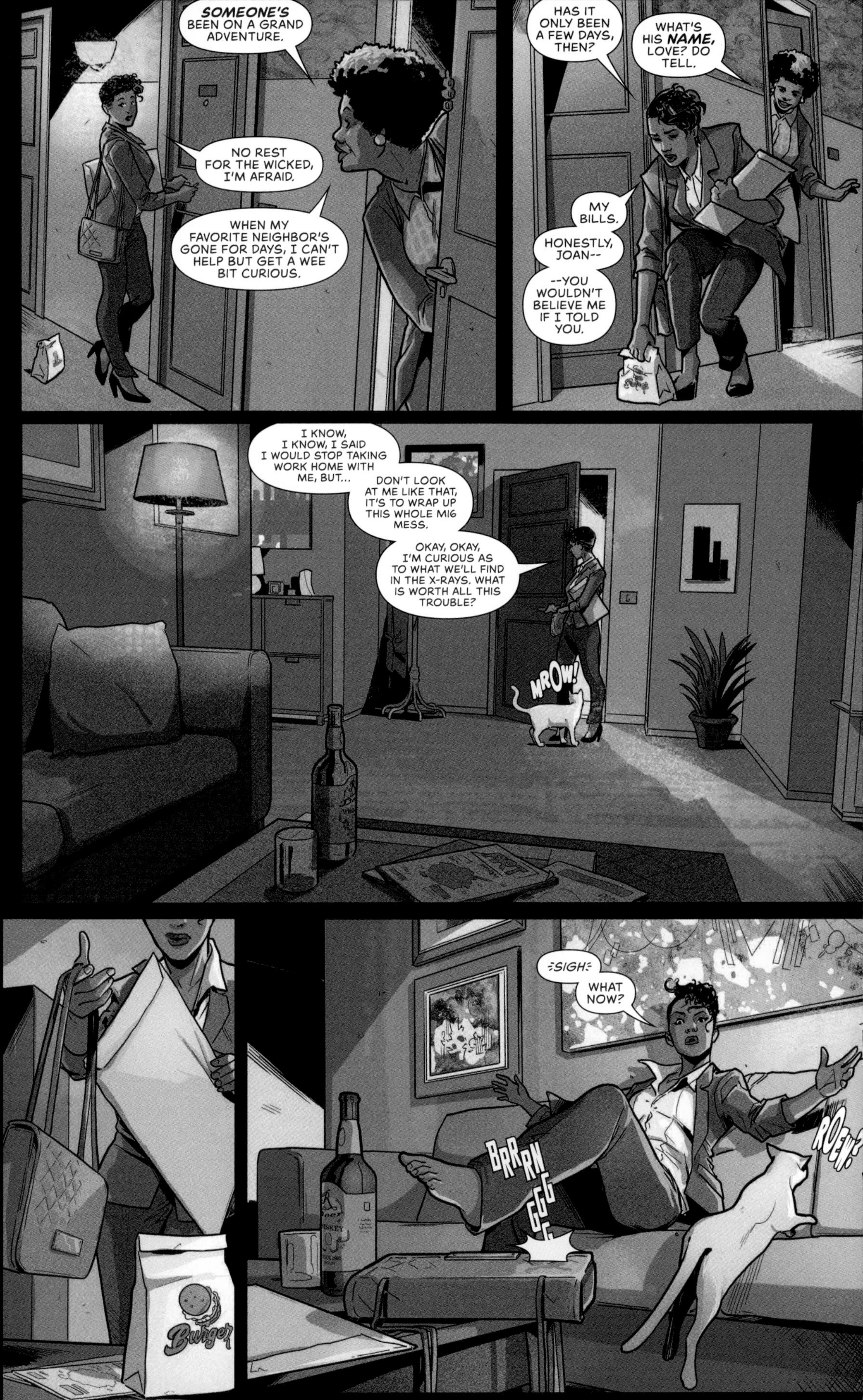
SOMEONE'S BEEN ON A GRAND ADVENTURE.
NO REST FOR THE WICKED, I'M AFRAID.
WHEN MY FAVORITE NEIGHBOR'S GONE FOR DAYS, I CAN'T HELP BUT GET A WEE BIT CURIOUS.
HAS IT ONLY BEEN A FEW DAYS, THEN?
WHAT'S HIS NAME, LOVE? DO TELL.
MY BILLS.
HONESTLY, JOAN--
--YOU WOULDN'T BELIEVE ME IF I TOLD YOU.
I KNOW, I KNOW, I SAID I WOULD STOP TAKING WORK HOME WITH ME, BUT...
DON'T LOOK AT ME LIKE THAT, IT'S TO WRAP UP THIS WHOLE MI6 MESS.
OKAY, OKAY, I'M CURIOUS AS TO WHAT WE'LL FIND IN THE X-RAYS. WHAT IS WORTH ALL THIS TROUBLE?
MROW!
Burger
SIGH
WHAT NOW?
BRRRRNGGG
ROEW?

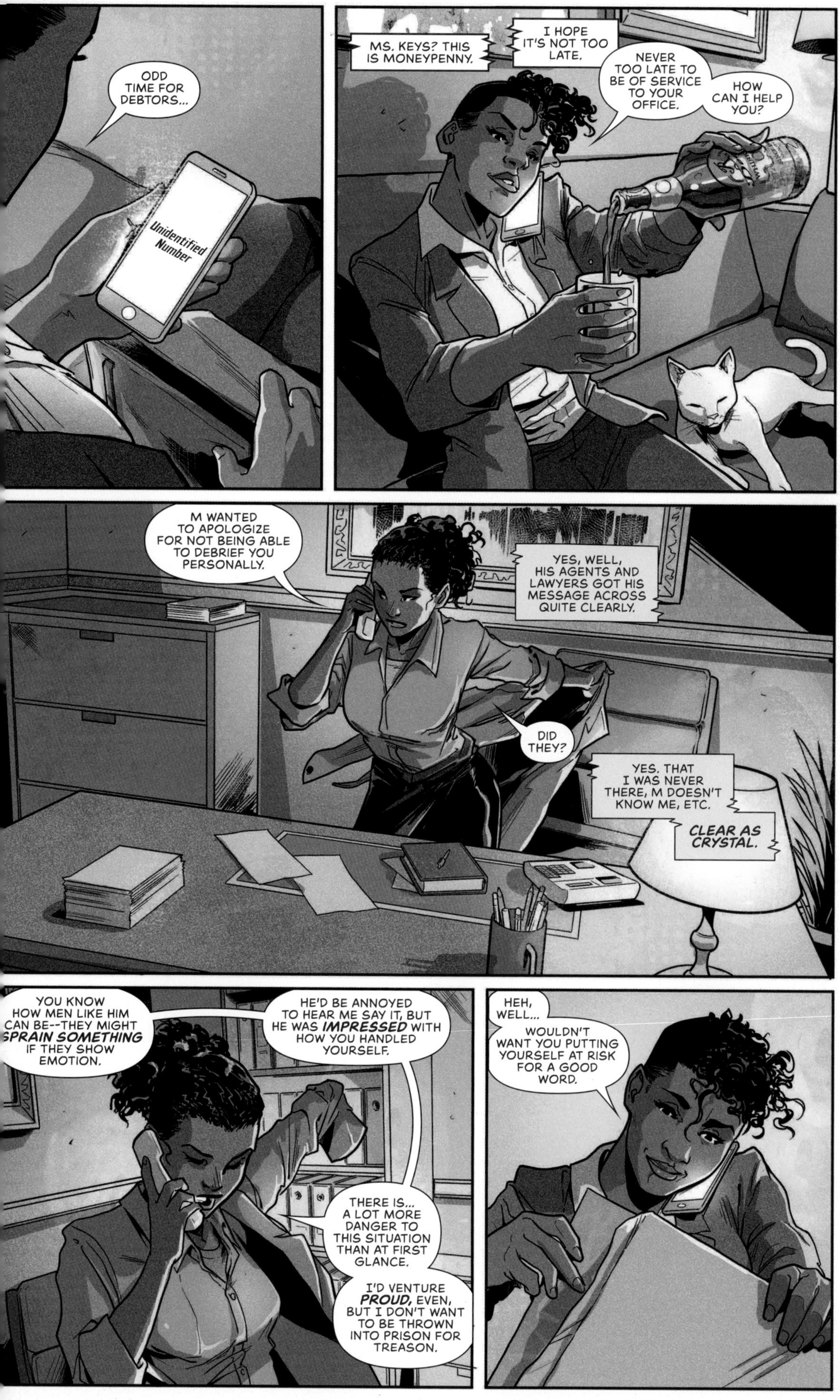
ODD TIME FOR DEBTORS...
Unidentified Number
MS. KEYS? THIS IS MONEYPENNY.
I HOPE IT'S NOT TOO LATE.
NEVER TOO LATE TO BE OF SERVICE TO YOUR OFFICE.
HOW CAN I HELP YOU?
M WANTED TO APOLOGIZE FOR NOT BEING ABLE TO DEBRIEF YOU PERSONALLY.
YES, WELL, HIS AGENTS AND LAWYERS GOT HIS MESSAGE ACROSS QUITE CLEARLY.
DID THEY?
YES. THAT I WAS NEVER THERE, M DOESN'T KNOW ME, ETC.
CLEAR AS CRYSTAL.
YOU KNOW HOW MEN LIKE HIM CAN BE--THEY MIGHT SPRAIN SOMETHING IF THEY SHOW EMOTION.
HE'D BE ANNOYED TO HEAR ME SAY IT, BUT HE WAS IMPRESSED WITH HOW YOU HANDLED YOURSELF.
THERE IS... A LOT MORE DANGER TO THIS SITUATION THAN AT FIRST GLANCE.
I'D VENTURE PROUD, EVEN, BUT I DON'T WANT TO BE THROWN INTO PRISON FOR TREASON.
HEH, WELL...
WOULDN'T WANT YOU PUTTING YOURSELF AT RISK FOR A GOOD WORD.

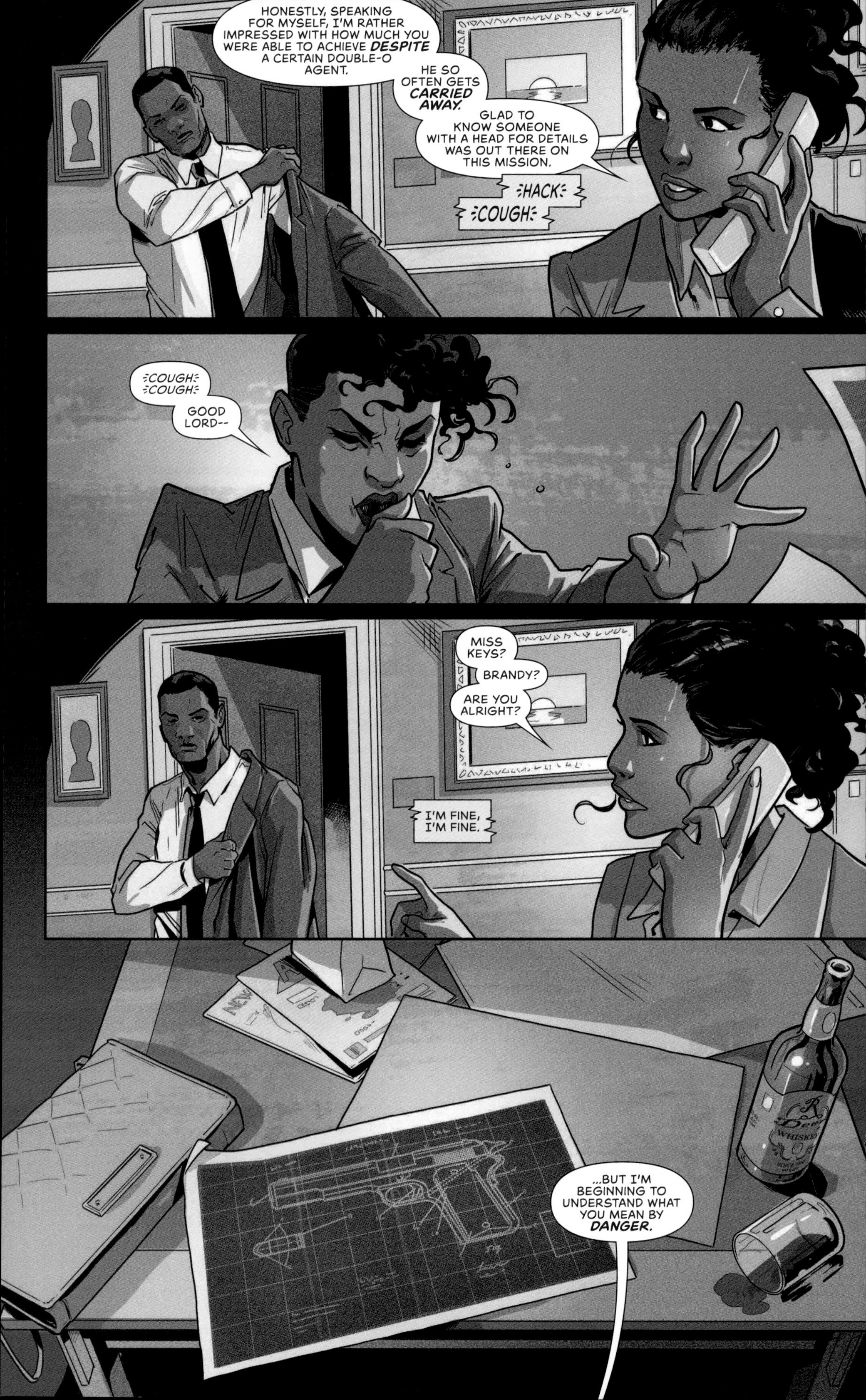
HONESTLY, SPEAKING FOR MYSELF, I'M RATHER IMPRESSED WITH HOW MUCH YOU WERE ABLE TO ACHIEVE *DESPITE* A CERTAIN DOUBLE-O AGENT.
HE SO OFTEN GETS *CARRIED AWAY.*
GLAD TO KNOW SOMEONE WITH A HEAD FOR DETAILS WAS OUT THERE ON THIS MISSION.
HACK
COUGH
COUGH
COUGH
GOOD LORD--
MISS KEYS?
BRANDY?
ARE YOU ALRIGHT?
I'M FINE, I'M FINE.
...BUT I'M BEGINNING TO UNDERSTAND WHAT YOU MEAN BY *DANGER.*

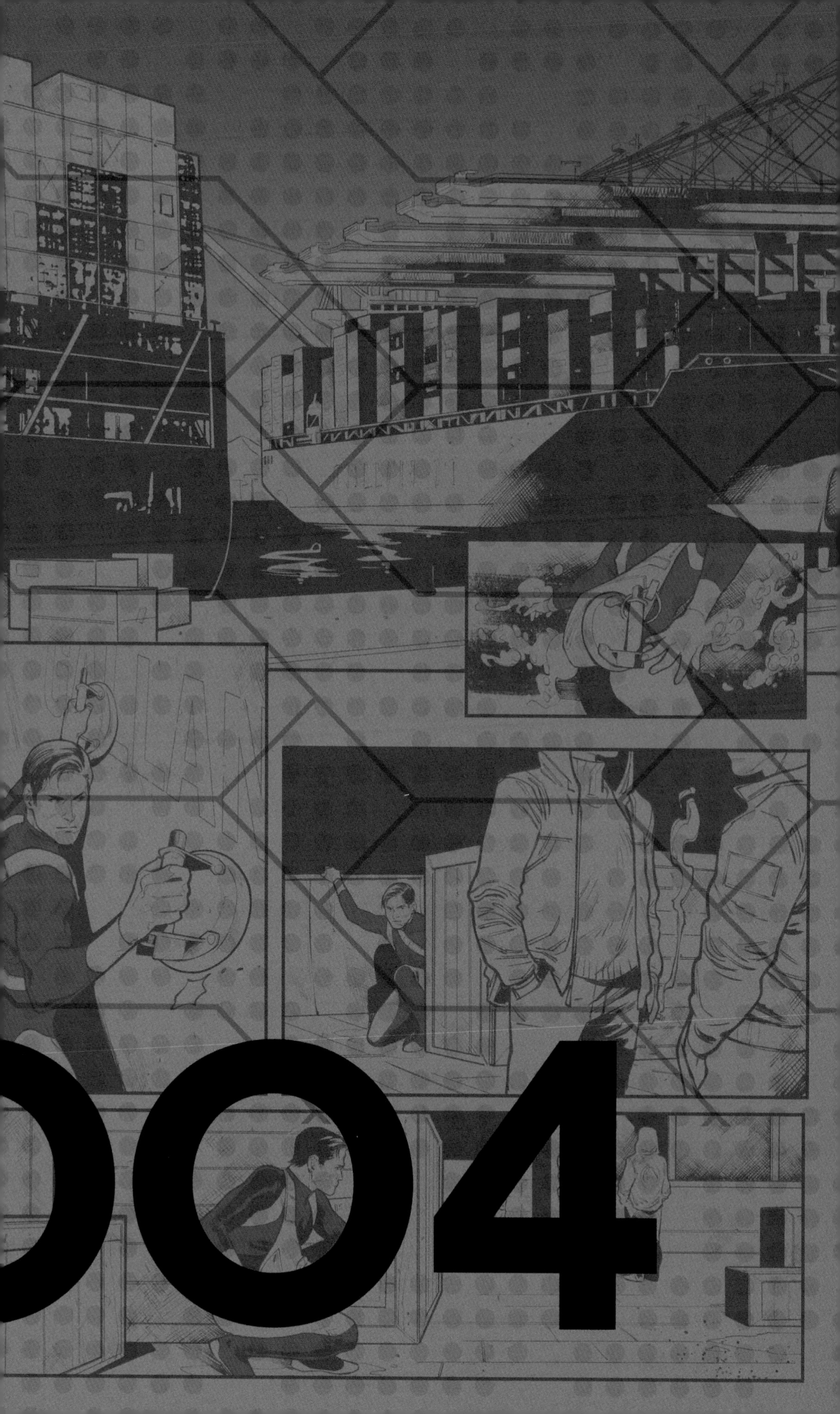
004.

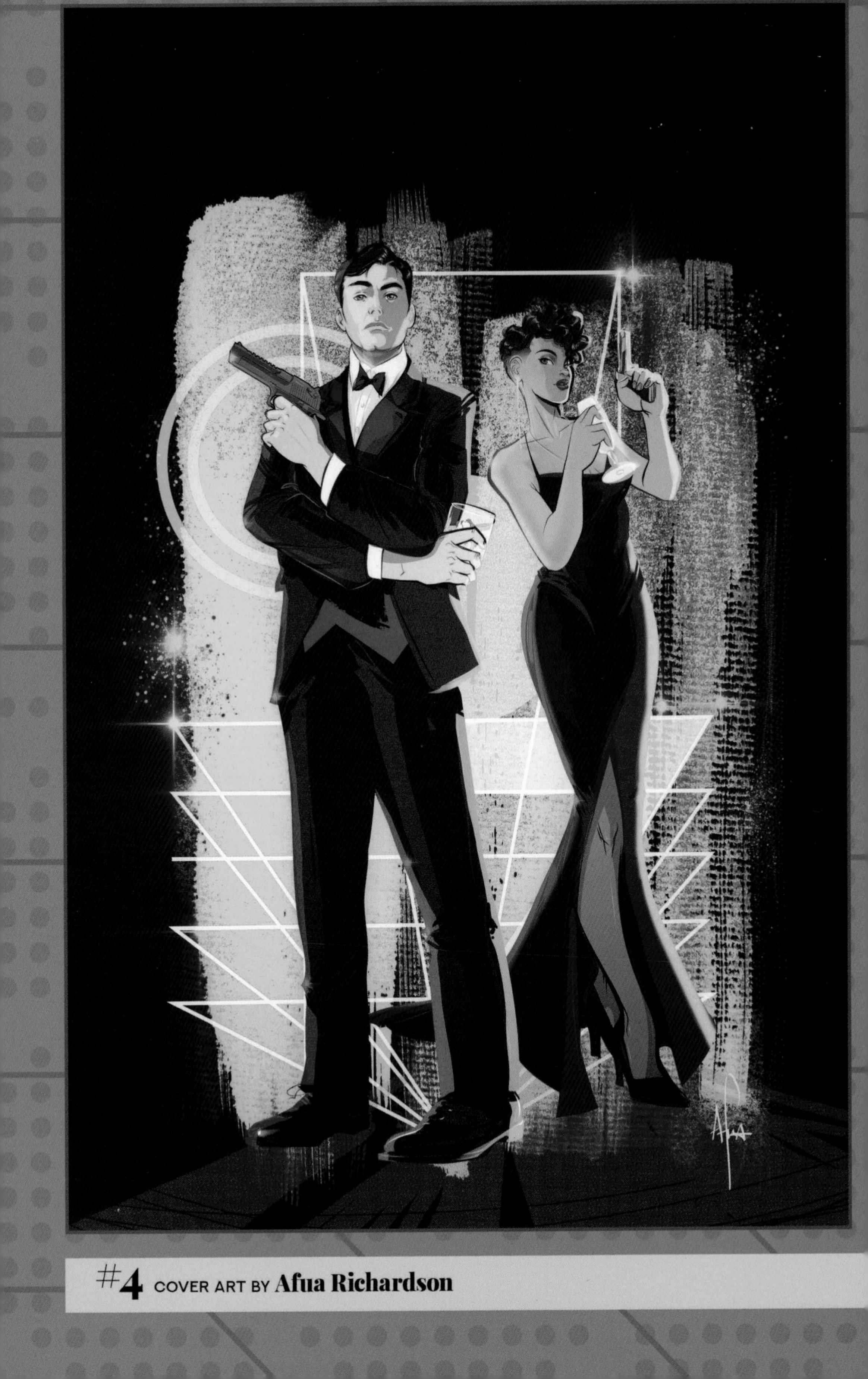

#4 COVER ART BY Afua Richardson

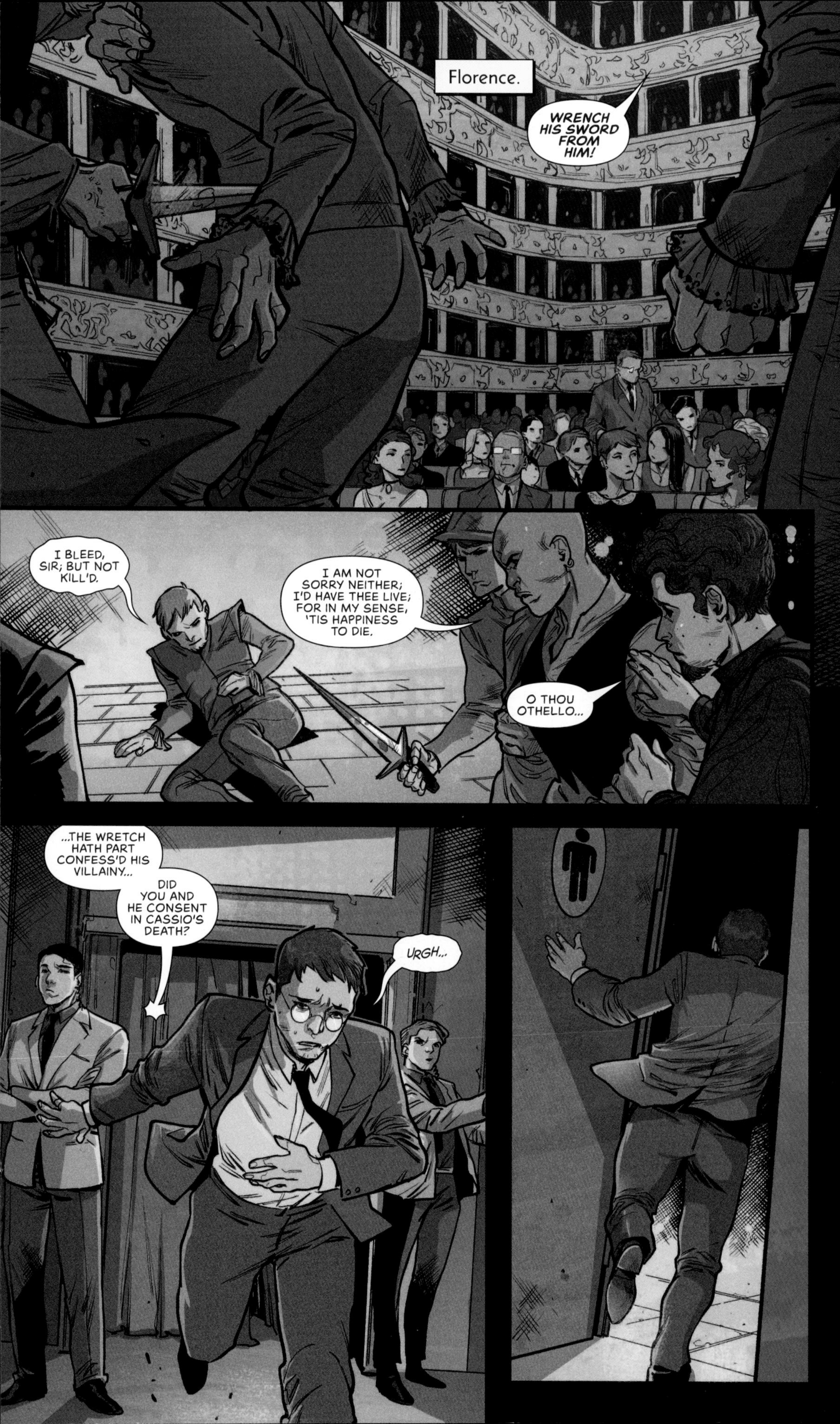
Florence.
WRENCH HIS SWORD FROM HIM!
I BLEED, SIR; BUT NOT KILL'D.
I AM NOT SORRY NEITHER; I'D HAVE THEE LIVE; FOR IN MY SENSE, 'TIS HAPPINESS TO DIE.
O THOU OTHELLO...
...THE WRETCH HATH PART CONFESS'D HIS VILLAINY...
DID YOU AND HE CONSENT IN CASSIO'S DEATH?
URGH...

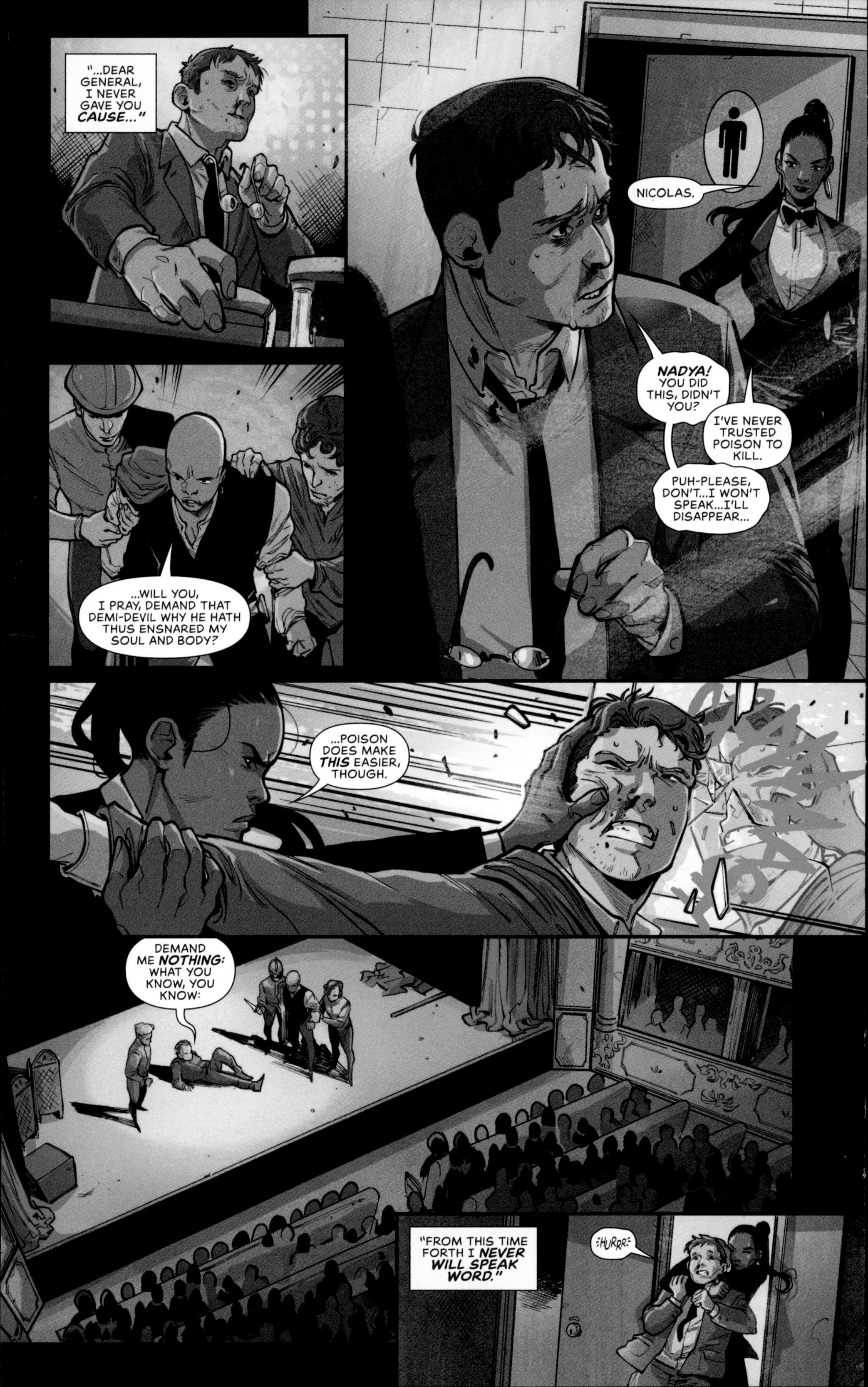
"...DEAR GENERAL, I NEVER GAVE YOU CAUSE..."
NICOLAS.
NADYA! YOU DID THIS, DIDN'T YOU?
I'VE NEVER TRUSTED POISON TO KILL.
PUH-PLEASE, DON'T...I WON'T SPEAK...I'LL DISAPPEAR...
...WILL YOU, I PRAY, DEMAND THAT DEMI-DEVIL WHY HE HATH THUS ENSNARED MY SOUL AND BODY?
...POISON DOES MAKE THIS EASIER, THOUGH.
DEMAND ME NOTHING: WHAT YOU KNOW, YOU KNOW:
"FROM THIS TIME FORTH I NEVER WILL SPEAK WORD."
HURRR

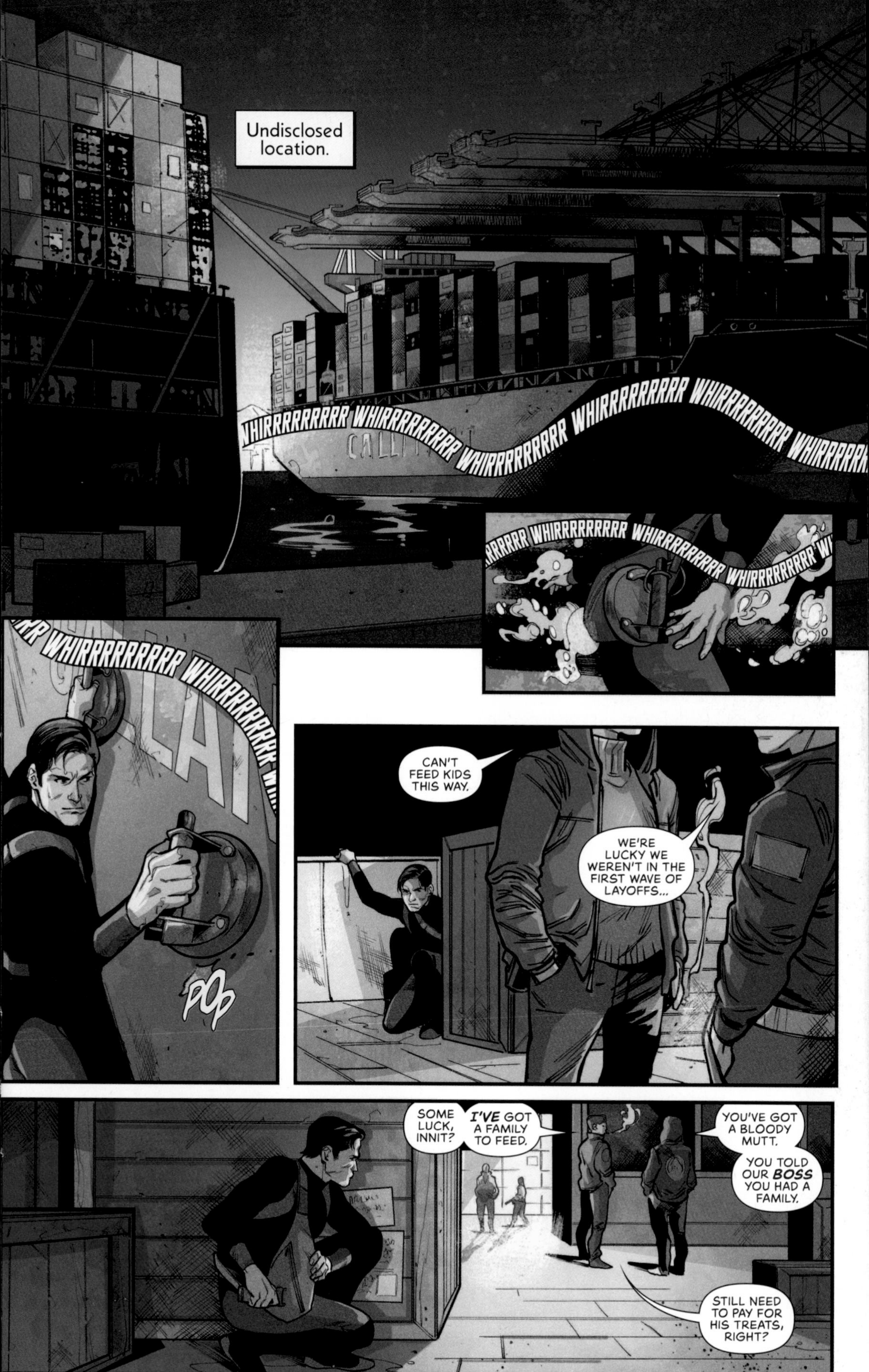
Undisclosed location.
WHIRRRRRRRR WHIRRRRRRRR WHIRRRRRRRR WHIRRRRRRRR
WHIRRRRRRRR WHIRRRRRRRR WHIRRRRRRRR
WHIRRRRRRRR WHIRRRRRRRR
POP
CAN'T FEED KIDS THIS WAY.
WE'RE LUCKY WE WEREN'T IN THE FIRST WAVE OF LAYOFFS...
SOME LUCK, INNIT?
I'VE GOT A FAMILY TO FEED.
YOU'VE GOT A BLOODY MUTT.
YOU TOLD OUR BOSS YOU HAD A FAMILY.
STILL NEED TO PAY FOR HIS TREATS, RIGHT?

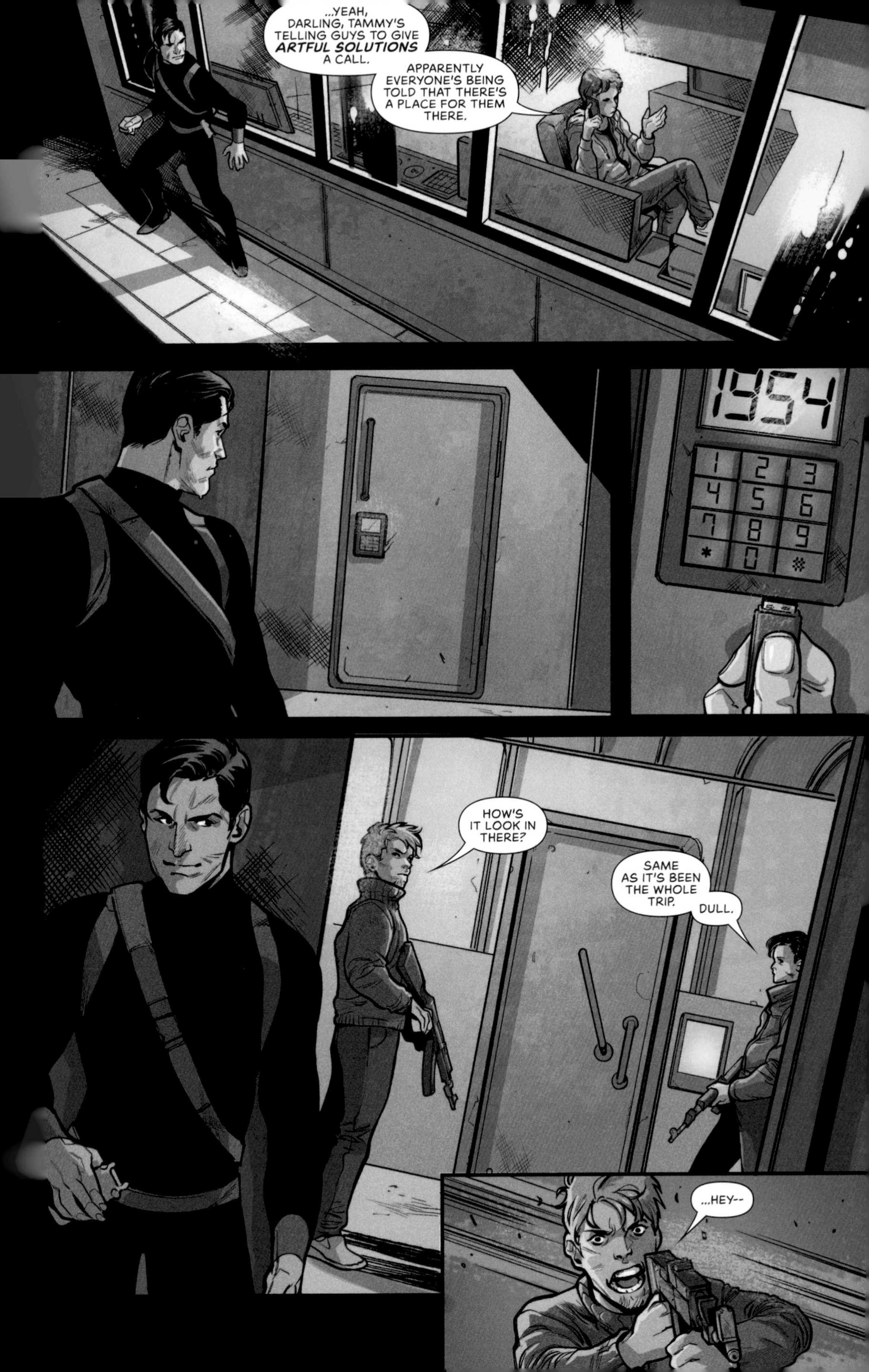
...YEAH, DARLING, TAMMY'S TELLING GUYS TO GIVE ***ARTFUL SOLUTIONS*** A CALL.
APPARENTLY EVERYONE'S BEING TOLD THAT THERE'S A PLACE FOR THEM THERE.
1954
1 2 3
4 5 6
7 8 9
* 0 #
HOW'S IT LOOK IN THERE?
SAME AS IT'S BEEN THE WHOLE TRIP.
DULL.
...HEY--

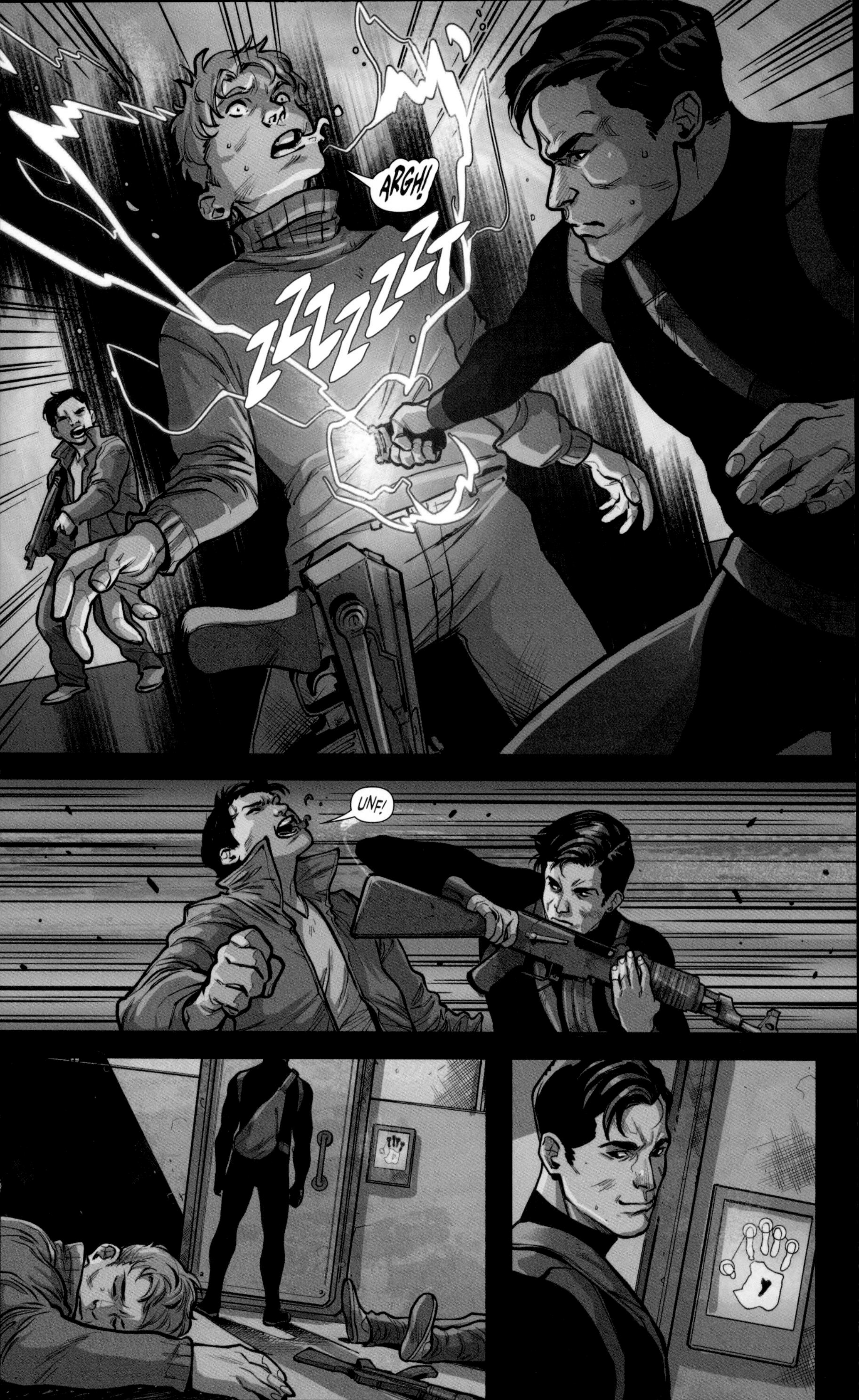
ARGH!
ZZZZZZZZT
UNF!

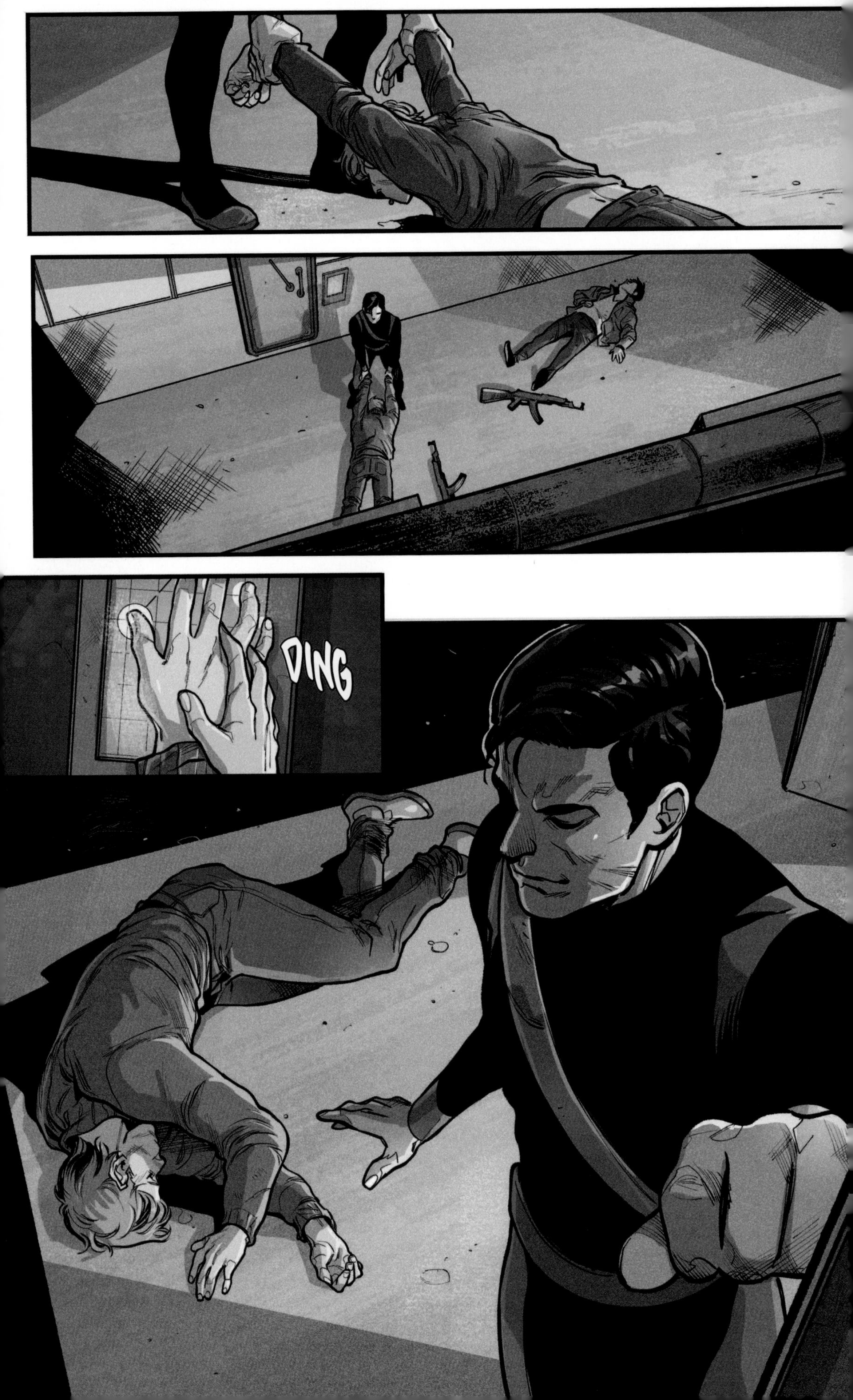
DING

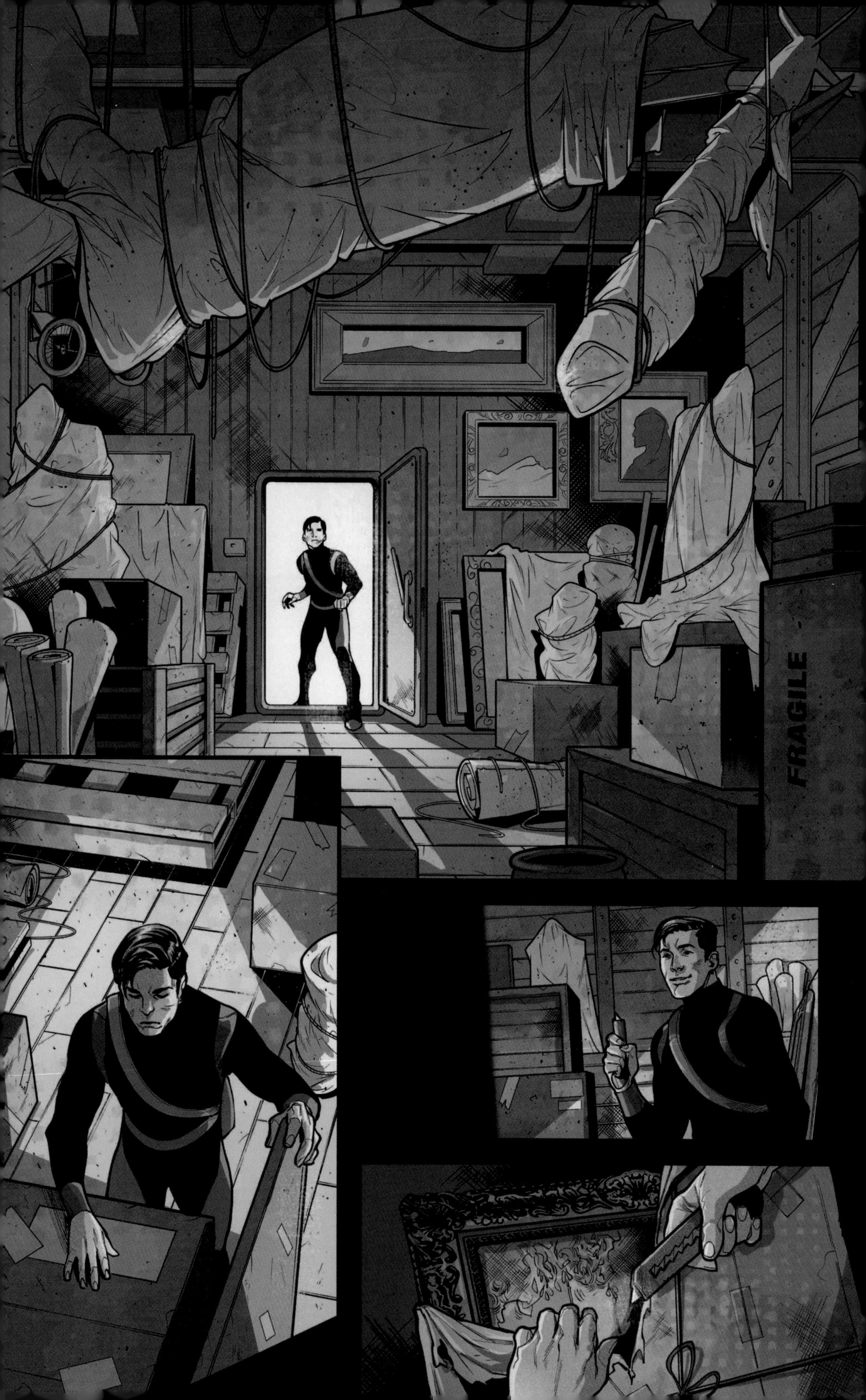
FRAGILE

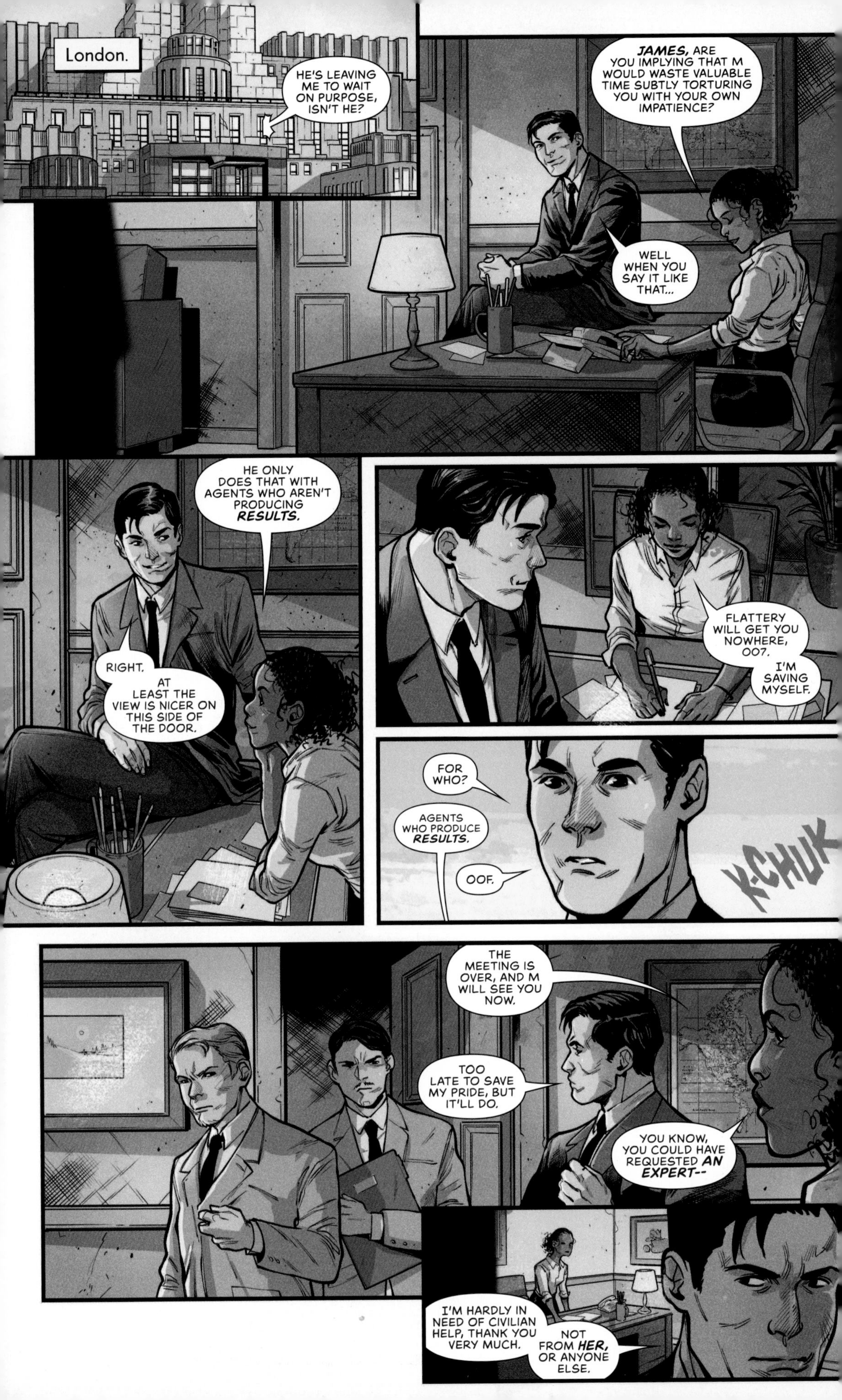
London.
HE'S LEAVING ME TO WAIT ON PURPOSE, ISN'T HE?
JAMES, ARE YOU IMPLYING THAT M WOULD WASTE VALUABLE TIME SUBTLY TORTURING YOU WITH YOUR OWN IMPATIENCE?
WELL WHEN YOU SAY IT LIKE THAT...
HE ONLY DOES THAT WITH AGENTS WHO AREN'T PRODUCING RESULTS.
RIGHT.
AT LEAST THE VIEW IS NICER ON THIS SIDE OF THE DOOR.
FLATTERY WILL GET YOU NOWHERE, 007.
I'M SAVING MYSELF.
FOR WHO?
AGENTS WHO PRODUCE RESULTS.
OOF.
K-CHUK
THE MEETING IS OVER, AND M WILL SEE YOU NOW.
TOO LATE TO SAVE MY PRIDE, BUT IT'LL DO.
YOU KNOW, YOU COULD HAVE REQUESTED AN EXPERT--
I'M HARDLY IN NEED OF CIVILIAN HELP, THANK YOU VERY MUCH.
NOT FROM HER, OR ANYONE ELSE.

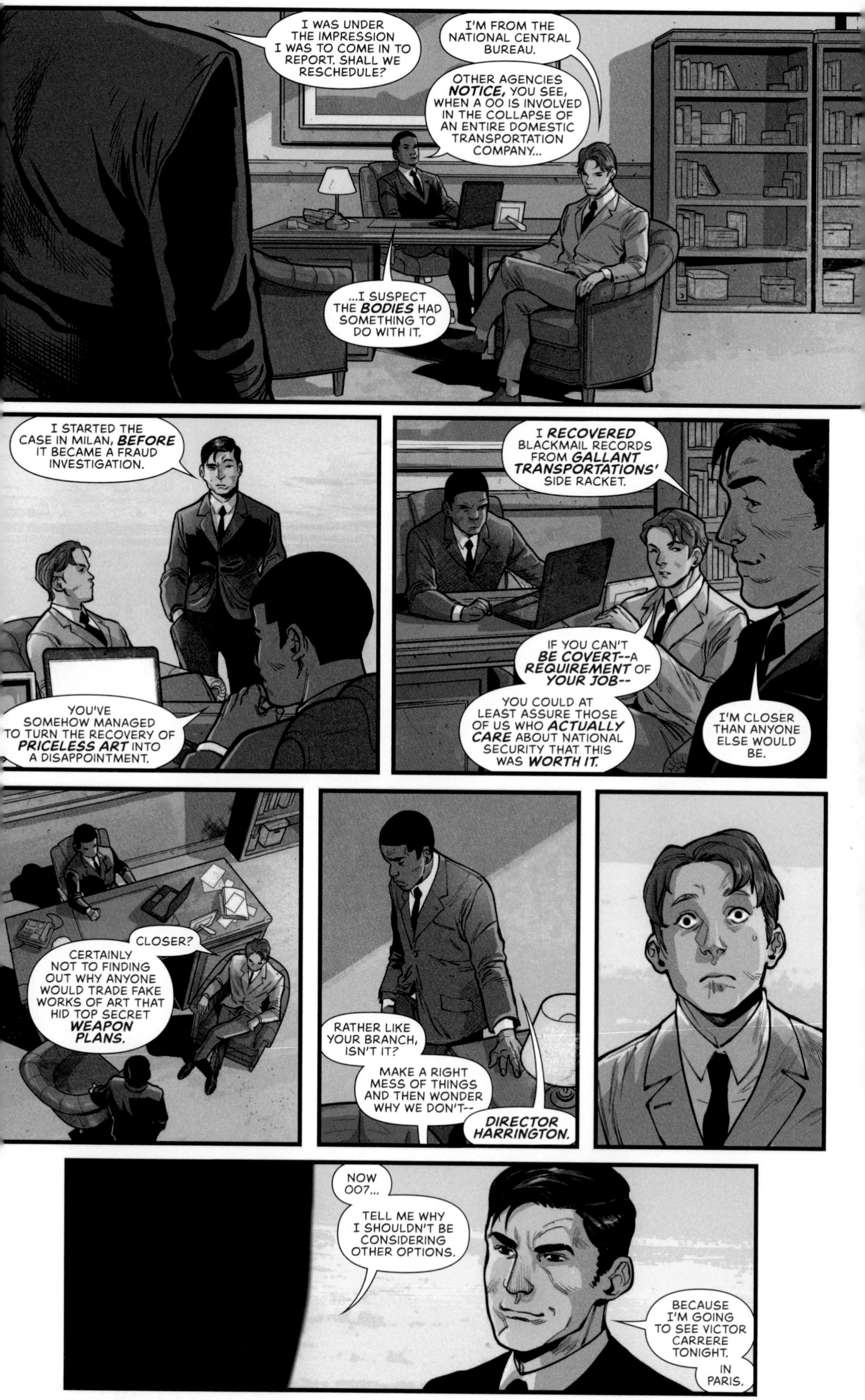
I WAS UNDER THE IMPRESSION I WAS TO COME IN TO REPORT. SHALL WE RESCHEDULE?
I'M FROM THE NATIONAL CENTRAL BUREAU.
OTHER AGENCIES NOTICE, YOU SEE, WHEN A 00 IS INVOLVED IN THE COLLAPSE OF AN ENTIRE DOMESTIC TRANSPORTATION COMPANY...
...I SUSPECT THE BODIES HAD SOMETHING TO DO WITH IT.
I STARTED THE CASE IN MILAN, BEFORE IT BECAME A FRAUD INVESTIGATION.
YOU'VE SOMEHOW MANAGED TO TURN THE RECOVERY OF PRICELESS ART INTO A DISAPPOINTMENT.
I RECOVERED BLACKMAIL RECORDS FROM GALLANT TRANSPORTATIONS' SIDE RACKET.
IF YOU CAN'T BE COVERT--A REQUIREMENT OF YOUR JOB--
YOU COULD AT LEAST ASSURE THOSE OF US WHO ACTUALLY CARE ABOUT NATIONAL SECURITY THAT THIS WAS WORTH IT.
I'M CLOSER THAN ANYONE ELSE WOULD BE.
CLOSER?
CERTAINLY NOT TO FINDING OUT WHY ANYONE WOULD TRADE FAKE WORKS OF ART THAT HID TOP SECRET WEAPON PLANS.
RATHER LIKE YOUR BRANCH, ISN'T IT?
MAKE A RIGHT MESS OF THINGS AND THEN WONDER WHY WE DON'T--
DIRECTOR HARRINGTON.
NOW 007...
TELL ME WHY I SHOULDN'T BE CONSIDERING OTHER OPTIONS.
BECAUSE I'M GOING TO SEE VICTOR CARRERE TONIGHT.
IN PARIS.

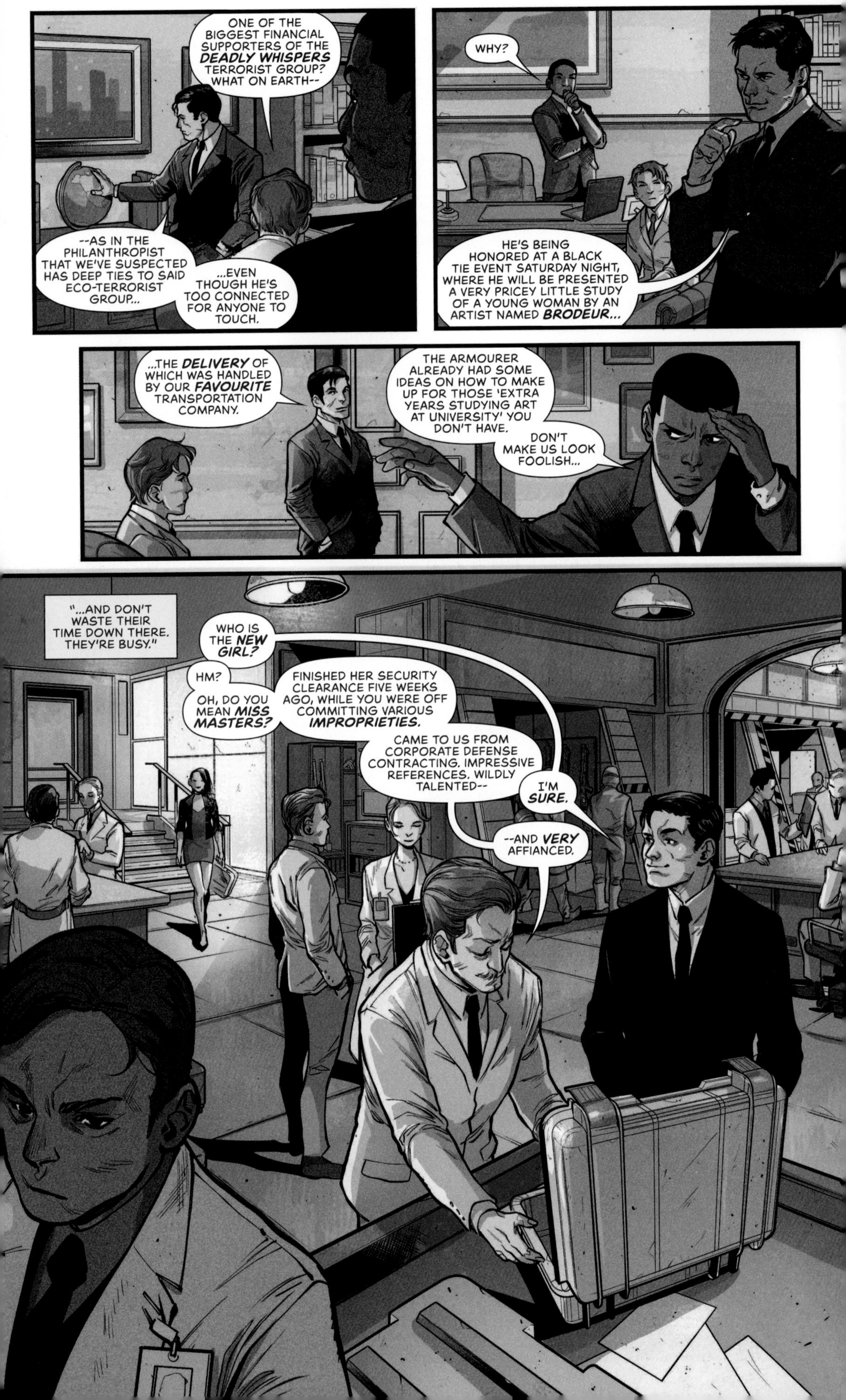
ONE OF THE BIGGEST FINANCIAL SUPPORTERS OF THE DEADLY WHISPERS TERRORIST GROUP? WHAT ON EARTH--
--AS IN THE PHILANTHROPIST THAT WE'VE SUSPECTED HAS DEEP TIES TO SAID ECO-TERRORIST GROUP...
...EVEN THOUGH HE'S TOO CONNECTED FOR ANYONE TO TOUCH.
WHY?
HE'S BEING HONORED AT A BLACK TIE EVENT SATURDAY NIGHT, WHERE HE WILL BE PRESENTED A VERY PRICEY LITTLE STUDY OF A YOUNG WOMAN BY AN ARTIST NAMED BRODEUR...
...THE DELIVERY OF WHICH WAS HANDLED BY OUR FAVOURITE TRANSPORTATION COMPANY.
THE ARMOURER ALREADY HAD SOME IDEAS ON HOW TO MAKE UP FOR THOSE 'EXTRA YEARS STUDYING ART AT UNIVERSITY' YOU DON'T HAVE.
DON'T MAKE US LOOK FOOLISH...
"...AND DON'T WASTE THEIR TIME DOWN THERE. THEY'RE BUSY."
WHO IS THE NEW GIRL?
HM?
OH, DO YOU MEAN MISS MASTERS?
FINISHED HER SECURITY CLEARANCE FIVE WEEKS AGO, WHILE YOU WERE OFF COMMITTING VARIOUS IMPROPRIETIES.
CAME TO US FROM CORPORATE DEFENSE CONTRACTING. IMPRESSIVE REFERENCES. WILDLY TALENTED--
I'M SURE.
--AND VERY AFFIANCED.

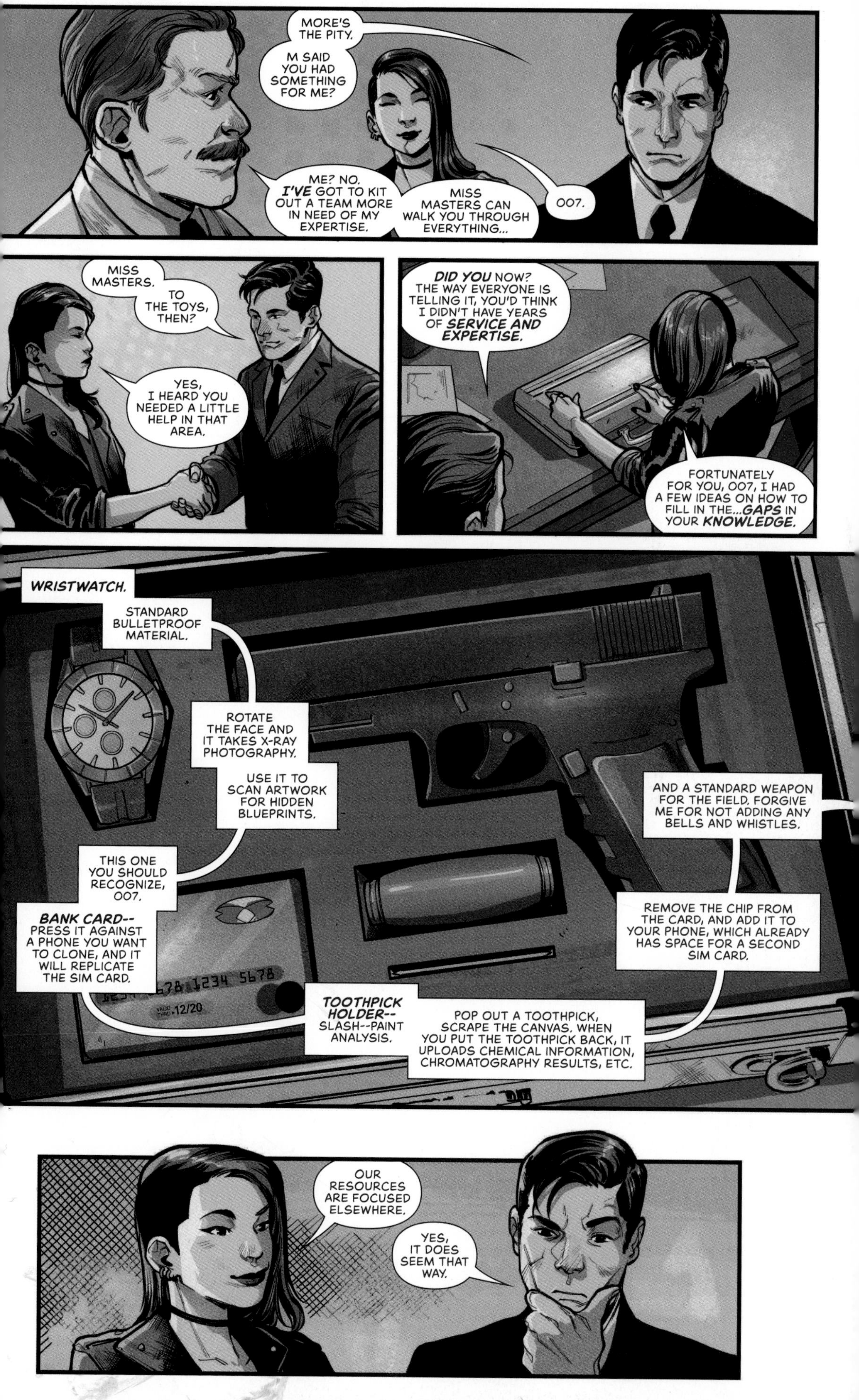
MORE'S THE PITY.
M SAID YOU HAD SOMETHING FOR ME?
ME? NO. *I'VE* GOT TO KIT OUT A TEAM MORE IN NEED OF MY EXPERTISE.
MISS MASTERS CAN WALK YOU THROUGH EVERYTHING...
007.
MISS MASTERS.
TO THE TOYS, THEN?
YES, I HEARD YOU NEEDED A LITTLE HELP IN THAT AREA.
DID YOU NOW? THE WAY EVERYONE IS TELLING IT, YOU'D THINK I DIDN'T HAVE YEARS OF ***SERVICE AND EXPERTISE.***
FORTUNATELY FOR YOU, 007, I HAD A FEW IDEAS ON HOW TO FILL IN THE...***GAPS*** IN YOUR ***KNOWLEDGE.***
WRISTWATCH.
STANDARD BULLETPROOF MATERIAL.
ROTATE THE FACE AND IT TAKES X-RAY PHOTOGRAPHY.
USE IT TO SCAN ARTWORK FOR HIDDEN BLUEPRINTS.
AND A STANDARD WEAPON FOR THE FIELD. FORGIVE ME FOR NOT ADDING ANY BELLS AND WHISTLES.
THIS ONE YOU SHOULD RECOGNIZE, 007.
BANK CARD-- PRESS IT AGAINST A PHONE YOU WANT TO CLONE, AND IT WILL REPLICATE THE SIM CARD.
REMOVE THE CHIP FROM THE CARD, AND ADD IT TO YOUR PHONE, WHICH ALREADY HAS SPACE FOR A SECOND SIM CARD.
TOOTHPICK HOLDER-- SLASH--PAINT ANALYSIS.
POP OUT A TOOTHPICK, SCRAPE THE CANVAS. WHEN YOU PUT THE TOOTHPICK BACK, IT UPLOADS CHEMICAL INFORMATION, CHROMATOGRAPHY RESULTS, ETC.
OUR RESOURCES ARE FOCUSED ELSEWHERE.
YES, IT DOES SEEM THAT WAY.

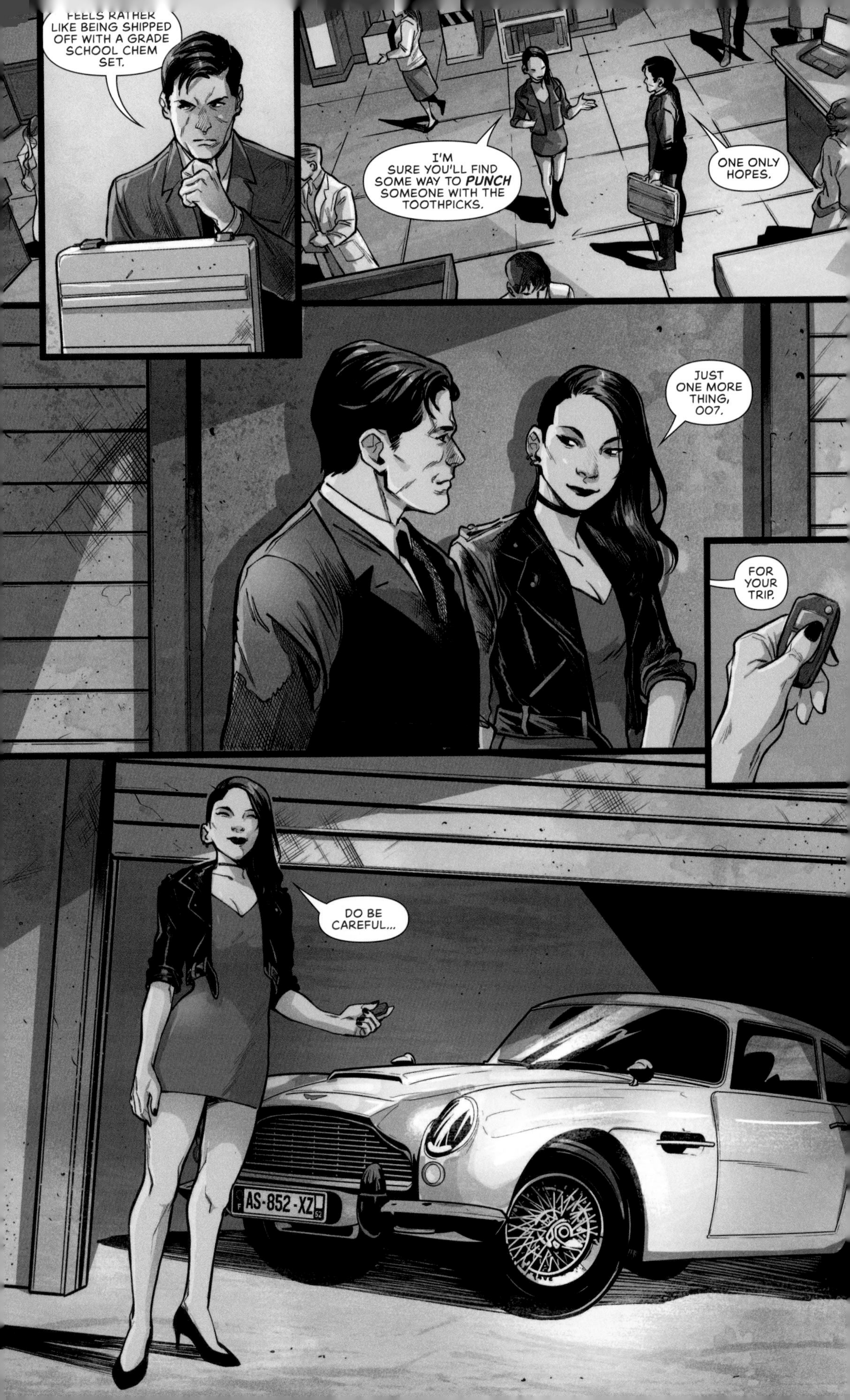
FEELS RATHER LIKE BEING SHIPPED OFF WITH A GRADE SCHOOL CHEM SET.
I'M SURE YOU'LL FIND SOME WAY TO PUNCH SOMEONE WITH THE TOOTHPICKS.
ONE ONLY HOPES.
JUST ONE MORE THING, 007.
FOR YOUR TRIP.
DO BE CAREFUL...
AS-852-XZ

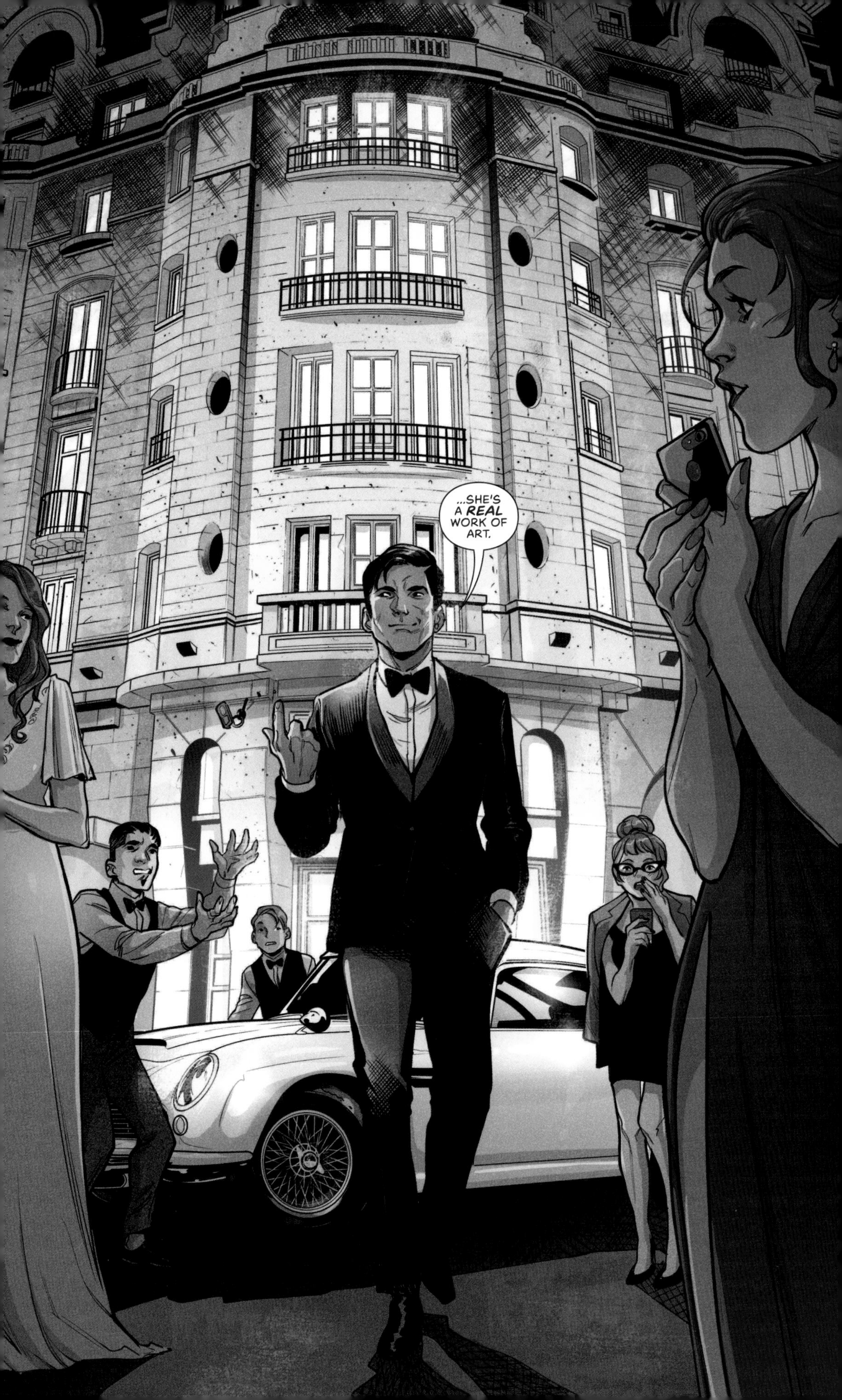
...SHE'S A REAL WORK OF ART.

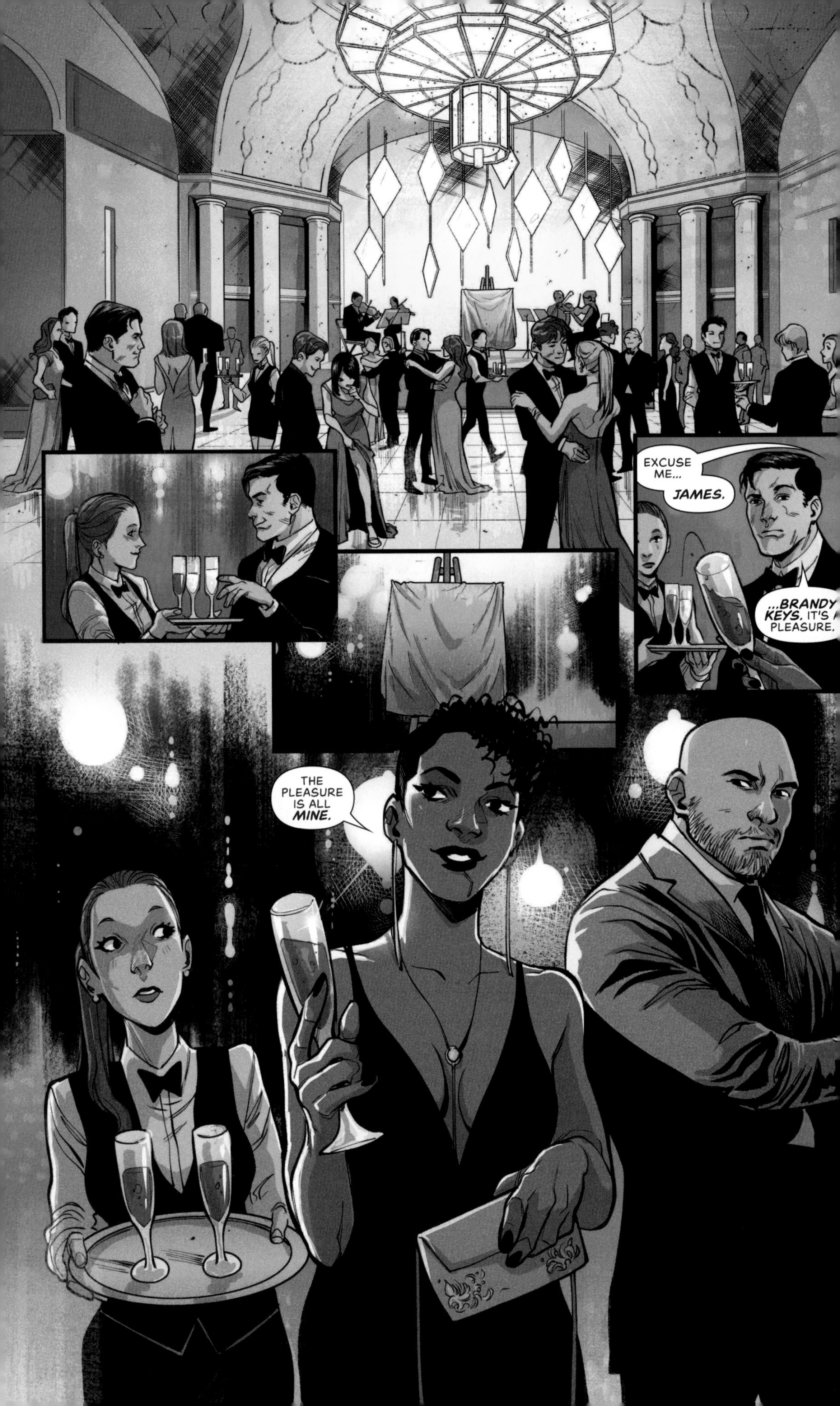

EXCUSE ME... JAMES.
...BRANDY KEYS. IT'S PLEASURE.
THE PLEASURE IS ALL MINE.

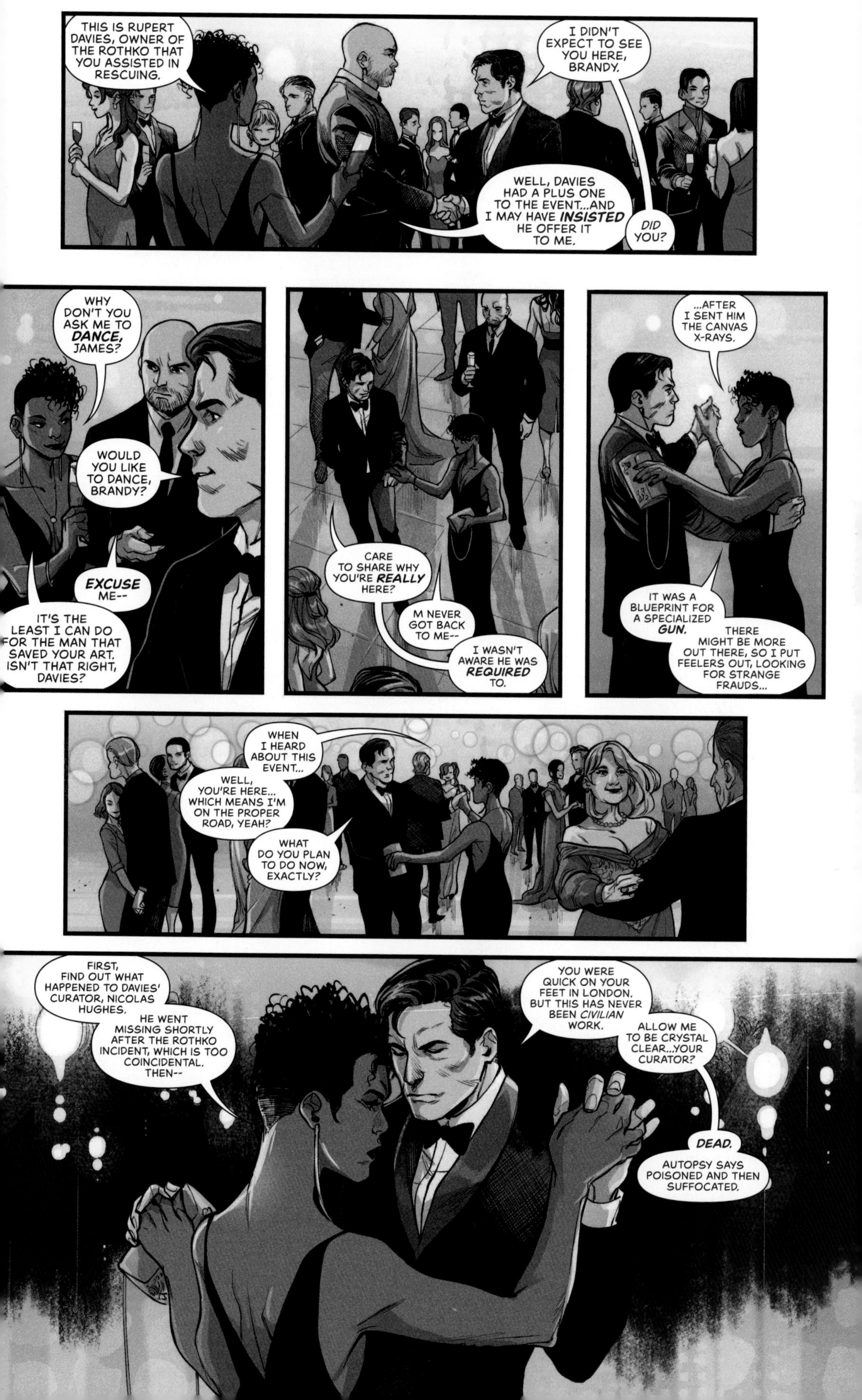
THIS IS RUPERT DAVIES, OWNER OF THE ROTHKO THAT YOU ASSISTED IN RESCUING.
I DIDN'T EXPECT TO SEE YOU HERE, BRANDY.
WELL, DAVIES HAD A PLUS ONE TO THE EVENT...AND I MAY HAVE *INSISTED* HE OFFER IT TO ME.
DID YOU?
WHY DON'T YOU ASK ME TO *DANCE,* JAMES?
WOULD YOU LIKE TO DANCE, BRANDY?
EXCUSE ME--
IT'S THE LEAST I CAN DO FOR THE MAN THAT SAVED YOUR ART. ISN'T THAT RIGHT, DAVIES?
CARE TO SHARE WHY YOU'RE *REALLY* HERE?
M NEVER GOT BACK TO ME--
I WASN'T AWARE HE WAS *REQUIRED* TO.
...AFTER I SENT HIM THE CANVAS X-RAYS.
IT WAS A BLUEPRINT FOR A SPECIALIZED *GUN.*
THERE MIGHT BE MORE OUT THERE, SO I PUT FEELERS OUT, LOOKING FOR STRANGE FRAUDS...
WHEN I HEARD ABOUT THIS EVENT...
WELL, YOU'RE HERE... WHICH MEANS I'M ON THE PROPER ROAD, YEAH?
WHAT DO YOU PLAN TO DO NOW, EXACTLY?
FIRST, FIND OUT WHAT HAPPENED TO DAVIES' CURATOR, NICOLAS HUGHES.
HE WENT MISSING SHORTLY AFTER THE ROTHKO INCIDENT, WHICH IS TOO COINCIDENTAL. THEN--
YOU WERE QUICK ON YOUR FEET IN LONDON. BUT THIS HAS NEVER BEEN *CIVILIAN* WORK.
ALLOW ME TO BE CRYSTAL CLEAR...YOUR CURATOR?
DEAD.
AUTOPSY SAYS POISONED AND THEN SUFFOCATED.

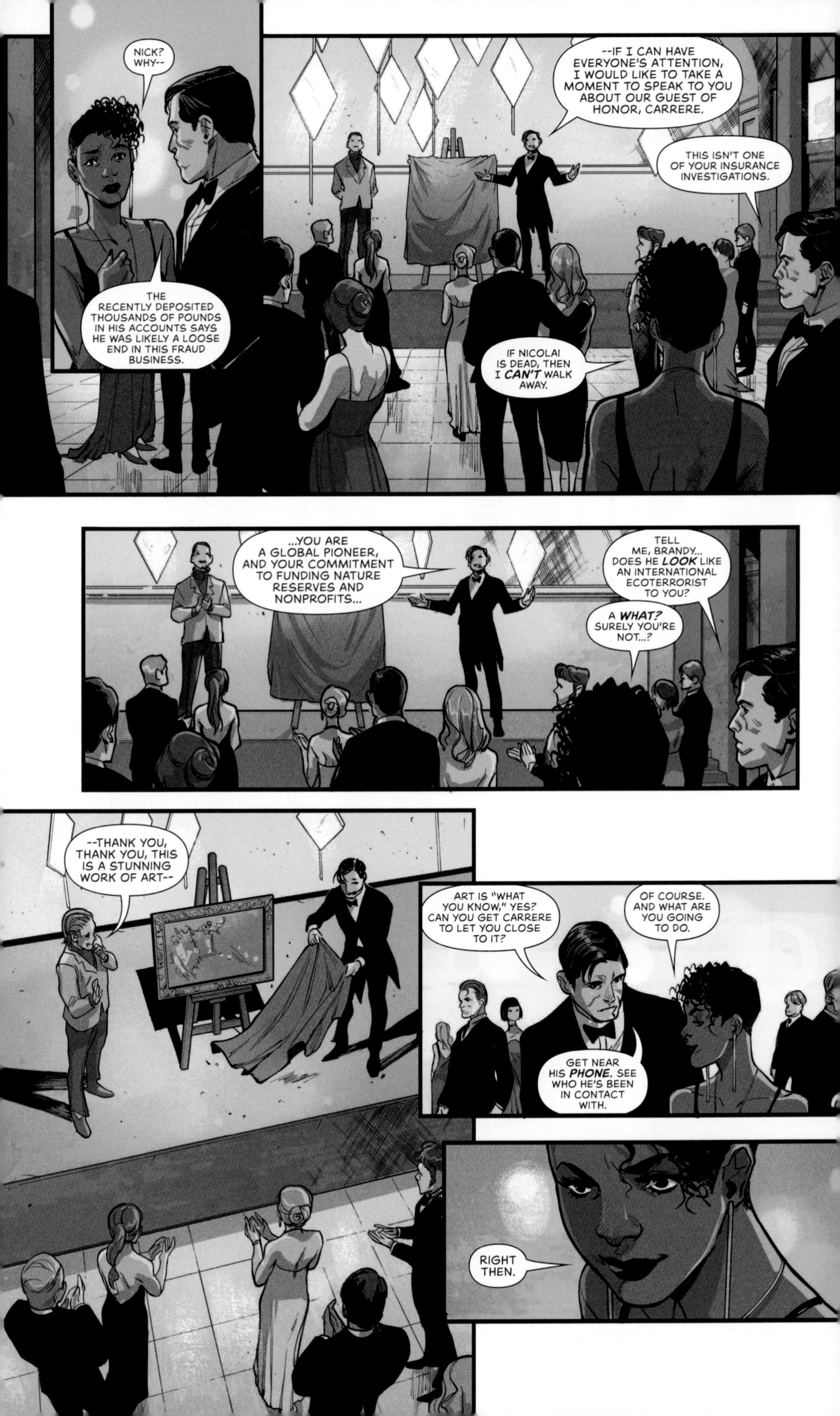
NICK? WHY--
THE RECENTLY DEPOSITED THOUSANDS OF POUNDS IN HIS ACCOUNTS SAYS HE WAS LIKELY A LOOSE END IN THIS FRAUD BUSINESS.
--IF I CAN HAVE EVERYONE'S ATTENTION, I WOULD LIKE TO TAKE A MOMENT TO SPEAK TO YOU ABOUT OUR GUEST OF HONOR, CARRERE.
THIS ISN'T ONE OF YOUR INSURANCE INVESTIGATIONS.
IF NICOLAI IS DEAD, THEN I CAN'T WALK AWAY.
...YOU ARE A GLOBAL PIONEER, AND YOUR COMMITMENT TO FUNDING NATURE RESERVES AND NONPROFITS...
TELL ME, BRANDY... DOES HE LOOK LIKE AN INTERNATIONAL ECOTERRORIST TO YOU?
A WHAT? SURELY YOU'RE NOT...?
--THANK YOU, THANK YOU, THIS IS A STUNNING WORK OF ART--
ART IS "WHAT YOU KNOW," YES? CAN YOU GET CARRERE TO LET YOU CLOSE TO IT?
OF COURSE. AND WHAT ARE YOU GOING TO DO.
GET NEAR HIS PHONE. SEE WHO HE'S BEEN IN CONTACT WITH.
RIGHT THEN.

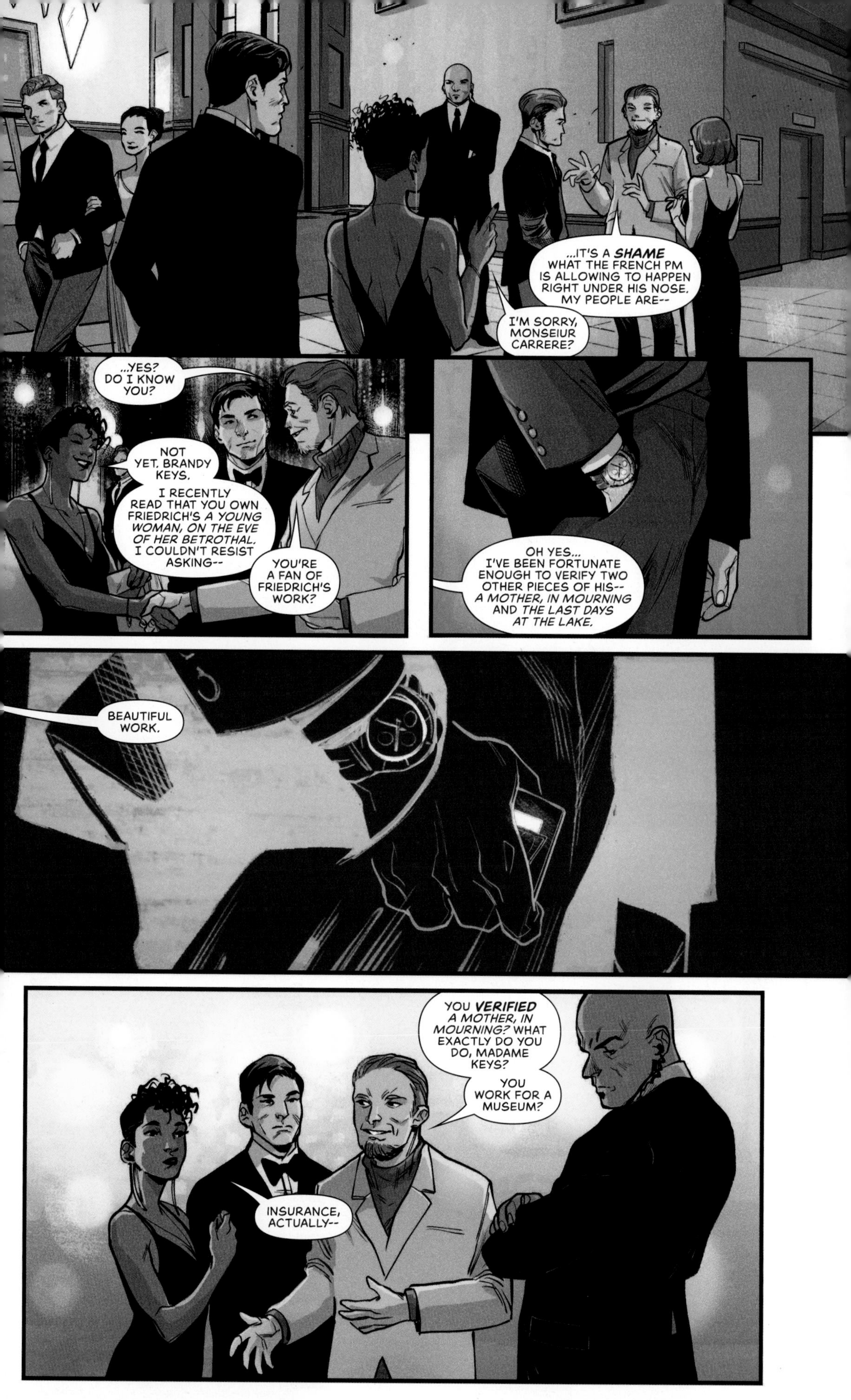

...IT'S A SHAME WHAT THE FRENCH PM IS ALLOWING TO HAPPEN RIGHT UNDER HIS NOSE. MY PEOPLE ARE--
I'M SORRY, MONSEIUR CARRERE?
...YES? DO I KNOW YOU?
NOT YET. BRANDY KEYS.
I RECENTLY READ THAT YOU OWN FRIEDRICH'S A YOUNG WOMAN, ON THE EVE OF HER BETROTHAL. I COULDN'T RESIST ASKING--
YOU'RE A FAN OF FRIEDRICH'S WORK?
OH YES... I'VE BEEN FORTUNATE ENOUGH TO VERIFY TWO OTHER PIECES OF HIS-- A MOTHER, IN MOURNING AND THE LAST DAYS AT THE LAKE.
BEAUTIFUL WORK.
YOU VERIFIED A MOTHER, IN MOURNING? WHAT EXACTLY DO YOU DO, MADAME KEYS?
YOU WORK FOR A MUSEUM?
INSURANCE, ACTUALLY--

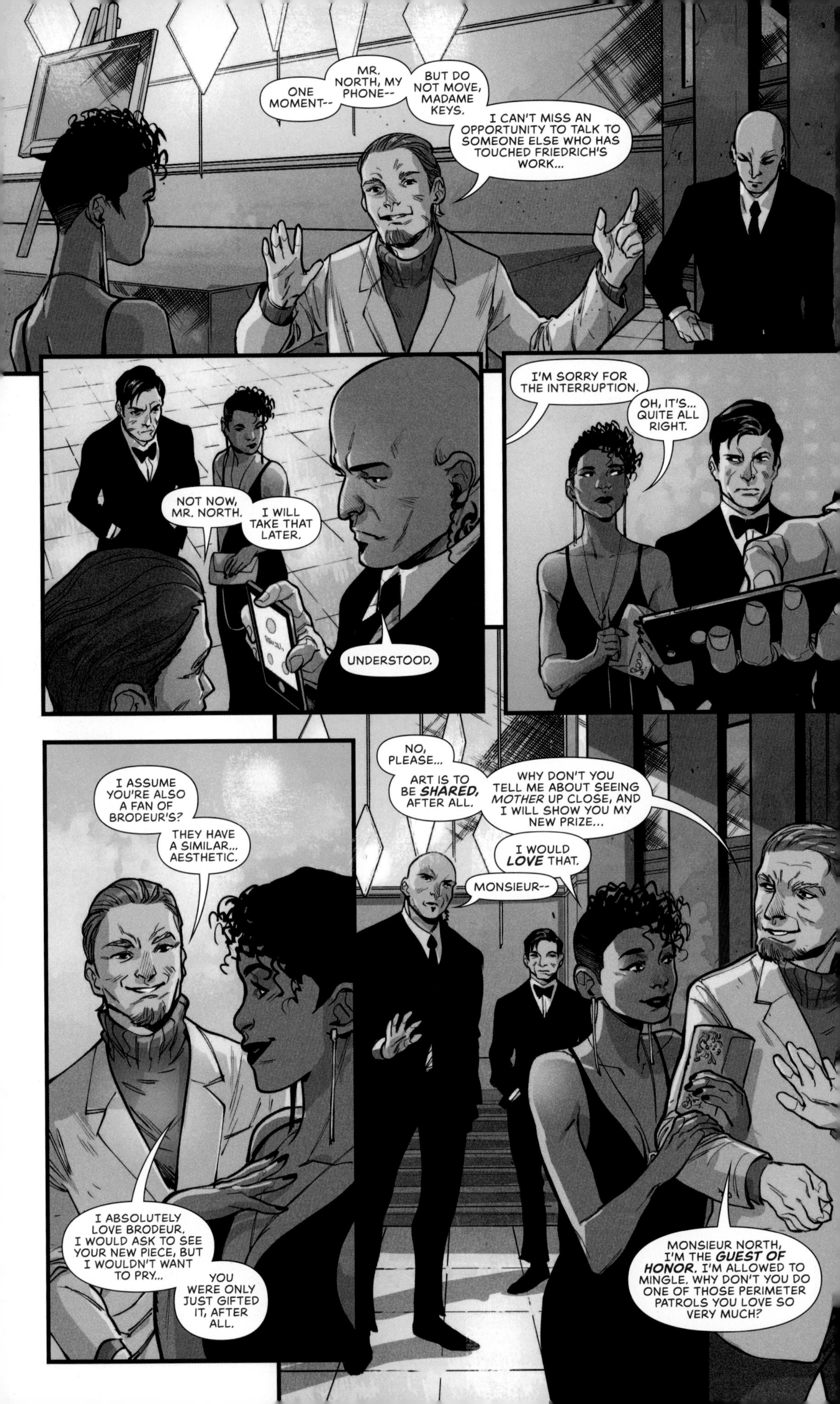
ONE MOMENT--
MR. NORTH, MY PHONE--
BUT DO NOT MOVE, MADAME KEYS.
I CAN'T MISS AN OPPORTUNITY TO TALK TO SOMEONE ELSE WHO HAS TOUCHED FRIEDRICH'S WORK...
NOT NOW, MR. NORTH.
I WILL TAKE THAT LATER.
UNDERSTOOD.
I'M SORRY FOR THE INTERRUPTION.
OH, IT'S... QUITE ALL RIGHT.
I ASSUME YOU'RE ALSO A FAN OF BRODEUR'S?
THEY HAVE A SIMILAR... AESTHETIC.
I ABSOLUTELY LOVE BRODEUR. I WOULD ASK TO SEE YOUR NEW PIECE, BUT I WOULDN'T WANT TO PRY...
YOU WERE ONLY JUST GIFTED IT, AFTER ALL.
NO, PLEASE...
ART IS TO BE **SHARED**, AFTER ALL.
WHY DON'T YOU TELL ME ABOUT SEEING *MOTHER* UP CLOSE, AND I WILL SHOW YOU MY NEW PRIZE...
I WOULD **LOVE** THAT.
MONSIEUR--
MONSIEUR NORTH, I'M THE **GUEST OF HONOR**. I'M ALLOWED TO MINGLE. WHY DON'T YOU DO ONE OF THOSE PERIMETER PATROLS YOU LOVE SO VERY MUCH?

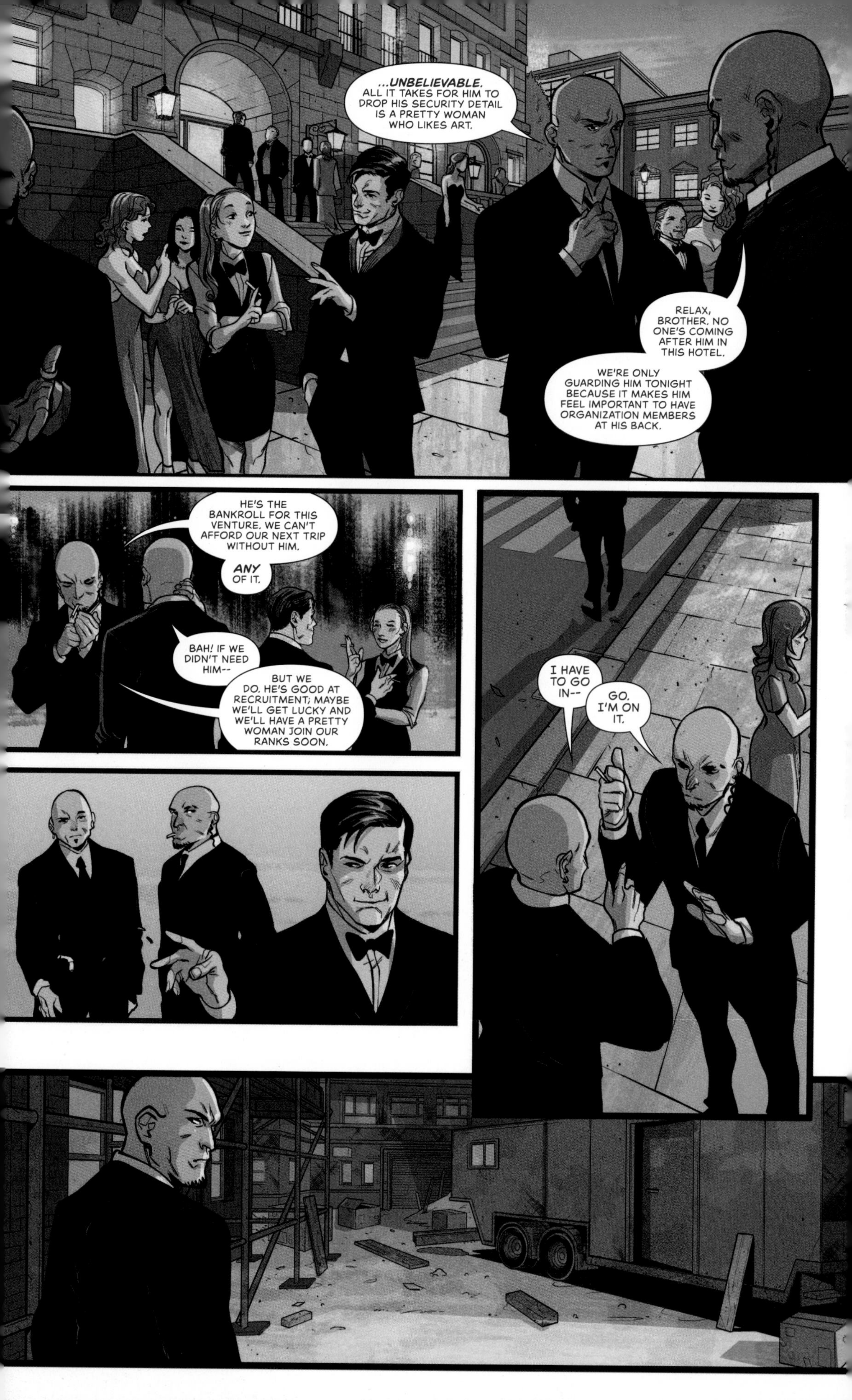
...UNBELIEVABLE. ALL IT TAKES FOR HIM TO DROP HIS SECURITY DETAIL IS A PRETTY WOMAN WHO LIKES ART.
RELAX, BROTHER. NO ONE'S COMING AFTER HIM IN THIS HOTEL.
WE'RE ONLY GUARDING HIM TONIGHT BECAUSE IT MAKES HIM FEEL IMPORTANT TO HAVE ORGANIZATION MEMBERS AT HIS BACK.
HE'S THE BANKROLL FOR THIS VENTURE. WE CAN'T AFFORD OUR NEXT TRIP WITHOUT HIM.
ANY OF IT.
BAH! IF WE DIDN'T NEED HIM--
BUT WE DO. HE'S GOOD AT RECRUITMENT; MAYBE WE'LL GET LUCKY AND WE'LL HAVE A PRETTY WOMAN JOIN OUR RANKS SOON.
I HAVE TO GO IN--
GO. I'M ON IT.

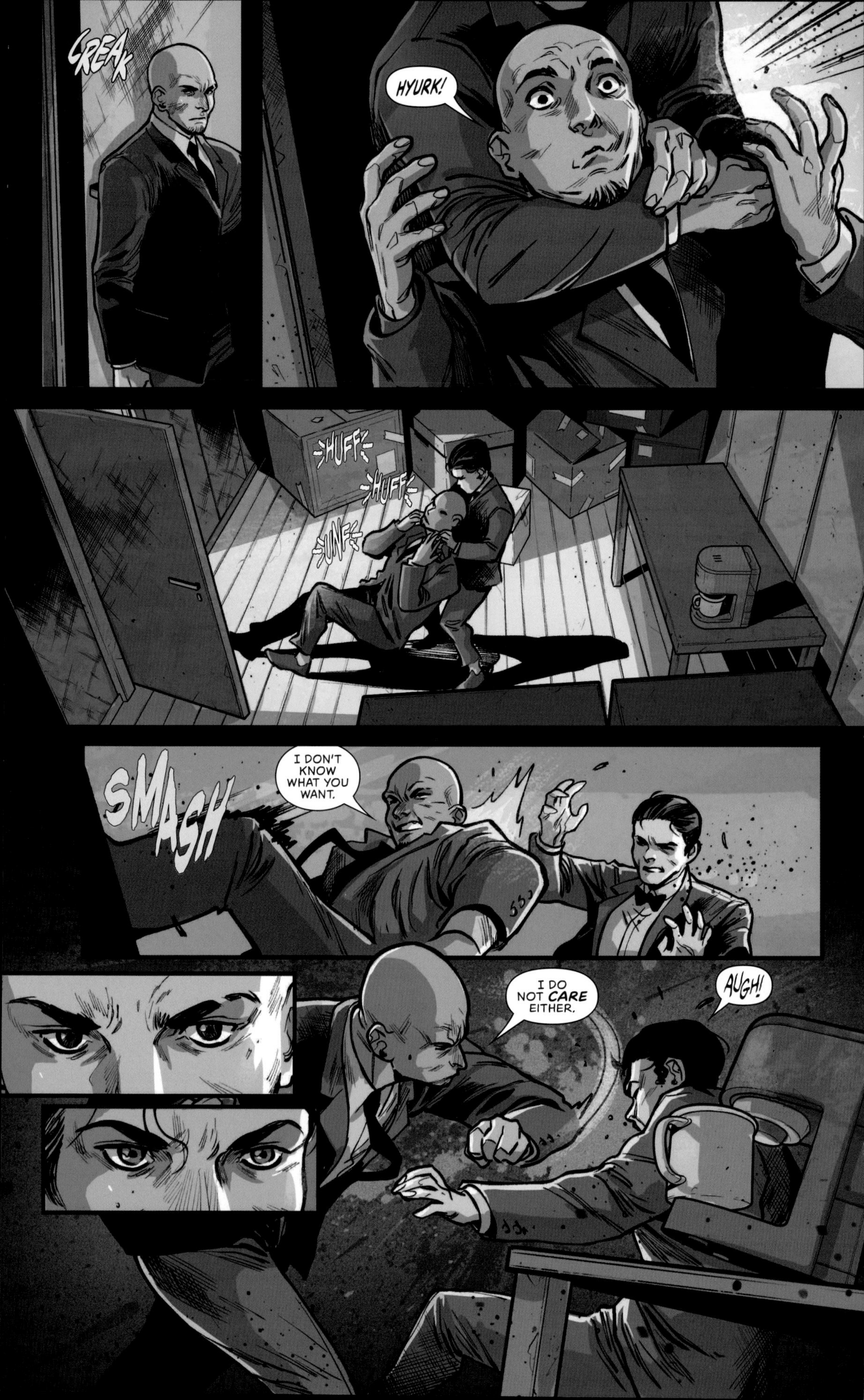
CREAK
HYURK!
HUFF
HUFF
UNF
SMASH
I DON'T KNOW WHAT YOU WANT.
I DO NOT CARE EITHER.
AUGH!

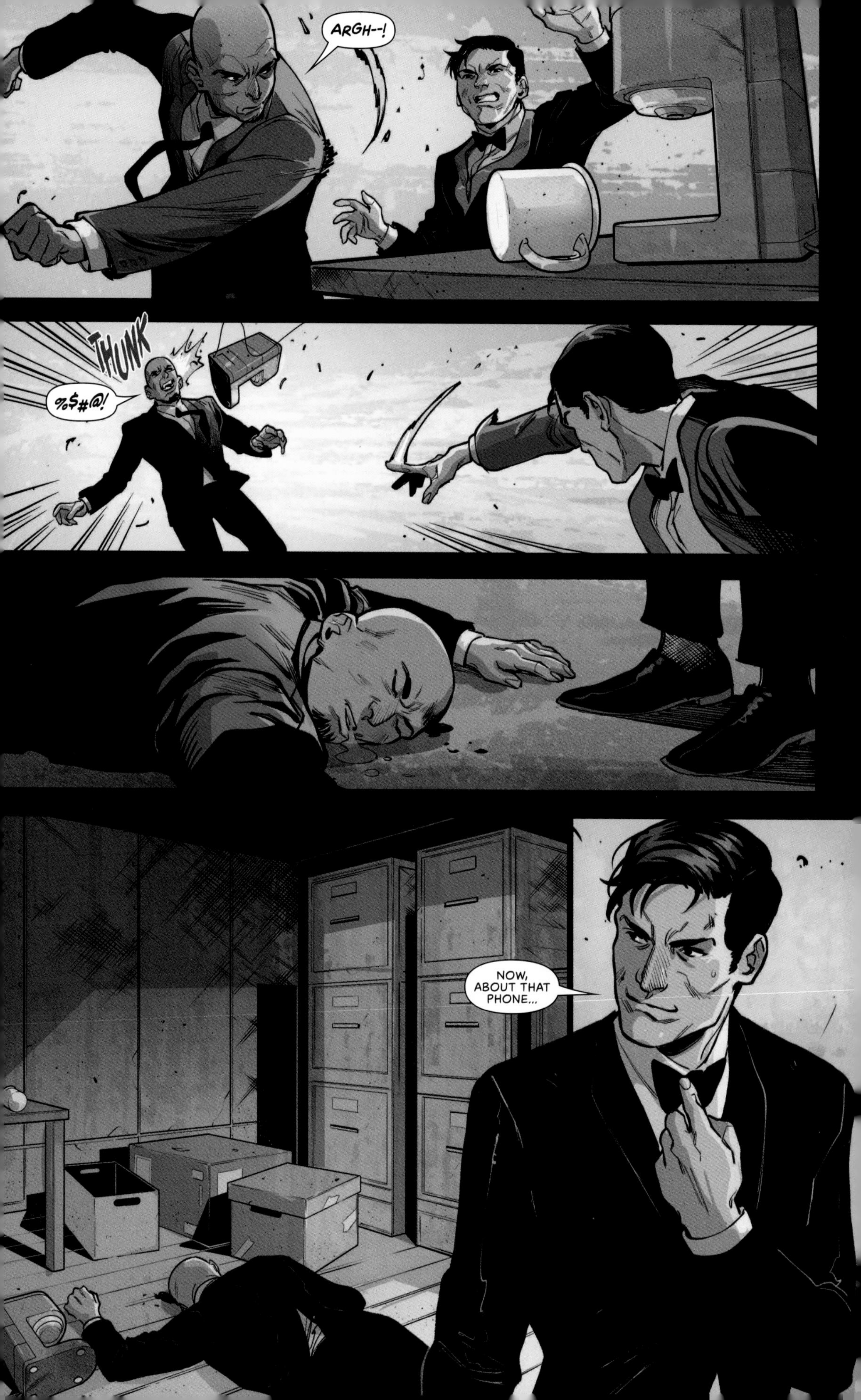
ARGH--!
THUNK
%$#@!
NOW, ABOUT THAT PHONE...

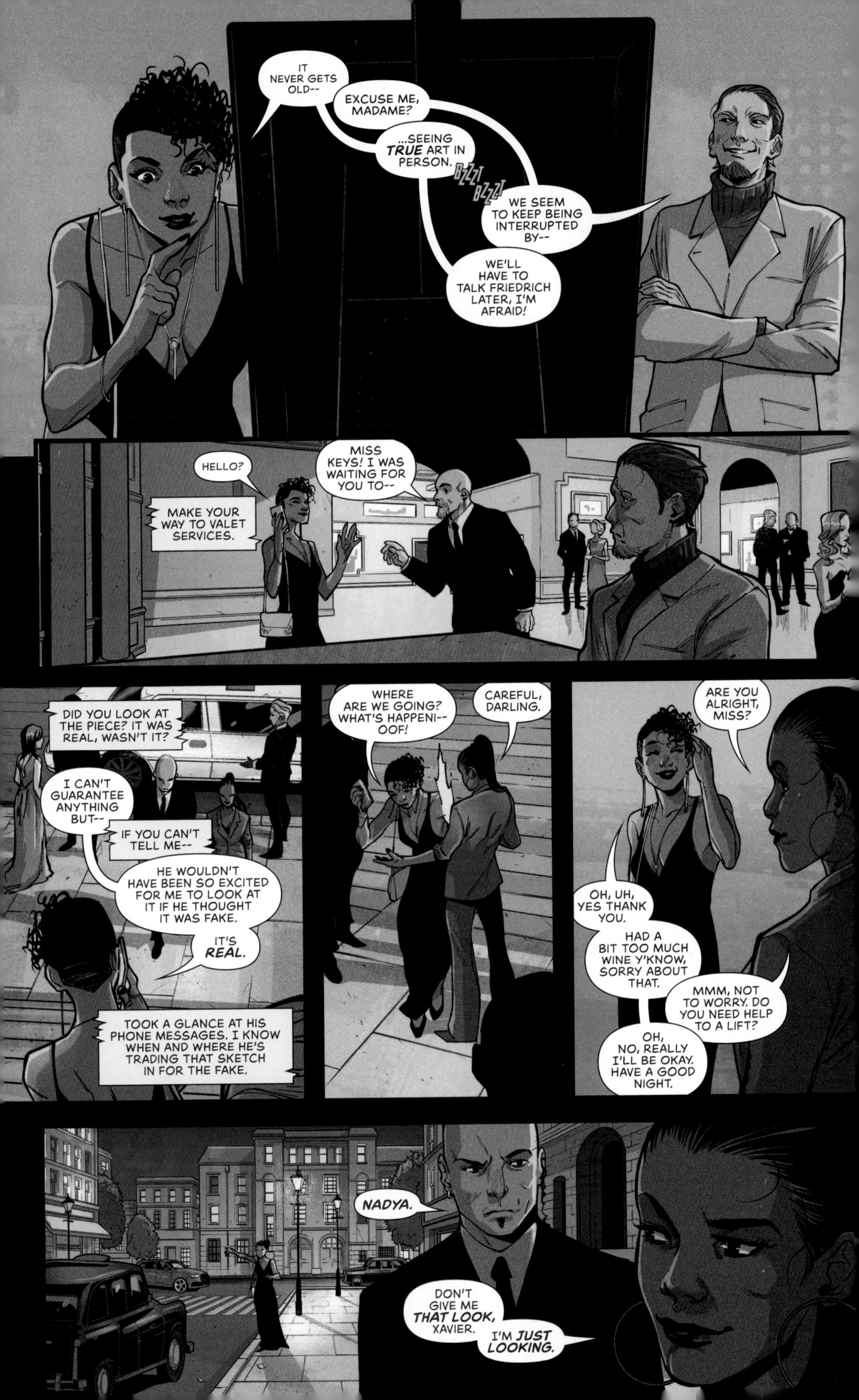

IT NEVER GETS OLD--
EXCUSE ME, MADAME?
...SEEING TRUE ART IN PERSON.
BZZZT BZZZT
WE SEEM TO KEEP BEING INTERRUPTED BY--
WE'LL HAVE TO TALK FRIEDRICH LATER, I'M AFRAID!
HELLO?
MAKE YOUR WAY TO VALET SERVICES.
MISS KEYS! I WAS WAITING FOR YOU TO--
DID YOU LOOK AT THE PIECE? IT WAS REAL, WASN'T IT?
I CAN'T GUARANTEE ANYTHING BUT--
IF YOU CAN'T TELL ME--
HE WOULDN'T HAVE BEEN SO EXCITED FOR ME TO LOOK AT IT IF HE THOUGHT IT WAS FAKE.
IT'S REAL.
TOOK A GLANCE AT HIS PHONE MESSAGES. I KNOW WHEN AND WHERE HE'S TRADING THAT SKETCH IN FOR THE FAKE.
WHERE ARE WE GOING? WHAT'S HAPPENI-- OOF!
CAREFUL, DARLING.
ARE YOU ALRIGHT, MISS?
OH, UH, YES THANK YOU.
HAD A BIT TOO MUCH WINE Y'KNOW, SORRY ABOUT THAT.
MMM, NOT TO WORRY. DO YOU NEED HELP TO A LIFT?
OH, NO, REALLY I'LL BE OKAY. HAVE A GOOD NIGHT.
NADYA.
DON'T GIVE ME THAT LOOK, XAVIER.
I'M JUST LOOKING.

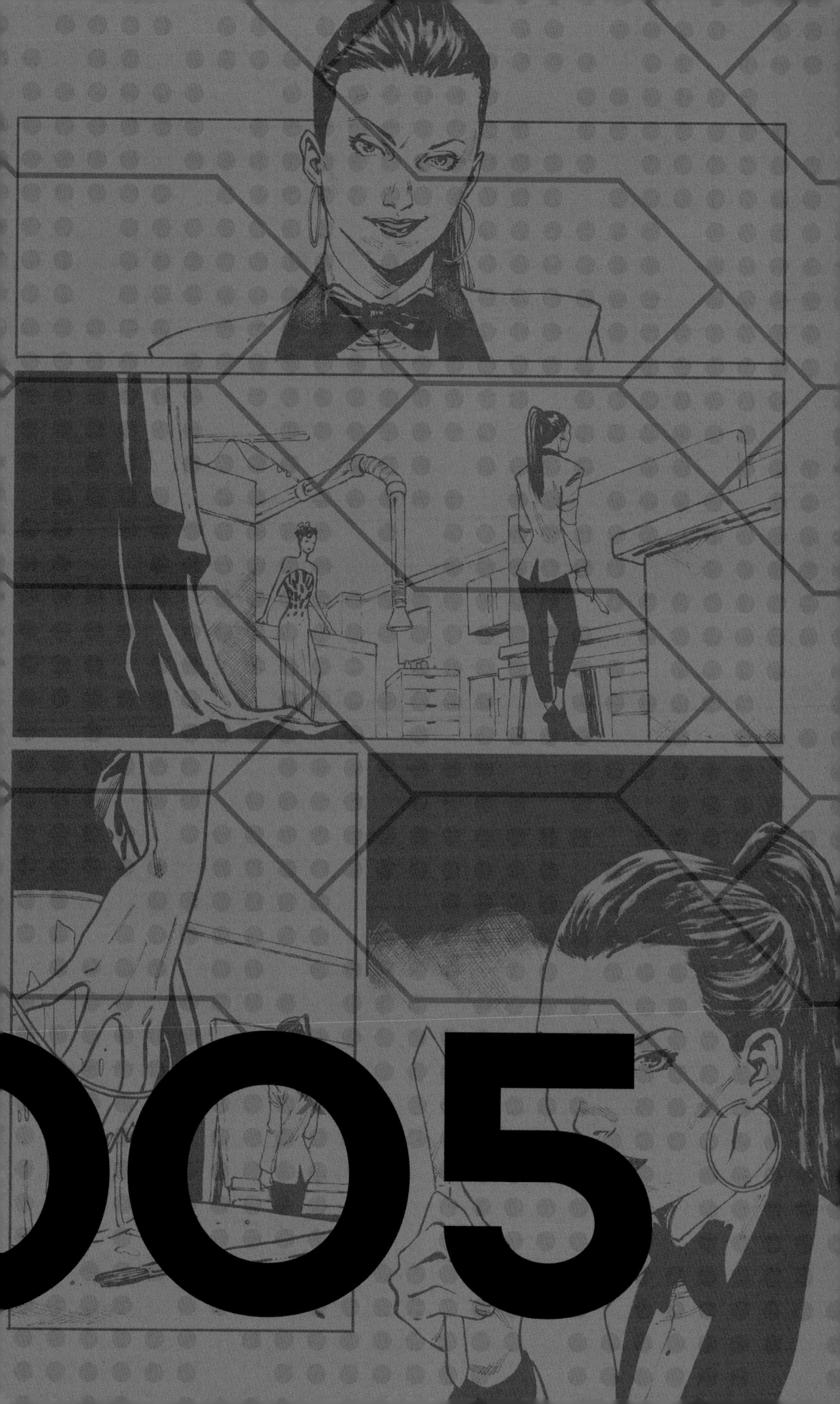
005

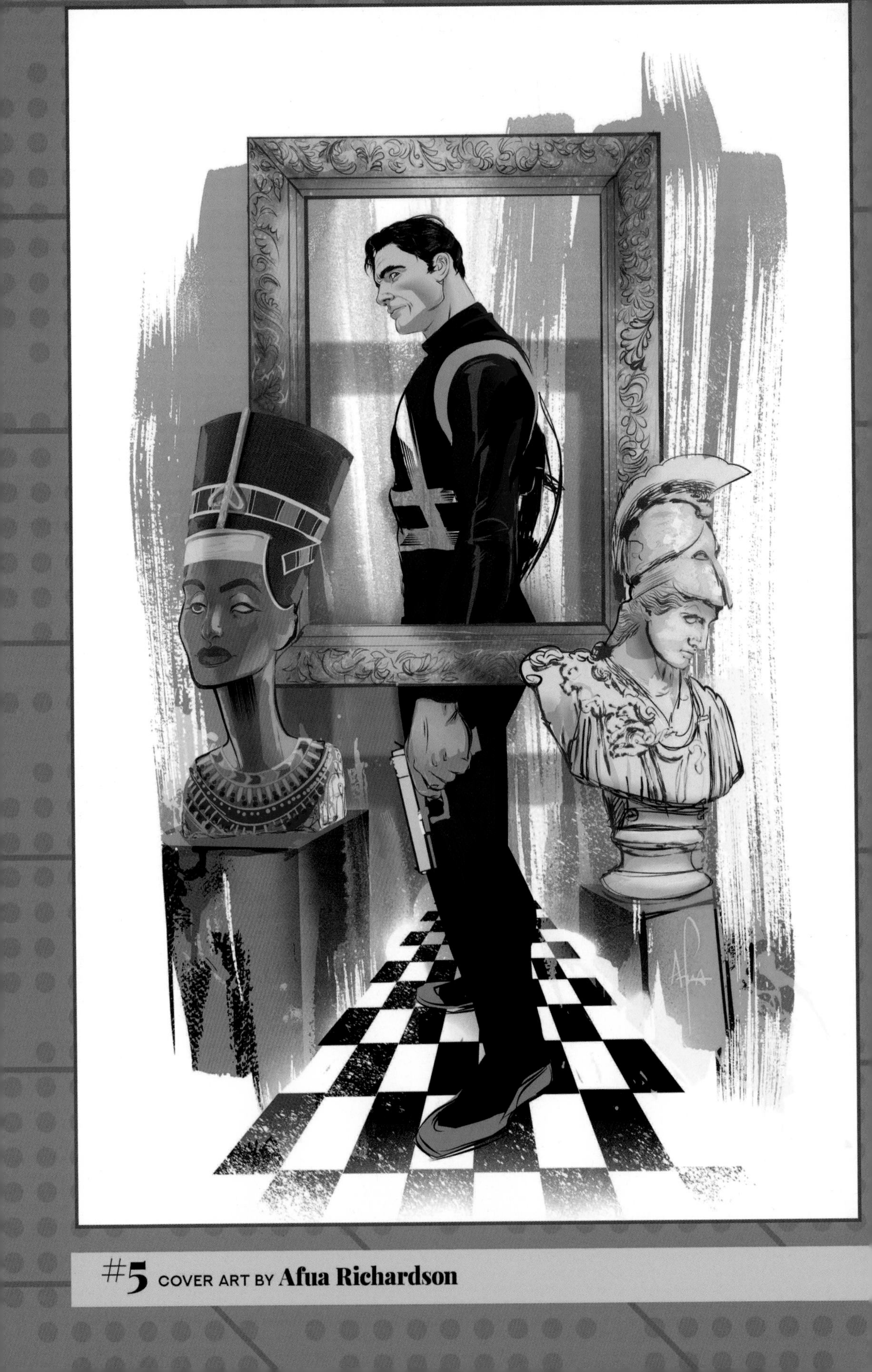
Afua

#5 COVER ART BY **Afua Richardson**

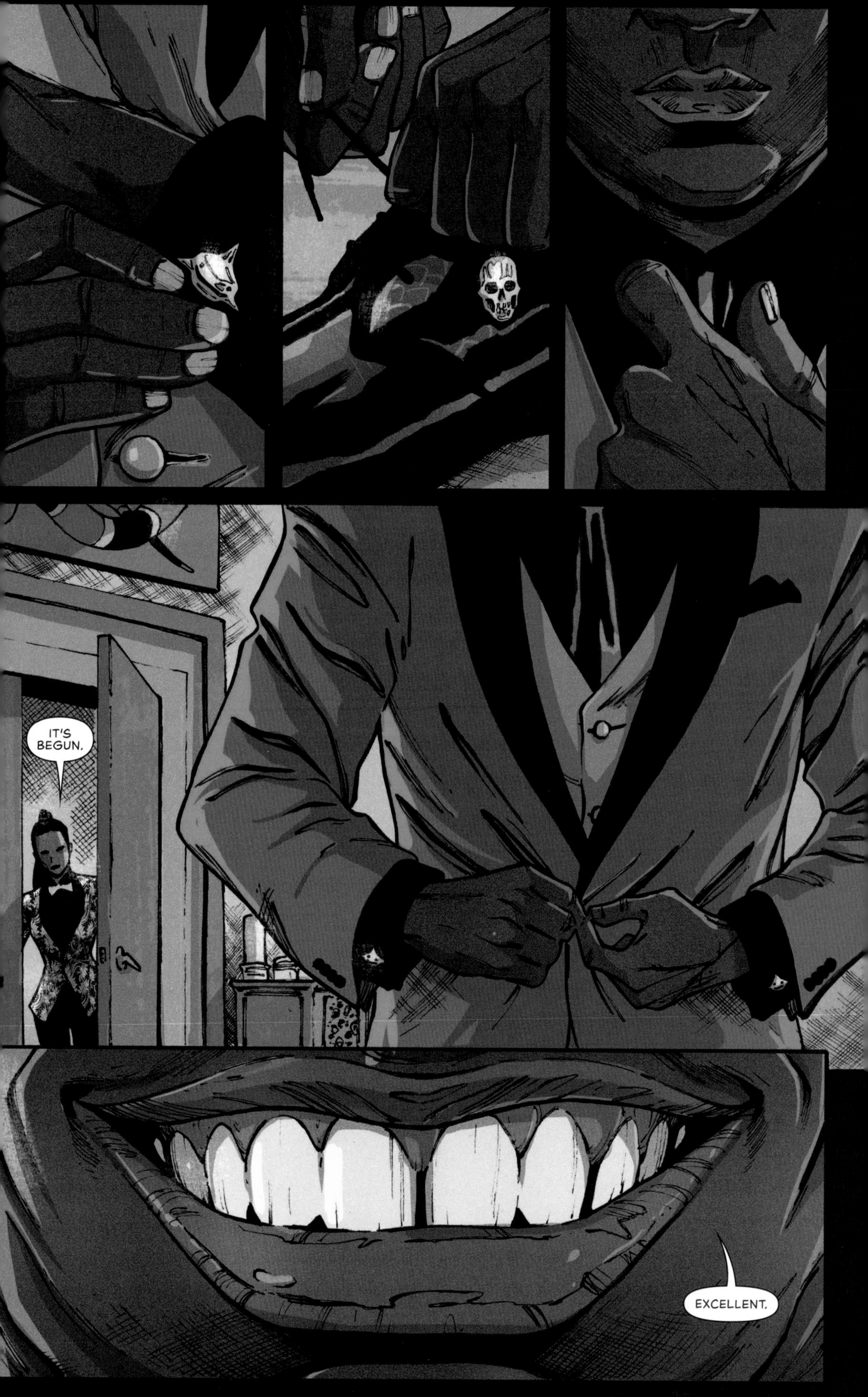
IT'S BEGUN.
EXCELLENT.

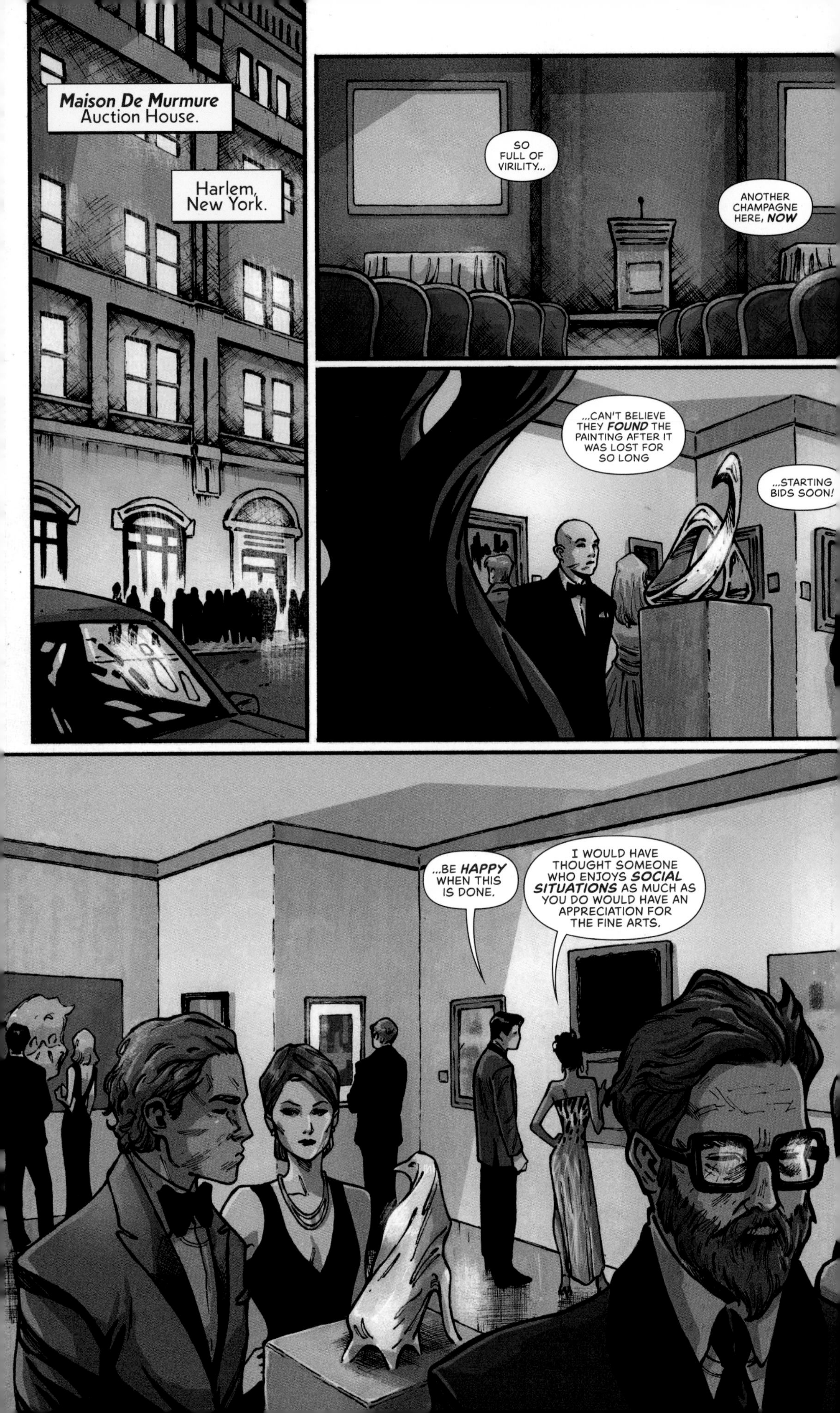

Maison De Murmure Auction House.
Harlem, New York.
SO FULL OF VIRILITY...
ANOTHER CHAMPAGNE HERE, NOW
...CAN'T BELIEVE THEY FOUND THE PAINTING AFTER IT WAS LOST FOR SO LONG
...STARTING BIDS SOON!
...BE HAPPY WHEN THIS IS DONE.
I WOULD HAVE THOUGHT SOMEONE WHO ENJOYS SOCIAL SITUATIONS AS MUCH AS YOU DO WOULD HAVE AN APPRECIATION FOR THE FINE ARTS.

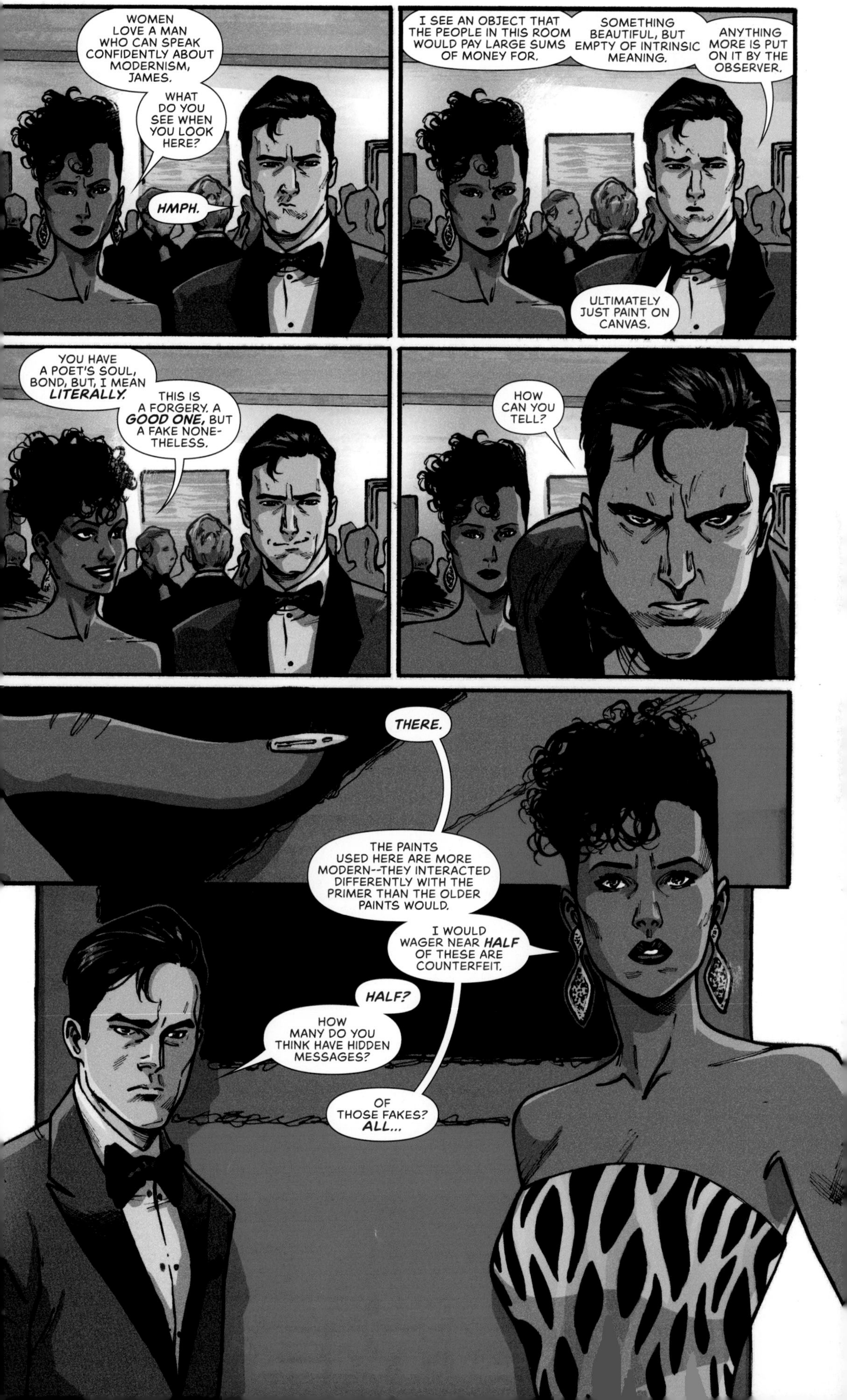
WOMEN LOVE A MAN WHO CAN SPEAK CONFIDENTLY ABOUT MODERNISM, JAMES.
WHAT DO YOU SEE WHEN YOU LOOK HERE?
HMPH.
I SEE AN OBJECT THAT THE PEOPLE IN THIS ROOM WOULD PAY LARGE SUMS OF MONEY FOR.
SOMETHING BEAUTIFUL, BUT EMPTY OF INTRINSIC MEANING.
ANYTHING MORE IS PUT ON IT BY THE OBSERVER.
ULTIMATELY JUST PAINT ON CANVAS.
YOU HAVE A POET'S SOUL, BOND, BUT, I MEAN LITERALLY.
THIS IS A FORGERY. A GOOD ONE, BUT A FAKE NONE-THELESS.
HOW CAN YOU TELL?
THERE.
THE PAINTS USED HERE ARE MORE MODERN--THEY INTERACTED DIFFERENTLY WITH THE PRIMER THAN THE OLDER PAINTS WOULD.
I WOULD WAGER NEAR HALF OF THESE ARE COUNTERFEIT.
HALF?
HOW MANY DO YOU THINK HAVE HIDDEN MESSAGES?
OF THOSE FAKES? ALL...

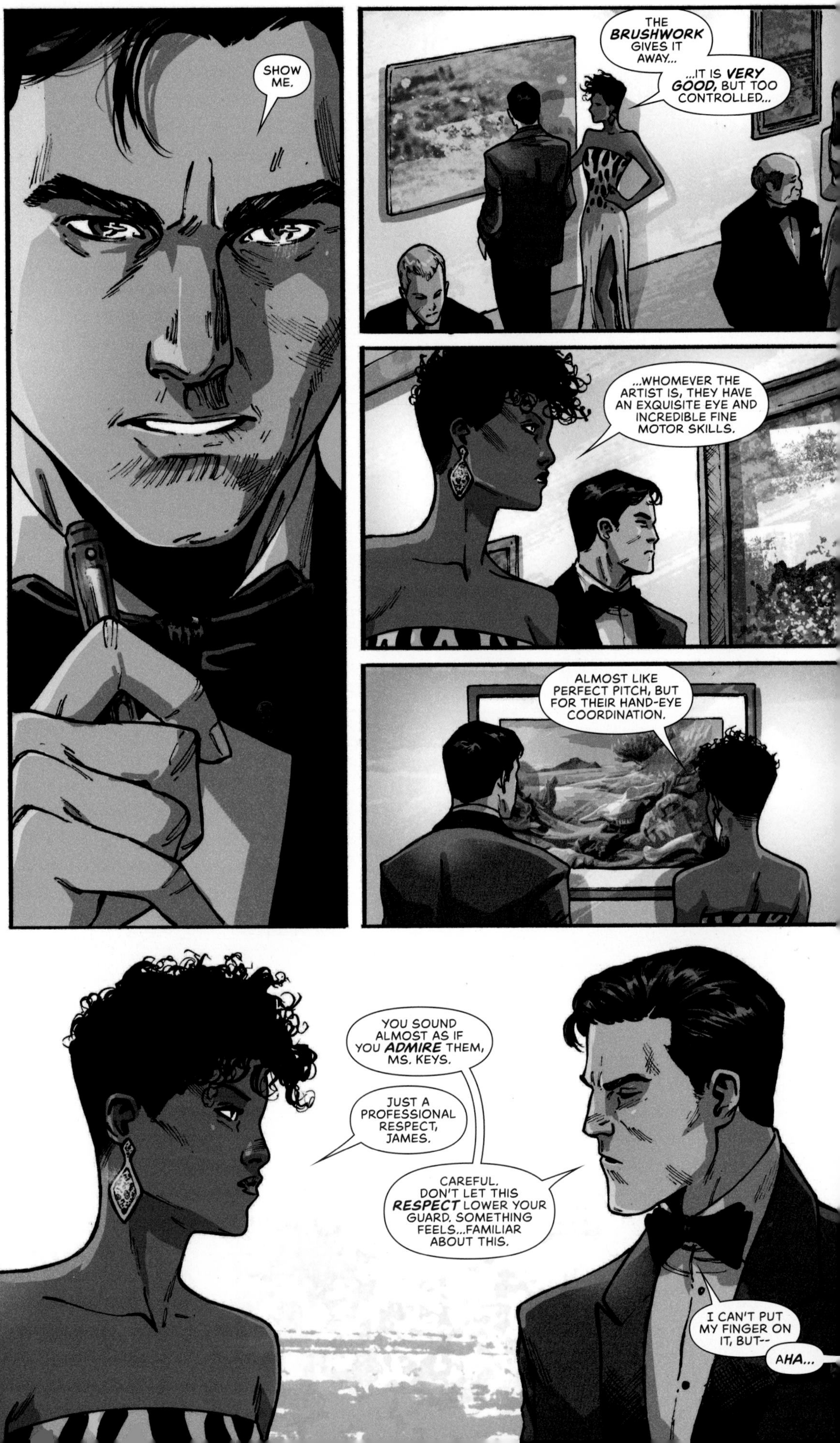
SHOW ME.
THE BRUSHWORK GIVES IT AWAY...
...IT IS VERY GOOD, BUT TOO CONTROLLED...
...WHOMEVER THE ARTIST IS, THEY HAVE AN EXQUISITE EYE AND INCREDIBLE FINE MOTOR SKILLS.
ALMOST LIKE PERFECT PITCH, BUT FOR THEIR HAND-EYE COORDINATION.
YOU SOUND ALMOST AS IF YOU ADMIRE THEM, MS. KEYS.
JUST A PROFESSIONAL RESPECT, JAMES.
CAREFUL. DON'T LET THIS RESPECT LOWER YOUR GUARD. SOMETHING FEELS...FAMILIAR ABOUT THIS.
I CAN'T PUT MY FINGER ON IT, BUT--
AHA...

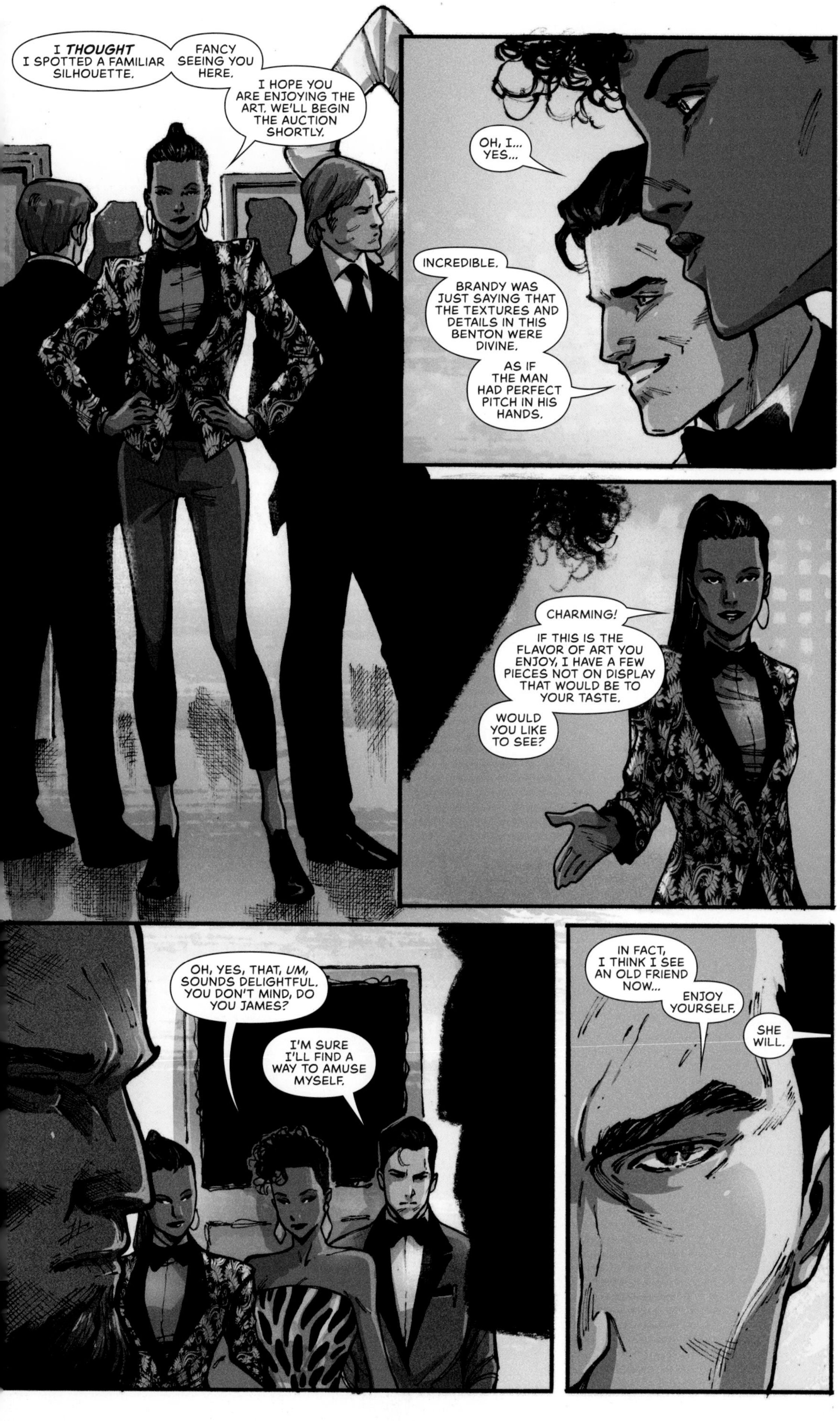
I *THOUGHT* I SPOTTED A FAMILIAR SILHOUETTE.
FANCY SEEING YOU HERE.
I HOPE YOU ARE ENJOYING THE ART. WE'LL BEGIN THE AUCTION SHORTLY.
OH, I... YES...
INCREDIBLE.
BRANDY WAS JUST SAYING THAT THE TEXTURES AND DETAILS IN THIS BENTON WERE DIVINE.
AS IF THE MAN HAD PERFECT PITCH IN HIS HANDS.
CHARMING!
IF THIS IS THE FLAVOR OF ART YOU ENJOY, I HAVE A FEW PIECES NOT ON DISPLAY THAT WOULD BE TO YOUR TASTE.
WOULD YOU LIKE TO SEE?
OH, YES, THAT, *UM*, SOUNDS DELIGHTFUL. YOU DON'T MIND, DO YOU JAMES?
I'M SURE I'LL FIND A WAY TO AMUSE MYSELF.
IN FACT, I THINK I SEE AN OLD FRIEND NOW...
ENJOY YOURSELF.
SHE WILL.

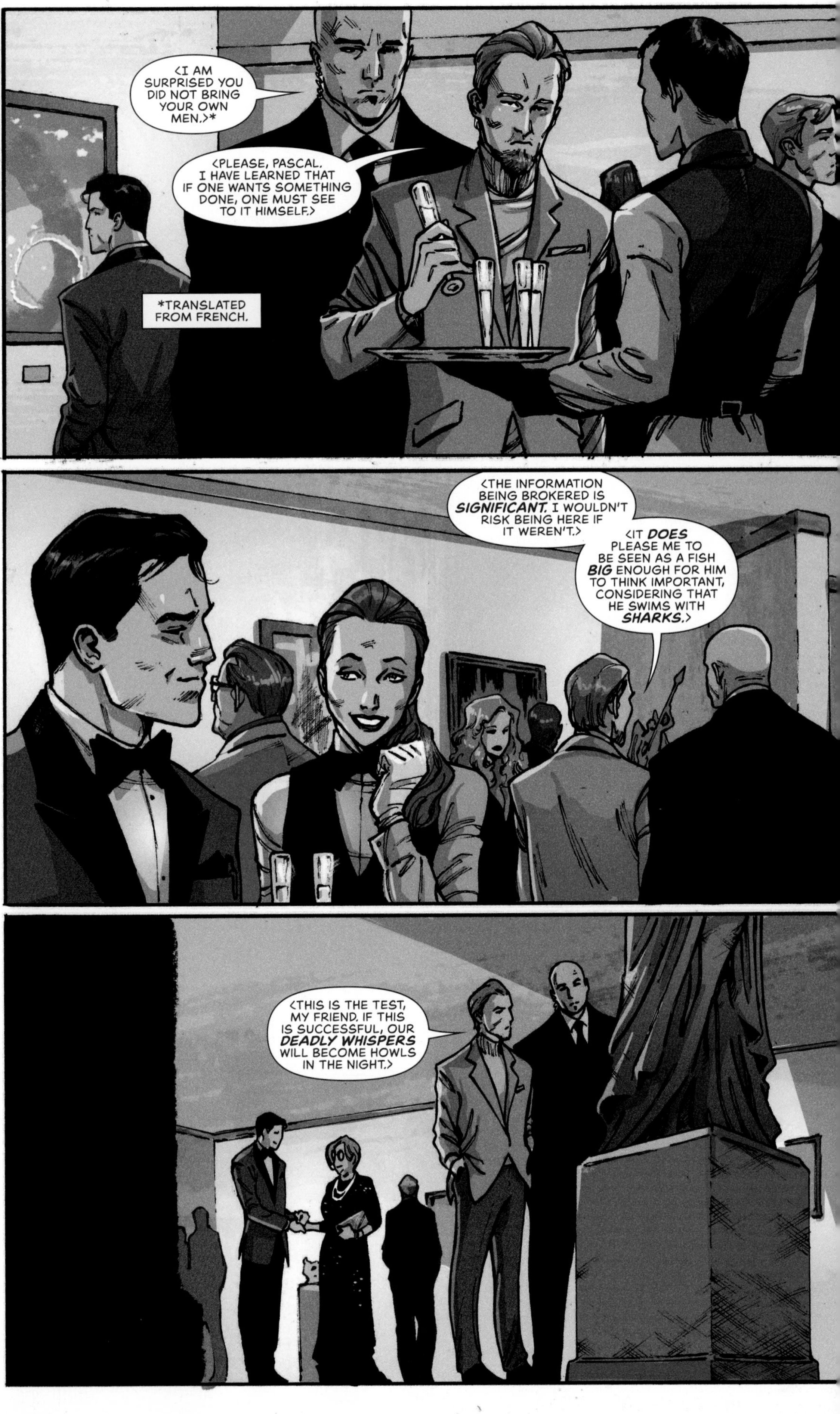
<I AM SURPRISED YOU DID NOT BRING YOUR OWN MEN.>*
<PLEASE, PASCAL. I HAVE LEARNED THAT IF ONE WANTS SOMETHING DONE, ONE MUST SEE TO IT HIMSELF.>
*TRANSLATED FROM FRENCH.
<THE INFORMATION BEING BROKERED IS SIGNIFICANT. I WOULDN'T RISK BEING HERE IF IT WEREN'T.>
<IT DOES PLEASE ME TO BE SEEN AS A FISH BIG ENOUGH FOR HIM TO THINK IMPORTANT, CONSIDERING THAT HE SWIMS WITH SHARKS.>
<THIS IS THE TEST, MY FRIEND. IF THIS IS SUCCESSFUL, OUR DEADLY WHISPERS WILL BECOME HOWLS IN THE NIGHT.>

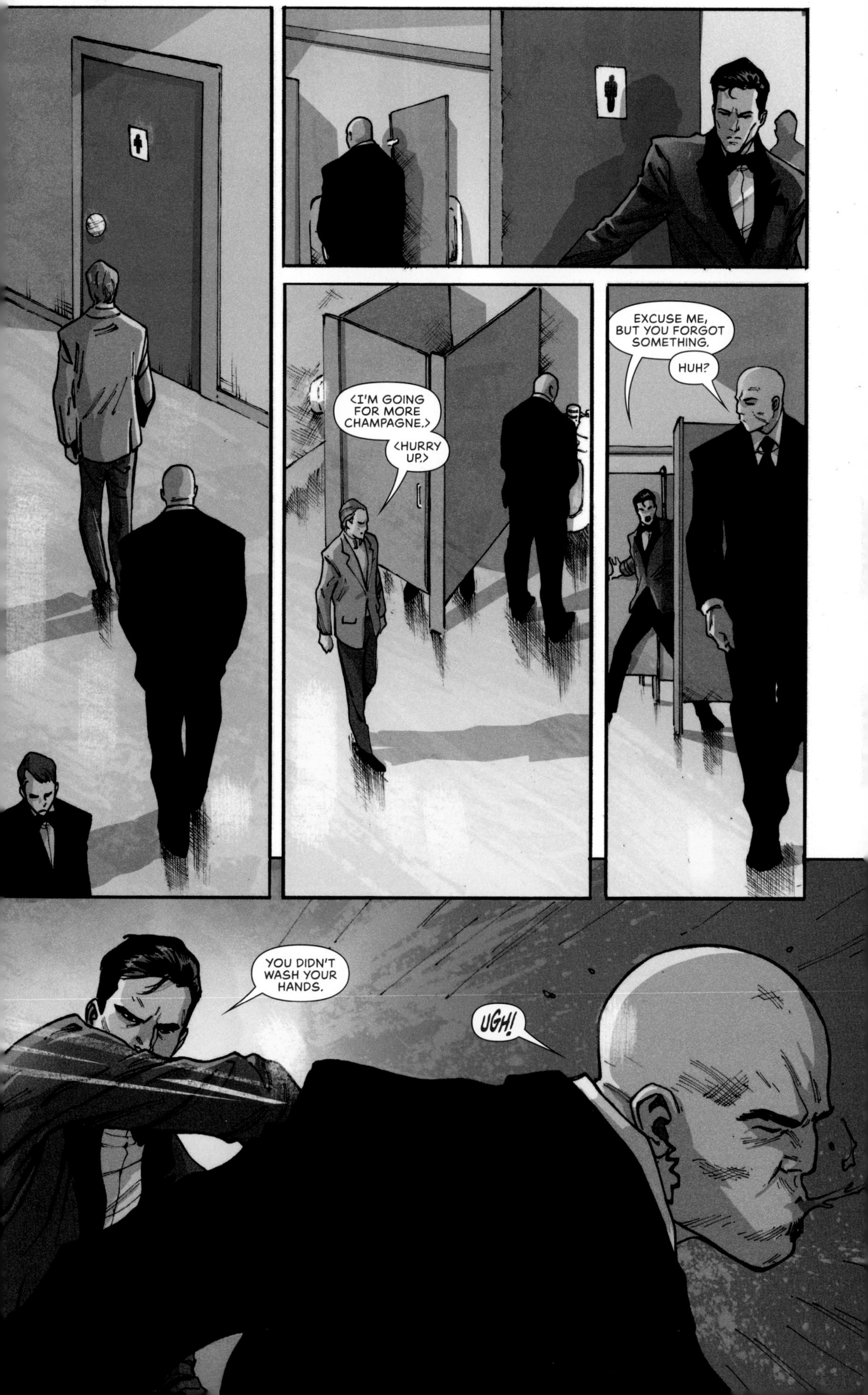
<I'M GOING FOR MORE CHAMPAGNE.>
<HURRY UP.>
EXCUSE ME, BUT YOU FORGOT SOMETHING.
HUH?
YOU DIDN'T WASH YOUR HANDS.
UGH!

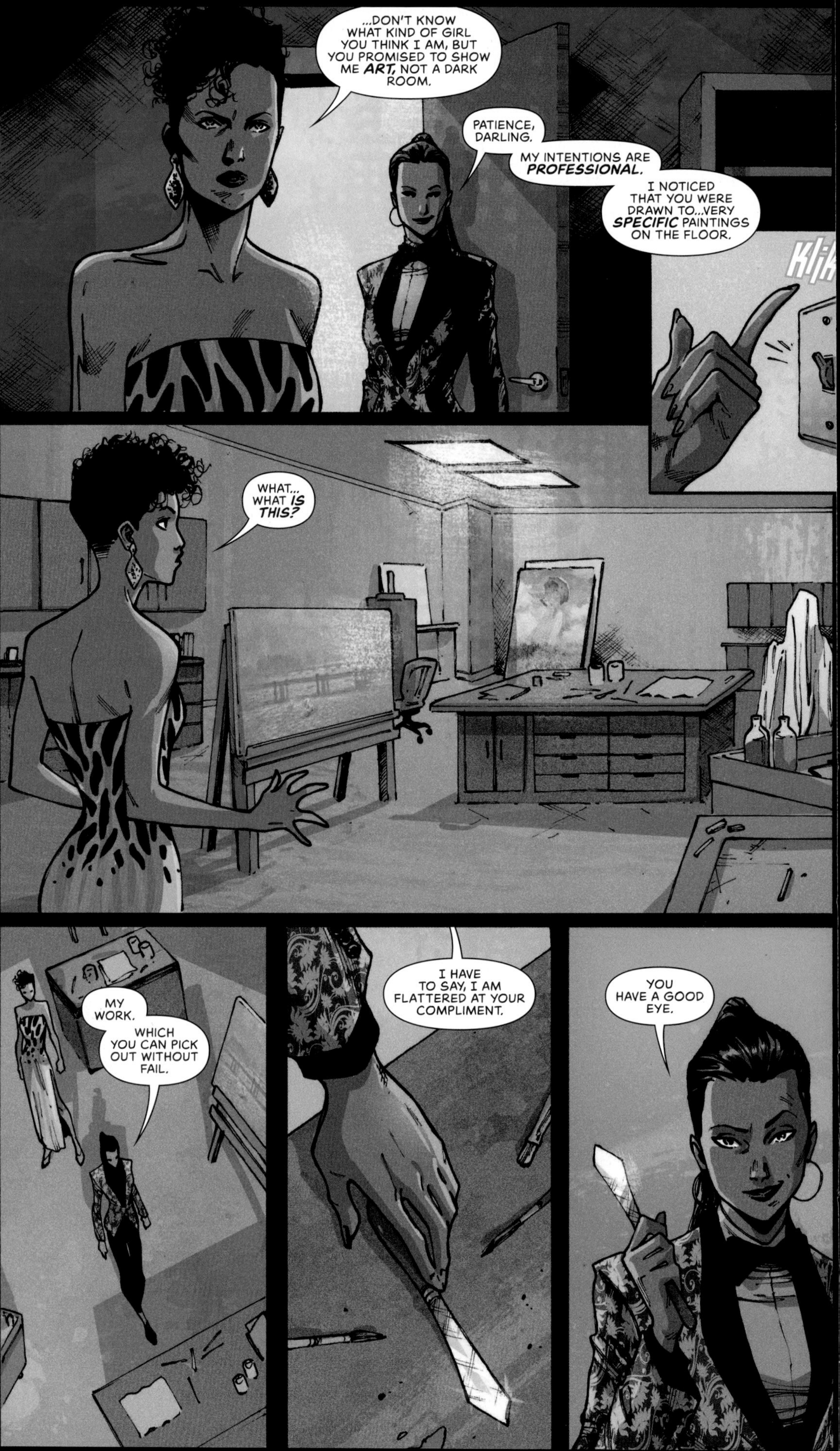
...DON'T KNOW WHAT KIND OF GIRL YOU THINK I AM, BUT YOU PROMISED TO SHOW ME **ART,** NOT A DARK ROOM.
PATIENCE, DARLING.
MY INTENTIONS ARE **PROFESSIONAL.**
I NOTICED THAT YOU WERE DRAWN TO...VERY **SPECIFIC** PAINTINGS ON THE FLOOR.
WHAT... WHAT **IS THIS?**
MY WORK.
WHICH YOU CAN PICK OUT WITHOUT FAIL.
I HAVE TO SAY, I AM FLATTERED AT YOUR COMPLIMENT.
YOU HAVE A GOOD EYE.

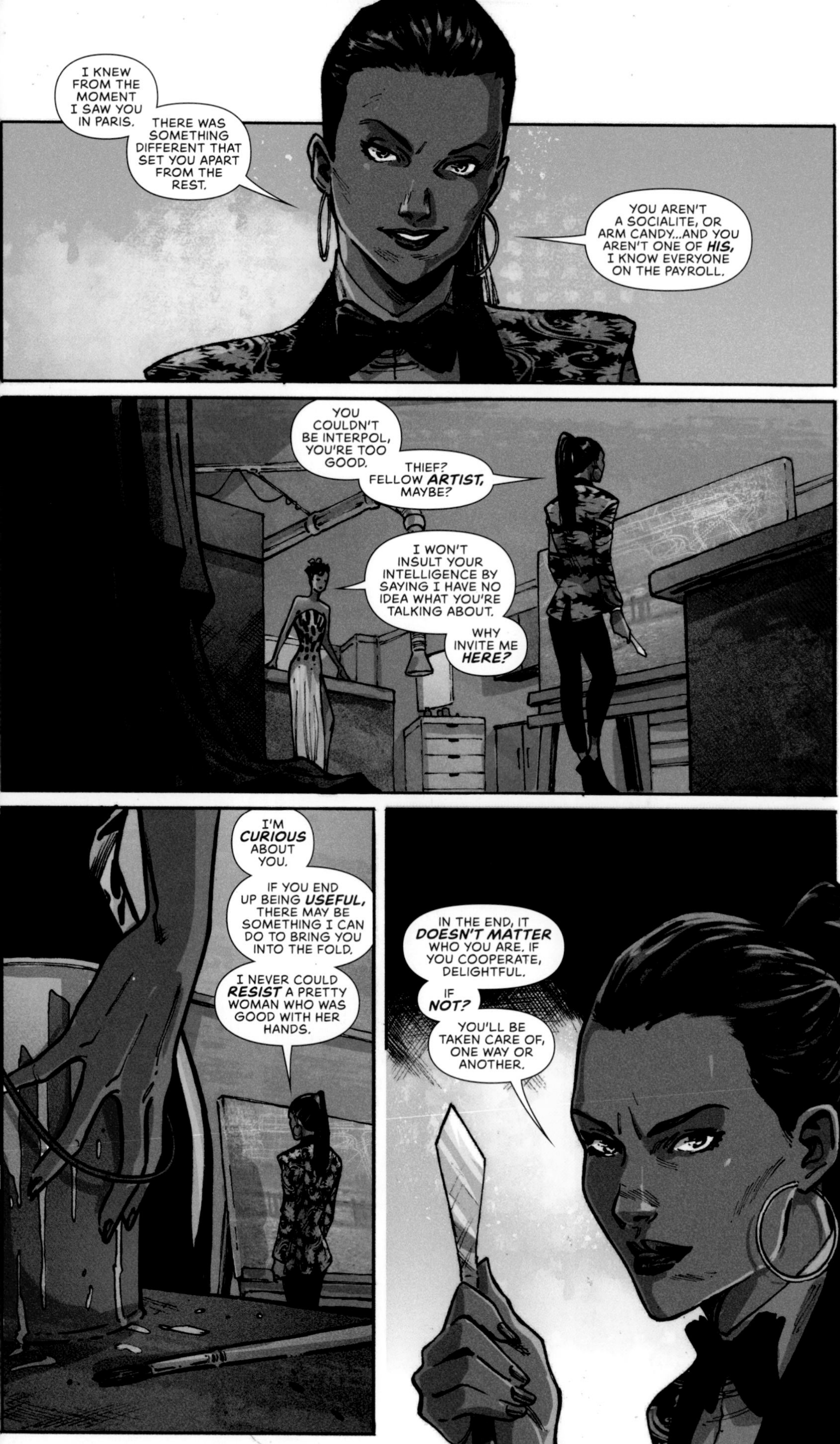

I KNEW FROM THE MOMENT I SAW YOU IN PARIS.
THERE WAS SOMETHING DIFFERENT THAT SET YOU APART FROM THE REST.
YOU AREN'T A SOCIALITE, OR ARM CANDY...AND YOU AREN'T ONE OF HIS, I KNOW EVERYONE ON THE PAYROLL.
YOU COULDN'T BE INTERPOL, YOU'RE TOO GOOD.
THIEF? FELLOW ARTIST, MAYBE?
I WON'T INSULT YOUR INTELLIGENCE BY SAYING I HAVE NO IDEA WHAT YOU'RE TALKING ABOUT.
WHY INVITE ME HERE?
I'M CURIOUS ABOUT YOU.
IF YOU END UP BEING USEFUL, THERE MAY BE SOMETHING I CAN DO TO BRING YOU INTO THE FOLD.
I NEVER COULD RESIST A PRETTY WOMAN WHO WAS GOOD WITH HER HANDS.
IN THE END, IT DOESN'T MATTER WHO YOU ARE. IF YOU COOPERATE, DELIGHTFUL.
IF NOT?
YOU'LL BE TAKEN CARE OF, ONE WAY OR ANOTHER.

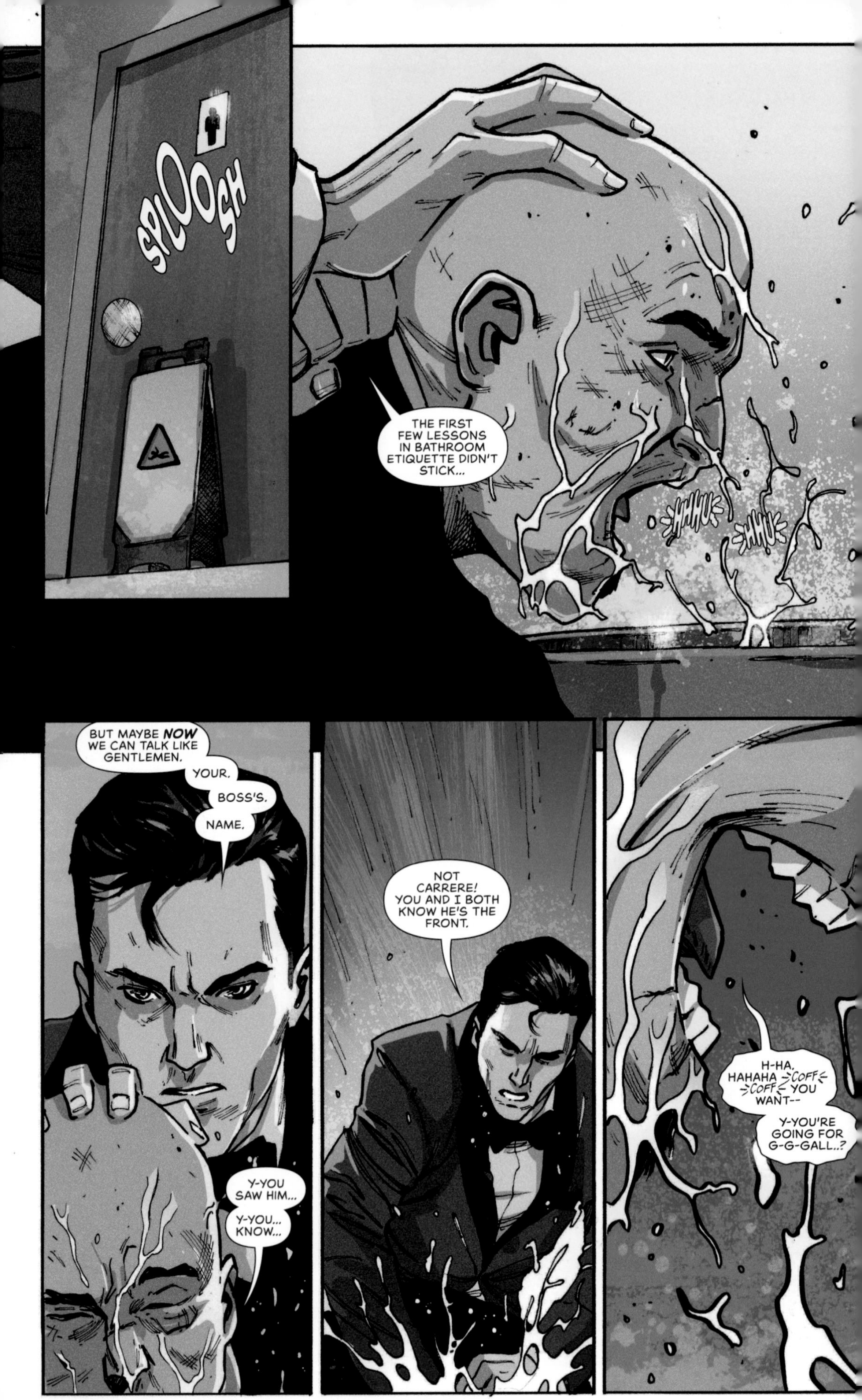
SPLOOSH
THE FIRST FEW LESSONS IN BATHROOM ETIQUETTE DIDN'T STICK...
HHHU
HHU
BUT MAYBE NOW WE CAN TALK LIKE GENTLEMEN.
YOUR.
BOSS'S.
NAME.
Y-YOU SAW HIM...
Y-YOU... KNOW...
NOT CARRERE! YOU AND I BOTH KNOW HE'S THE FRONT.
H-HA. HAHAHA COFF COFF YOU WANT--
Y-YOU'RE GOING FOR G-G-GALL..?

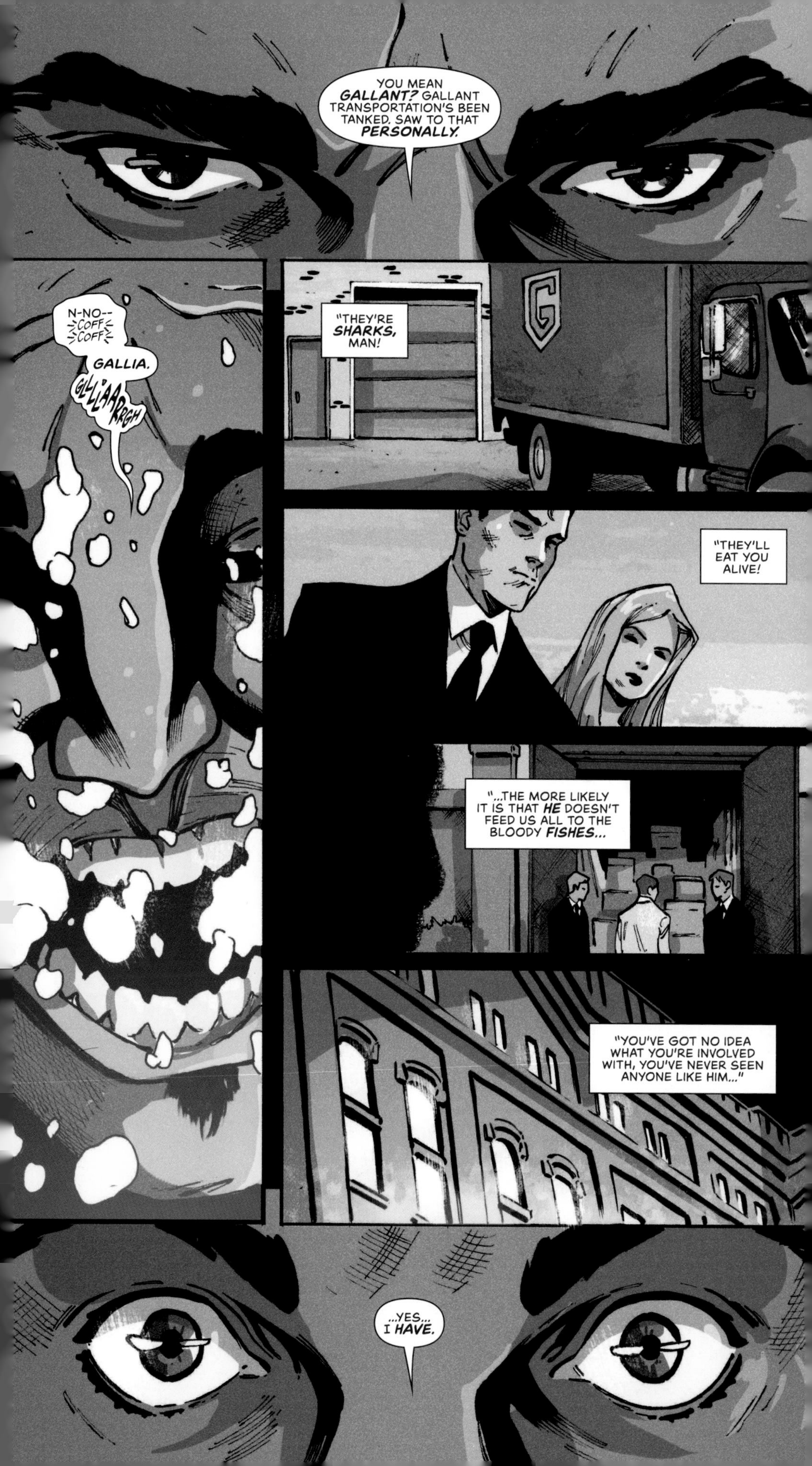

YOU MEAN GALLANT? GALLANT TRANSPORTATION'S BEEN TANKED. SAW TO THAT PERSONALLY.
N-NO-- COFF COFF
GALLIA.
GLLLIAARRGH
"THEY'RE SHARKS, MAN!
"THEY'LL EAT YOU ALIVE!
"...THE MORE LIKELY IT IS THAT HE DOESN'T FEED US ALL TO THE BLOODY FISHES...
"YOU'VE GOT NO IDEA WHAT YOU'RE INVOLVED WITH, YOU'VE NEVER SEEN ANYONE LIKE HIM..."
...YES... I HAVE.

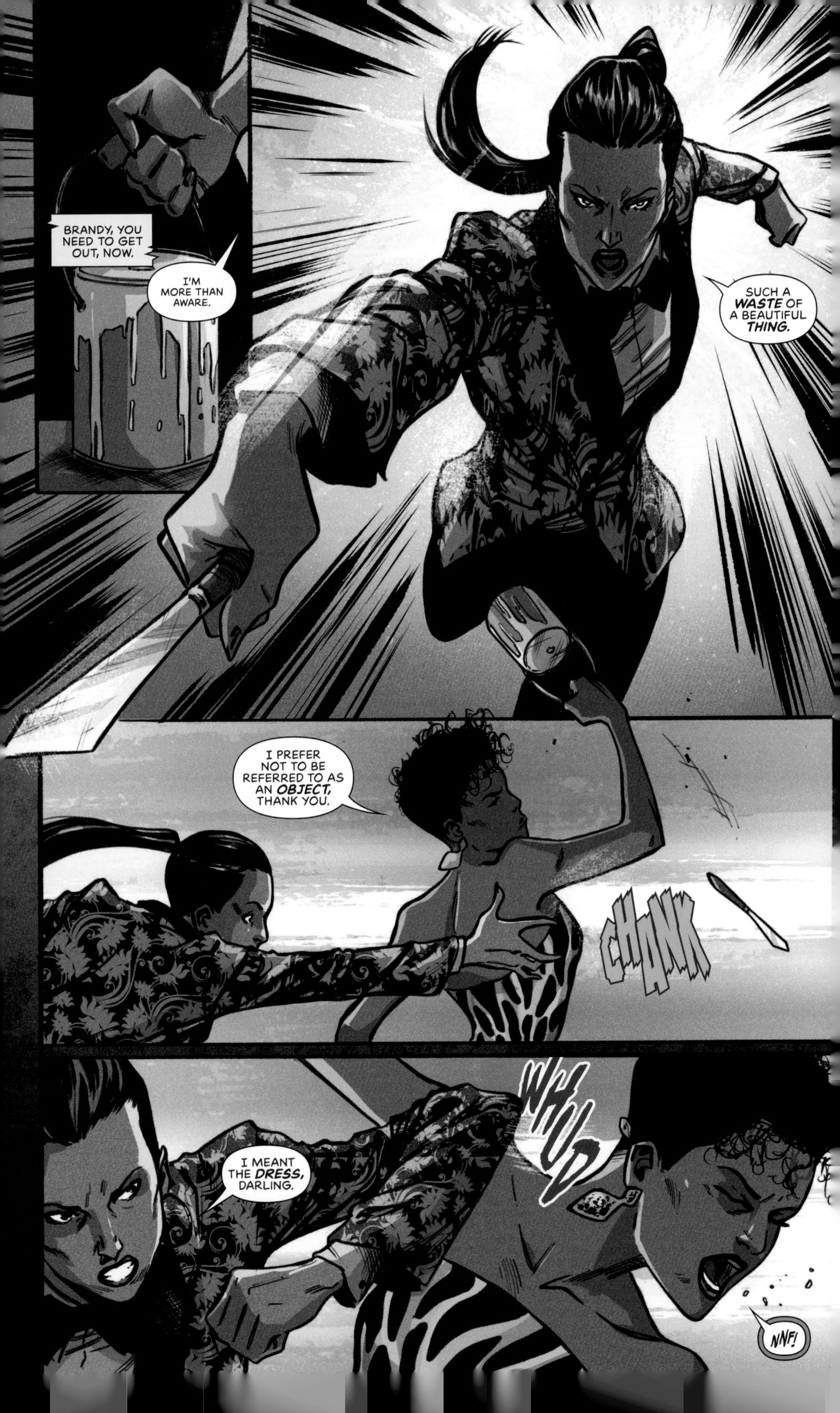
BRANDY, YOU NEED TO GET OUT, NOW.
I'M MORE THAN AWARE.
SUCH A WASTE OF A BEAUTIFUL THING.
I PREFER NOT TO BE REFERRED TO AS AN OBJECT, THANK YOU.
CHANK
I MEANT THE DRESS, DARLING.
WHUD
NNF!

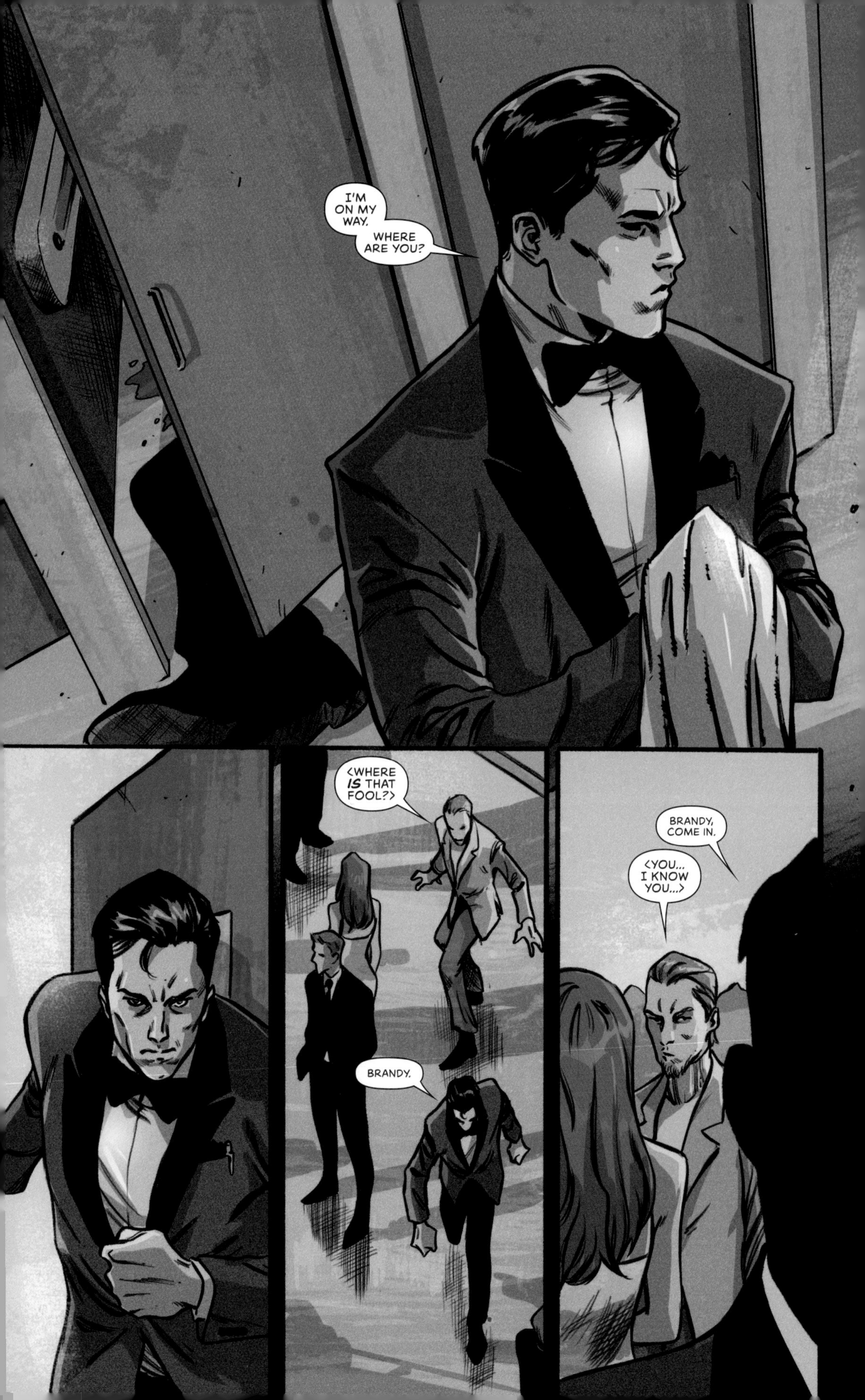
I'M ON MY WAY.
WHERE ARE YOU?
<WHERE *IS* THAT FOOL?>
BRANDY.
BRANDY, COME IN.
<YOU... I KNOW YOU...>

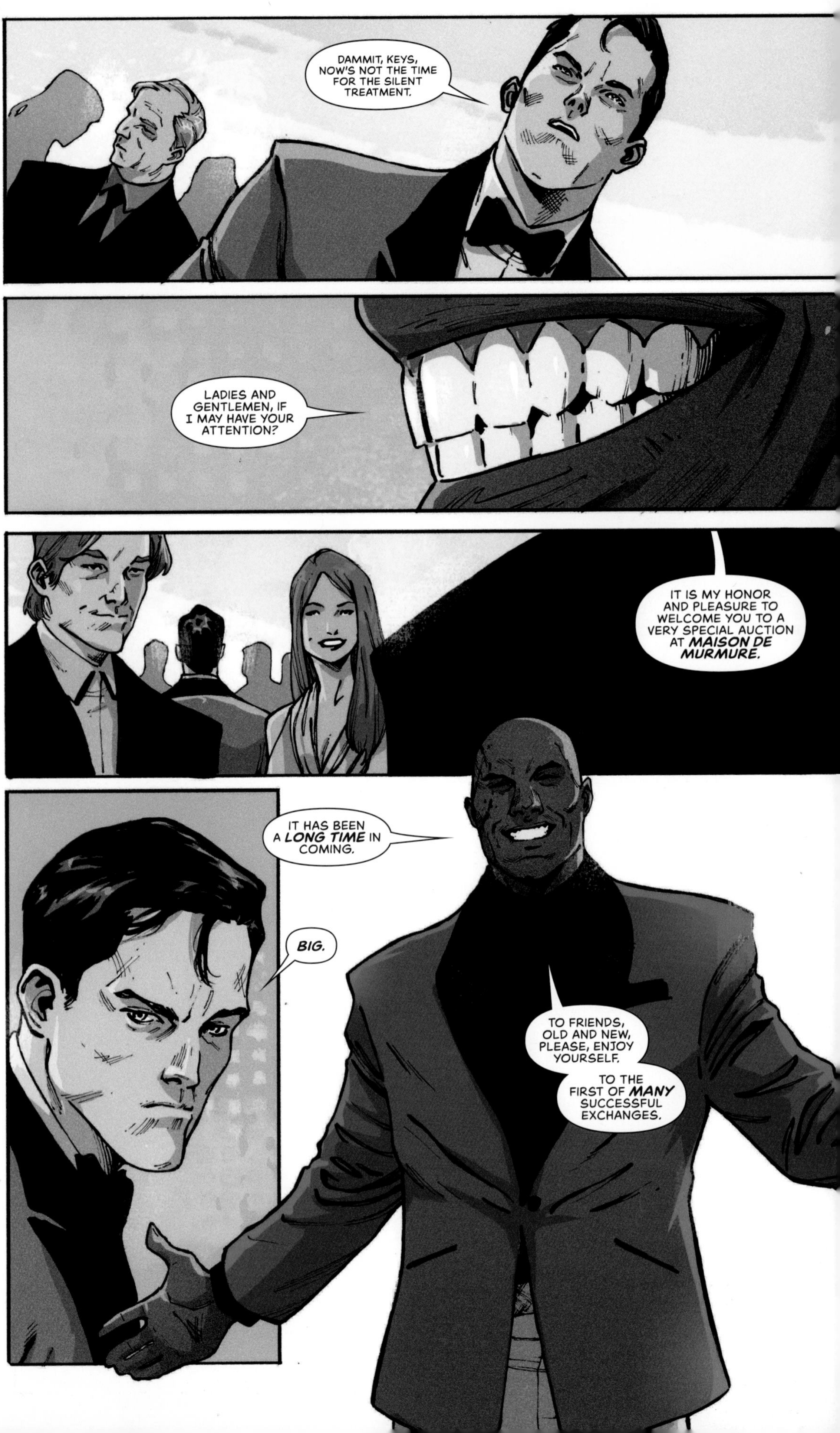
DAMMIT, KEYS, NOW'S NOT THE TIME FOR THE SILENT TREATMENT.
LADIES AND GENTLEMEN, IF I MAY HAVE YOUR ATTENTION?
IT IS MY HONOR AND PLEASURE TO WELCOME YOU TO A VERY SPECIAL AUCTION AT MAISON DE MURMURE.
IT HAS BEEN A LONG TIME IN COMING.
BIG.
TO FRIENDS, OLD AND NEW, PLEASE, ENJOY YOURSELF.
TO THE FIRST OF MANY SUCCESSFUL EXCHANGES.

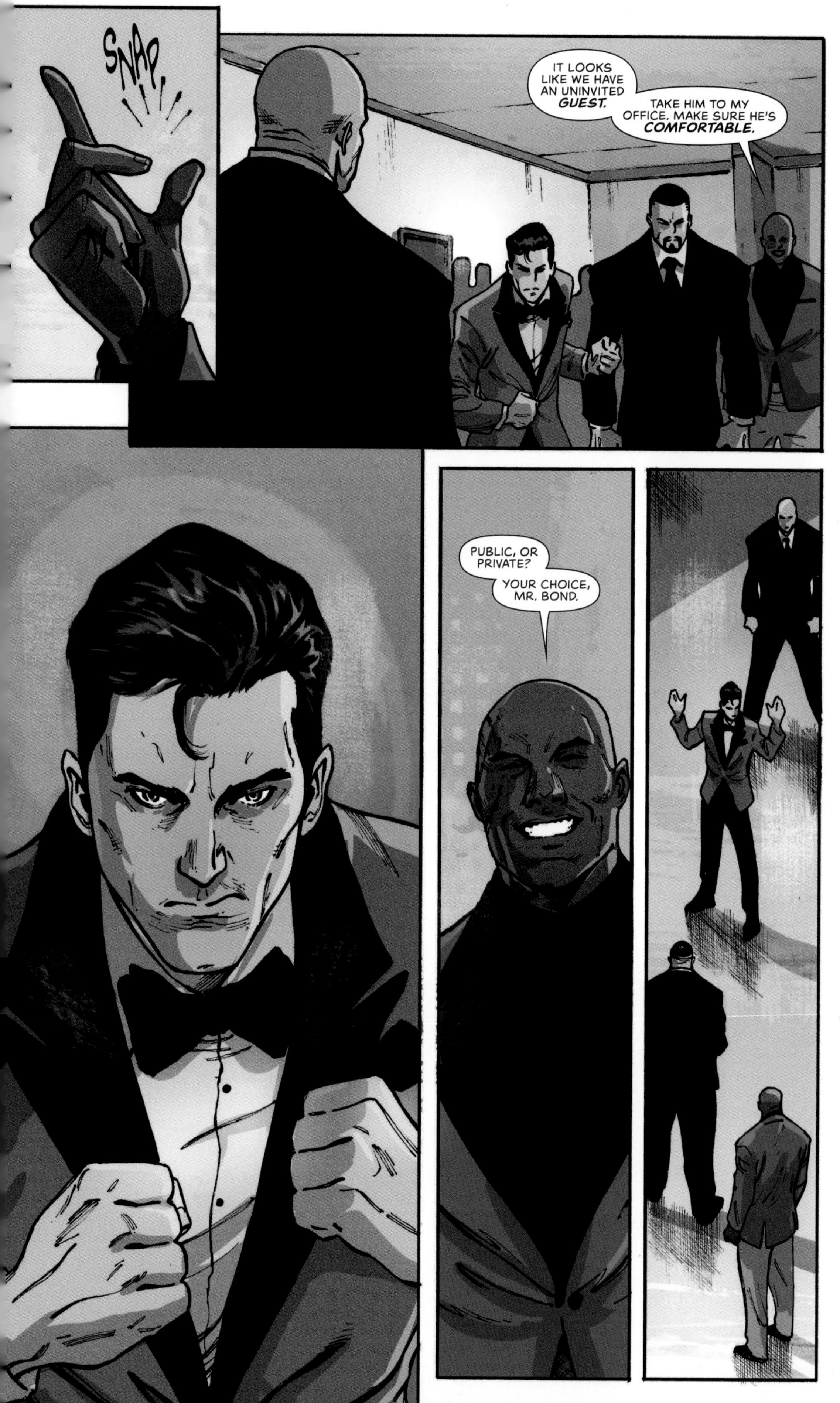
SNAP
IT LOOKS LIKE WE HAVE AN UNINVITED GUEST.
TAKE HIM TO MY OFFICE. MAKE SURE HE'S COMFORTABLE.
PUBLIC, OR PRIVATE?
YOUR CHOICE, MR. BOND.

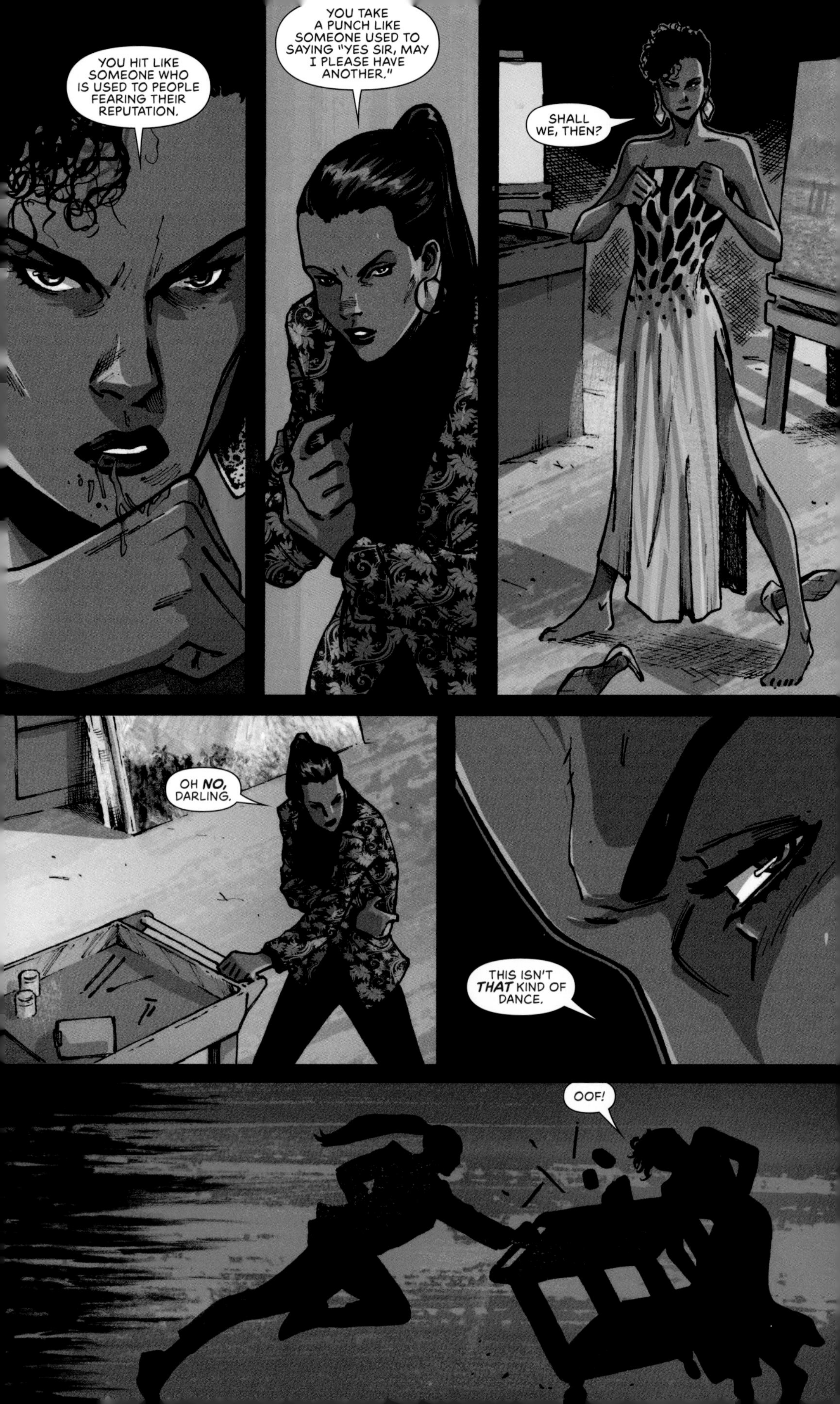
YOU HIT LIKE SOMEONE WHO IS USED TO PEOPLE FEARING THEIR REPUTATION.
YOU TAKE A PUNCH LIKE SOMEONE USED TO SAYING "YES SIR, MAY I PLEASE HAVE ANOTHER."
SHALL WE, THEN?
OH NO, DARLING.
THIS ISN'T THAT KIND OF DANCE.
OOF!

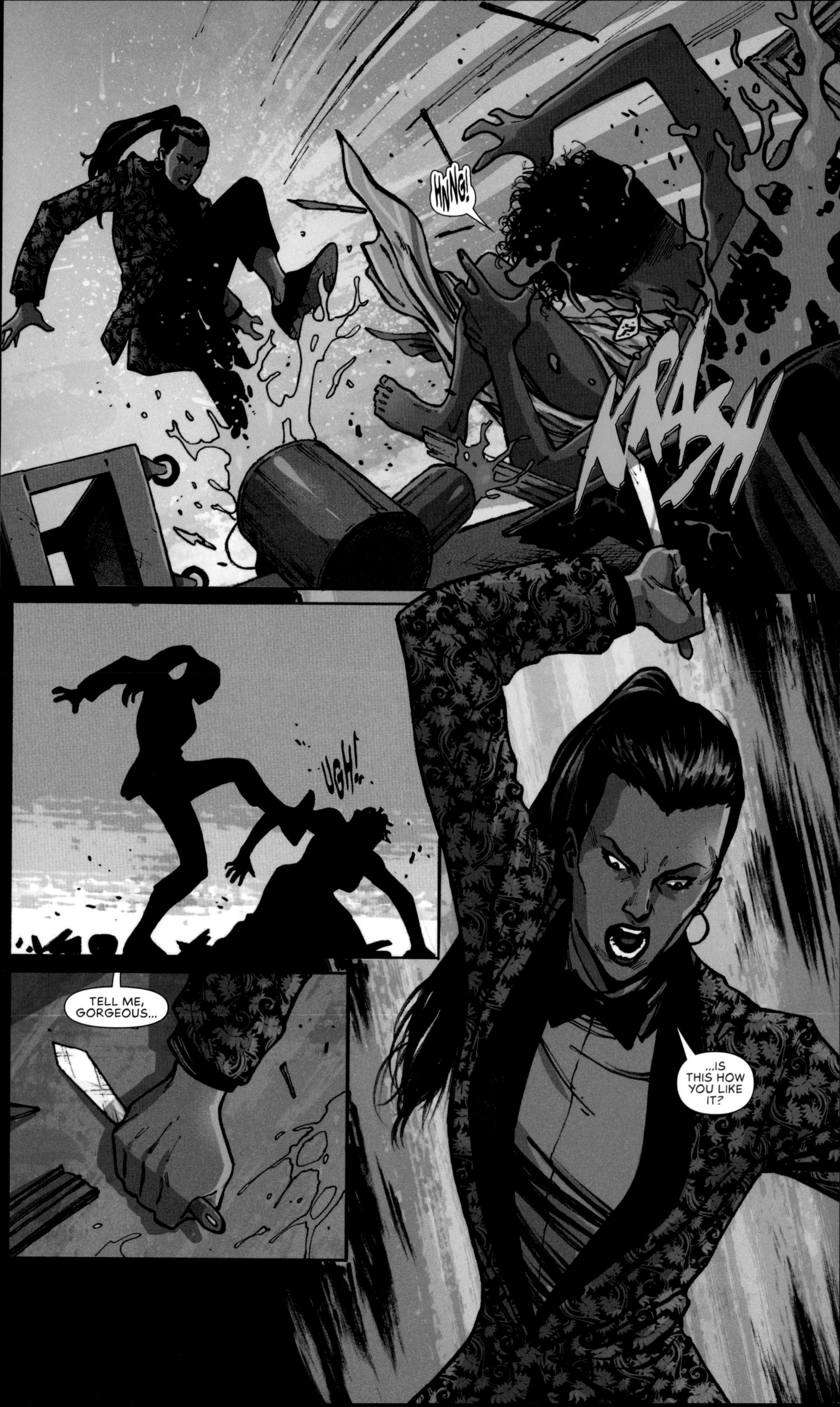
HNNG!
KRASH
UGH!
TELL ME, GORGEOUS...
...IS THIS HOW YOU LIKE IT?

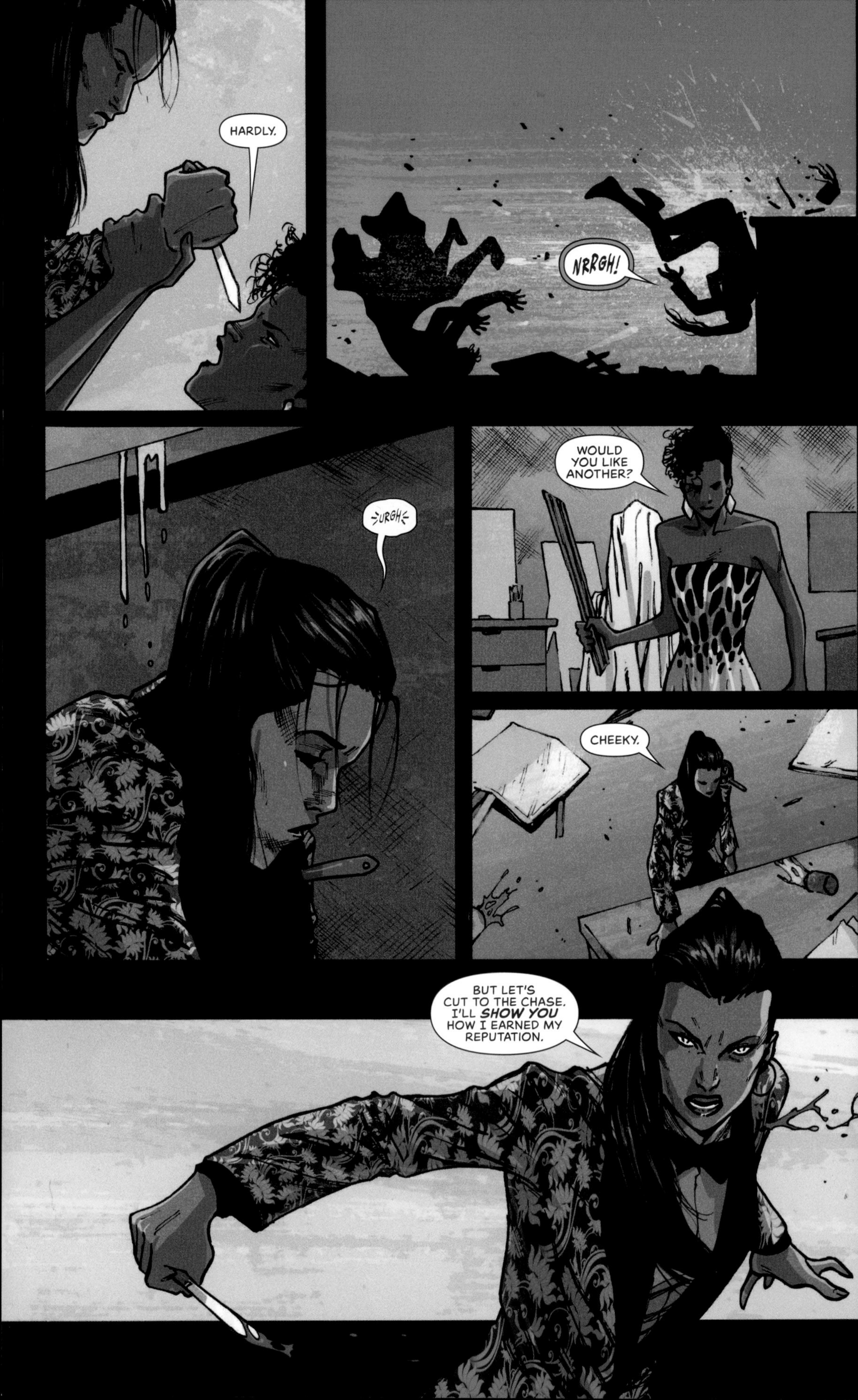
HARDLY.
NRRGH!
URGH
WOULD YOU LIKE ANOTHER?
CHEEKY.
BUT LET'S CUT TO THE CHASE. I'LL SHOW YOU HOW I EARNED MY REPUTATION.

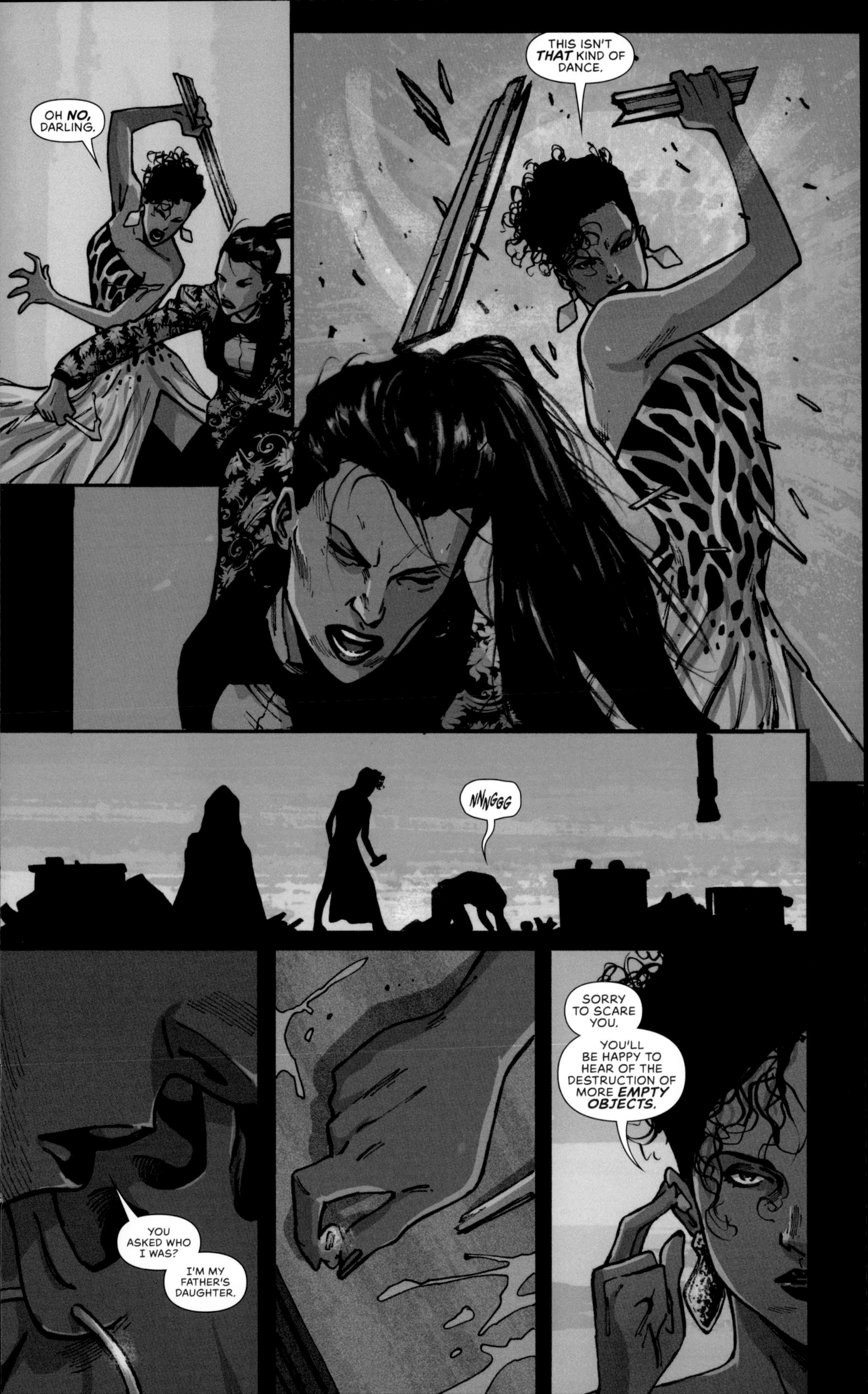
OH **NO,** DARLING.
THIS ISN'T **THAT** KIND OF DANCE.
NNNGGG
YOU ASKED WHO I WAS?
I'M MY FATHER'S DAUGHTER.
SORRY TO SCARE YOU.
YOU'LL BE HAPPY TO HEAR OF THE DESTRUCTION OF MORE **EMPTY OBJECTS.**

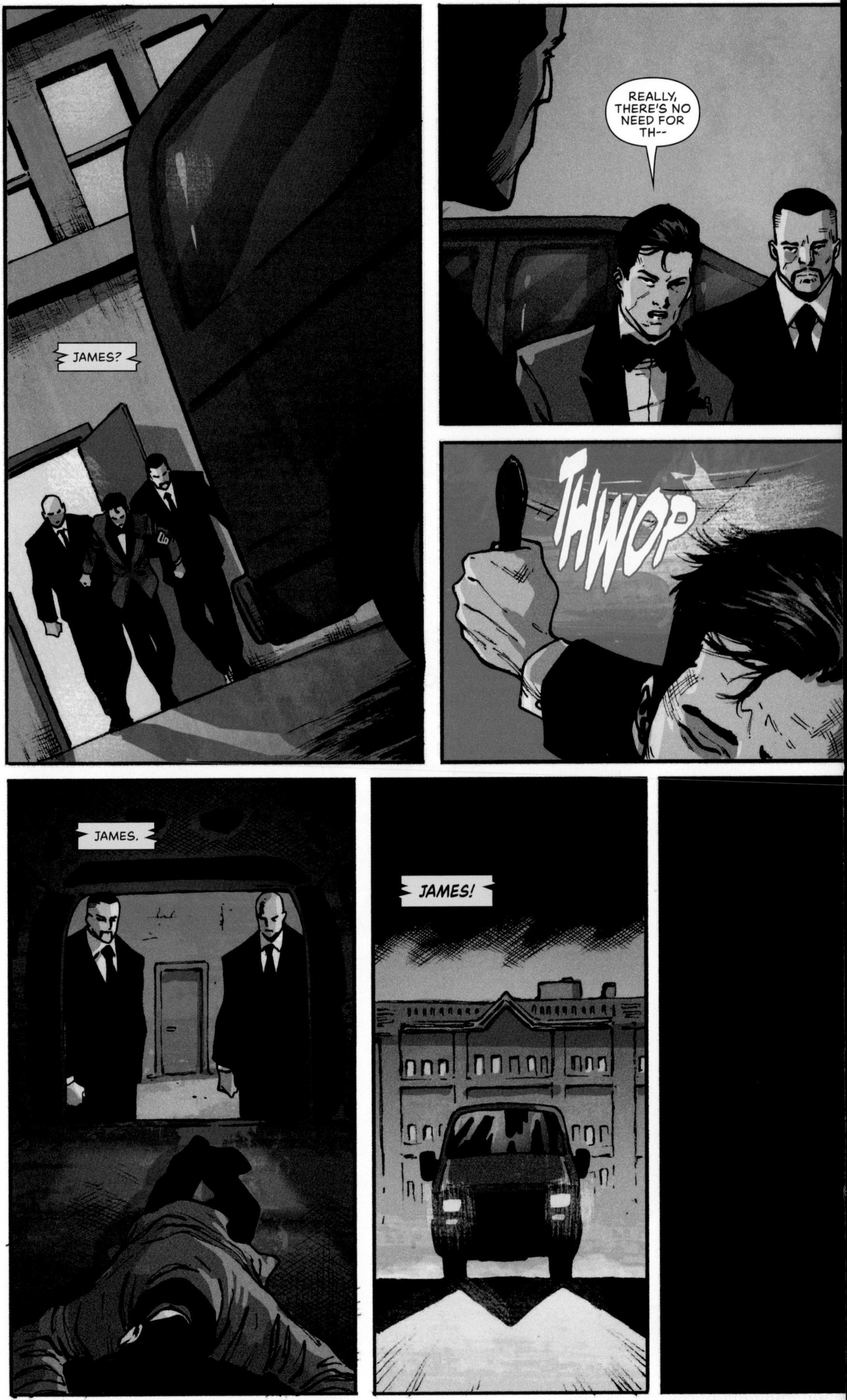

JAMES?
REALLY, THERE'S NO NEED FOR TH--
THWOP
JAMES.
JAMES!

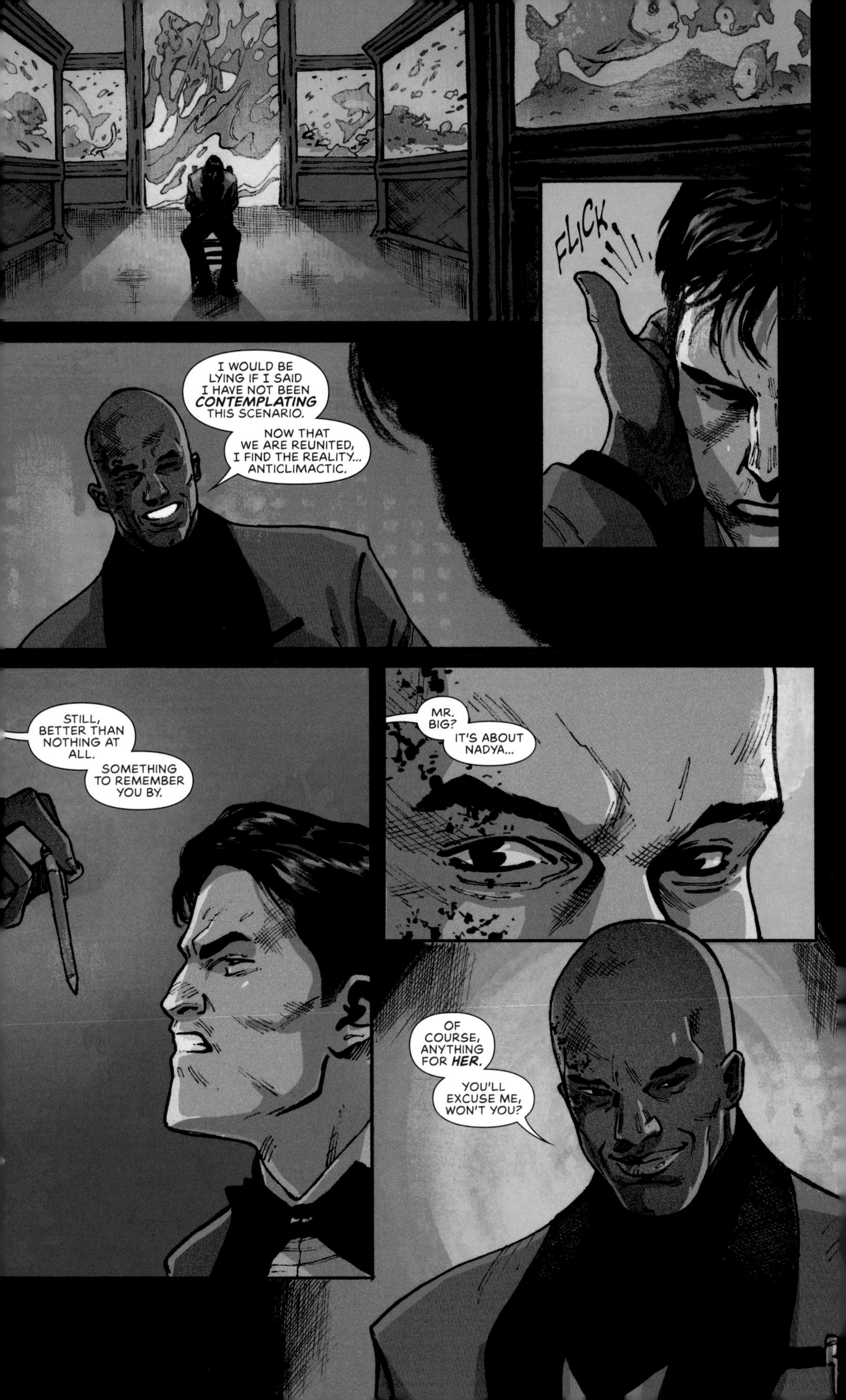
FLICK
I WOULD BE LYING IF I SAID I HAVE NOT BEEN CONTEMPLATING THIS SCENARIO.
NOW THAT WE ARE REUNITED, I FIND THE REALITY... ANTICLIMACTIC.
STILL, BETTER THAN NOTHING AT ALL.
SOMETHING TO REMEMBER YOU BY.
MR. BIG?
IT'S ABOUT NADYA...
OF COURSE, ANYTHING FOR HER.
YOU'LL EXCUSE ME, WON'T YOU?

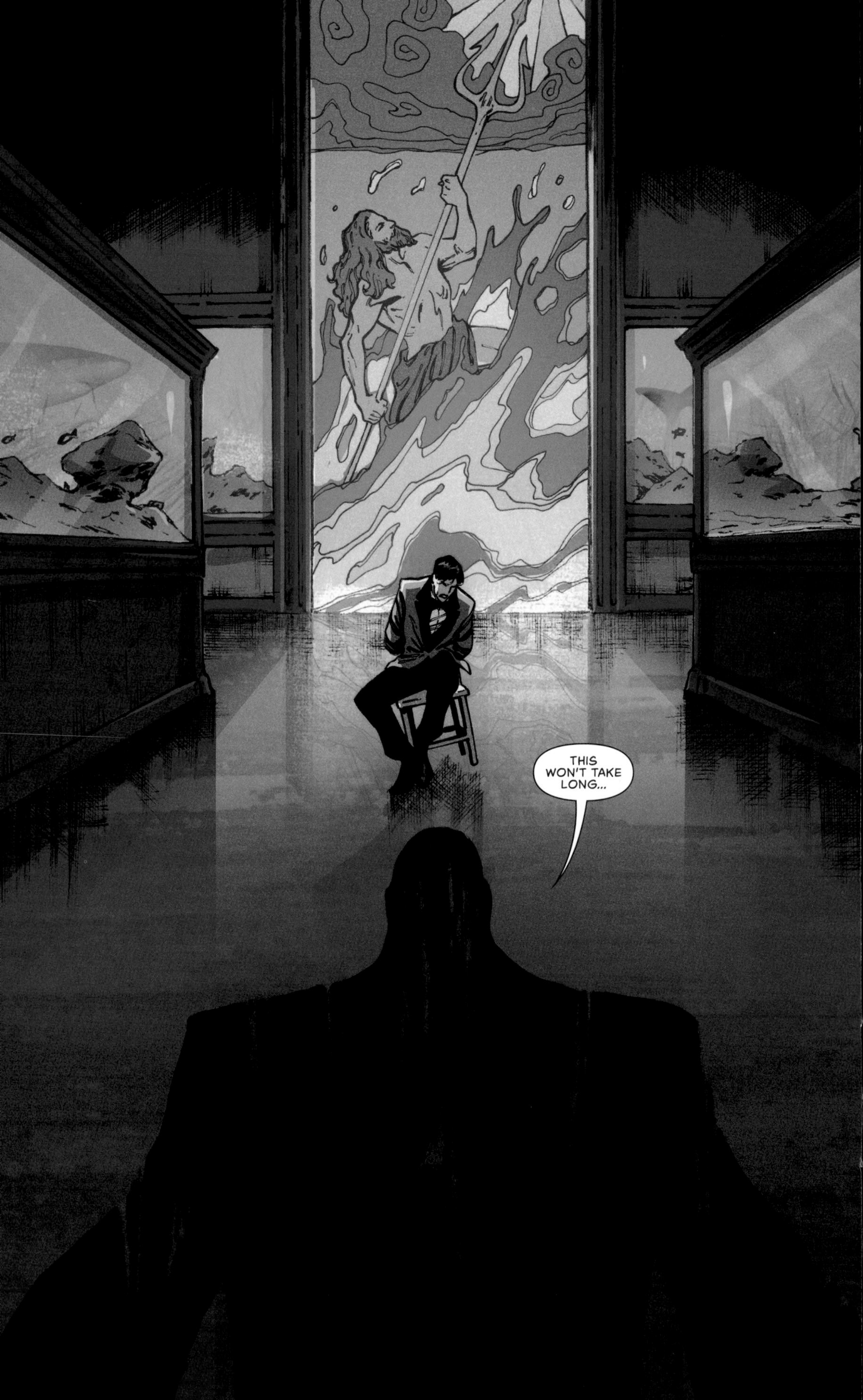
THIS WON'T TAKE LONG...

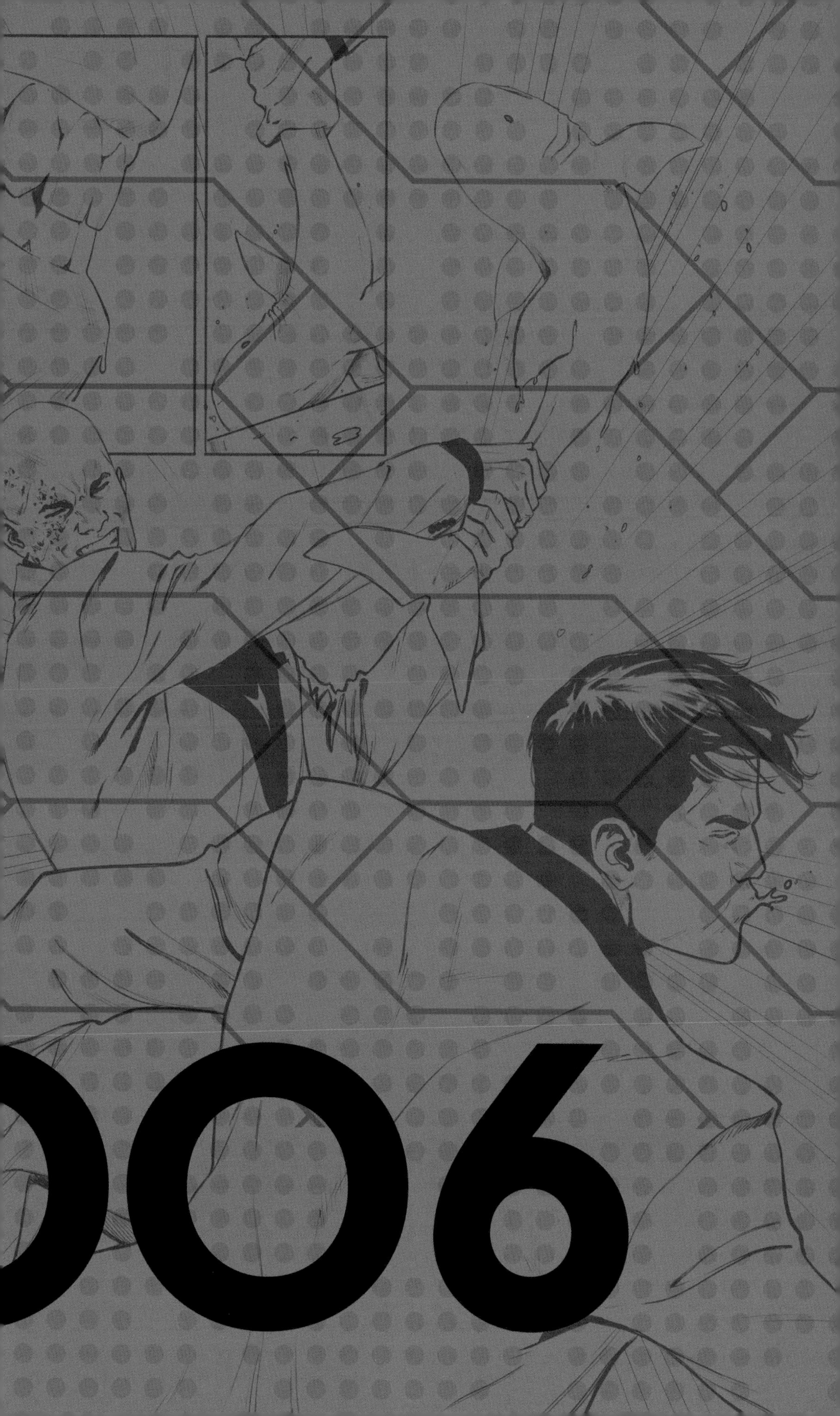
006

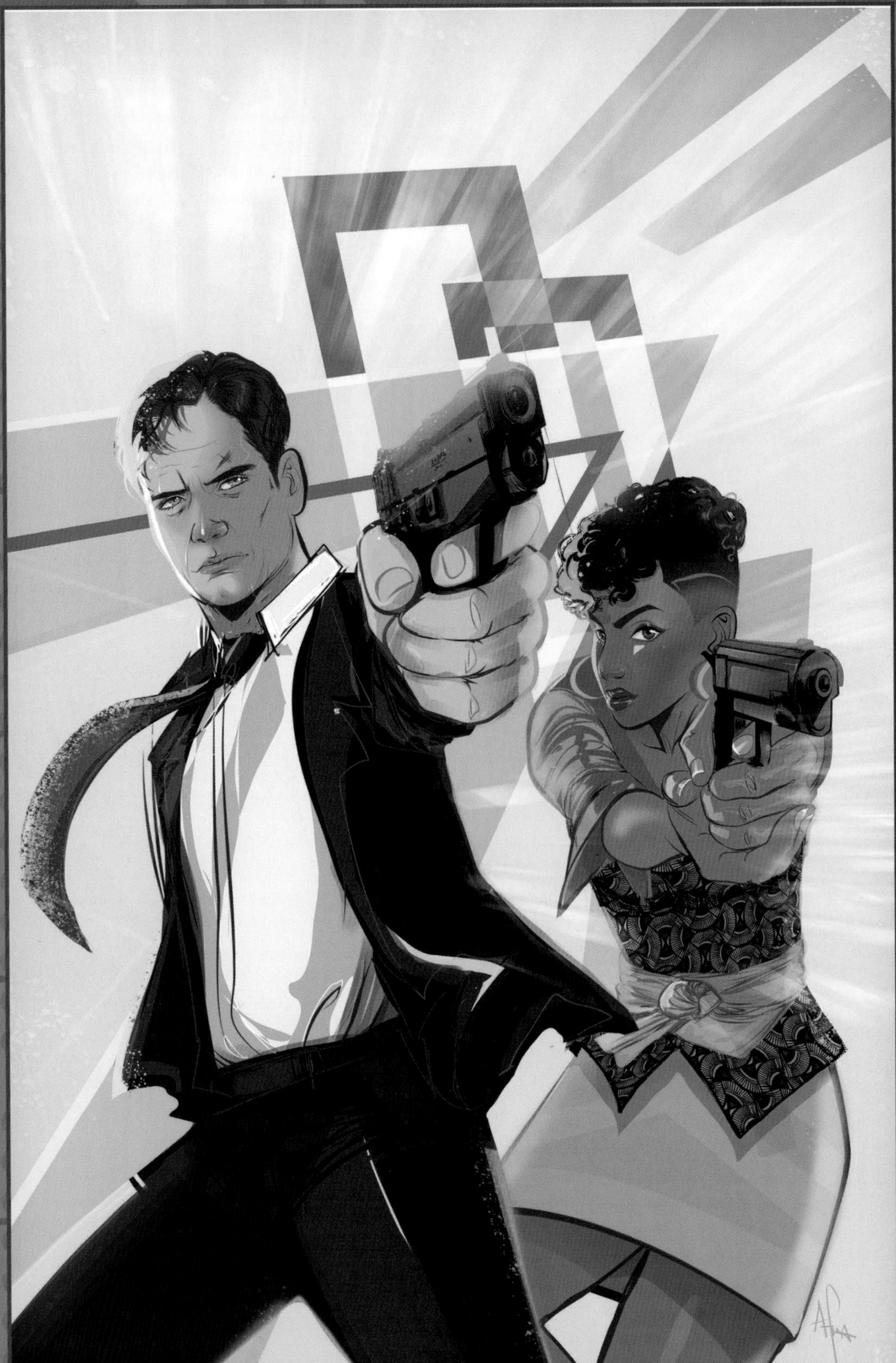
Afua

#6 COVER ART BY **Afua Richardson**

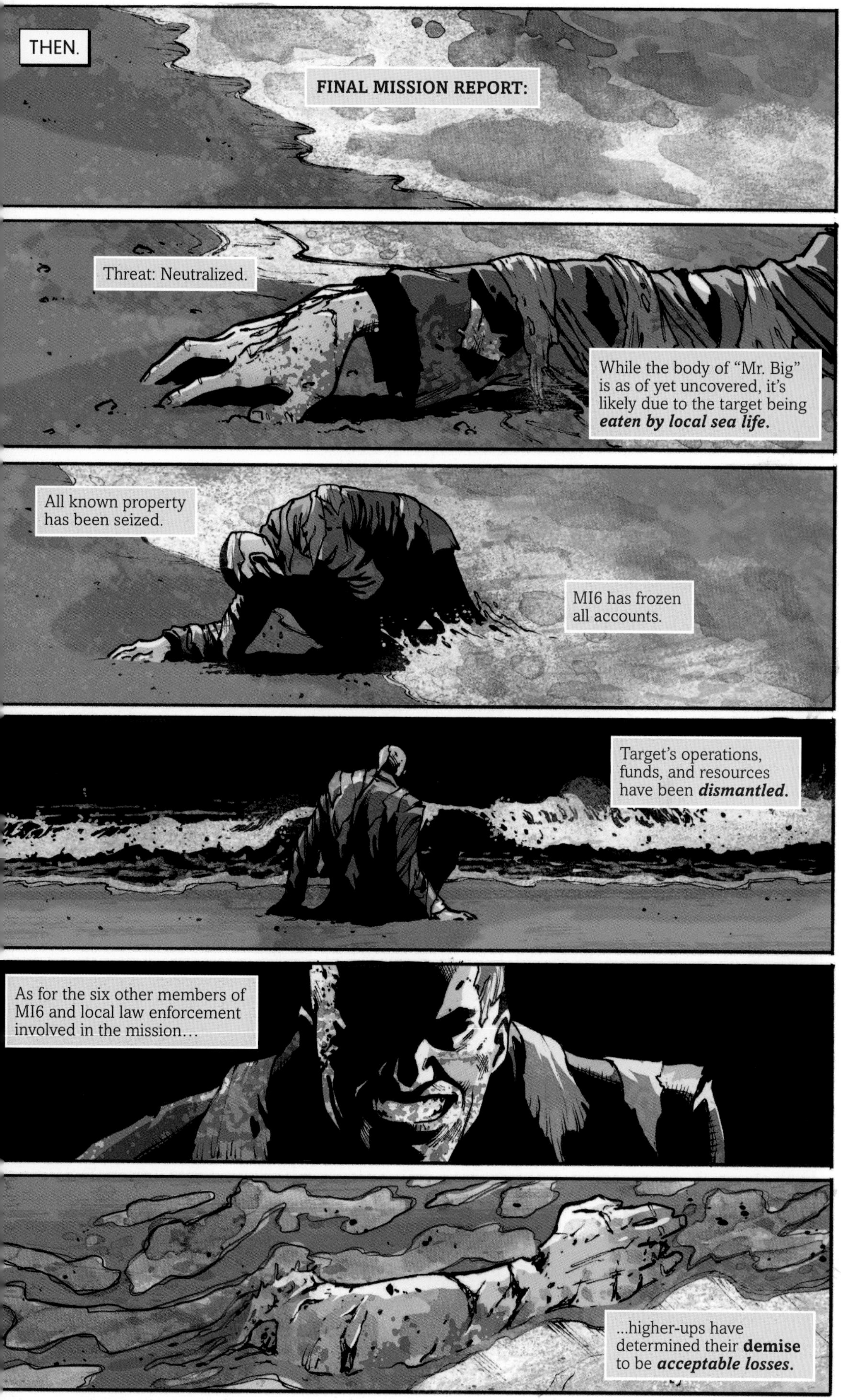
THEN.
FINAL MISSION REPORT:
Threat: Neutralized.
While the body of "Mr. Big" is as of yet uncovered, it's likely due to the target being ***eaten by local sea life.***
All known property has been seized.
MI6 has frozen all accounts.
Target's operations, funds, and resources have been ***dismantled.***
As for the six other members of MI6 and local law enforcement involved in the mission...
...higher-ups have determined their **demise** to be ***acceptable losses.***

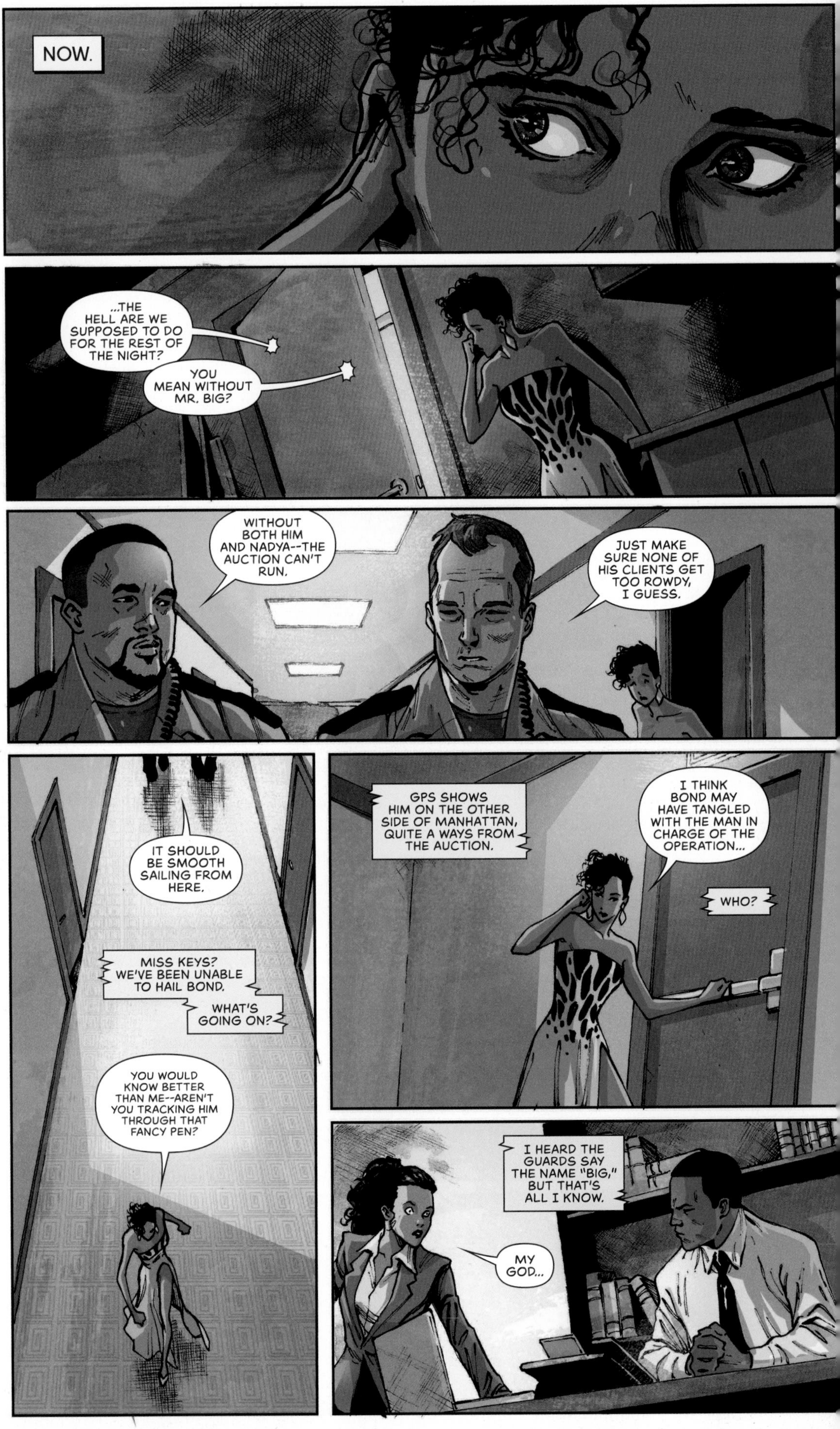
NOW.
...THE HELL ARE WE SUPPOSED TO DO FOR THE REST OF THE NIGHT?
YOU MEAN WITHOUT MR. BIG?
WITHOUT BOTH HIM AND NADYA--THE AUCTION CAN'T RUN.
JUST MAKE SURE NONE OF HIS CLIENTS GET TOO ROWDY, I GUESS.
IT SHOULD BE SMOOTH SAILING FROM HERE.
MISS KEYS? WE'VE BEEN UNABLE TO HAIL BOND.
WHAT'S GOING ON?
YOU WOULD KNOW BETTER THAN ME--AREN'T YOU TRACKING HIM THROUGH THAT FANCY PEN?
GPS SHOWS HIM ON THE OTHER SIDE OF MANHATTAN, QUITE A WAYS FROM THE AUCTION.
I THINK BOND MAY HAVE TANGLED WITH THE MAN IN CHARGE OF THE OPERATION...
WHO?
I HEARD THE GUARDS SAY THE NAME "BIG," BUT THAT'S ALL I KNOW.
MY GOD...

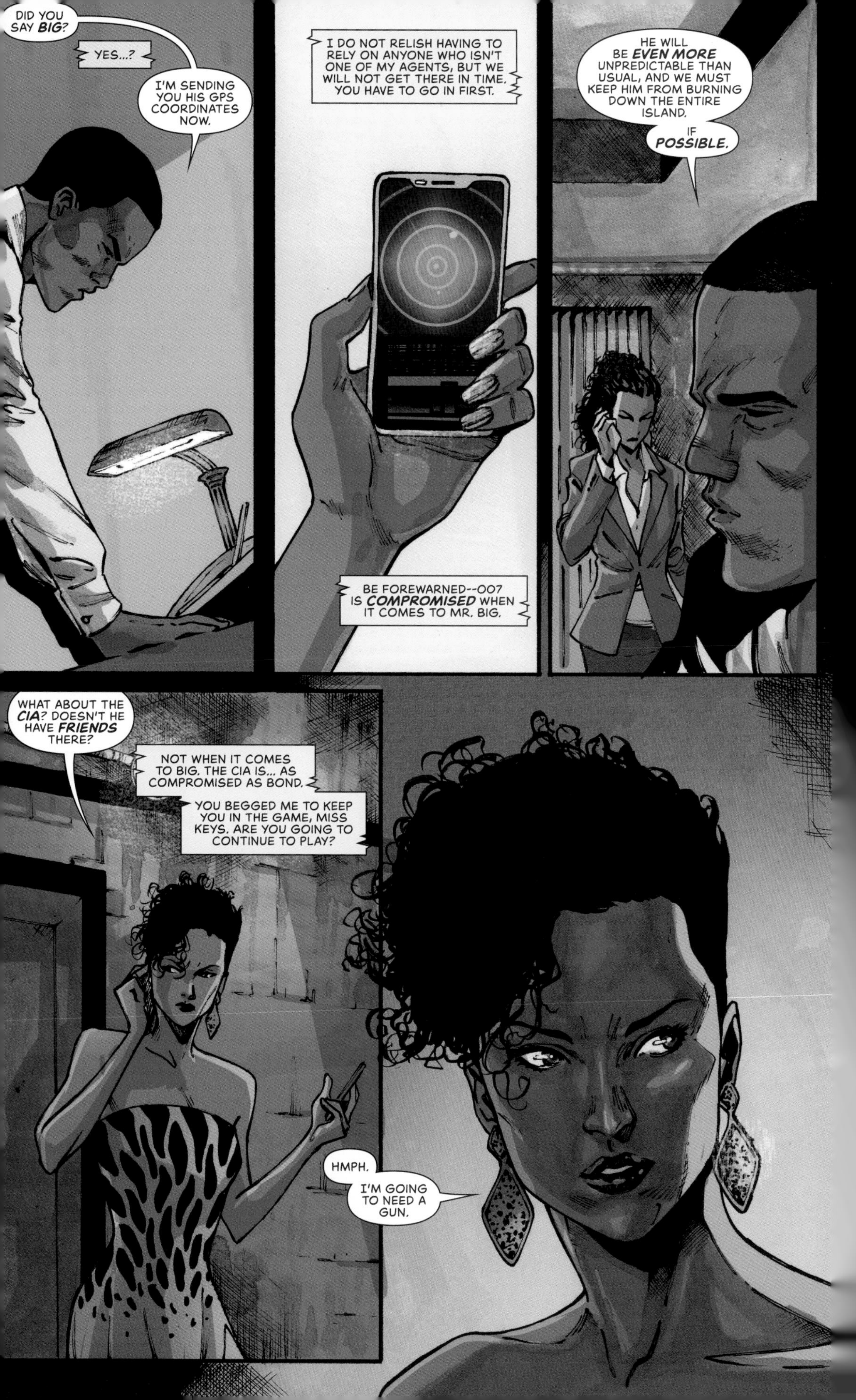
DID YOU SAY *BIG?*
YES...?
I'M SENDING YOU HIS GPS COORDINATES NOW.
I DO NOT RELISH HAVING TO RELY ON ANYONE WHO ISN'T ONE OF MY AGENTS, BUT WE WILL NOT GET THERE IN TIME. YOU HAVE TO GO IN FIRST.
BE FOREWARNED--007 IS *COMPROMISED* WHEN IT COMES TO MR. BIG.
HE WILL BE *EVEN MORE* UNPREDICTABLE THAN USUAL, AND WE MUST KEEP HIM FROM BURNING DOWN THE ENTIRE ISLAND.
IF *POSSIBLE.*
WHAT ABOUT THE *CIA?* DOESN'T HE HAVE *FRIENDS* THERE?
NOT WHEN IT COMES TO BIG. THE CIA IS... AS COMPROMISED AS BOND.
YOU BEGGED ME TO KEEP YOU IN THE GAME, MISS KEYS. ARE YOU GOING TO CONTINUE TO PLAY?
HMPH.
I'M GOING TO NEED A GUN.

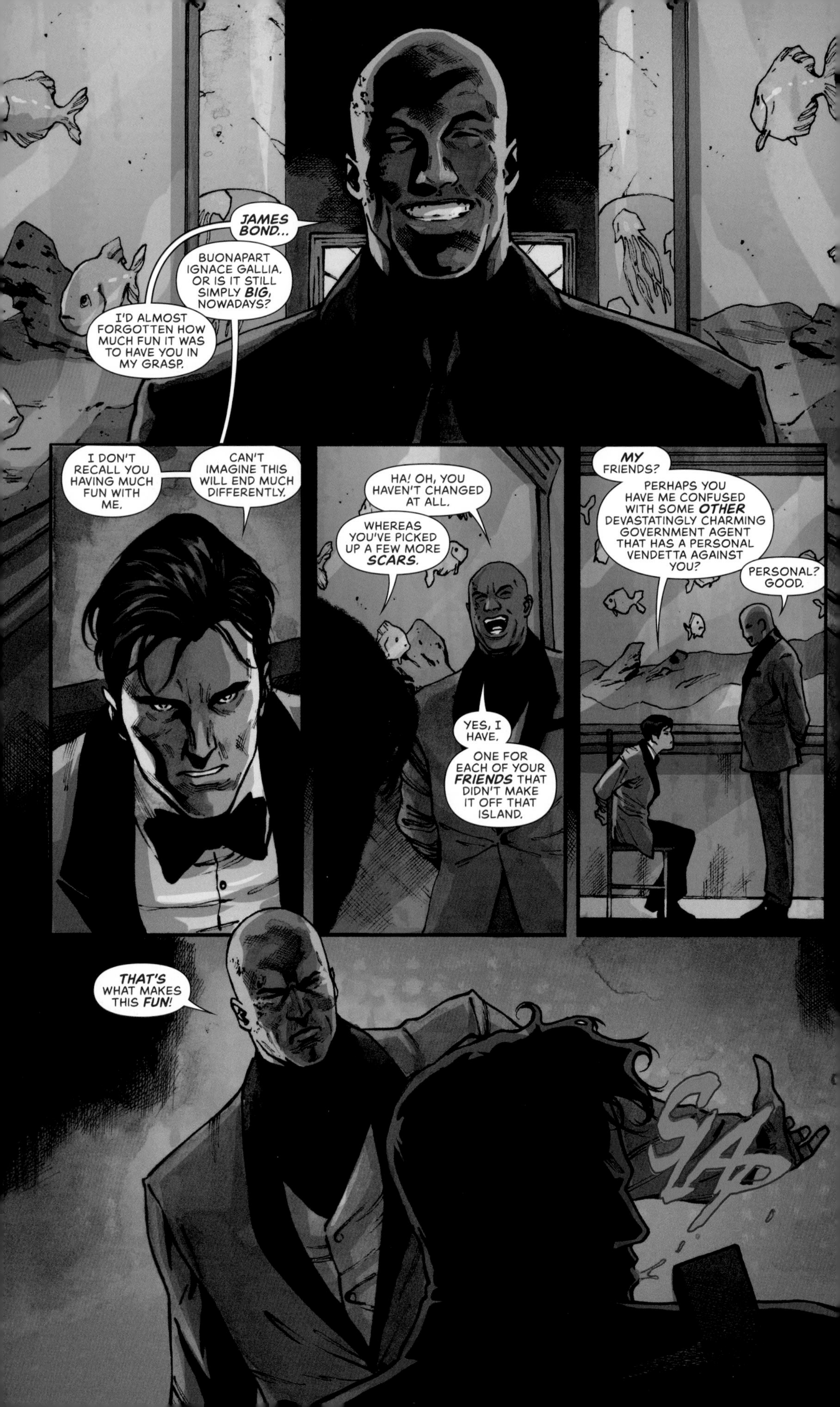
JAMES BOND...
BUONAPART IGNACE GALLIA. OR IS IT STILL SIMPLY BIG, NOWADAYS?
I'D ALMOST FORGOTTEN HOW MUCH FUN IT WAS TO HAVE YOU IN MY GRASP.
CAN'T IMAGINE THIS WILL END MUCH DIFFERENTLY.
I DON'T RECALL YOU HAVING MUCH FUN WITH ME.
HA! OH, YOU HAVEN'T CHANGED AT ALL.
WHEREAS YOU'VE PICKED UP A FEW MORE SCARS.
YES, I HAVE.
ONE FOR EACH OF YOUR FRIENDS THAT DIDN'T MAKE IT OFF THAT ISLAND.
MY FRIENDS?
PERHAPS YOU HAVE ME CONFUSED WITH SOME OTHER DEVASTATINGLY CHARMING GOVERNMENT AGENT THAT HAS A PERSONAL VENDETTA AGAINST YOU?
PERSONAL? GOOD.
THAT'S WHAT MAKES THIS FUN!
SLAP

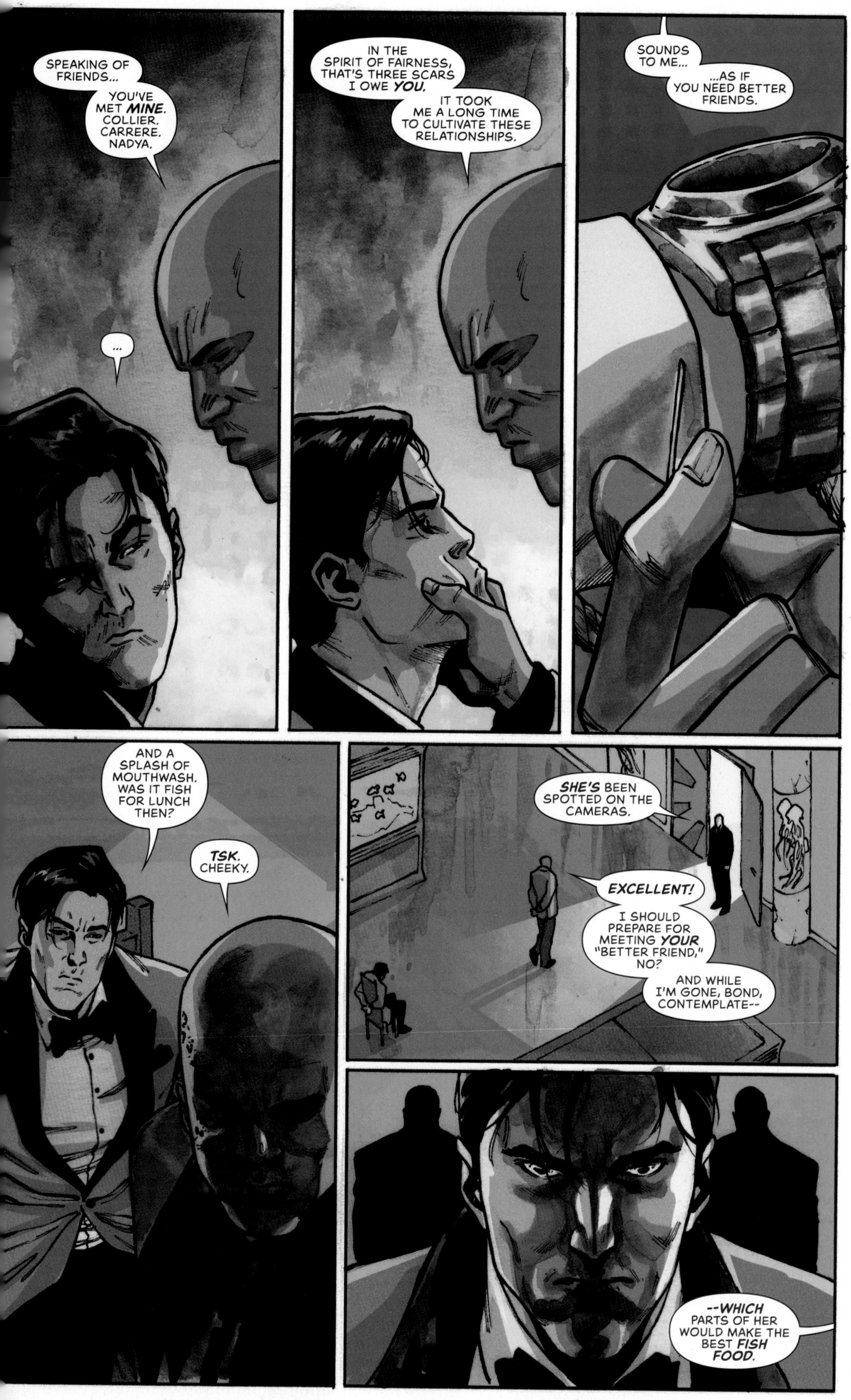
SPEAKING OF FRIENDS...
YOU'VE MET **MINE**. COLLIER. CARRERE. NADYA.
...
IN THE SPIRIT OF FAIRNESS, THAT'S THREE SCARS I OWE **YOU**.
IT TOOK ME A LONG TIME TO CULTIVATE THESE RELATIONSHIPS.
SOUNDS TO ME...
...AS IF YOU NEED BETTER FRIENDS.
AND A SPLASH OF MOUTHWASH. WAS IT FISH FOR LUNCH THEN?
TSK. CHEEKY.
SHE'S BEEN SPOTTED ON THE CAMERAS.
EXCELLENT!
I SHOULD PREPARE FOR MEETING **YOUR** "BETTER FRIEND," NO?
AND WHILE I'M GONE, BOND, CONTEMPLATE--
--**WHICH** PARTS OF HER WOULD MAKE THE BEST **FISH FOOD**.

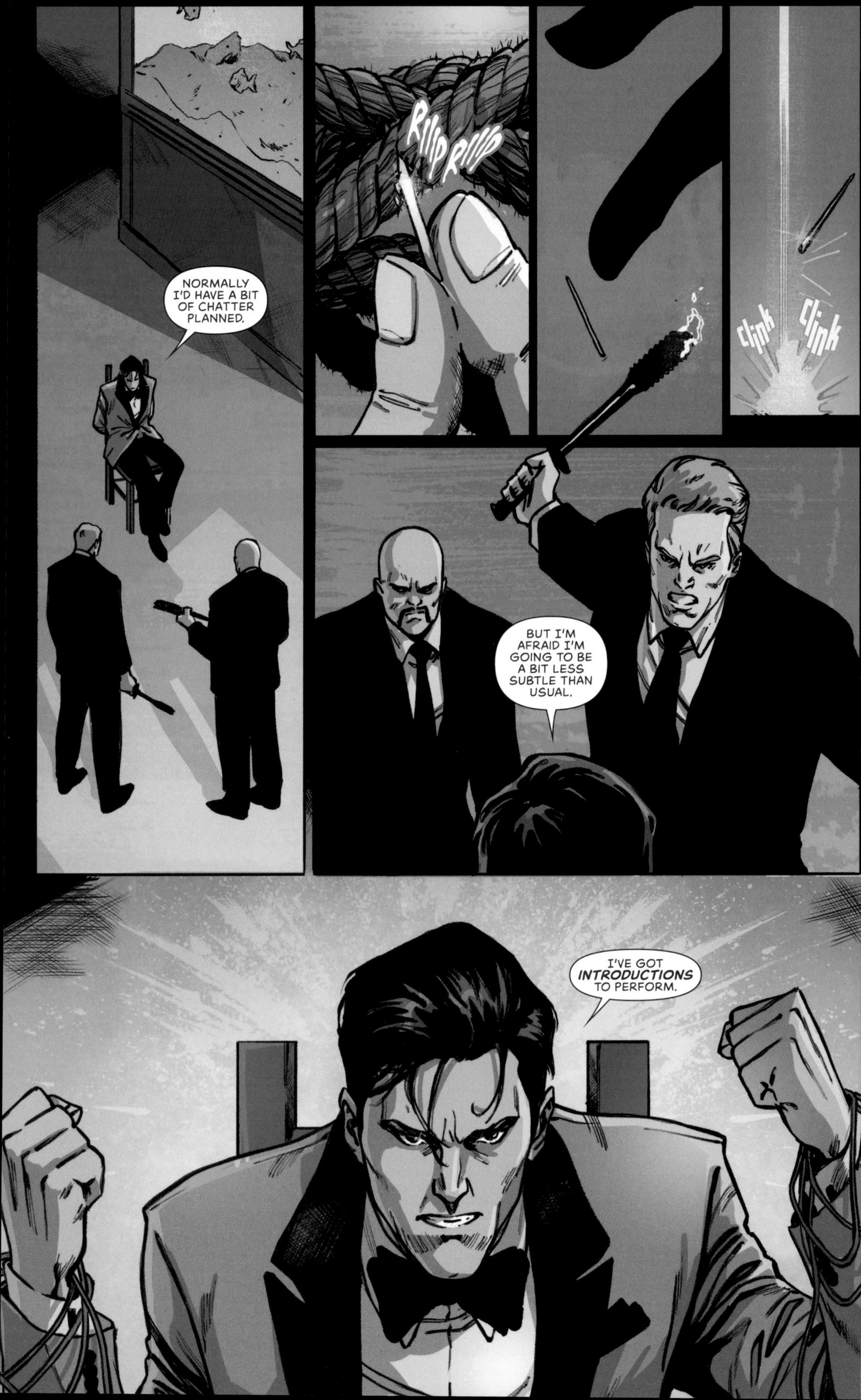

NORMALLY I'D HAVE A BIT OF CHATTER PLANNED.
RIIIP RIIIP
CLINK CLINK
BUT I'M AFRAID I'M GOING TO BE A BIT LESS SUBTLE THAN USUAL.
I'VE GOT *INTRODUCTIONS* TO PERFORM.

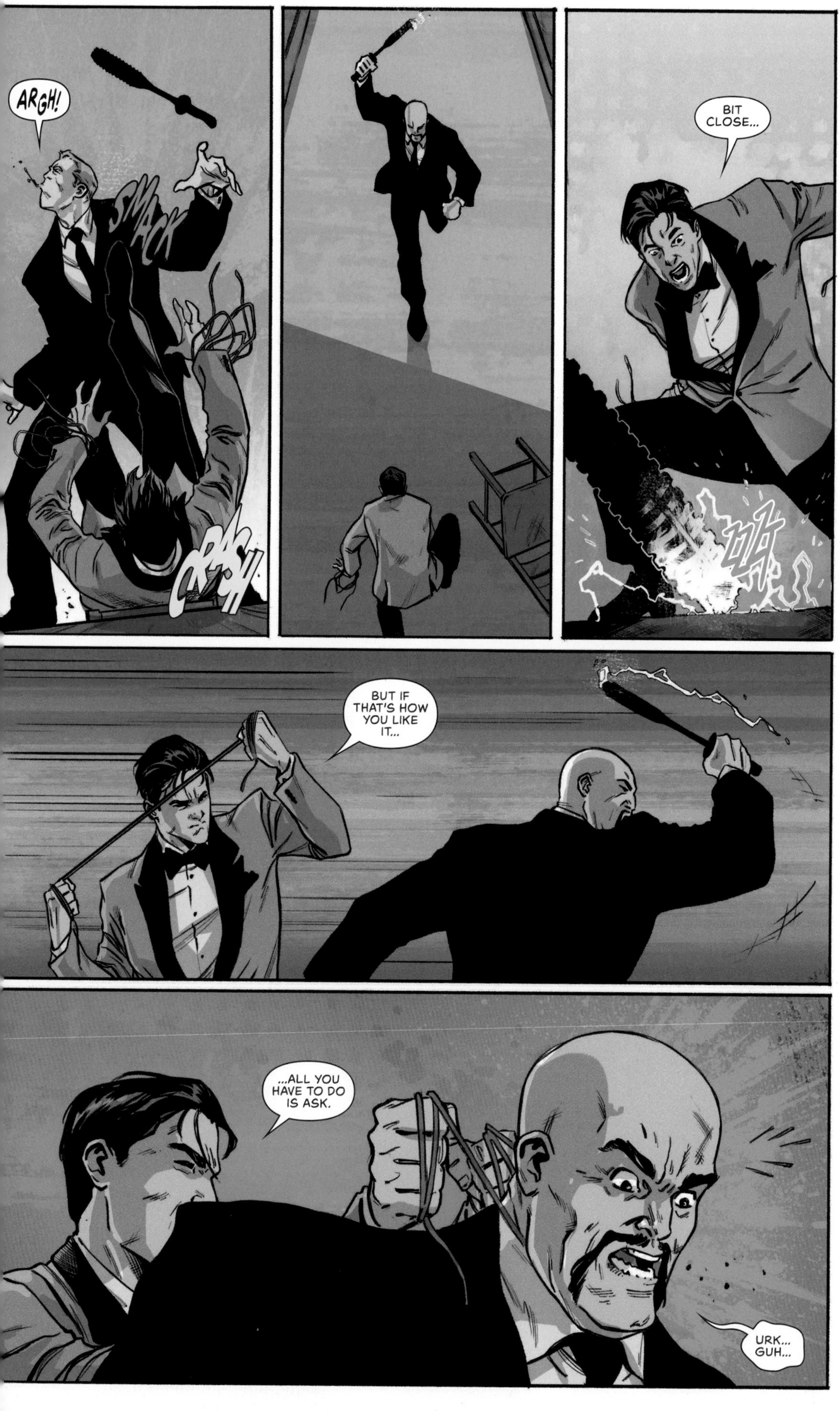
ARGH!
SMACK
CRASH
BIT CLOSE...
BUT IF THAT'S HOW YOU LIKE IT...
...ALL YOU HAVE TO DO IS ASK.
URK... GUH...

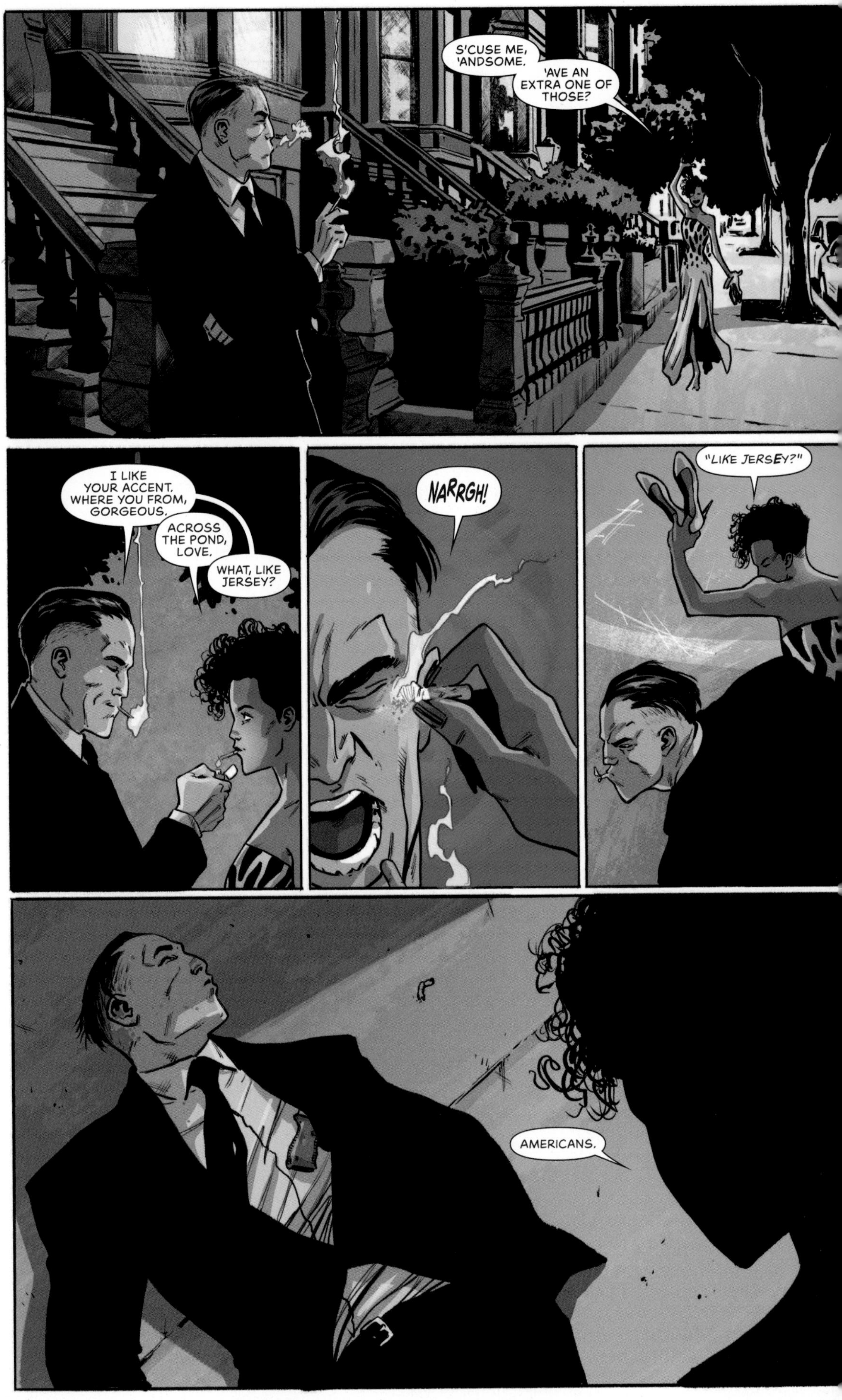
S'CUSE ME, 'ANDSOME.
'AVE AN EXTRA ONE OF THOSE?
I LIKE YOUR ACCENT. WHERE YOU FROM, GORGEOUS.
ACROSS THE POND, LOVE.
WHAT, LIKE JERSEY?
NARRGH!
"LIKE JERSEY?"
AMERICANS.

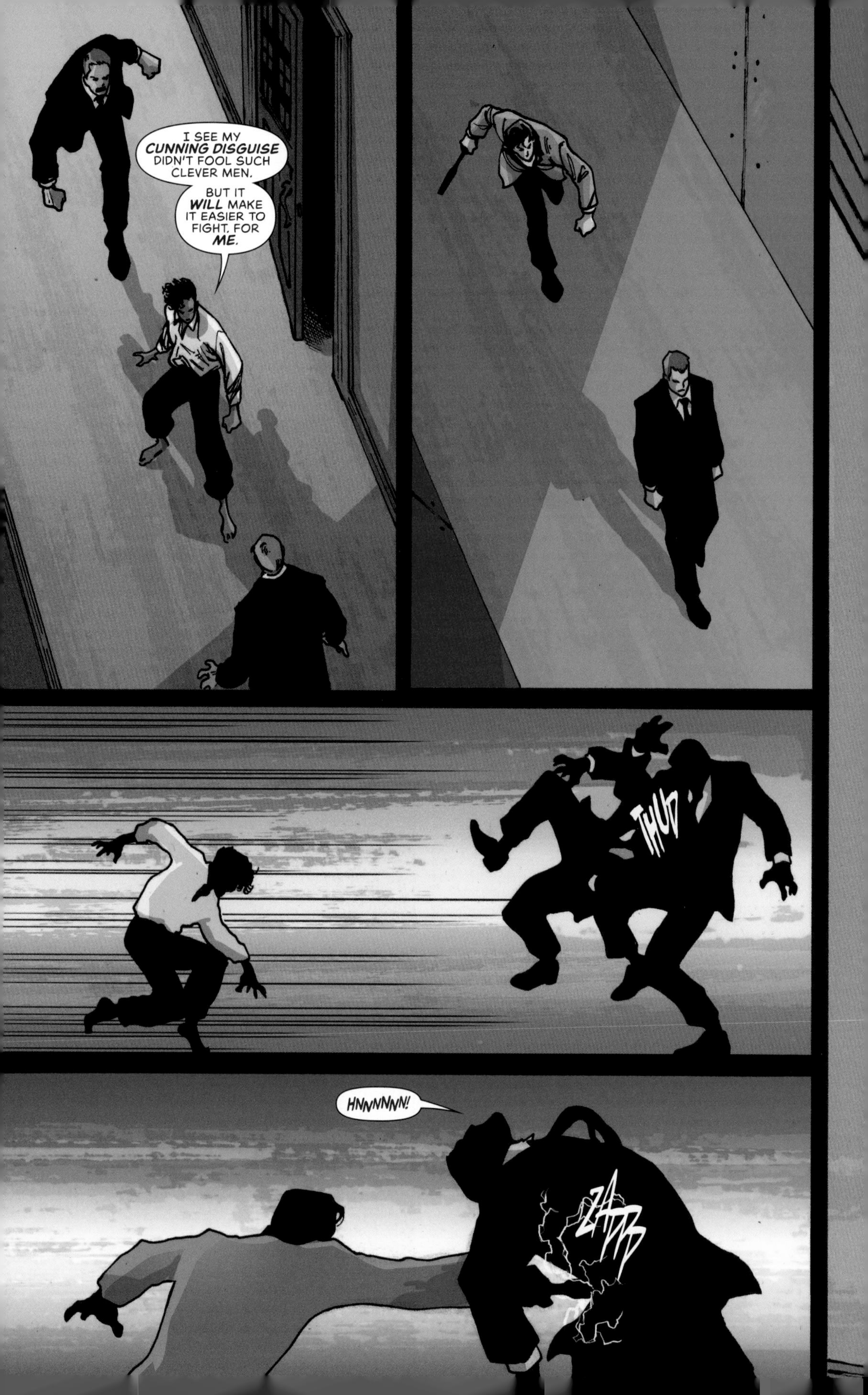

I SEE MY *CUNNING DISGUISE* DIDN'T FOOL SUCH CLEVER MEN.
BUT IT *WILL* MAKE IT EASIER TO FIGHT, FOR *ME*.
THUD
HNNNNNN!
ZAPP

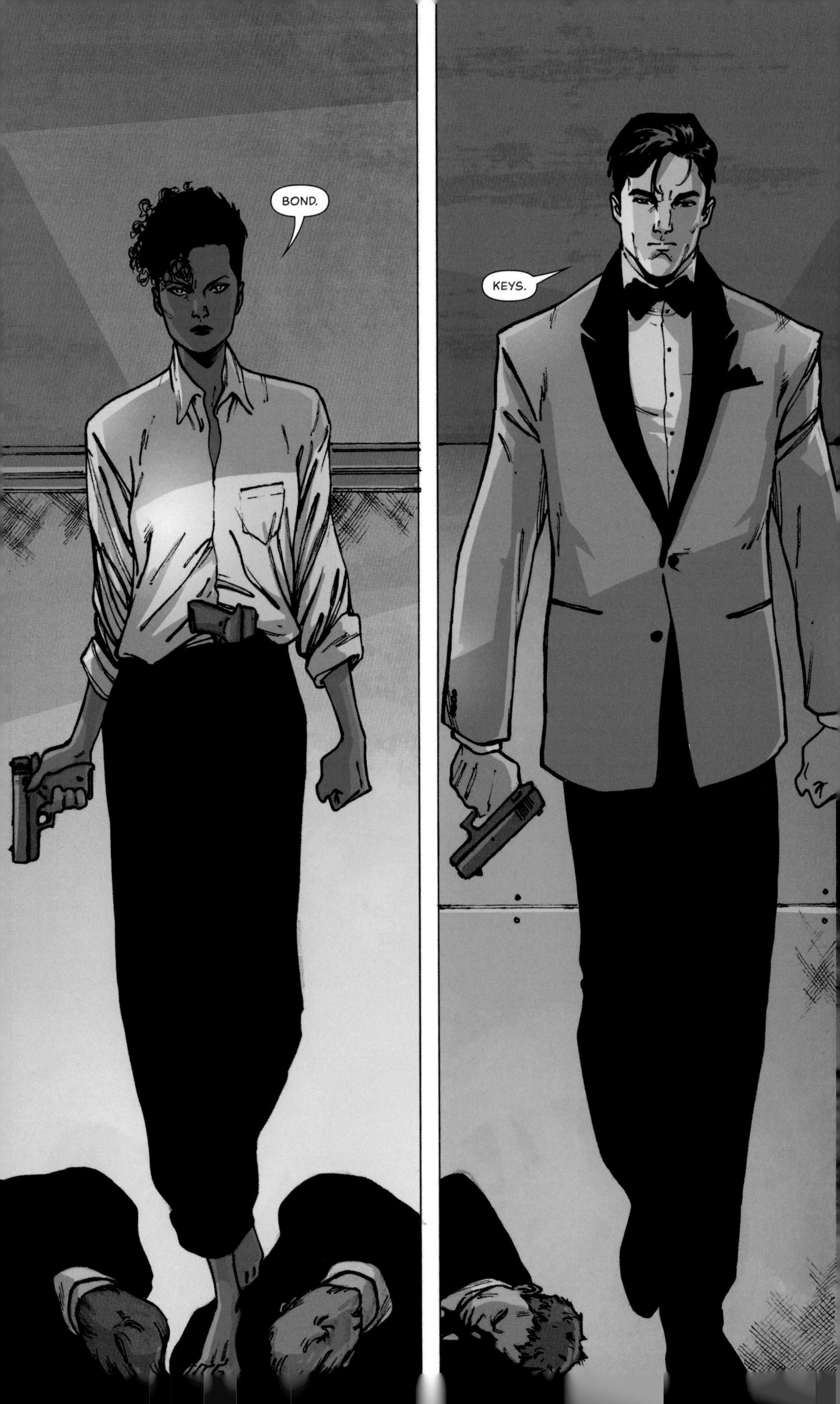
BOND.
KEYS.

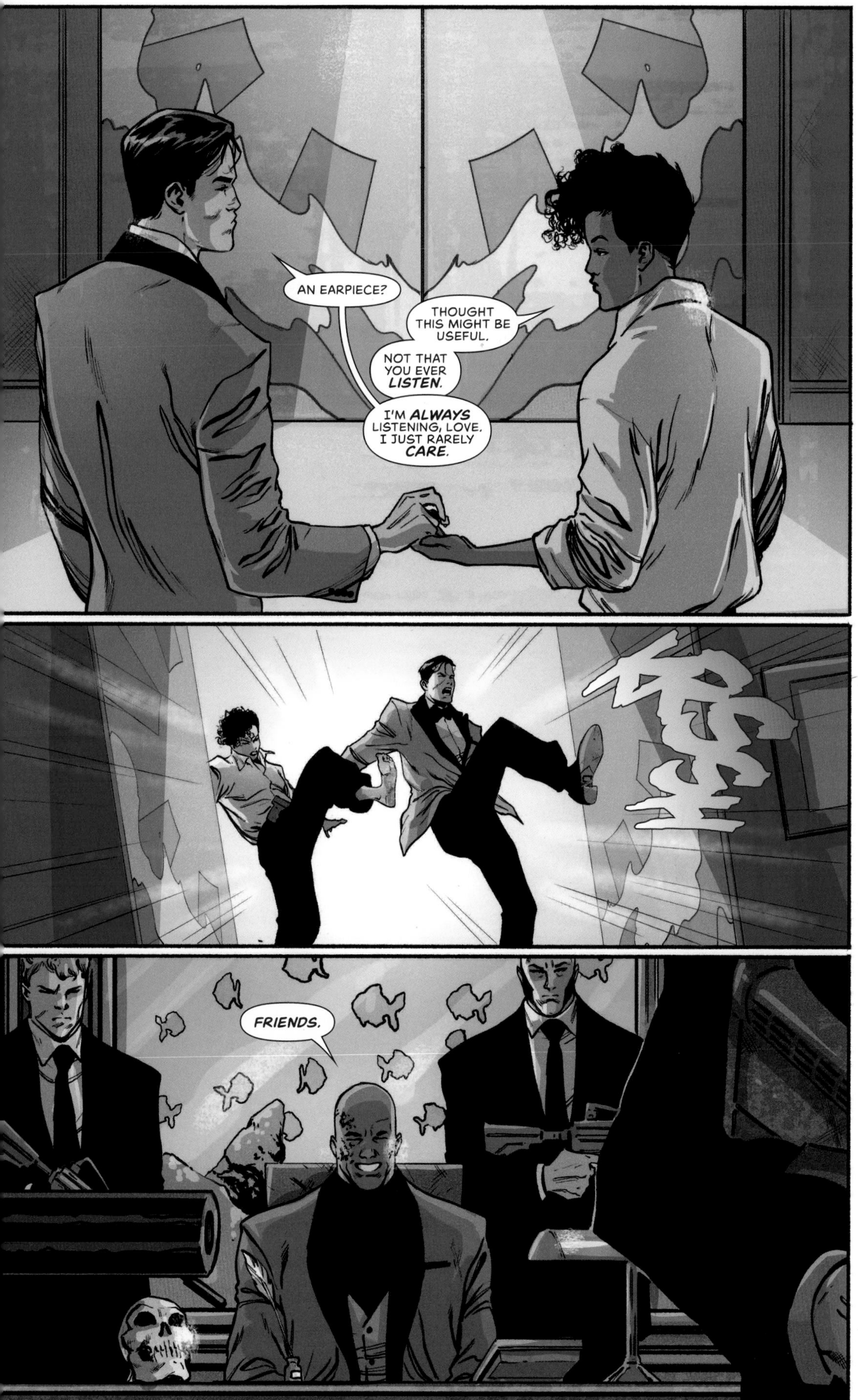
AN EARPIECE?
THOUGHT THIS MIGHT BE USEFUL.
NOT THAT YOU EVER LISTEN.
I'M ALWAYS LISTENING, LOVE. I JUST RARELY CARE.
FRIENDS.

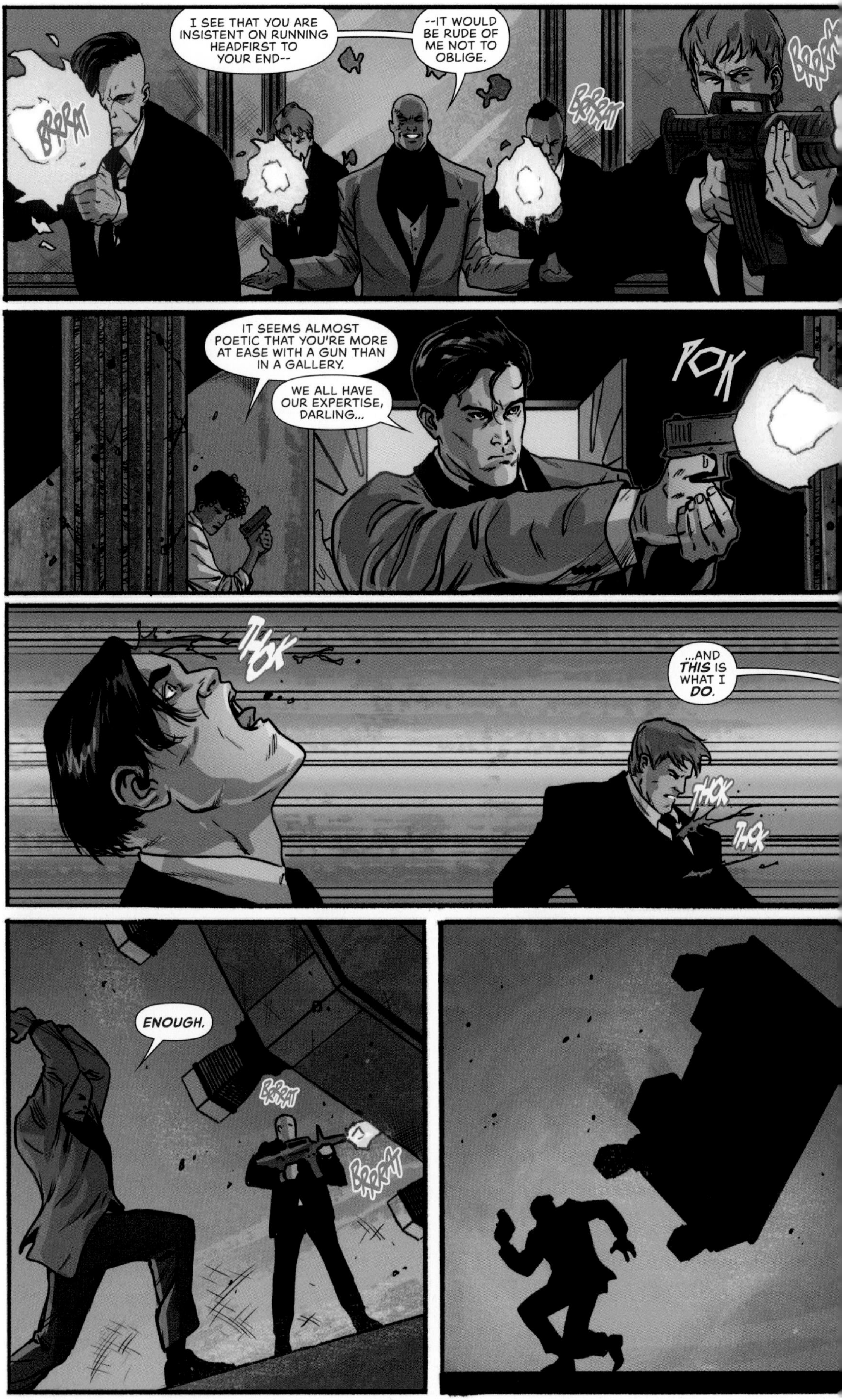
I SEE THAT YOU ARE INSISTENT ON RUNNING HEADFIRST TO YOUR END--
--IT WOULD BE RUDE OF ME NOT TO OBLIGE.
BRRRAT
BRRRAT
IT SEEMS ALMOST POETIC THAT YOU'RE MORE AT EASE WITH A GUN THAN IN A GALLERY.
WE ALL HAVE OUR EXPERTISE, DARLING...
POK
THOK
...AND THIS IS WHAT I DO.
THOK
THOK
ENOUGH.
BRRRAT
BRRRAT

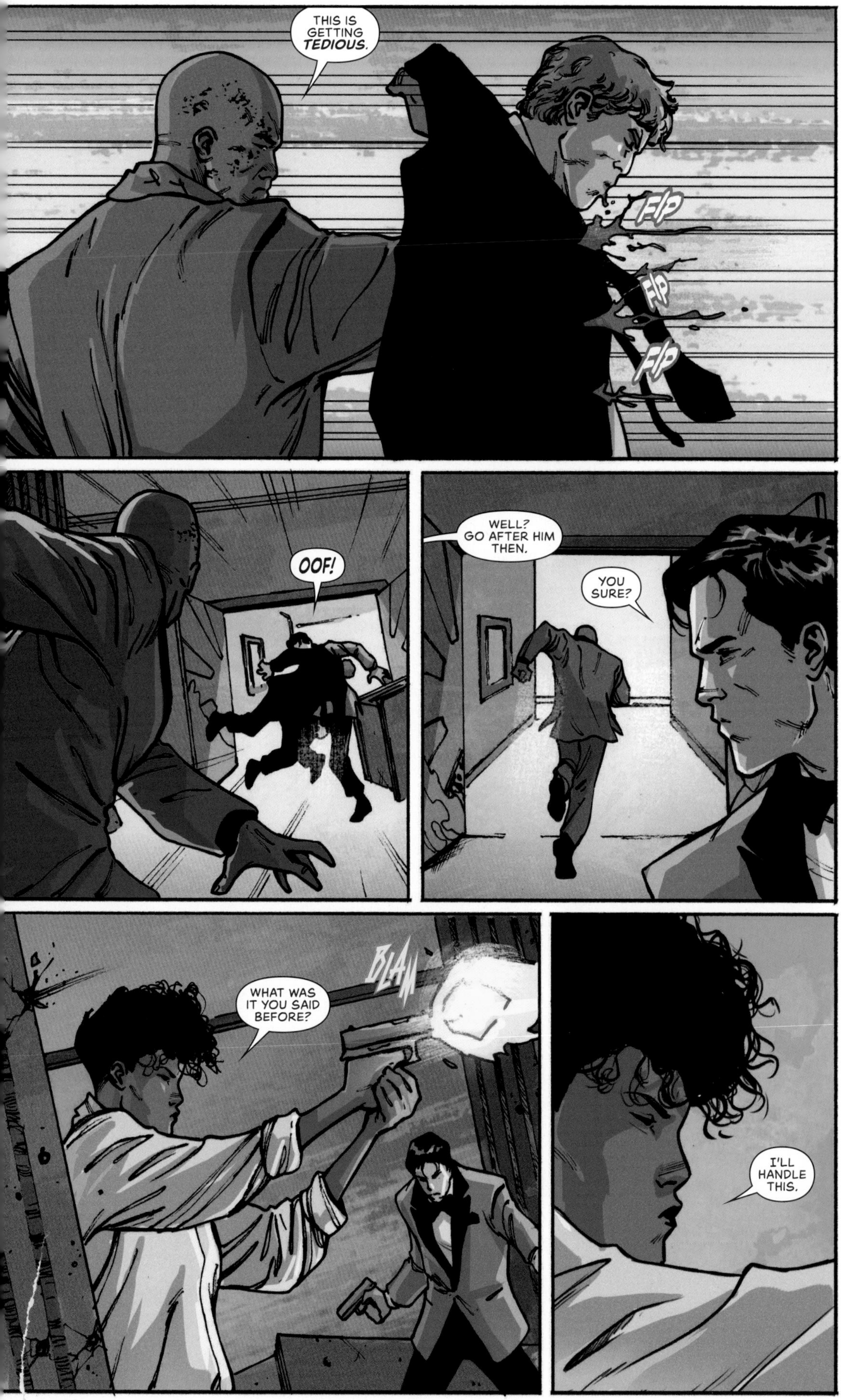
THIS IS GETTING *TEDIOUS*.
F/P
F/P
F/P
OOF!
WELL? GO AFTER HIM THEN.
YOU SURE?
BLAM
WHAT WAS IT YOU SAID BEFORE?
I'LL HANDLE THIS.

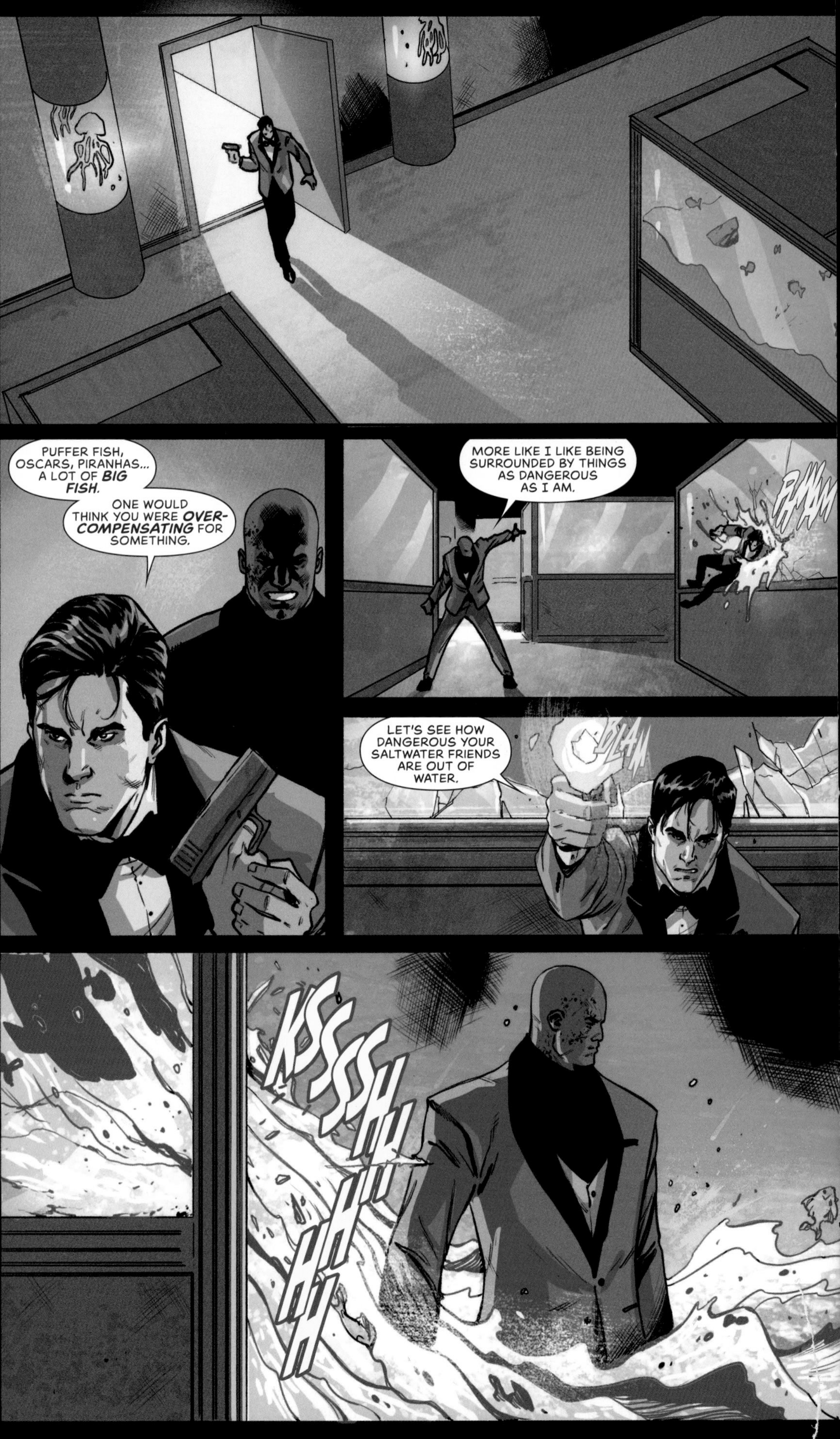
PUFFER FISH, OSCARS, PIRANHAS... A LOT OF BIG FISH.
ONE WOULD THINK YOU WERE OVER-COMPENSATING FOR SOMETHING.
MORE LIKE I LIKE BEING SURROUNDED BY THINGS AS DANGEROUS AS I AM.
PHAM
LET'S SEE HOW DANGEROUS YOUR SALTWATER FRIENDS ARE OUT OF WATER.
BLAM
KSSSHHHHHH

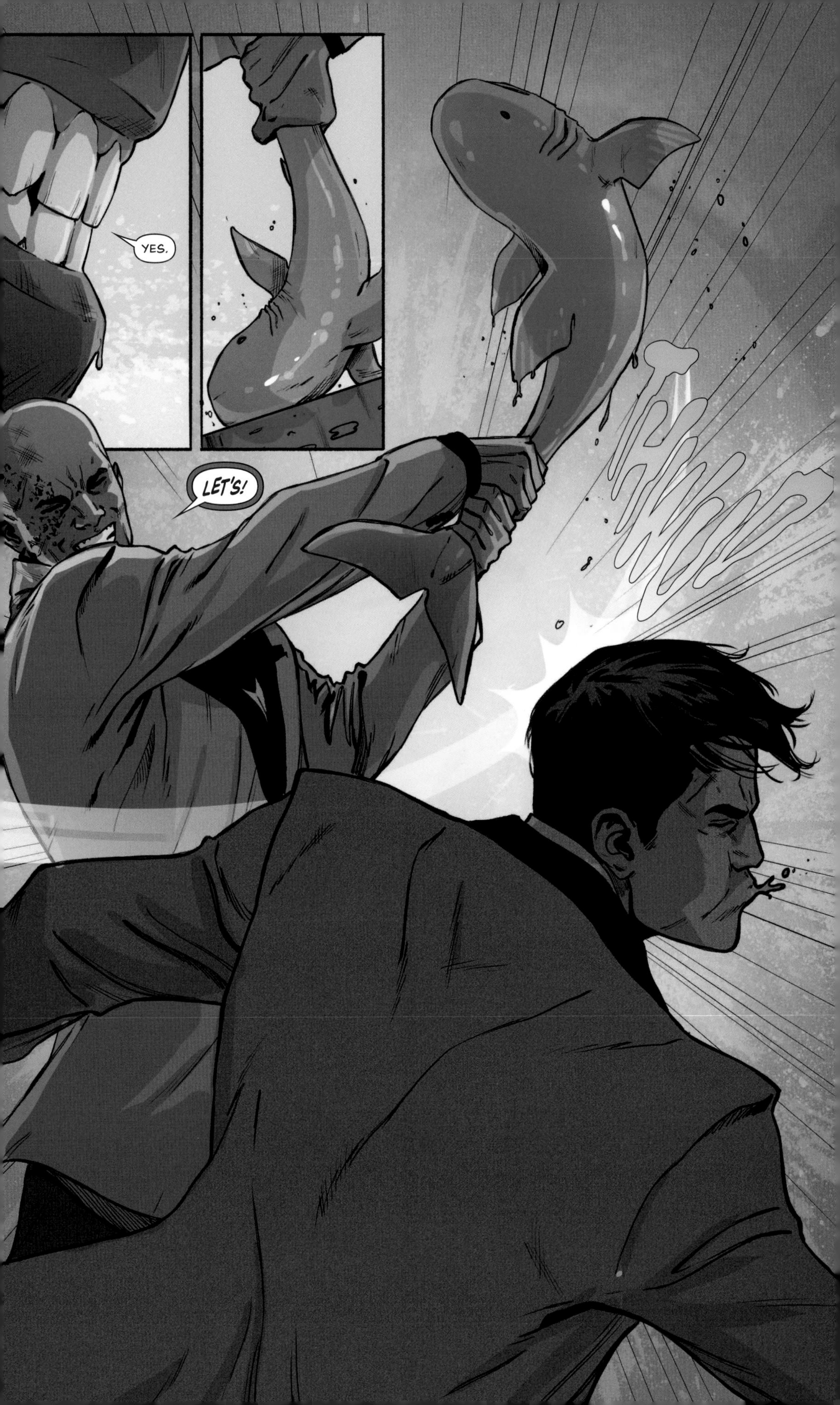
YES.
LET'S!
THWOK

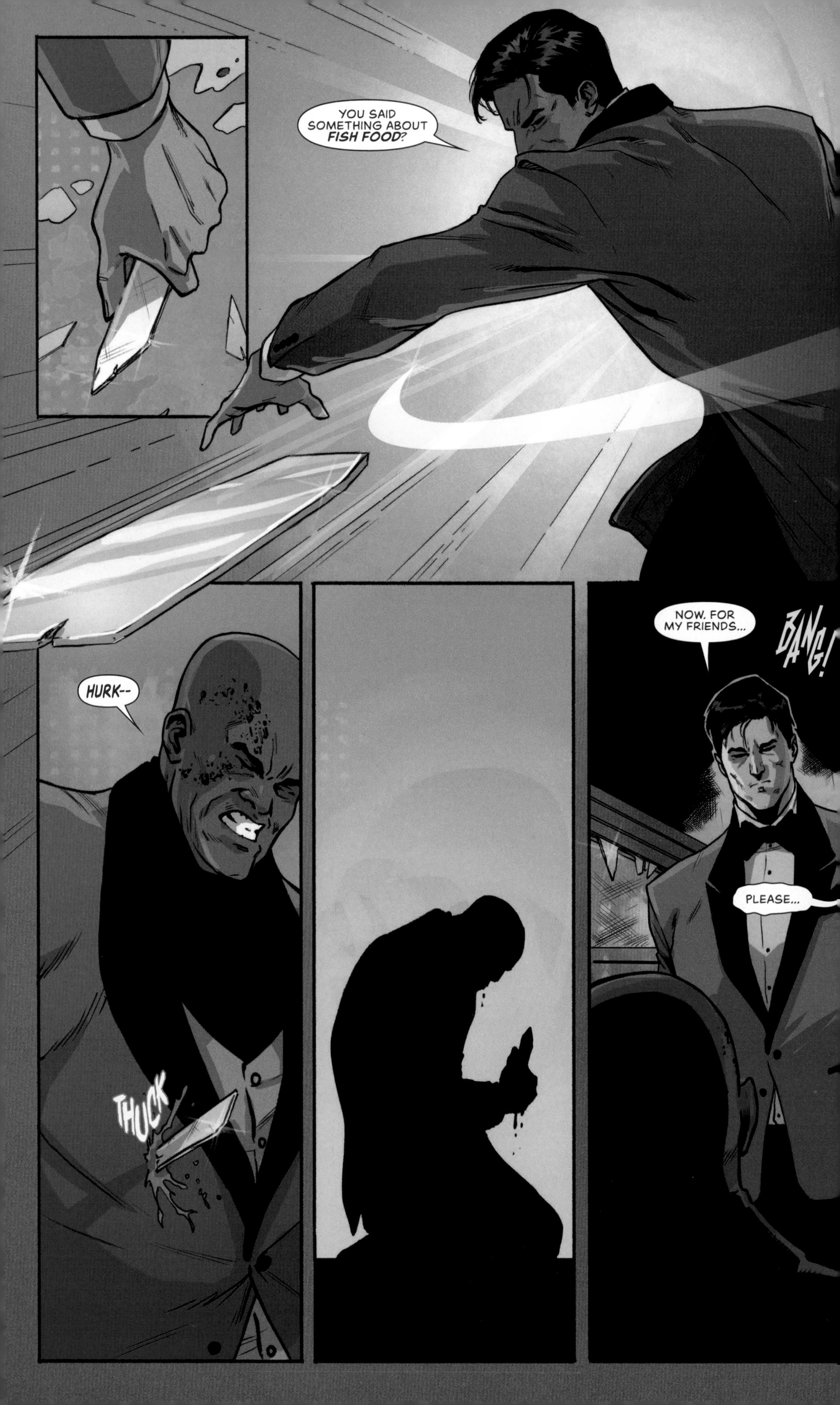

YOU SAID SOMETHING ABOUT *FISH FOOD?*
HURK--
THUCK
NOW. FOR MY FRIENDS...
BANG!
PLEASE...

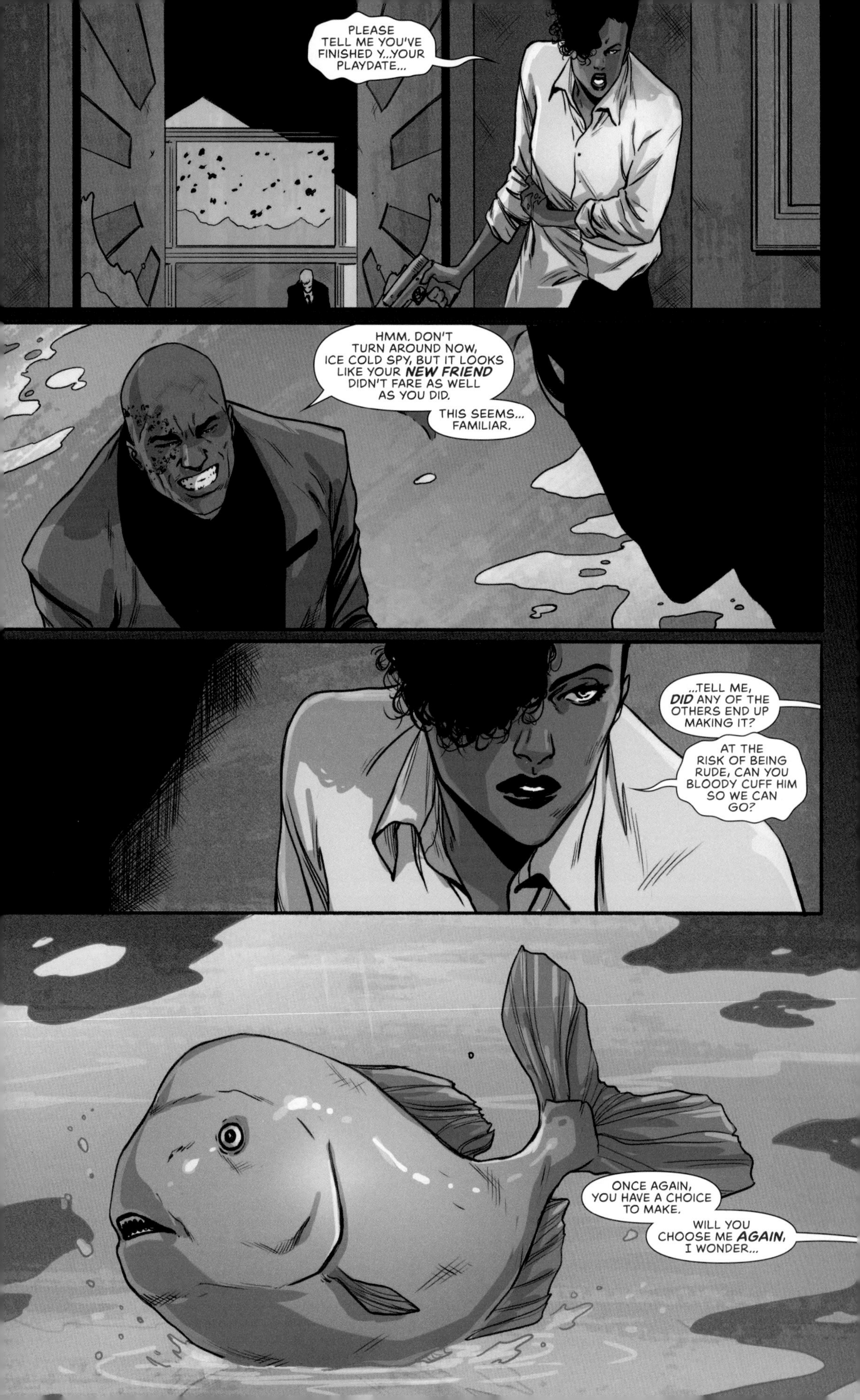

PLEASE TELL ME YOU'VE FINISHED Y...YOUR PLAYDATE...
HMM. DON'T TURN AROUND NOW, ICE COLD SPY, BUT IT LOOKS LIKE YOUR NEW FRIEND DIDN'T FARE AS WELL AS YOU DID.
THIS SEEMS... FAMILIAR.
...TELL ME, DID ANY OF THE OTHERS END UP MAKING IT?
AT THE RISK OF BEING RUDE, CAN YOU BLOODY CUFF HIM SO WE CAN GO?
ONCE AGAIN, YOU HAVE A CHOICE TO MAKE.
WILL YOU CHOOSE ME AGAIN, I WONDER...

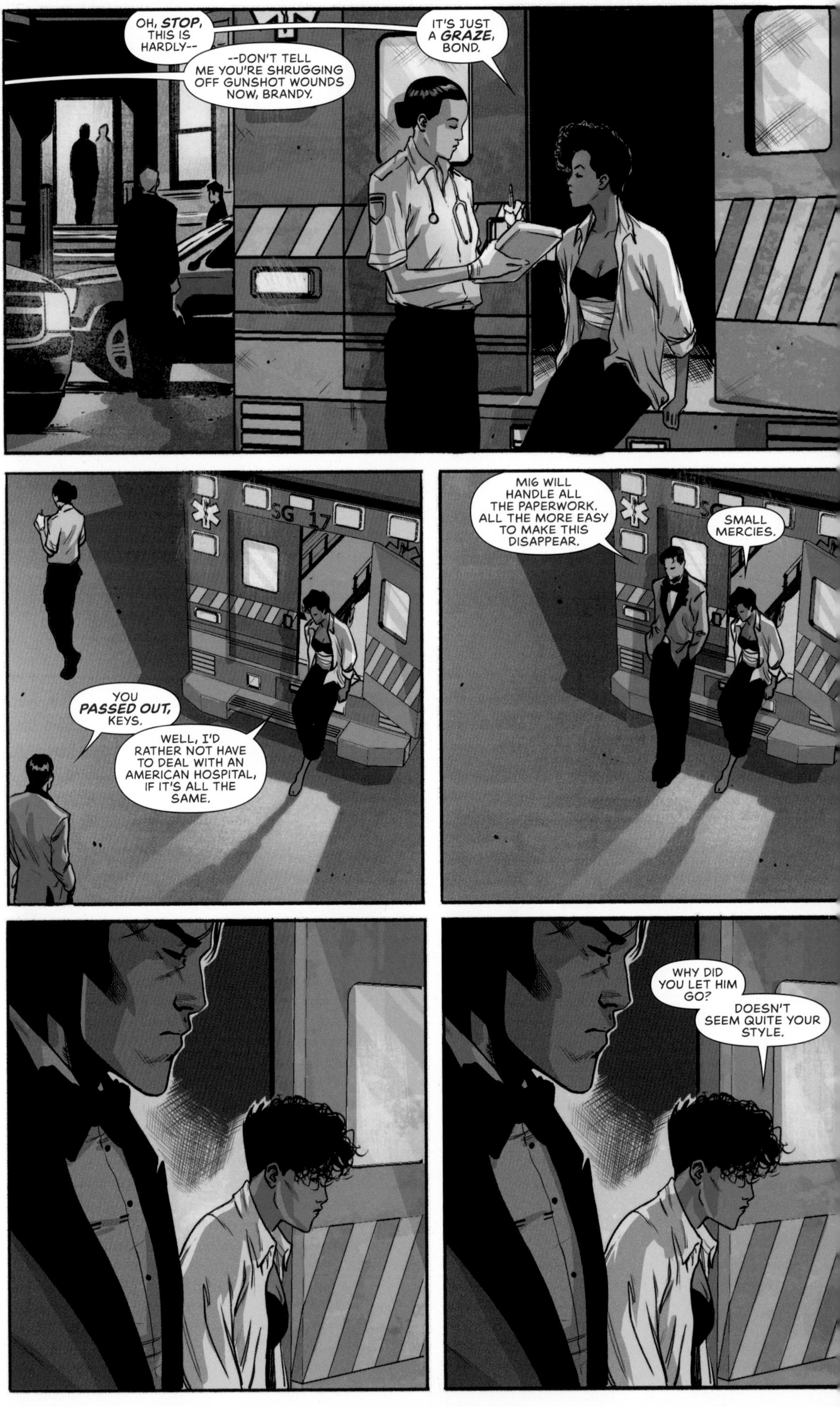
OH, **STOP**, THIS IS HARDLY--
IT'S JUST A **GRAZE**, BOND.
--DON'T TELL ME YOU'RE SHRUGGING OFF GUNSHOT WOUNDS NOW, BRANDY.
SG 17
YOU **PASSED OUT**, KEYS.
WELL, I'D RATHER NOT HAVE TO DEAL WITH AN AMERICAN HOSPITAL, IF IT'S ALL THE SAME.
MI6 WILL HANDLE ALL THE PAPERWORK. ALL THE MORE EASY TO MAKE THIS DISAPPEAR.
SMALL MERCIES.
WHY DID YOU LET HIM GO?
DOESN'T SEEM QUITE YOUR STYLE.

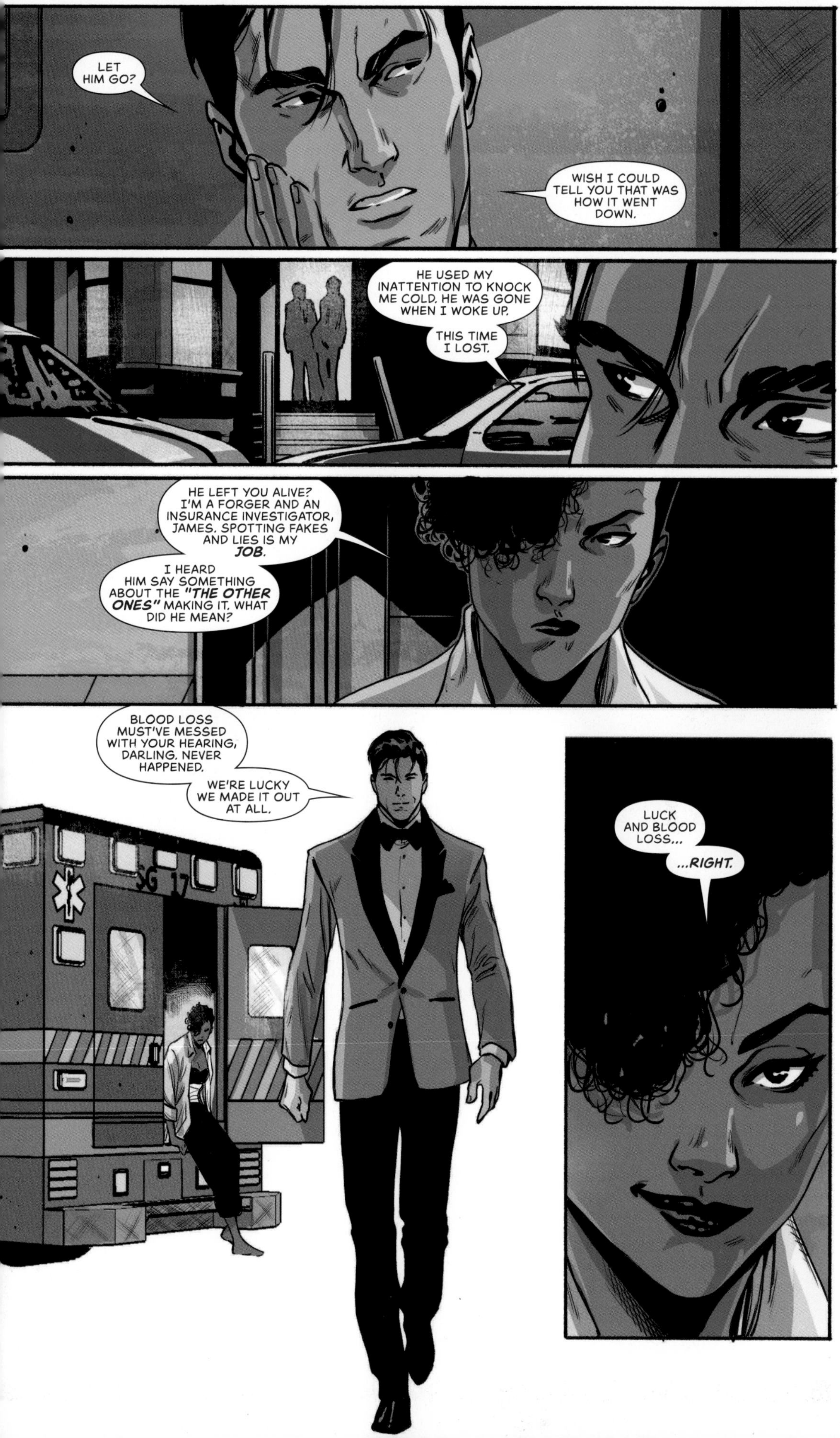
LET HIM GO?
WISH I COULD TELL YOU THAT WAS HOW IT WENT DOWN.
HE USED MY INATTENTION TO KNOCK ME COLD. HE WAS GONE WHEN I WOKE UP.
THIS TIME I LOST.
HE LEFT YOU ALIVE? I'M A FORGER AND AN INSURANCE INVESTIGATOR, JAMES. SPOTTING FAKES AND LIES IS MY *JOB*.
I HEARD HIM SAY SOMETHING ABOUT THE ***"THE OTHER ONES"*** MAKING IT. WHAT DID HE MEAN?
BLOOD LOSS MUST'VE MESSED WITH YOUR HEARING, DARLING. NEVER HAPPENED.
WE'RE LUCKY WE MADE IT OUT AT ALL.
SG 17
LUCK AND BLOOD LOSS...
...RIGHT.

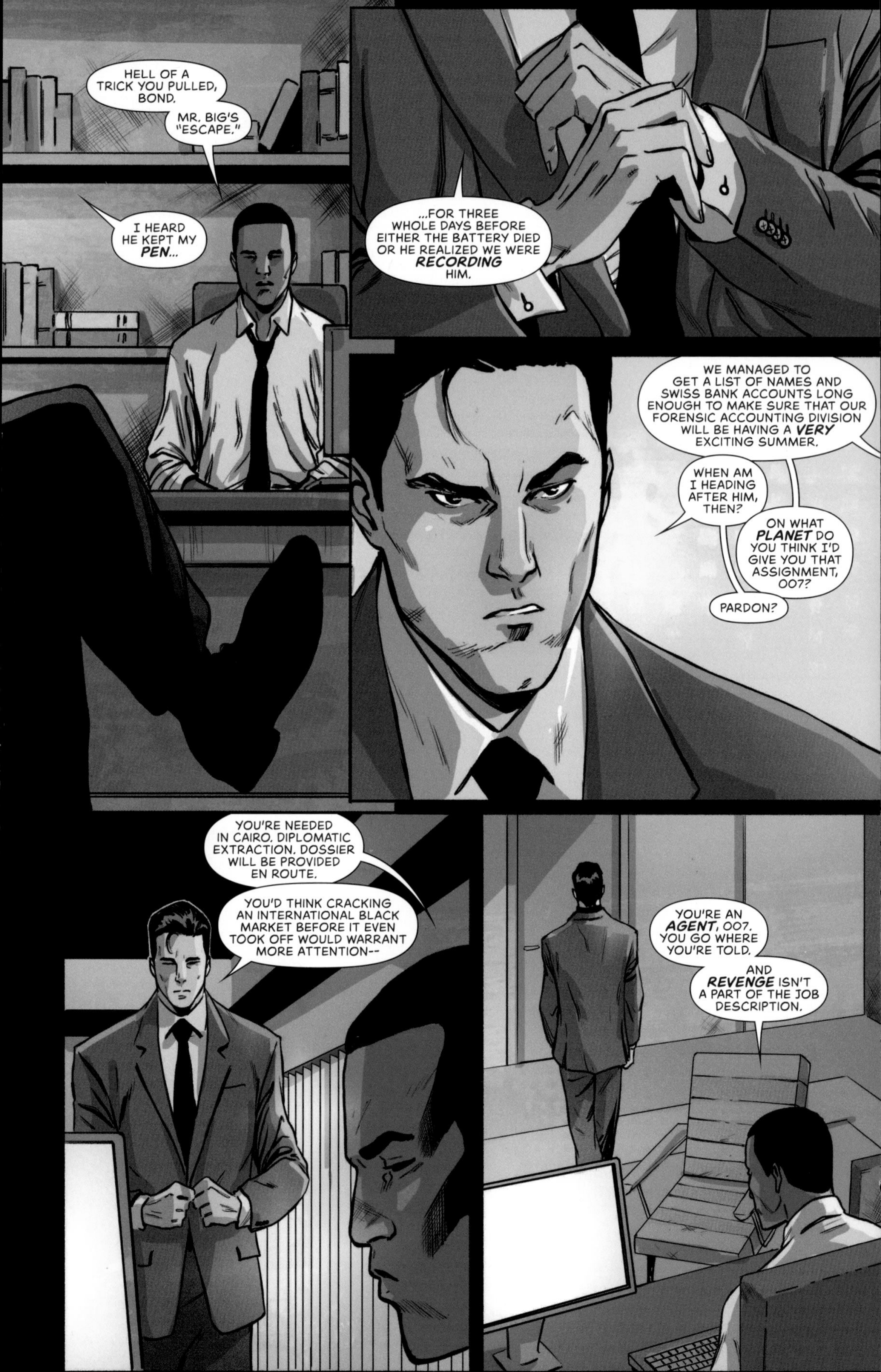
HELL OF A TRICK YOU PULLED, BOND.
MR. BIG'S "ESCAPE."
I HEARD HE KEPT MY PEN...
...FOR THREE WHOLE DAYS BEFORE EITHER THE BATTERY DIED OR HE REALIZED WE WERE RECORDING HIM.
WE MANAGED TO GET A LIST OF NAMES AND SWISS BANK ACCOUNTS LONG ENOUGH TO MAKE SURE THAT OUR FORENSIC ACCOUNTING DIVISION WILL BE HAVING A VERY EXCITING SUMMER.
WHEN AM I HEADING AFTER HIM, THEN?
ON WHAT PLANET DO YOU THINK I'D GIVE YOU THAT ASSIGNMENT, 007?
PARDON?
YOU'RE NEEDED IN CAIRO. DIPLOMATIC EXTRACTION. DOSSIER WILL BE PROVIDED EN ROUTE.
YOU'D THINK CRACKING AN INTERNATIONAL BLACK MARKET BEFORE IT EVEN TOOK OFF WOULD WARRANT MORE ATTENTION--
YOU'RE AN AGENT, 007. YOU GO WHERE YOU'RE TOLD.
AND REVENGE ISN'T A PART OF THE JOB DESCRIPTION.

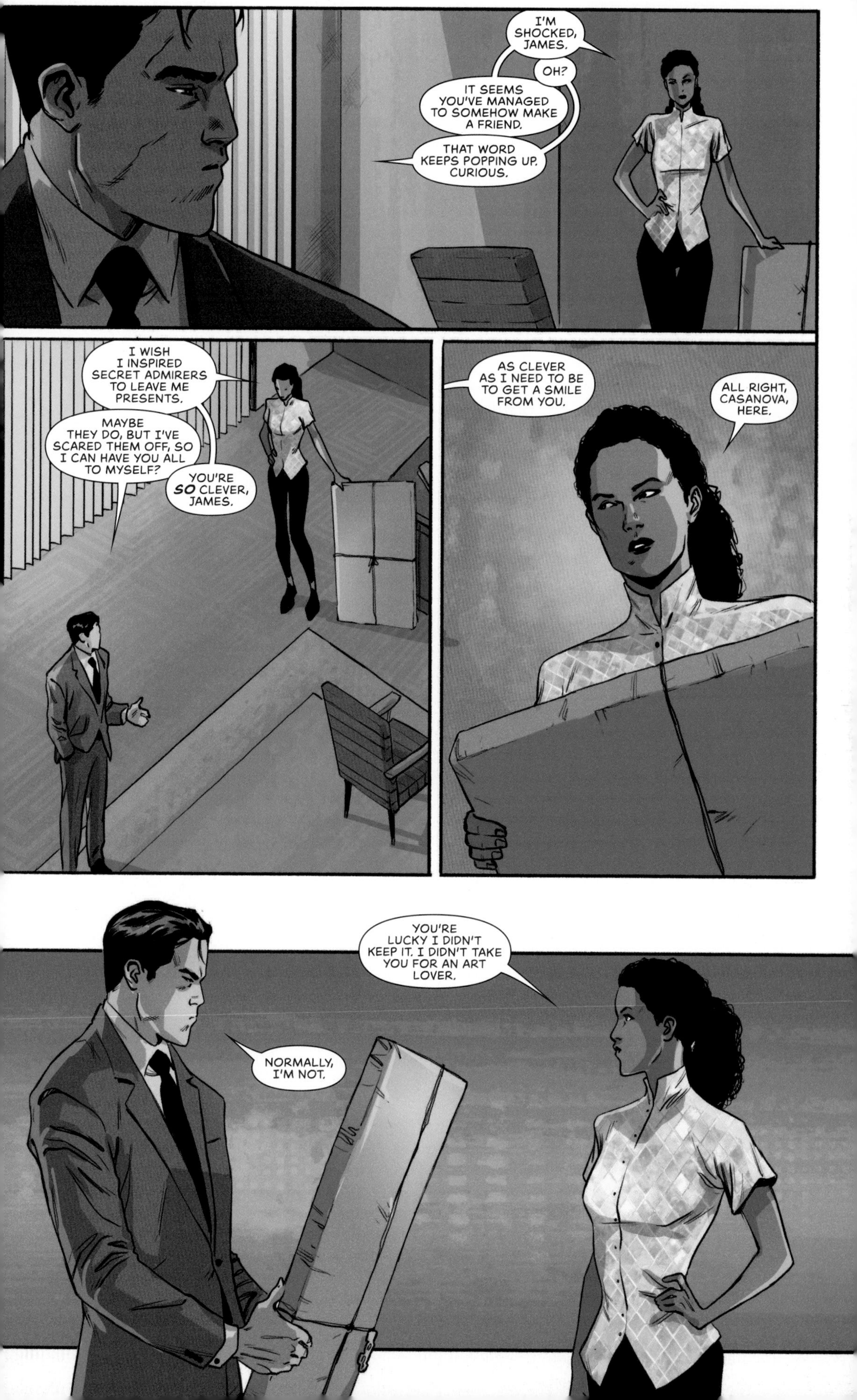
I'M SHOCKED, JAMES.
OH?
IT SEEMS YOU'VE MANAGED TO SOMEHOW MAKE A FRIEND.
THAT WORD KEEPS POPPING UP. CURIOUS.
I WISH I INSPIRED SECRET ADMIRERS TO LEAVE ME PRESENTS.
MAYBE THEY DO, BUT I'VE SCARED THEM OFF, SO I CAN HAVE YOU ALL TO MYSELF?
YOU'RE SO CLEVER, JAMES.
AS CLEVER AS I NEED TO BE TO GET A SMILE FROM YOU.
ALL RIGHT, CASANOVA, HERE.
YOU'RE LUCKY I DIDN'T KEEP IT. I DIDN'T TAKE YOU FOR AN ART LOVER.
NORMALLY, I'M NOT.

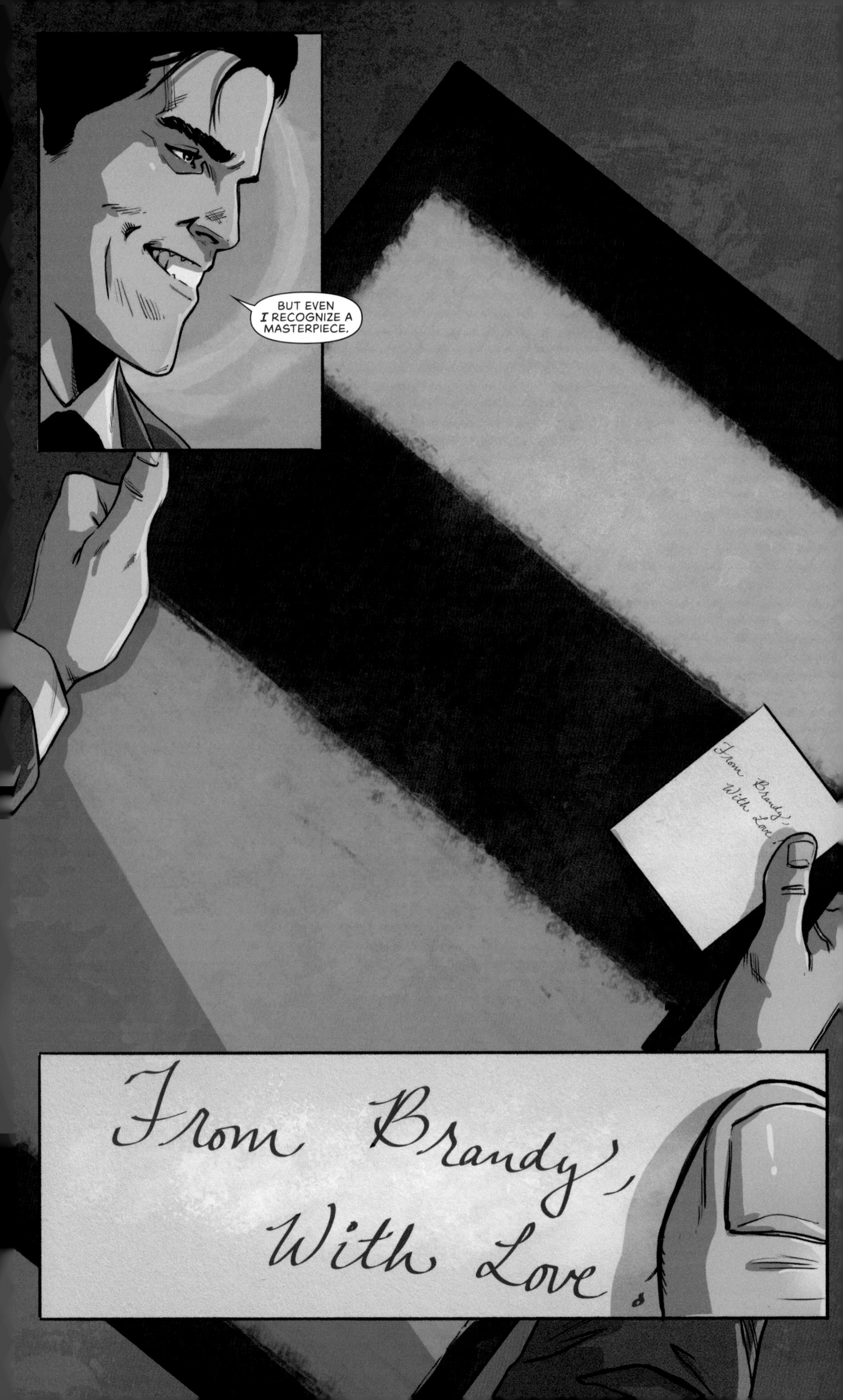
BUT EVEN *I* RECOGNIZE A MASTERPIECE.
From Brandy, With Love
From Brandy, With Love.

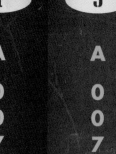

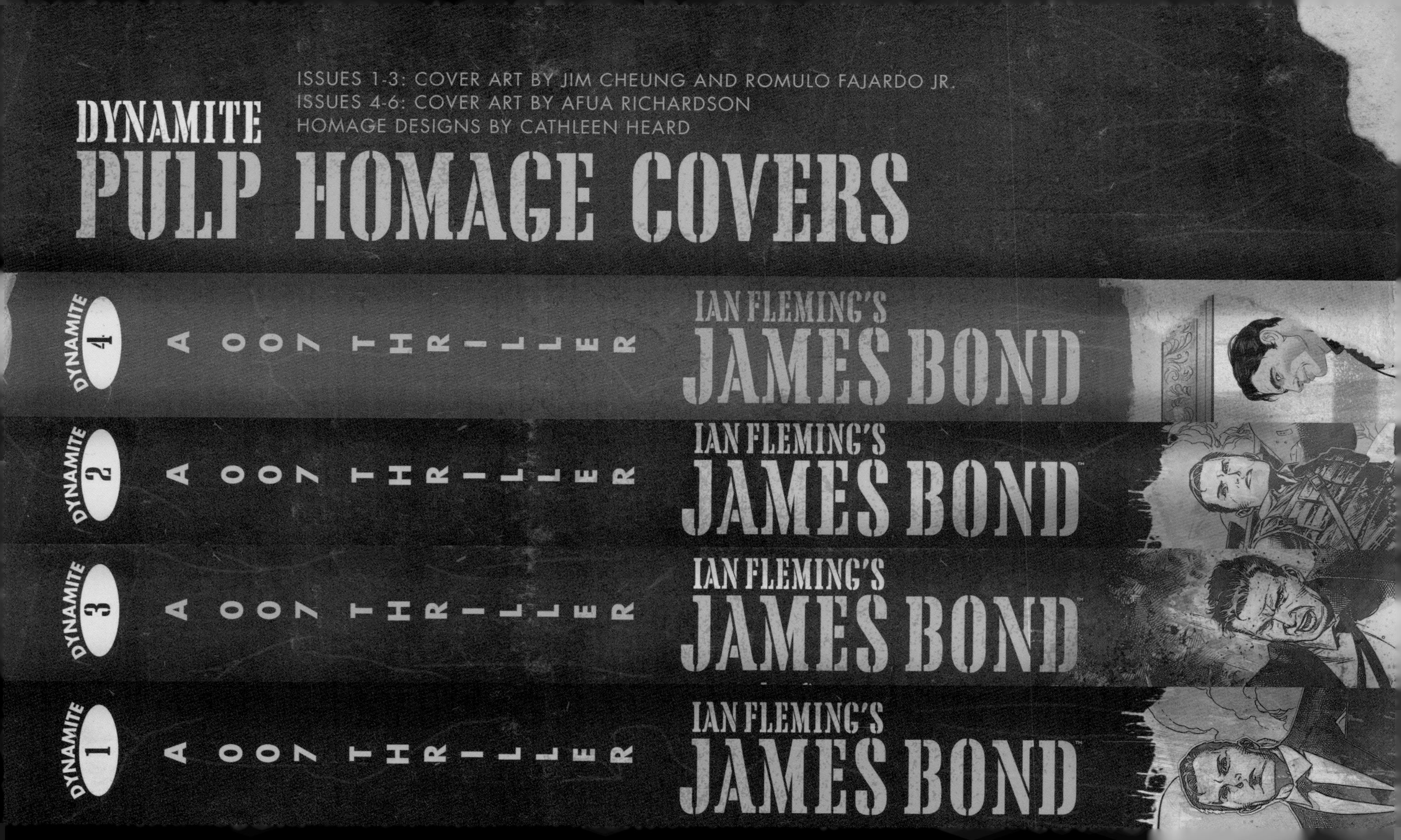

DYNAMITE
1

A 007 THRILLER

IAN FLEMING'S JAMES BOND

DYNAMITE
3

A 007 THRILLER

IAN FLEMING'S JAMES BOND

DYNAMITE
2

A 007 THRILLER

IAN FLEMING'S JAMES BOND

DYNAMITE
4

A 007 THRILLER

IAN FLEMING'S JAMES BOND

DYNAMITE

PULP HOMAGE COVERS

ISSUES 1-3: COVER ART BY JIM CHEUNG AND ROMULO FAJARDO JR.
ISSUES 4-6: COVER ART BY AFUA RICHARDSON

HOMAGE DESIGNS BY CATHLEEN HEARD

DYNAMITE
$3.99

A 007 THRILLER

IAN FLEMING'S
JAMES BOND™

AYALA   LORE   GAPSTUR   ROSH   MAHER

02

DYNAMITE
$3.99

A 007 THRILLER

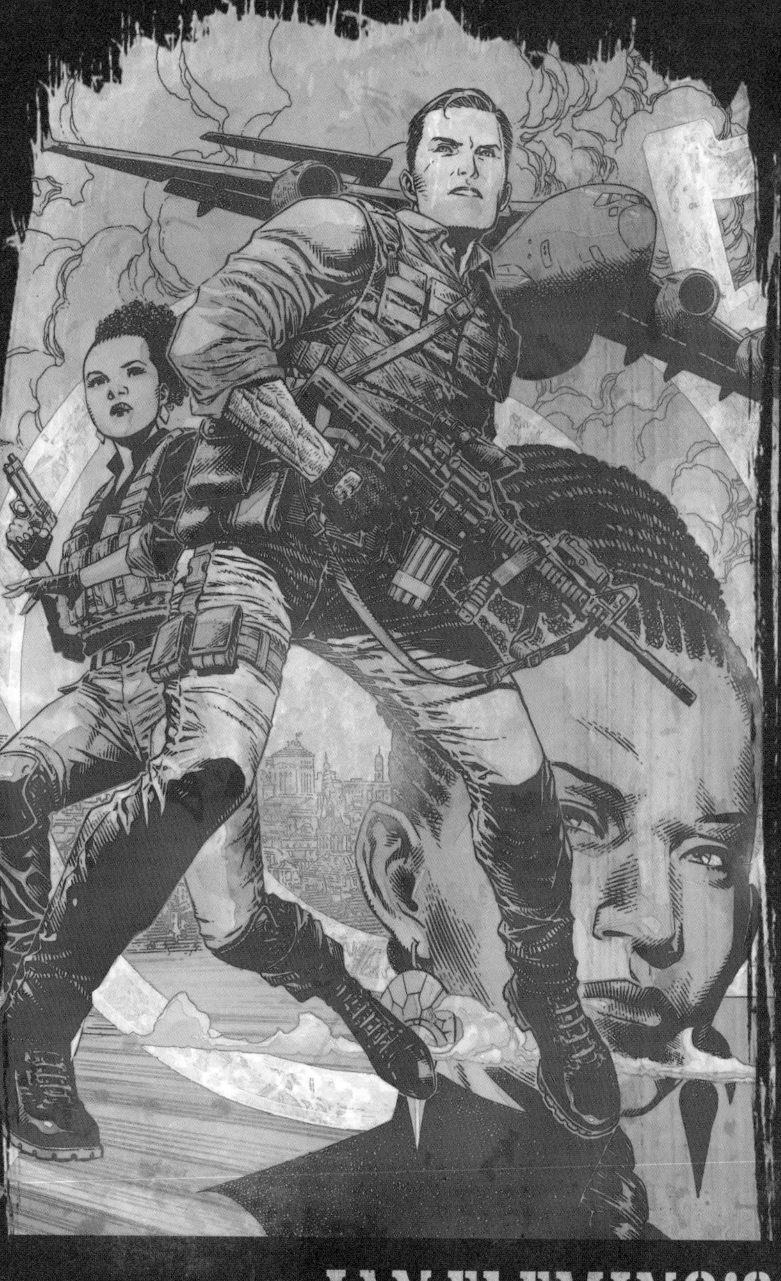

IAN FLEMING'S JAMES BOND™

AYALA LORE GAPSTUR ROSH OTSMANE-ELHAOU

003

DYNAMITE $3.99

A 007 THRILLER

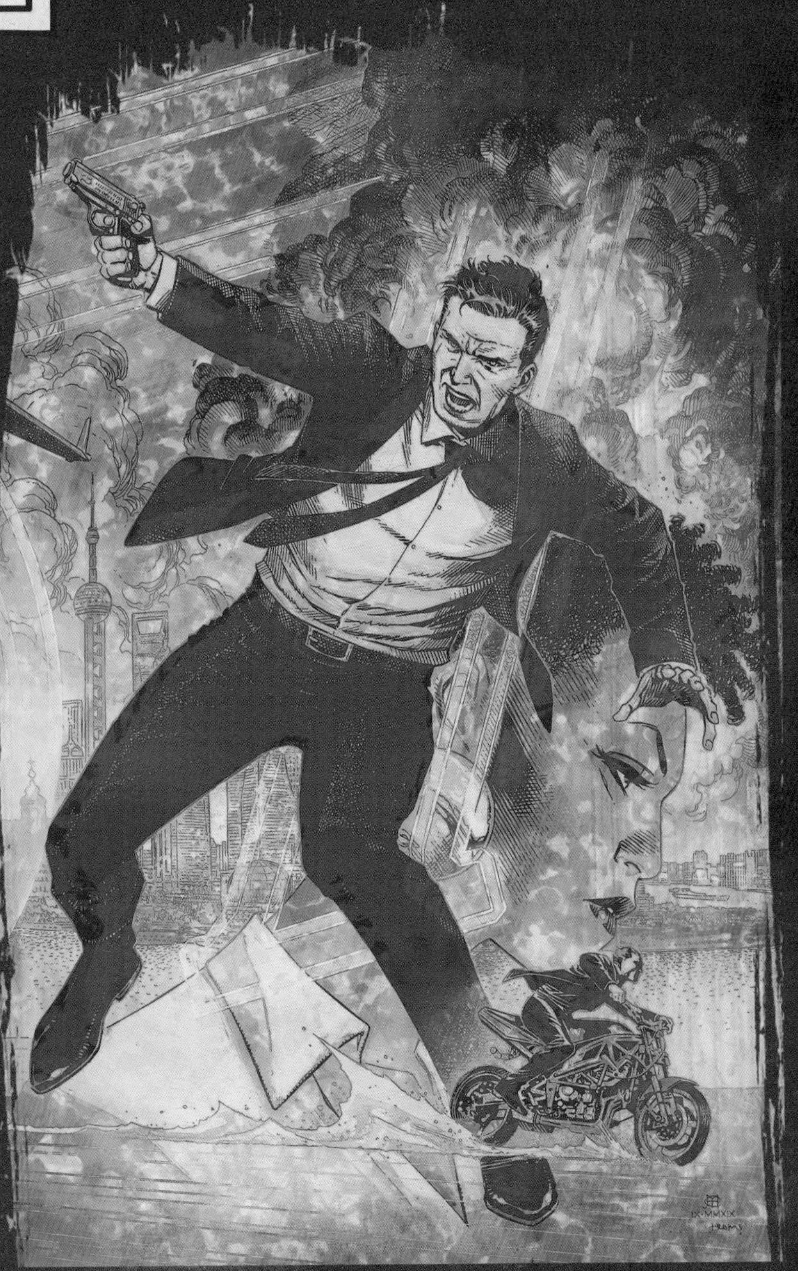

IAN FLEMING'S JAMES BOND™

AYALA LORE D'URSO RENNA ROSH MAHER

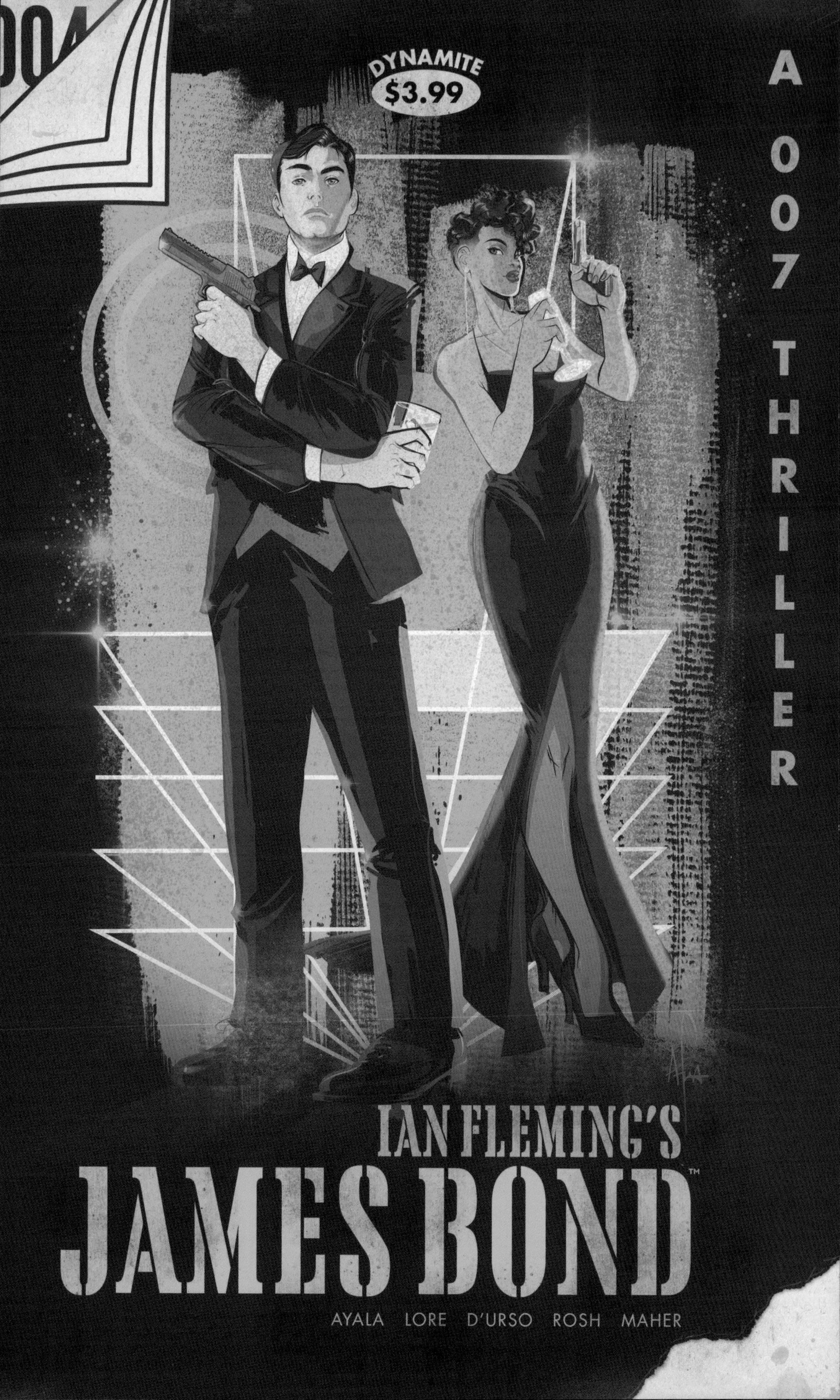

DYNAMITE
$3.99
A 007 THRILLER
IAN FLEMING'S
JAMES BOND™
AYALA LORE D'URSO ROSH MAHER

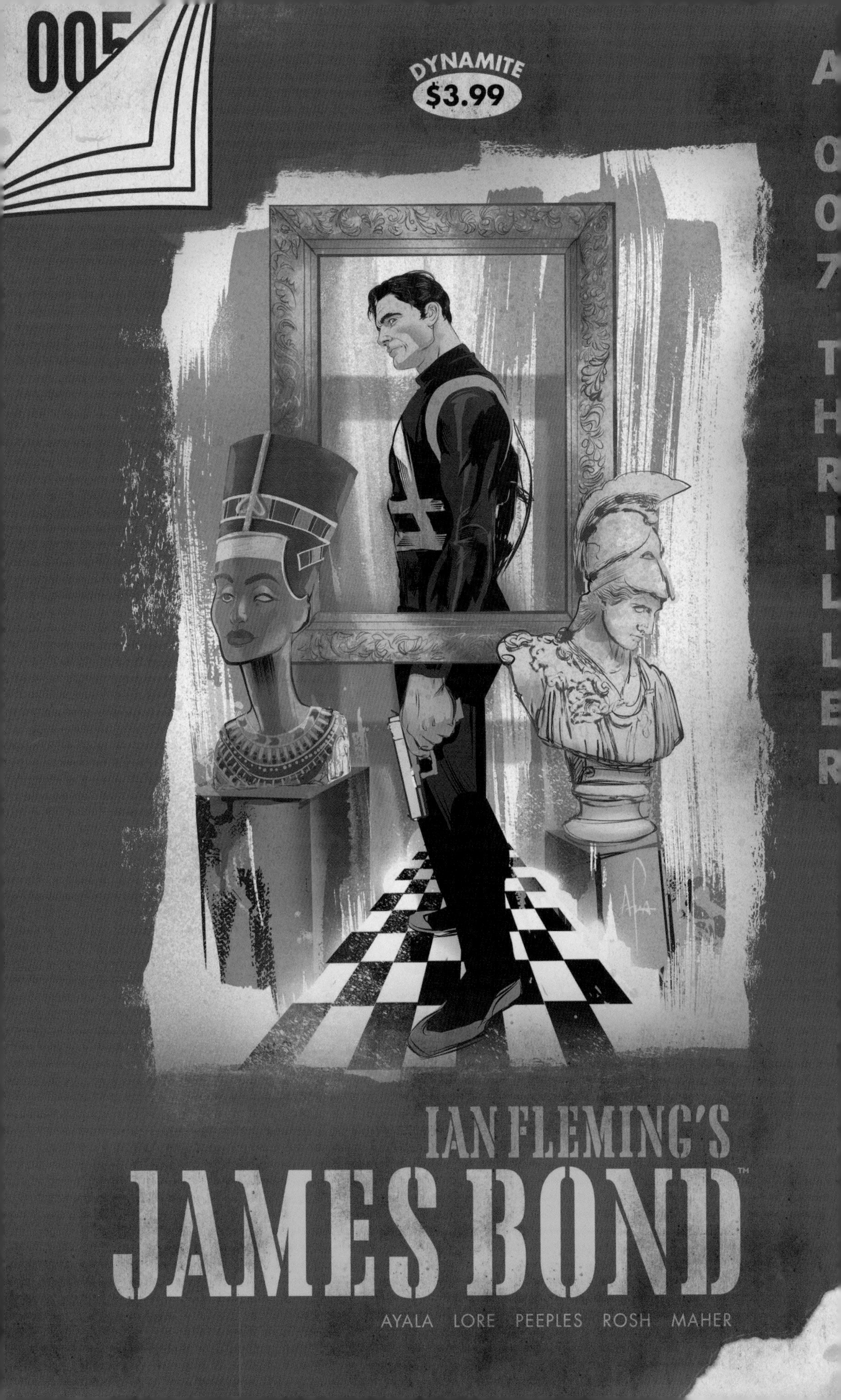
005
DYNAMITE
$3.99
A 007 THRILLER
IAN FLEMING'S
JAMES BOND™
AYALA LORE PEEPLES ROSH MAHER

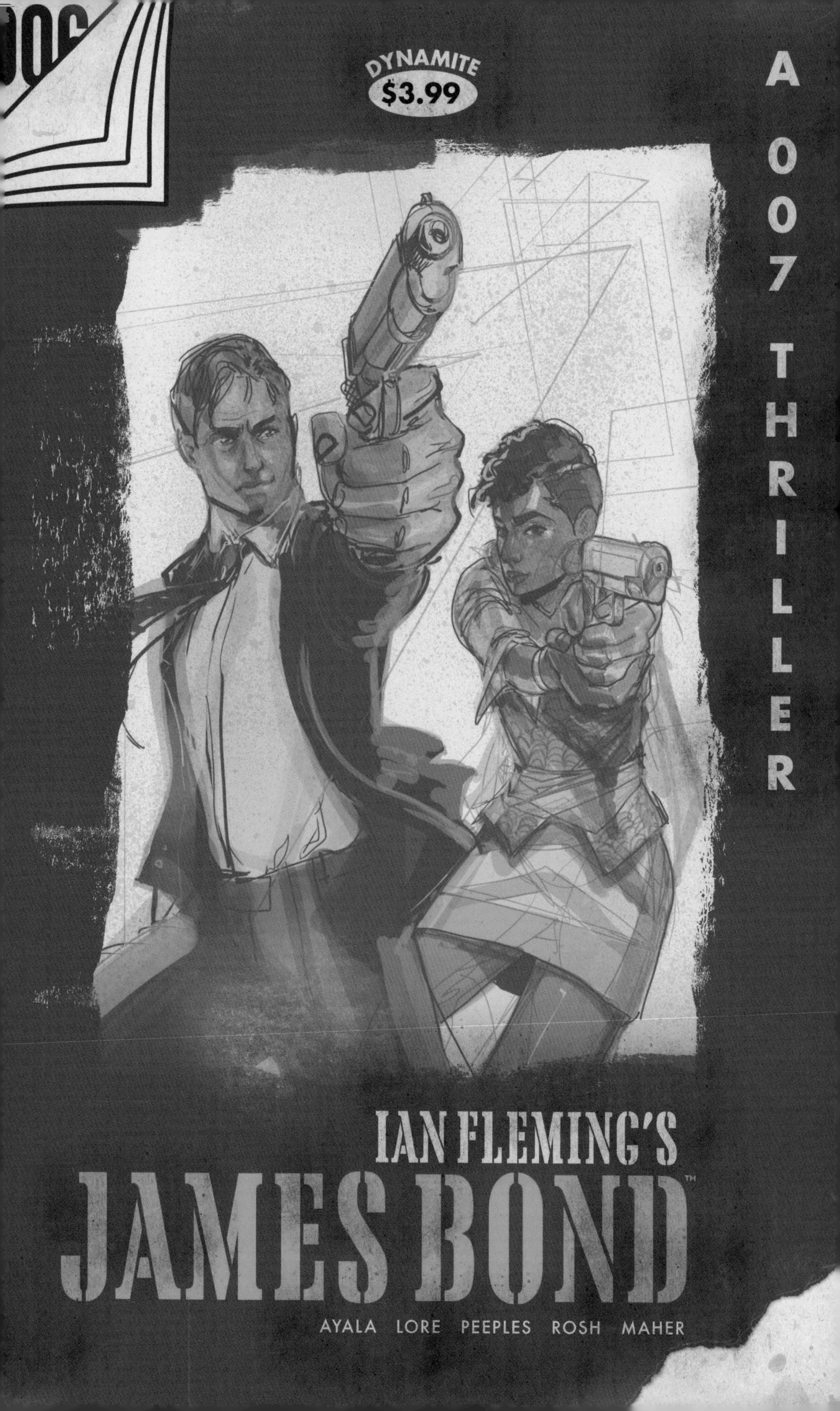
DYNAMITE
$3.99
A 007 THRILLER
IAN FLEMING'S
JAMES BOND™
AYALA LORE PEEPLES ROSH MAHER

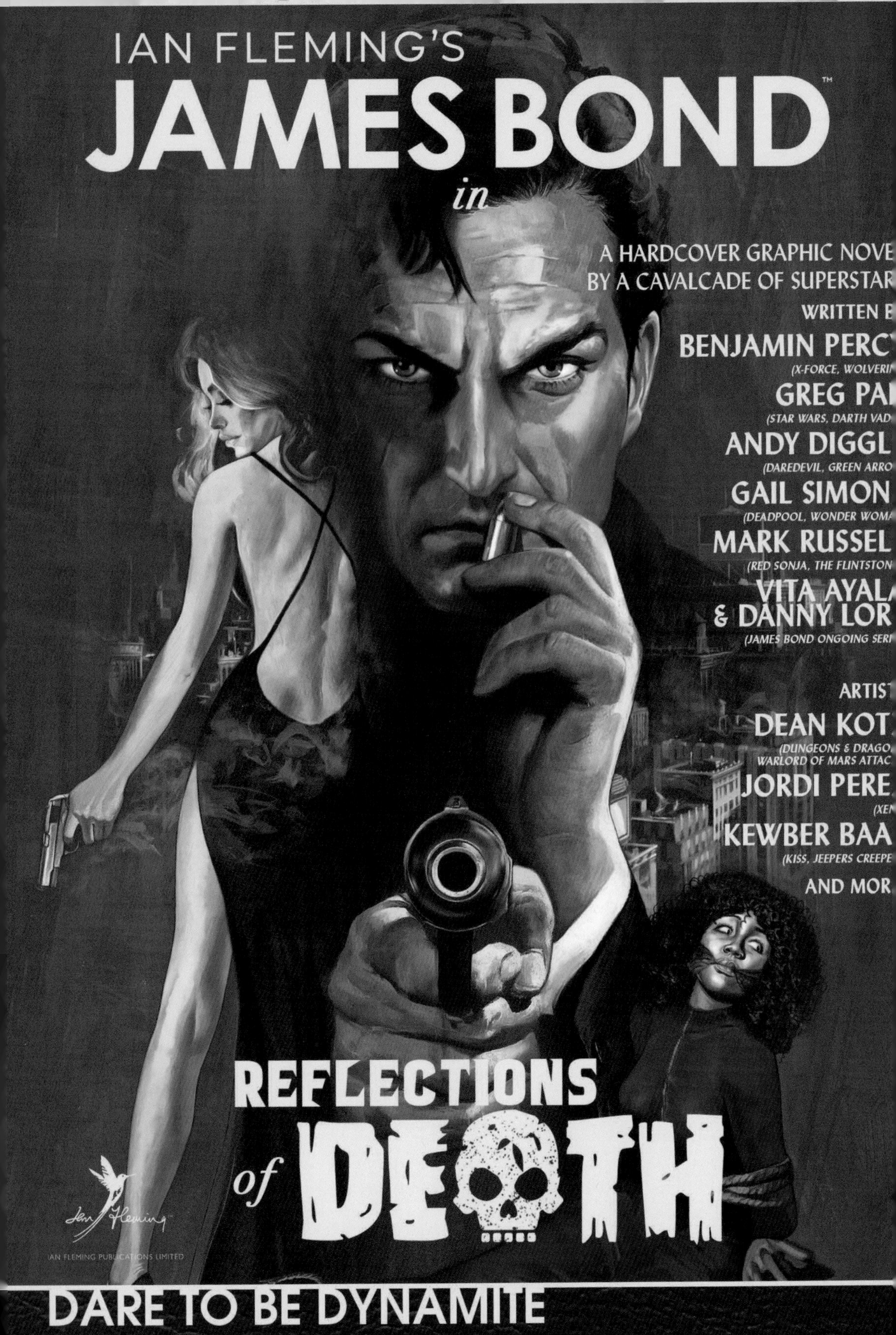

IAN FLEMING'S
JAMES BOND™
in
A HARDCOVER GRAPHIC NOVE
BY A CAVALCADE OF SUPERSTAR
WRITTEN B
BENJAMIN PERC
(X-FORCE, WOLVERI
GREG PA
(STAR WARS, DARTH VAD
ANDY DIGGL
(DAREDEVIL, GREEN ARRO
GAIL SIMON
(DEADPOOL, WONDER WOM
MARK RUSSEL
(RED SONJA, THE FLINTSTON
VITA AYAL
& DANNY LOR
(JAMES BOND ONGOING SER
ARTIS
DEAN KOT
(DUNGEONS & DRAGO
WARLORD OF MARS ATTAC
JORDI PERE
(XE
KEWBER BAA
(KISS, JEEPERS CREEPE
AND MOR
REFLECTIONS
of DEATH
IAN FLEMING PUBLICATIONS LIMITED
DARE TO BE DYNAMITE
DYNAMITE
#DareToBeDynamite
Join the discussion at dynamite.com
/dynamitecomics
@dynamitecomic

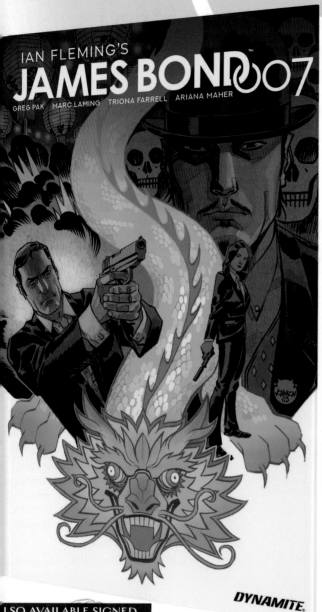

THESE GREAT JAMES BOND COLLECTIONS ALSO AVAILABLE

ELLIS · MASTERS
IAN FLEMING'S
JAMES BOND 007
VARGR
DYNAMITE

JAMES BOND: VARGR
HARDCOVER: 978-1-60690-901-0
TRADE PAPERBACK: 978-1-5241-0480-1

ELLIS · MASTERS
IAN FLEMING'S
JAMES BOND 007
EIDOLON
DYNAMITE

JAMES BOND: EIDOLON
HARDCOVER: 978-1-5241-0272-2
TRADE PAPERBACK: 978-1-5241-0694-2

PERCY · LOBOSCO
IAN FLEMING'S
JAMES BOND 007
BLACK BOX
DYNAMITE

JAMES BOND: BLACK BOX
HARDCOVER: 978-1-5241-0409-2

DIGGLE · CASALANGUIDA
IAN FLEMING'S
JAMES BOND 007
HAMMERHEAD
DYNAMITE

JAMES BOND: HAMMERHEAD
HARDCOVER: 978-1-5241-0322-4

DIGGLE · CASALANGUIDA
IAN FLEMING'S
JAMES BOND 007
KILL CHAIN
DYNAMITE
AVAILABLE SIGNED BY ANDY DIGGLE!

JAMES BOND: KILL CHAIN
HARDCOVER: 978-1-5241-0595-2

JAMES BOND 007
FELIX LEITER
DYNAMITE

JAMES BOND: FELIX LEITER
HARDCOVER: 978-1-5241-0470-2

Ian Fleming's
JAMES BOND
Agent 007
CASINO ROYALE
AVAILABLE SIGNED BY VAN JENSEN!
ALSO AVAILABLE SIGNED & REMARKED BY DENNIS CALERO!

JAMES BOND: CASINO ROYALE
HARDCOVER: 978-1-5241-0068-1

IAN FLEMING'S
JAMES BOND 007
CASE FILES
DYNAMITE
4 STORIES IN ONE COLLECTION

JAMES BOND: CASE FILES
HARDCOVER: 978-1-5241-0678-2

VARGR:

"This is classic Bond here."
– Bleeding Cool

EIDOLON:

"Not only are the characters great, the story itself is engaging as hell."
– Newsarama

BLACK BOX:

"Percy's got the voice right for Bond and Lobosco definitely has some really strong design work here with characters and locations."
– The Fandom Post

HAMMERHEAD:

"This comic is all the best parts of a Fleming book accompanied with visuals that only a comic can provide."
– Weird Science

KILL CHAIN:

"Dynamite Entertainment continues to show that when it comes to James Bond, nobody does it better."
- Comic Crusaders

FELIX LEITER:

"James Bond: Felix Leiter...still stands as a neatly compact solo outing for the fan-favorite co-star."
- Newsarama

CASINO ROYALE:

"The bourbon is gone. The triumph of "Casino Royale" remains."
- The Oregonian

CASE FILES:

" "There's no wonder Moustafa is Eisner nominated."
- Comic Bastards
(Solstice)

IAN FLEMING PUBLICATIONS LIMITED

DYNAMITE®

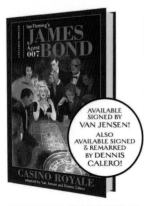